MCITP 70-663
Exam Ref:

Designing and Deploying Messaging
Solutions with Microsoft® Exchange
Server 2010

Orin Thomas

Published with the authorization of Microsoft Corporation by:

O'Reilly Media, Inc.
1005 Gravenstein Highway North
Sebastopol, California 95472

ISBN: 978-0-7356-5808-0

1 2 3 4 5 6 7 8 9 QG 6 5 4 3 2 1

Printed and bound in the United States of America.

Microsoft Press books are available through booksellers and distributors worldwide. If you need support related to this book, email Microsoft Press Book Support at *mspinput@microsoft.com*. Please tell us what you think of this book at *http://www.microsoft.com/learning/booksurvey*.

Acquisitions and Developmental Editor: Ken Jones
Production Editor: Adam Zaremba
Editorial Production: S4Carlisle Publishing Services
Technical Reviewer: Ian McLean
Copyeditor: Becka McKay
Indexer: Potomac Indexing, LLC
Cover Composition: Karen Montgomery
Illustrator: S4Carlisle Publishing Services

Contents at a Glance

Introduction   *xvii*

Preparing for the Exam   *xxi*

CHAPTER 1   Planning the Exchange Server 2010 Infrastructure   1

CHAPTER 2   Deploying the Exchange Server 2010 Infrastructure   95

CHAPTER 3   Designing and Deploying Security for the Exchange
             Organization   215

CHAPTER 4   Designing and Deploying Exchange Server 2010
             Availability and Recovery   287

CHAPTER 5   Designing and Deploying Messaging Compliance,
             System Monitoring, and Reporting   351

Index   *401*

Contents

Introduction   **xvii**

Microsoft Certified Professional Program   *xviii*

Acknowledgments   *xviii*

Support and Feedback   *xix*

Preparing for the Exam   **xxi**

Chapter 1   Planning the Exchange Server 2010 Infrastructure   1

Objective 1.1: Design the Exchange Server 2010 Installation 2

    Choosing Exchange Server Locations   3

    Planning Exchange DNS Support   5

    Service Level Agreement Considerations   8

    Active Directory and Network Topology   10

    Multiple Domains   11

    Multiple Forests   11

    Directory Synchronization with the Cloud   12

    Exchange Federation   14

    Exchange Pre-Deployment Analyzer   15

    Exchange Deployment Assistant   15

    Objective Summary   17

    Objective Review   17

What do you think of this book? We want to hear from you!

Microsoft is interested in hearing your feedback so we can continually improve our
books and learning resources for you. To participate in a brief online survey, please visit:

www.microsoft.com/learning/booksurvey/

Objective 1.2: Design Message Routing 20

   Design Message Transport   20

   Modifying Default Message Routing Topology   21

   Transport Server Scalability   22

   Message Queues and Shadow Redundancy   25

   Transport Storage Requirements   26

   Planning Accepted and Remote Domains   28

   Planning Send and Receive Connectors   29

   Planning DNS   32

   Planning Transport Server Ports   34

   Objective Summary   35

   Objective Review   36

Objective 1.3: Design the Mailbox Server Role 39

   Plan Database Sizing   39

   Plan Log Sizing   42

   Storage Performance Requirements   42

   Mailboxes in Multiple-Forest Topologies   44

   Recipient Policies   46

   Distribution Group Policies   49

   Public Folders   53

   Mailbox Provisioning Policies   54

   Objective Summary   55

   Objective Review   56

Objective 1.4: Design Client Access 59

   Planning Client Access Servers Location   59

   CAS Proxying and Remote Access   60

   Planning Client Access Server Services   60

   Exchange Control Panel   61

   Exchange ActiveSync   63

   Testing Client Access Server Performance   63

   Client Access Server Hardware Requirements   64

Planning Autodiscover   64

Autodiscover in Multiple-Forest Environments   65

Planning Client Access Server Certificates   66

Objective Summary   67

Objective Review   68

Objective 1.5: Plan for Transition and Coexistence 70

Exchange Consolidation   70

Upgrade Approaches   71

Multiple Sites   72

Exchange 2003 Upgrade or Coexistence   72

Exchange 2007 Upgrade or Coexistence   74

Mixed Exchange 2003 and Exchange 2007 Environments   75

Exchange Server Deployment Assistant   76

Coexistence with SMTP-Based Messaging Systems   77

Coexistence with non-SMTP Messaging Systems   77

Global Address List Synchronization   78

Objective Summary   78

Objective Review   79

Chapter Summary 82

Answers 83

Objective 1.1: Review   83

Objective 1.1: Thought Experiment   85

Objective 1.2: Review   85

Objective 1.2: Thought Experiment   87

Objective 1.3: Review   87

Objective 1.3: Thought Experiment   89

Objective 1.4: Review   89

Objective 1.4: Thought Experiment   91

Objective 1.5: Review   91

Objective 1.5: Thought Experiment   93

Chapter 2   Deploying the Exchange Server 2010 Infrastructure   95

Objective 2.1: Prepare the Infrastructure for Exchange Server
    2010 Deployment 96

    Active Directory Functional Level Requirements   97

    Domain Controller Role Requirements   98

    Preparing Active Directory with an Existing Exchange
        Deployment   99

    Preparing the Active Directory Schema   100

    Preparing Active Directory   101

    Preparing Domains   102

    Preparing Federation   103

    Active Directory Synchronization   106

    Configuring DNS Support for SMTP   107

    Objective Summary   108

    Objective Review   108

Objective 2.2: Deploy Edge Transport Server Role 111

    Edge Transport Role   111

    Edge Subscriptions   112

    Direct Configuration   115

    Clone Edge Transport Configuration   116

    Configure Transport Agents   117

    Third-Party Email Gateways   118

    Configure Address Rewriting   120

    Objective Summary   121

    Objective Review   122

Objective 2.3: Deploy Client Access Server Role 125

    Deploying the Client Access Role   125

    Requesting a CAS Certificate   126

    Configuring Outlook Web App   128

    Outlook Anywhere   133

ActiveSync   134

Autodiscover   134

Availability Service   136

POP3 and IMAP4 Access   137

Verifying Client Access Server Functionality   137

Objective Summary   140

Objective Review   140

Objective 2.4: Deploy Hub Transport Server Role. 143

Hub Transport Servers in Multi-Site and
    Multi-Forest Environments   143

Configuring Accepted Domains   144

Configuring Transport Rules   145

Configuring Remote Domains   148

Manage Send Connectors   149

Manage Receive Connectors   151

Message Size Restrictions   153

Special Case Scenarios   155

Objective Summary   157

Objective Review   158

Objective 2.5: Deploy Mailbox Server Role 161

Deploy Mailbox Servers   161

Deploy Mailbox Databases   162

Database Configuration and Quota Policies   165

Database Mailbox Provisioning Policies   166

Deploy Address Lists   167

Deploy Offline Address Books   170

Deploy Public Folders   172

Validate Mailbox Server Access   178

Objective Summary   179

Objective Review   179

Objective 2.6: Deploy Server Roles for Coexistence and Migration. 182

    Upgrading and Coexistence with Exchange 2003   182

    Upgrading and Coexistence with Exchange 2007   184

    Installing Exchange 2010 in a Mixed Exchange 2003 and
        Exchange 2007 Environment   186

    Validating Exchange Server Deployment   187

    Coexistence with Third-Party Email Systems   188

    Transport Rule Coexistence   191

    Converting LDAP to OPATH Filters   192

    Routing Group Connector Configuration   193

    Objective Summary   194

    Objective Review   195

Chapter Summary. 199

Answers. 201

    Objective 2.1: Review   201

    Objective 2.1: Thought Experiment   202

    Objective 2.2: Review   203

    Objective 2.2: Thought Experiment   205

    Objective 2.3: Review   205

    Objective 2.3: Thought Experiment   207

    Objective 2.4: Review   207

    Objective 2.4: Thought Experiment   209

    Objective 2.5: Review   209

    Objective 2.5: Thought Experiment   211

    Objective 2.6: Review   211

    Objective 2.6: Thought Experiment   213

**Chapter 3 Designing and Deploying Security for the
Exchange Organization   215**

Objective 3.1: Design and Deploy Messaging Security 216

　Define Message Security Requirements   217

　Certificates   217

　Secure Relaying   218

　Signing, Encrypting, and S/MIME   220

　MTLS and Domain Security   221

　Information Rights Management (IRM)   223

　IRM in Multiple-Forest Environments   225

　Transport Protection and Decryption   226

　Outlook Protection Rule   227

　Objective Summary   228

　Objective Review   229

Objective 3.2: Design and Deploy Exchange Permissions Model. 231

　Role-Based Access Control   232

　Exchange Control Panel   238

　Split Permissions Model   239

　Objective Summary   240

　Objective Review   241

Objective 3.3: Design and Deploy Message Hygiene. 243

　Antivirus Features   243

　Anti-Spam Features   244

　Objective Summary   254

　Objective Review   254

Objective 3.4: Design and Deploy Client Access Security 257

　ActiveSync Policies   257

　OWA Authentication   260

　OWA Segmentation   262

　Objective Summary   265

　Objective Review   265

Objective 3.5: Design and Deploy Exchange Object Permissions 268

    Public Folder Security   268

    Mailbox Permissions   270

    Distribution Group Security   270

    Objective Summary   273

    Objective Review   274

Chapter Summary 276

Answers 278

    Objective 3.1: Review   278

    Objective 3.1: Thought Experiment   279

    Objective 3.2: Review   280

    Objective 3.2: Thought Experiment   281

    Objective 3.3: Review   281

    Objective 3.3: Thought Experiment   283

    Objective 3.4: Review   283

    Objective 3.4: Thought Experiment   284

    Objective 3.5: Review   285

    Objective 3.5: Thought Experiment   286

Chapter 4   Designing and Deploying Exchange Server 2010 Availability and Recovery   287

Objective 4.1: Design and Deploy High Availability and Disaster Recovery for Exchange Dependencies 288

    Active Directory Redundancy and Recovery   288

    DNS   290

    Storage   292

    Site   292

    Updates   293

    Change Management   295

    Backup and Recovery Objectives   295

    Objective Summary   296

    Objective Review   296

Objective 4.2: Design and Deploy High Availability and
    Disaster Recovery for CAS Role. 298

    Back Up CAS   299

    Recover CAS   300

    Deploy CAS Arrays   301

    Design Multi-Site CAS Deployment   302

    CAS Site Failover   302

    Objective Summary   303

    Objective Review   304

Objective 4.3: Design and Deploy High Availability and
    Disaster Recovery for Mailbox Server Role. 306

    Back Up Mailbox Servers   306

    Recover Mailbox Servers   307

    Recover Mailbox Databases and Data   308

    Design Database Availability Groups   309

    Design and Deploy Public Folder Replication   319

    Repair Mailbox Databases   320

    Objective Summary   321

    Objective Review   321

Objective 4.4: Design and Deploy High Availability and
    Disaster Recovery for Hub Transport Role 324

    Hub Transport Backup   325

    Hub Transport Server Recovery   325

    Redundant Hub Transport Deployment   326

    Resilient Receive Connectors   328

    Send Connector Resiliency   328

    Objective Summary   330

    Objective Review   330

Objective 4.5: Design and Deploy High Availability and
    Disaster Recovery for Edge Transport Role. 332

        Edge Transport Server Backup and Recovery   333

        Redundant Edge Transport Server Deployment   334

        Configure DNS to Support Redundant Edge Transport   335

        Objective Summary   336

        Objective Review   336

Chapter Summary. 339

Answers. 340

        Objective 4.1: Review   340

        Objective 4.1: Thought Experiment   341

        Objective 4.2: Review   342

        Objective 4.2: Thought Experiment   343

        Objective 4.3: Review   344

        Objective 4.3: Thought Experiment   345

        Objective 4.4: Review   346

        Objective 4.4: Thought Experiment   347

        Objective 4.5: Review   348

        Objective 4.5: Thought Experiment   349

**Chapter 5   Designing and Deploying Messaging
Compliance, System Monitoring, and Reporting   351**

Objective 5.1: Design and Deploy Auditing and Discovery. 352

        Administrator Audit Logging   352

        Mailbox Audit Logging   354

        Message Tracking   354

        Protocol Logging   356

        Discovery Searches   357

        Records Management   359

        Information Rights Management Logging   360

        Objective Summary   361

        Objective Review   362

Objective 5.2: Design and Deploy Message Archival 363

    Understanding Recoverable Items   364

    Single Item Recovery   365

    Litigation Hold   366

    Personal Archives   368

    Managed Folders   369

    Retention Tags and Policies   371

    Migrate from Managed Folders to Retention Policies   372

    Retention Hold   372

    Objective Summary   373

    Objective Review   374

Objective 5.3: Design and Deploy Transport Rules for
Message Compliance 376

    Ethical Firewalls   377

    Message Journaling   378

    Alternate Journaling Mailbox   379

    MailTips   379

    Disclaimers   380

    Objective Summary   381

    Objective Review   382

Objective 5.4: Design and Deploy for Monitoring and Reporting 384

    Monitoring Exchange   384

    Connectivity Logging   385

    Exchange 2010 Performance Monitoring   386

    ActiveSync Reporting   388

    Objective Summary   389

    Objective Review   390

Chapter Summary. 392

Answers. 393

    Objective 5.1: Review   393

    Objective 5.1: Thought Experiment   394

    Objective 5.2: Review   394

    Objective 5.2: Thought Experiment   396

    Objective 5.3: Review   396

    Objective 5.3: Thought Experiment   397

    Objective 5.4: Review   398

    Objective 5.4: Thought Experiment   399

Index   *401*

What do you think of this book? We want to hear from you!

Microsoft is interested in hearing your feedback so we can continually improve our books and learning resources for you. To participate in a brief online survey, please visit:

www.microsoft.com/learning/booksurvey/

Introduction

This Exam Ref is designed to assist you with studying for the MCITP exam 70-663, "Designing and Deploying Messaging Solutions with Microsoft Exchange Server 2010." This Exchange Server 2010 exam focuses on which technology to use to meet a particular design objective; the MCTS exam 70-662, "Microsoft Exchange Server 2010, Configuring" (*http://www.microsoft.com/learning/en/us/exam.aspx?id=70-662#tab2*) involves knowing how to configure that technology to meet a specific operational objective.

The 70-663 exam is aimed at messaging administrators in medium to large organizations. By passing the exam, you will demonstrate that you have the knowledge and experience to design complex, multi-site and multi-forest Exchange Server 2010 deployments. If you've also passed the 70-662 exam, passing this exam will earn you the MCITP: Enterprise Messaging Administrator 2010 certification.

This book will review every concept described in the following exam objective domains:

- Planning the Exchange Server 2010 Infrastructure
- Deploying the Exchange Server 2010 Infrastructure
- Designing and Deploying Security for the Exchange Organization
- Designing and Deploying Exchange Server 2010 Availability and Recovery
- Designing and Deploying Messaging Compliance, System Monitoring, and Reporting

This book covers every exam objective, but it does not necessarily cover every exam question. Microsoft regularly adds new questions to the exam, making it impossible for this (or any) book to provide every answer. Instead, this book is designed to supplement your relevant independent study and real-world experience with the product. If you encounter a topic in this book that you do not feel completely comfortable with, you should visit any links described in the text and spend several hours researching the topic further using TechNet, Exchange Server team blogs, and support forums. Ideally, you should also deploy your own complex Exchange environment. This involves deploying multiple servers across multiple sites and domains. The simplest way of doing this is to build your own virtualized lab.

Microsoft Certified Professional Program

Microsoft certifications provide the best method for proving your command of current Microsoft products and technologies. The exams and corresponding certifications are developed to validate your mastery of critical competencies as you design and develop, or implement and support, solutions with Microsoft products and technologies. Computer professionals who become Microsoft certified are recognized as experts and are sought after industry-wide. Certification brings a variety of benefits to the individual and to employers and organizations.

> **MORE INFO**   **OTHER MICROSOFT CERTIFICATIONS**
>
> For a full list of Microsoft certifications, go to *www.microsoft.com/learning/mcp/ default.asp.*

Acknowledgments

I'd like to thank my good mate Ken Jones at O'Reilly for his support in getting the Exam Ref series off the ground. It's always a pleasure to work with Ken and I'm forever thankful for the opportunities that he presents me with as an author. Readers have Ken to thank for ensuring that Pro-level exams like 70-663 are now getting Microsoft Press coverage.

I'd also like to thank technical reviewer Ian McLean, production editor Jean Smith, production manager Dan Fauxsmith, and copy editor Rebecca McKay. Without your assistance and professionalism, the book wouldn't have come together as well as it has!

As always I'd like to thank my wife, Oksana, and son, Rooslan, for their patience with me during the writing process. I'd also like to thank Scott Schnoll for his excellent technical presentations, which really bring features such as how Exchange handles datacenter failover to life. I'd also like to thank Chris Brown for his feedback and Paul Cunningham for his great website *http://exchangeserverpro.com.*

I'd also like to thank you, the reader, for picking up this book. If you have any questions about anything and you want to get in touch with me, you can find me on twitter *http://twitter.com/OrinThomas.*

Support and Feedback

The following sections provide information on errata, book support, feedback, and contact information.

Errata

We've made every effort to ensure the accuracy of this book and its companion content. Any errors that have been reported since this book was published are listed on our Microsoft Press site at oreilly.com:

> *http://go.microsoft.com/FWLink/?Linkid=235193*

If you find an error that is not already listed, you can report it to us through the same page.

If you need additional support, email Microsoft Press Book Support at *mspinput@microsoft.com*.

Please note that product support for Microsoft software is not offered through the addresses above.

We Want to Hear from You

At Microsoft Press, your satisfaction is our top priority, and your feedback our most valuable asset. Please tell us what you think of this book at:

> *http://www.microsoft.com/learning/booksurvey*

The survey is short, and we read every one of your comments and ideas. Thanks in advance for your input!

Stay in Touch

Let's keep the conversation going! We're on Twitter: *http://twitter.com/MicrosoftPress*

Preparing for the Exam

Microsoft certification exams are a great way to build your resume and let the world know about your level of expertise. Certification exams validate your on-the-job experience and product knowledge. Although there is no substitute for on-the-job experience, preparation through study and hands-on practice can help you prepare for the exam. We recommend that you augment your exam preparation plan by using a combination of available study materials and courses. For example, you might use the Exam Ref and another study guide for your "at home" preparation, and take a Microsoft Official Curriculum course for the classroom experience. Choose the combination that you think works best for you.

CHAPTER 1

Planning the Exchange Server 2010 Infrastructure

You have probably heard the expression "Measure twice, cut once." When it comes to the deployment of Exchange Server 2010, taking time with your organization's deployment can save you a lot of trouble later. In this chapter you'll learn about the different models for on-premises and cloud-based deployments, DNS requirements, how to translate Service Level Agreement (SLA) requirements into design decisions, and whether you need to plan Exchange federation. You'll learn how to design an appropriate topology to meet your organization's message routing requirements, design a Mailbox server deployment that is appropriate given your organization's topology, design a Client Access Server deployment to support your proposed Exchange deployment, and plan a deployment to meet any transition and coexistence requirements. This chapter is primarily about design considerations prior to deploying Exchange Server 2010. Chapter 2, "Deploying the Exchange Server 2010 Infrastructure," deals more with the specifics of configuring these technologies on the organizational network.

> **IMPORTANT**
>
> ### Have you read page xxi?
>
> It contains valuable information regarding the skills you need to pass the exam.

Objectives in this chapter:

- Objective 1.1: Design the Exchange Server 2010 installation
- Objective 1.2: Design Message routing
- Objective 1.3: Design the mailbox server role
- Objective 1.4: Design client access
- Objective 1.5: Plan for transition and coexistence

Real World

Most organizations don't get to deploy a brand new Exchange infrastructure from scratch, but instead have to perform a deployment based on the constraints imposed by an existing infrastructure. That makes the objectives in this chapter a little tricky because they involve testing your knowledge of a theoretical Exchange Server 2010 deployment rather than what you may encounter when actually deploying Exchange Server 2010. A good example of this is when I discuss preparing the schema and domains for the Active Directory deployment. As a friend of mine in the Exchange product team pointed out, it isn't actually necessary to run these commands separately because the Exchange Server 2010 installation wizard makes these preparations automatically the first time you install Exchange. If it all happens automatically, why mention it and why put it on an exam? Microsoft's aim in testing this knowledge on the exam is to ensure that you have an understanding of what is going on in the background—so you understand how the schema and domains are prepared even if you do just decide to run the installation wizard instead of carefully going through the Active Directory preparation first.

EXAM TIP

In reality crafting an Exchange design involves dealing with nuance and complexity, but actual exam questions are in a multiple-choice format where answers are either right or wrong. In reality some answers are better than others. If, in the exam, you have an option where it seems as though two answers could be right, but you can only choose one answer as correct, you've likely missed a clue in the question text that would allow you to discard one of these answers. This is because when exams are authored, not only does the question writer have to provide good reasons why one answer is correct, but he also has to provide good reasons as to why the other answers are incorrect. Although there is a small chance that you've come across a bad question that got through proofreading and peer review, it's more likely that in a stressful exam situation you've overlooked a vital bit of evidence that discounts an answer you suspect is correct.

Objective 1.1: Design the Exchange Server 2010 Installation

Microsoft provides guidance for IT professionals on the factors they should consider when planning to deploy Exchange Server 2010. In this objective you'll learn about the factors you need to consider when planning your Exchange deployment. In Chapter 2, "Deploying the Exchange Server 2010 Infrastructure," you'll learn about the practical steps you need to take to perform an Exchange Server 2010 deployment.

This objective covers:

- Define Exchange server locations.
- Determine Exchange DNS requirements.
- Consider SLA requirements.
- Consider Network and Active Directory site topologies.
- Plan for Exchange federation.
- Consider complex Active Directory requirements.
- Understand the Exchange Deployment Assistant.

Choosing Exchange Server Locations

You can choose between three general Exchange design options when deploying Exchange Server 2010: an on-premises deployment, a cloud deployment, or a coexistence deployment. In the real world, decisions about whether to go with an on-premises or cloud-based deployment are rarely technical in nature. These decisions are usually driven by business needs and cost and you are unlikely to encounter a question on the 70-663 exam that directly asks you whether a cloud-based or on-premises deployment is appropriate. You are more likely to be asked about what design considerations are involved if it becomes necessary to configure your organization to support an on-premises and cloud-based coexistence scenario. You'll need to know what steps you'd need to take to get such a deployment working, not whether an organization would be better off shunting everything to the cloud or keeping everything in-house.

On-Premises Deployments

The 70-663 exam primarily deals with the design of on-premises Exchange Server 2010 deployments and infrastructure. In part this is because a lot less design work is required if you go with an entirely cloud-based Exchange deployment than there is in deciding where to place hub transport, client access, and mailbox servers on a per-site basis. The focus is on local deployments because the vast majority of organizations who use Exchange still choose to go with on-premises rather than coexistence or entirely cloud-based deployments.

When choosing where to place Exchange servers, you need to take into account issues such as number of mailboxes, server capacity, and available bandwidth. While it might be possible to place an Exchange server that hosts the mailbox, client access, and hub transport server roles at each location, even in the biggest organizations such an approach isn't always necessary. For example, one multinational company I know of has approximately 2,000 employees spread across the capital cities of Australia and another 500 or so in New Zealand. All of these employees use Exchange servers hosted in Singapore and there is no local Exchange deployment. Each office has local domain controllers and global catalog servers to handle authentication, but the client access, hub transport, and mailbox servers are thousands of miles away in another country.

Cloud-Only Deployments

A completely cloud-based deployment involves your organization's Exchange server being hosted online, most likely through Exchange Online, which is a part of Microsoft Office 365. Cloud-only deployments have the following characteristics:

- The cloud-based Exchange deployment is completely separate from any local on-premises messaging system.
- Users need separate credentials to authenticate and access their cloud-hosted mailboxes.
- The local Active Directory infrastructure does not synchronize with the cloud-based deployments. User mailboxes and distribution groups are administered independently of any local on-premises mailbox and distribution groups.

Cloud-only deployments are often used for new organizations or organizations that want to move from a third-party mail system to a cloud-based Exchange mail system.

> ***MORE INFO*** **UNDERSTANDING CLOUD-ONLY DEPLOYMENTS**
>
> For more information on cloud-only deployments, consult the following TechNet webpage: *http://technet.microsoft.com/en-us/library/gg583832.aspx.*

Coexistence

Coexistence deployments involve both an on-premises Exchange deployment and a cloud-hosted Exchange deployment. Coexistence is generally used when an organization wants to transition from an existing Exchange Server 2003 or Exchange Server 2007 deployment to an entirely cloud-hosted Exchange 2010 deployment, though it is possible to configure coexistence between a local Exchange 2010 deployment and a cloud-hosted Exchange 2010 deployment as well.

When you deploy Exchange in a coexistence configuration, you need to deploy an on-premises coexistence server. A coexistence server is a computer running Exchange Server 2010 that you configure with the necessary Exchange Server 2010 roles that allow it to manage communication between the on-premises Exchange deployment and the cloud-based deployment. You also need to configure a directory synchronization server. This server synchronizes account information between the local and hosted Exchange deployments.

Hosted Exchange 2010 supports two types of coexistence. The difference between these is as follows:

- **Simple coexistence**   Provides a unified Global Address List (GAL) and mail routing between the local and hosted Exchange organization.
- **Rich coexistence**   Provides a unified GAL, mail routing, sharing availability information, and the ability to move mailboxes between the local and hosted Exchange organization. Rich coexistence requires that you configure a federation trust with the Microsoft Federation Gateway.

MORE INFO   **COEXISTENCE**

To learn more about coexistence, consult the following page on TechNet: *http://technet. microsoft.com/en-us/library/gg476106.aspx.*

Planning Exchange DNS Support

Although it is possible to use Active Directory and Exchange with a third-party DNS solution such as BIND, doing so requires substantial administrative overhead. Microsoft recommends that you use Active Directory–integrated DNS zones to support your internal Active Directory and Exchange name resolution requirements. You should configure Active Directory–integrated zones to accept secure dynamic updates only, you should enable scavenging, and you should configure DNS zones to replicate to all domain controllers in the forest. Configuring DNS in this way ensures that internal DNS is updated appropriately when you introduce new servers hosting Exchange Server 2010 roles into your Active Directory environment.

Many organizations split the hosting of their externally resolvable DNS hosts from their internal DNS. For example, an organization might use the contoso.com Active Directory Integrated DNS zone to support the contoso.com forest. The problem is that while it will be fine for external clients to resolve hostnames like www.contoso.com and smtp.contoso.com, most organizations would not want internal host names such as SYD-FS1.contoso.com and SYD-EX1.contoso.com to be resolvable by hosts on the Internet.

You can deal with the problem by configuring DNS delegation to point to an externally hosted DNS zone that only holds records that you want available to hosts on the Internet, such as the host and MX records that point to your organization's SMTP server. A separate internal DNS infrastructure holds all records that should be accessible to internal hosts.

Rather than having the same zone hosted in two different locations, another option is to configure a split DNS namespace, where your organization's internal DNS domain name is a delegated sub-domain of the external DNS namespace. For example, the external DNS namespace might be adatum.com and the internal DNS namespace be configured as corp. adatum.com. When taking this approach it is necessary to ensure that you configure the root domain as an accepted domain, so that recipients can receive email using the root domain as their mail domain. For example, being able to accept email @adatum.com rather than only at @corp.adatum.com.

Common Shared Namespace

Some organizations use multiple mail systems, but only have a single address space. For example, an email message sent to kim.akers@contoso.com might need to be routed to an Exchange Server 2010 mailbox, whereas an email message to sam.abolrous@contoso.com might need to be routed to a mailbox hosted on a third-party messaging system. You can solve this design challenge within Exchange by configuring what is known as an *internal relay domain* and then creating a send connector to route email to the shared domain.

Disjointed Namespace

A disjointed namespace exists when the primary DNS suffix of a computer does not match the DNS domain name of the domain of which the computer is a member. Microsoft supports three different scenarios for deploying Exchange in an environment where there is a disjointed namespace:

- The primary DNS suffix of all domain controllers differs from the DNS domain name. Computers that are members of this domain may or may not be disjointed. In this situation, you can have Exchange servers that use either the primary DNS suffix or the DNS domain name.

- One or more member computers in the domain have primary DNS suffixes that differ from the DNS domain name even though all domain controllers are not disjointed. In this situation, you can have Exchange servers that use either the primary DNS suffix or the DNS domain name.

- The NetBIOS name of domain controllers differs from the subdomain of the DNS domain name of those domain controllers. For example, the NetBIOS name might be SOUTHPACIFIC, but the primary DNS suffix and the DNS domain name might be contoso.com.

For servers running Exchange Server 2010 to have access to domain controllers in environments that have a disjointed namespace, it is necessary to modify the *msDS-AllowedDNSSuffixes* Active Directory attribute on the domain object container so that it includes both the DNS domain name and the primary DNS suffix, as shown in Figure 1-1.

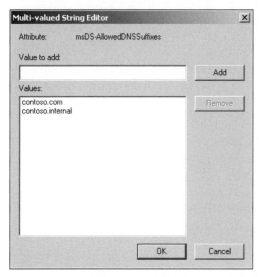

FIGURE 1-1 msDS-AllowedDNSSuffixes

You also need to ensure that the DNS suffix search list for computers includes all DNS namespaces used within your organization. This can be done by configuring the DNS Suffix Search List group policy item, located in the Computer Configuration\Policies\Administrative Templates\Network\DNS Client node.

To view the primary DNS suffix and DNS domain name of a computer running Windows Server 2008 or Windows Server 2008 R2, click the Computer Name tab of the System Properties dialog box, as shown in Figure 1-2. In the figure the namespace is disjointed as the primary DNS suffix is adatum.internal where the domain name is adatum.com.

> **MORE INFO** **DISJOINTED NAMESPACE SCENARIOS**
>
> To learn more about disjointed namespace scenarios, consult the following TechNet document: *http://technet.microsoft.com/en-us/library/bb676377.aspx*.

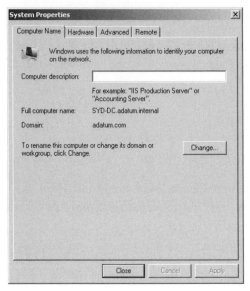

FIGURE 1-2 Disjointed namespace

Service Level Agreement Considerations

A Service Level Agreement (SLA) is an arrangement between the IT service provider and an organization that specifies measurable infrastructure performance levels. Although SLAs vary from organization to organization, they most commonly include goals related to the following service characteristics:

- **Availability**   A way of defining how reliable the service is in terms of the amount of time the service may be unavailable in a given period. For example, an SLA might specify that Exchange has an allowable downtime for planned maintenance and unplanned faults for a total of five hours a month.

- **Performance**   A way of defining minimum performance characteristics of the infrastructure. For example, an SLA might specify a maximum number of concurrent connections to a mailbox server. Performance may influence your design with relation to the hardware specifications of servers hosting Exchange.

- **Recovery**   This is a way of defining how quickly data or services can be recovered in the event of an outage. For example, an SLA might specify a maximum recovery time for deleted mailbox items. Recovery objectives influence the data protection technologies that you include in your Exchange design.

You must explicitly define each performance characteristic in the SLA. For example, you might be designing an Exchange deployment for an organization that has a head office and two branch offices. The branch offices are so small that you decide not to deploy Exchange at those sites, but instead have users connect to Exchange servers located at the head office site. If the site link between the head office and one of the branch office sites fails, blocking access to Exchange for the users at that branch office site, but all other users in the organization are able to access the centrally located Exchange servers, how will that outage be measured by the terms of the SLA?

Internal SLAs are arrangements between an organization's IT department and business units within the organization. In most organizations, internal SLAs tend to be less formal and the performance metrics less explicitly defined. External SLAs are contracts created between the organization and a third-party provider, such as a cloud service provider. External SLAs tend to be a lot more complicated and are generally legally binding contracts including cost, bonus, and penalty clauses. External SLAs are increasingly important for organizations that use a hybrid approach to their Exchange deployment, with some services hosted internally and other services hosted in the public cloud.

When you have an SLA in place, you will need to regularly attend to certain ongoing tasks, including:

- **Service catalog maintenance**   A service catalog defines the services provided to the organization. It provides detailed descriptions of the service components and the IT functionality utilized by the business. You need to ensure that this is both comprehensive and up to date.

- **Service level monitoring**   It is important to have a monitoring solution in place that verifies that the IT service provider is complying with the conditions of the SLA. Products such as System Center Operations Manager 2012 are designed to monitor Exchange Server 2010 deployments.

- **Service level reporting**   You should regularly generate and distribute reports. These reports should describe metrics related to the performance levels specified in the SLA. SLA objectives must be specific and measurable. If you cannot measure an SLA objective, it is impossible to impartially determine whether that objective has been met. Having an SLA objective that is open to interpretation can lead to disagreements between the IT department and the organization as to whether the objective has been met.

- **SLA review**   Plan to review the SLA periodically with all involved stakeholders. Use these reviews to determine whether you should modify the SLA to better meet the needs of the organization.

You should have an SLA in place before you complete the Exchange design process. Knowing what goals you need to meet allows you to ensure that your Exchange design suits the needs of your organization. For example, you might meet availability requirements by deploying multiple hub transport servers at each site, using Database Availability Groups and Client Access Server arrays. The terms of the SLA also impact the cost of the deployment. It is important to ensure that the terms of the SLA are realistic given the budgets involved. You can't realistically provide highly available redundant Exchange servers if your budget only allows you to deploy a single computer running Exchange at one central site.

Active Directory and Network Topology

Exchange Server 2010 generates its network topology information by querying Active Directory for site information. Each Active Directory site is defined as a collection of IPv4 or IPv6 networks. Usually that collection is a single local high-speed network. Most organizations have configured Active Directory so that each physical location is its own distinct Active Directory site. For example, you might have one site that represents a branch office at Sydney and another site that represents a branch office in Melbourne. As Active Directory does not automatically create additional sites, you may occasionally encounter organizations where Active Directory hasn't been properly maintained and there is only one site even though the organization itself is spread across multiple branch offices.

By using the Active Directory site topology, Exchange can determine how to transport messages and which global catalog servers and domain controllers should be used for processing Active Directory queries. When deploying Exchange, you don't need to worry about configuring routing topologies—this is all handled by using the Active Directory site topology. The only exception to this is if you are introducing Exchange 2010 into an environment that has Exchange 2003.

When considering your Exchange design, you should ensure that your organization's Active Directory site configuration is appropriate and reflects the realities of your organization's network infrastructure. At a minimum this means ensuring that IP networks at each branch office site are associated with and appropriate site within Active Directory. You associate IP networks with Active Directory sites by using the Active Directory Sites and Services console.

Multiple Domains

Exchange is designed to be deployed and used in multiple domains across a single forest. A single Exchange organization can span a forest that has a single or multiple domain trees. That means that you can have one Exchange organization supporting domains with different names, such as wingtiptoys.com and tailspintoys.com, as long as those domains are a part of the same Active Directory forest.

If you do have multiple domain trees in your forest, you might want to configure Exchange to accept email for more than one authoritative domain. That means that you can design a single Exchange organization so that it will be able to receive and process email for separate mail domains representing different trees in the same forest, such as wingtiptoys.com and tailspintoys.com, as long as Exchange has been properly configured. You configure accepted domains on transport servers. You will learn more about configuring accepted domains in Chapter 2.

> **MORE INFO** **GAL SEGMENTATION**
>
> Exchange Server 2010 service pack 2 will support GAL segmentation. GAL segmentation allows you to create smaller address lists on a per-domain or per-domain tree basis rather than including all addresses in an Exchange organization. To find out more about GAL segmentation, consult the following Exchange product team blog article at: *http://blogs. technet.com/b/exchange/archive/2011/01/27/3411882.aspx.*

Multiple Forests

Some organizations have more than one Active Directory forest, with trust relationships configured between forests to allow users who have accounts in one forest to access resources in another forest. As you are aware, a single Exchange Server 2010 organization can only span a single forest. If your organization has more than one forest, you will need to use one of the supported multiple forest topologies when you create your deployment design. Exchange Server 2010 supports the following multiple forest topologies:

- **Cross-forest** The cross-forest topology involves multiple Active Directory forests with an Exchange Server 2010 organization in each forest. When designing an Exchange deployment to support a cross-forest topology you need to configure recipient synchronization so that the GAL in each forest holds information for recipients in all forests. You also need to configure the Availability service so that users in each forest are able to view availability information for users in all of your organization's other forests.

- **Resource-forest** The resource-forest topology involves one Active Directory forest that has Exchange deployed and other Active Directory forests that host user accounts. In the resource-forest model, the forest that hosts Exchange often does not host user accounts and the accounts which have Exchange mailboxes are disabled. At least one forest that does not have an Exchange organization must host user accounts. Disabled user accounts in the forest that hosts Exchange are associated with user accounts in the account forest.

> **MORE INFO** **MULTIPLE-FOREST TOPOLOGIES**
>
> To learn more about supporting multiple-forest topologies with Exchange Server 2010, consult the following TechNet article: *http://technet.microsoft.com/en-us/library/bb124734.aspx.*

Microsoft recommends that you use a product such as Forefront Identity Lifecycle Manager (ILM) 2010 to ensure that the GAL in each forest in a cross-forest Exchange topology contains all the mail recipients from other forests. Enabling GAL synchronization requires that you create management agents that import mail-enabled groups, contacts, and users into a centralized metadirectory where they are represented as mail users. The management agents then synchronize these mail users to a specially configured OU in each target forest.

> **MORE INFO** **PLANNING ACTIVE DIRECTORY**
>
> To learn more about preparing Active Directory for the deployment of Exchange, consult the following webpage: *http://technet.microsoft.com/en-us/library/bb123715.aspx.*

Directory Synchronization with the Cloud

Active Directory synchronization allows you to configure an ongoing relationship between your organization's Active Directory infrastructure and a cloud service provider such as Office 365. Microsoft recommends that you configure single sign-on prior to setting up directory synchronization. Single sign-on allows a user to log on to cloud service providers, such as Office 365, using their organizational credentials. If single sign-on is not configured, it will be necessary to add and verify your organization's domains, and local password changes will not be synchronized with the hosted Exchange organization.

To configure your organization to support single sign-on, you need to take the following general steps:

1. Ensure that your organization's forest functional level is set to Windows Server 2003, Windows Server 2008, or Windows Server 2008 R2.

2. Ensure that the domain that you will be federating can be resolved by hosts on the Internet.

3. Configure User Principle Names (UPNs) for all users. UPNs used for single sign-on can only contain letters, numbers, periods, dashes, and underscore characters. The UPN domain suffix must be a publicly registered domain. Microsoft recommends using a user's email domain as her account's UPN suffix.

4. Deploy Active Directory Federation Services (AD FS) 2.0. AD FS is required to support single sign-on to cloud service providers such as Office 365. Microsoft recommends deploying two federation services in a load balanced configuration. Federation server proxies will be required if you want to support roaming clients or smartphone access to hosted Exchange.

> **MORE INFO**   **DEPLOY AD FS TO SUPPORT HOSTED EXCHANGE**
>
> To learn more about deploying AD FS to support Hosted Exchange, consult the following article: *http://onlinehelp.microsoft.com/en-us/office365-enterprises/ff652539.aspx*.

5. Install and configure the Microsoft Online Services Module for Windows PowerShell for Single Sign On. This module requires a host running Windows 7 or Windows Server 2008 R2 with the Microsoft .NET Framework 3.51 feature enabled.

6. Each domain that you want to synchronize with the cloud service provider must be added as a single sign-on domain or converted to become a single sign-on domain. To perform this conversion you use the *Connect-MsolService*, *Set-MsolAdfscontext*, and *Convert-MsolDomainToFederated* cmdlets.

> **MORE INFO**   **MICROSOFT ONLINE SERVICES MODULE FOR WINDOWS POWERSHELL**
>
> To learn more about the Microsoft Online Services Module for Windows PowerShell, consult the following webpage: *http://onlinehelp.microsoft.com/en-us/office365-enterprises/ff652560.aspx*.

Once you have configured single sign-on, you will need to designate a computer as your organization's directory synchronization computer. This computer can be a virtual machine, but it must meet the following criteria:

- The synchronization computer must be a member of the Active Directory forest that will host the Exchange organization.

- The synchronization computer cannot be a domain controller.

- The synchronization computer must have the .NET Framework 3.5 or later installed.

- The computer must run a 32-bit version of the Windows Server 2003, Windows Server 2003 R2, or Windows Server 2008 operating systems. At present the directory synchronization tool cannot be installed on a computer running Windows Server 2008 R2 because 64-bit environments are not supported.

You will also need to configure an Exchange Server 2010 coexistence server to support the coexistence scenario.

Exchange Federation

Exchange federation allows people in your organization to configure your Exchange infrastructure so that contact information and calendar availability can be shared with external recipients, vendors, and partners. If you want to configure Exchange federation, you need to set up a one-time federation trust between your organization and the Microsoft Federation Gateway. The Microsoft Federation Gateway is a cloud-based service that functions as a trust broker between a locally hosted Exchange 2010 organization and other organizations that have configured Exchange federation.

When creating a federation trust between your organization and the Microsoft Federation gateway, you need to either create a self-signed certificate or install an X.509 certificate signed by a trusted CA on the Exchange 2010 server that you will use to create the trust. Microsoft recommends using a self-signed certificate, which the New Federation Trust Wizard will automatically create and install, vastly simplifying this process.

After you have configured this trust relationship, the Microsoft Federation Gateway will issue Active Directory authenticated users in the local forest special Security Assertion Markup Language (SAML) delegation tokens. SAML delegation tokens allow organizations that have configured Exchange federation to trust users from other organizations that have configured Exchange federation. Instead of having to create each inter-organizational trust relationship separately, each organization configures a single trust with the Microsoft Federation Gateway, enabling them to share availability information with other organizations that have a trust with the Microsoft Federation Gateway.

When you establish a federation trust between your organization and the Microsoft Federation Gateway, an application identifier (AppID) is generated that will be used by the Federation Gateway to uniquely identify your Exchange organization. You use the AppID in conjunction with a text (TXT) record in DNS to prove that your organization is associated with the domain that is used with the Microsoft Federation Gateway. It is necessary to create a TXT record in the DNS zone for each federated domain in your organization.

You define which authoritative accepted domains in your organization are enabled for federation through the federated organization identifier (OrgID). Only those recipients that have email addresses associated with the OrgID will be able to use federated delegation features by the Microsoft Federation Gateway. Federation delegation uses a domain namespace for the OrgID that differs from the primary SMTP domain. This domain namespace should not be used for mailboxes, and Microsoft recommends that the namespace be called exchangedelegation. This subdomain works as the federated namespace for the Microsoft Federation Gateway, allowing it to manage unique identifiers for those recipients that need SAML delegation tokens. If you want to enable or disable all federation features for your Exchange organization, you can either enable or disable the OrgID.

> **MORE INFO** **EXCHANGE FEDERATION**
>
> For more information on Exchange Server 2010's federation features, consult the following TechNet article: *http://technet.microsoft.com/en-us/library/dd351109.aspx*.

Exchange Pre-Deployment Analyzer

The Exchange Pre-Deployment Analyzer is a tool that allows you to perform a readiness scan of your organization's environment to determine what modifications need to be made prior to the deployment of Exchange Server 2010. This tool will also perform a deep analysis of an existing Exchange 2003 and Exchange 2007 organization to determine whether the configuration will support an in-place upgrade to Exchange 2010. The end report includes critical and warning notifications. A critical notification is one that will block Exchange Server 2010 from being deployed and includes items such as the forest not running in Windows Server 2003 functional mode or higher. A warning notification indicates that some Exchange Server 2010 functionality may not be present if a deployment is performed given the current conditions.

> **MORE INFO** **PRE-DEPLOYMENT ANALYZER**
>
> To learn more about the Exchange Pre-Deployment Analyzer, download the tool from the following Microsoft website: *http://www.microsoft.com/download/en/details.aspx?displaylang=en&id=11636*.

Exchange Deployment Assistant

The Exchange Deployment Assistant, also known as ExDeploy and shown in Figure 1-3, is a web-based tool that you can use in the early stages of planning an Exchange Server 2010 deployment. ExDeploy works by asking a series of questions about your organization's current environment. Based on these questions, ExDeploy generates advice and a custom checklist to assist you with that deployment. Links are provided to relevant TechNet documentation and the output of ExDeploy can be saved for later review.

ExDeploy can provide you with a checklist and advice in the following scenarios:

- Locally hosted on-premise deployments:
    - Upgrade from Exchange Server 2003
    - Upgrade from Exchange Server 2007
    - Upgrade from mixed Exchange 2003 and Exchange 2007 environment
    - New Exchange Server 2010 deployment
- Coexistence of locally hosted on-premise and cloud:
    - Exchange 2003
    - Exchange 2007
    - Exchange 2010
    - Cloud-only deployments

FIGURE 1-3 Exchange Deployment Assistant

MORE INFO **EXCHANGE DEPLOYMENT ASSISTANT**

You can run the Exchange Deployment Assistant by navigating to the following address:
http://technet.microsoft.com/en-us/library/ee681665.aspx.

EXAM TIP

You should load the Exchange Server Deployment Assistant webpage and run through a few scenarios to understand how it functions and the advice it gives under changing conditions.

Objective Summary

- Exchange Server 2010 can be installed in an on-premise, cloud, or a coexistence configuration.
- The Active Directory Sites and Services console allows you to associate specific IP networks with specific Active Directory sites.
- SLA requirements determine parts of your Exchange design, primarily around high-availability features such as Database Availability Groups and Client Access Server Arrays.
- In multiple-forest environments, the resource-forest topology has Exchange deployed in one forest and accessed by users in other forests. The cross-forest topology has Exchange deployed in all forest and uses Forefront Identity Life Cycle Manager for GAL synchronization.
- Exchange Federation allows people in your organization to share contact and calendar availability information. Federation requires setting up a one-time federation trust between your organization and the Microsoft Federation Gateway.
- The Exchange Deployment Assistant (ExDeploy) is an online tool that provides advice and checklists to assist with planning an Exchange deployment based on answers to a set of questions about the current and intended environments.

Objective Review

Answer the following questions to test your knowledge of the information in this objective. You can find the answers to these questions and explanations of why each answer choice is correct or incorrect in the "Answers" section at the end of this chapter.

1. You are in the process of planning an Exchange Server 2010 installation. Which console should you use on a Windows Server 2008 R2 domain controller to verify that branch office network subnets are associated correctly with branch office sites in Active Directory?

    A. Active Directory Administrative Center

    B. Active Directory Users and Computers

    C. Active Directory Domains and Trusts

    D. Active Directory Sites and Services

2. Your organization has a single domain forest. The DNS domain name of the domain is contoso.com. The primary DNS suffix of all domain controllers is contoso.com, but the primary DNS suffix of all member servers—including the servers on which you intend to deploy Exchange Server 2010—is contoso.internal. Which of the following steps must you take to ensure that Exchange Server 2010 will function properly when deployed in this environment? (Choose all that apply.)

   A. Set the *msDS-AllowedDNSSuffixes* Active Directory attribute so that it only includes contoso.internal.

   B. Modify the *msDS-AllowedDNSSuffixes* Active Directory attribute on the domain object container so that it includes both contoso.com and contoso.internal.

   C. Configure the DNS suffix search list group policy item so that it includes both contoso.com and contoso.internal.

   D. Configure the DNS suffix search list group policy item so that it only includes contoso.internal.

3. You are in the process of consulting on an Exchange design for two companies. The first, Tailspin Toys, has a three-forest Active Directory infrastructure. The second company, Wingtip Toys, has a two-forest Active Directory infrastructure. You are in the process of determining which multiple-forest topology would suit each company. Tailspin Toys would be best suited by deploying Exchange in each forest. Wingtip Toys would be best suited by deploying Exchange in one forest and keeping user accounts in the other forest. Which of the following Exchange multiple-forest topology models best suits each organization? (Choose all that apply.)

   A. Tailspin Toys should use the cross-forest topology.

   B. Tailspin Toys should use the resource-forest topology.

   C. Wingtip Toys should use the cross-forest topology.

   D. Wingtip Toys should use the resource-forest topology.

4. You are interested in measuring service availability as a part of monitoring compliance with a Service Level Agreement (SLA). Which of the following products could you use to monitor service availability, configuring alerts to be sent in the event that any component in the Exchange infrastructure fails?

   A. System Center Configuration Manager 2012

   B. System Center Data Protection Manager 2012

   C. System Center Virtual Machine Manager 2012

   D. System Center Operations Manager 2012

5. Which of the following products can you use to assist with global address list (GAL) synchronization if your organization is intending to deploy Exchange Server 2010 in a cross-forest topology?

   A. Forefront Threat Management Gateway 2010

   B. Forefront Endpoint Protection 2012

   C. Forefront Identity Life Cycle Manager 2010

   D. Forefront Unified Access Gateway 2010

THOUGHT EXPERIMENT
Preparing Contoso for Directory Synchronization with the Cloud

In the following thought experiment, apply what you've learned about the "Design the Exchange Server 2010 installation" objective to predict what steps you need to take to prepare Contoso for directory synchronization with the cloud. You can find answers to these questions in the "Answers" section at the end of this chapter.

Contoso has a four-domain Active Directory forest that currently has a small Exchange Server 2007 deployment. You want to configure a coexistence scenario where Exchange Server 2007 will coexist with a cloud hosted Exchange deployment through Office 365.

With this in mind, answer the following questions:

1. What should you do prior to configuring directory synchronization to ensure that password changes are replicated to the cloud-hosted Exchange deployment?

2. What general steps must you take to configure single sign-on at Contoso?

3. Which two servers need to be deployed in the local organization to support the coexistence scenario?

Objective 1.2: Design Message Routing

Designing a message routing infrastructure involves determining where you need to put transport servers to effectively route messages inside and outside your organization. Not only do you need to decide where to put the transport servers, but you also need to ensure that these servers are sufficiently capable of handling the message traffic generated by your organization. Your design needs to include the mail domains that your organization will accept mail for, how to handle the routing of email to third-party messaging systems that might be used within your environment, and how messages will be forwarded from your organizations to destinations on the Internet. In this objective, you'll learn about message routing design. In Chapter 2 you'll learn about how to implement message routing with Edge Transport and Hub Transport servers.

This objective covers:

- Design message transport.
- Plan reverse lookup zones.
- Scale transport server performance.
- Plan accepted and remote domains.
- Design send and Receive connector configuration.

Design Message Transport

At the most basic level, when designing Exchange transport server deployment you need to ensure that you place at least one Hub Transport server in each Active Directory site that has an Exchange Mailbox server. When designing a traditional Exchange 2010 deployment, you will also place at least once Edge Transport server on a perimeter network that is adjacent to an Active Directory site with a Hub Transport server.

Messages are routed through an Exchange 2010 organization in the following general way:

- **Internal Message Routing**   When a message arrives at a Hub Transport server, processes within the Hub Transport server determine the Active Directory site location of the mailbox server that hosts the recipient's mailbox. If the destination Mailbox server is in another Active Directory site, the message is forwarded to the Hub Transport server in that site. If the destination Mailbox server is in the local Active Directory site, the message is queued for local delivery and delivered to the destination mailbox store using an Exchange remote procedure call (RPC).

- **External Message Routing**   When a message arrives at a Hub Transport server and the Hub Transport server determines that the recipient does not have a mailbox within the Exchange organization, the Hub Transport server attempts to select a Send connector through which to send the message. If the source server for that Send connector is in another Active Directory site, the Hub Transport server forwards the message to the Hub Transport server in that site. Through the configuration of Send connectors, you can also allow messages to be routed to other messaging systems within your organization. For example, if you have a cross-forest Exchange topology, you can configure a Send connector to route messages to the other internally hosted Exchange organization.

> **MORE INFO**   **MESSAGE ROUTING**
>
> To learn more about message routing, consult the following TechNet article: *http://technet. microsoft.com/en-us/library/aa998825.aspx.*

Modifying Default Message Routing Topology

If you don't modify the initial configuration, when a Hub Transport server needs to deliver a message to a recipient whose mailbox is hosted on a mailbox server in another Active Directory site, that Hub Transport server will initiate a direct connection to a Hub Transport server in that site. For example, if a Hub Transport server in the Melbourne site needs to deliver a message to a mailbox server in the Darwin site, it will initiate a connection to a Hub Transport server in the Darwin site. Although the default routing topology, based on Active Directory site topology, is suitable for most organizations, you can modify it in the following ways:

- Configure hub sites.
- Configure Exchange-specific routing costs.
- Configure expansion servers for distribution groups.

Configure Hub Sites

You can configure one or more Active Directory sites as hub sites. For example, you might configure the Sydney site as a hub site for all of the other Active Directory sites in your organization's Australian Exchange deployment. You should configure hub sites when your organization's network topology does not support direct connections between Hub Transport servers in different sites. When a hub site lies on a least-cost routing path between a source and destination Hub Transport server, the Hub Transport server at the hub site processes the messages before relaying them to the destination server.

You configure an Active Directory site as an Exchange hub site by using the *Set-AdSite* cmdlet. For example, to set the Sydney site as a hub site, use the following command:

```
Set-ADSite Sydney -HubSiteEnabled $true
```

Configure Exchange-Specific Routing Costs

You can alter the default routing topology by setting an Exchange cost on an Active Directory IP site link. Any set Exchange costs override the existing Active Directory assigned site cost. Use site-link costs to ensure that the least cost routing path between two sites goes through a hub site. You use the *Set-ADSiteLink* cmdlet to configure an Exchange-specific cost for an Active Directory IP site link. For example, to set the Exchange-specific cost of 20 to the IP site link IPSiteLinkMELSYD, use this command:

```
Set-ADSiteLink -Identity IPSiteLinkMELSYD -ExchangeCost 20
```

To remove the Exchange specific site cost from the IP site link IPSiteLinkMELSYD, use the following command:

```
Set-ADSiteLink -Identity IPSiteLinkMELSYD -ExchangeCost $null
```

> **MORE INFO**   **MODIFYING EXCHANGE COSTS ON IP SITE LINKS**
>
> To learn more about configuring Exchange costs on an Active Directory site link, consult the following TechNet document: *http://technet.microsoft.com/en-us/library/bb266946.aspx*.

Configure Expansion Servers for Distribution Groups

When a message is sent to a distribution group, the first Hub Transport server that intercepts the message performs the distribution group expansion, working out how to route messages to each member of the distribution group. With large distribution groups, this can cause a substantial performance hit on the Hub Transport server, slowing down all message routing operations. An alternative to allowing any Hub Transport server to perform distribution group expansion is to configure distribution groups to use specific Hub Transport servers to perform this task. You configure a specific Hub Transport server as a distribution group expansion server by modifying the properties of individual distribution groups. You'll learn more about configuring distribution groups in Chapter 2.

Transport Server Scalability

The simplest way to scale transport server performance is to add additional Hub transport servers at each Active Directory site. When you add additional Hub transport servers, messages route through each Hub transport server in a site in a load-balanced way. In theory, each Hub Transport server can queue a maximum of 500,000 messages. If your design calls for more than 500,000 messages to be queued in a single Active Directory site, you will need to add additional Hub Transport servers. Although the 500,000 figure represents the maximum number of messages that can be queued, most organizations will require a minimum inter-organizational delivery time frame for messages as a part of an SLA. You are more likely to have to add Hub Transport servers to ensure quick delivery than you are because you've reached the 500,000 message queue capacity.

Also remember that scalability is different from high availability. High availability involves adding additional servers to ensure that message routing continues in the event that a Hub Transport or Edge Transport server fails. You'll learn more about High Availability for transport servers in Chapter 4, "Designing and Deploying Exchange Server 2010 Availability and Recovery."

You can use several other technologies in your Exchange design to ensure that your transport server infrastructure isn't overwhelmed by excessive traffic. These include message throttling and back pressure.

Message Throttling

Message throttling allows you to limit the number of messages and connections that an Exchange 2010 Hub or Edge Transport server will accept. These limits ensure that the system resources of the transport server are not overwhelmed, either accidentally or intentionally. You can configure message throttling options on the transport server itself, on individual Send connectors, and on individual Receive connectors.

You can configure the following message throttling options:

- **Maximum concurrent mailbox deliveries**   This option determines the maximum number of delivery threads that a Hub Transport server can concurrently use to deliver messages to mailboxes. The default value is 20. This setting can be configured with the *MaxConcurrentMailboxDeliveries* parameter of the *Set-TransportServer* cmdlet.

- **Maximum concurrent mailbox submissions**   This option determines the maximum number of delivery threads that a Hub Transport server can concurrently use to accept messages from mailboxes. The default value is 20. This setting can be configured with the *MaxConcurrentMailboxSubmissions* parameter of the *Set-TransportServer* cmdlet.

- **Maximum connection rate per minute**   This option determines the maximum rate at which the Hub Transport or Edge Transport server will accept new inbound connections. The default value is 1200 connections per minute. This setting can be configured with the *MaxConnectionRatePerMinute* parameter of the *Set-TransportServer* cmdlet.

- **Maximum outbound connections**   This option determines the maximum number of outbound connections that a Hub or Edge Transport server can have open concurrently. The default value is 1000. You can configure this setting with the *MaxOutboundConnections* parameter of the *Set-TransportServer* cmdlet.

- **Maximum per domain outbound connections**   This option limits the number of connections that a transport server connected to the Internet—which will usually be an Edge Transport server but might in some cases be a Hub Transport server—can open to any individual remote domain. The default value is 20. You can configure this setting with the *MaxPerDomainOutboundConnections* parameter of the *Set-TransportServer* cmdlet.

- **Pick up directory maximum messages per minute**   This option limits the message processing rate for the Replay and Pickup directories. These directories are polled every five seconds and the default settings allows for eight messages to be processed every five-second interval. You can configure this setting with the *PickupDirectoryMax-MessagesPerMinute* parameter of the *Set-TransportServer* cmdlet. This figure you enter when using this parameter is for a 60-second duration, so you need to divide it by 12 to determine the number of messages processed during the polling interval.

- **Connection inactivity time out**   This option limits the maximum amount of time that an SMTP connection to a remote server will remain open while idle before closing. The default value is 10 minutes. You configure this option on Send connectors by using the *ConnectionInactivityTimeOut* parameter with the *Set-SendConnector* cmdlet.

- **Connection time out**   This option limits the maximum amount of time that an SMTP connection from a remote server will remain open, even if it is in the process of transmitting data. The default value on Hub Transport servers is 10 minutes and the default value on Edge Transport servers is 5 minutes. You configure this option on Receive connectors by using the *ConnectionTimeOut* parameter with the *Set-ReceiveConnector* cmdlet.

- **Maximum inbound connection**   This option limits the maximum number of concurrent inbound connections that the Receive connector will accept. The default is 5000. You configure this option on Receive connectors by using the *MaxInboundConnection* parameter with the *Set-ReceiveConnector* cmdlet.

- **Maximum inbound connection percentage per source**   This option limits the maximum number of SMTP connections that a Receive connector will accept from a single source as a percentage of available remaining connections. The default value is 2 percent. You configure this option on Receive connectors by using the *MaxInbound-ConnectionPErcentagePerSource* parameter with the *Set-ReceiveConnector* cmdlet.

- **Maximum inbound connection per source**   This option limits the maximum number of SMTP connections that a Receive connector will accept from a single source as a fixed value. The default value is 100. You configure this option on Receive connectors by using the *MaxInboundConnectionPerSource* parameter with the *Set-ReceiveConnector* cmdlet.

- **Maximum Protocol errors**   This option limits the maximum number of SMTP protocol errors that can occur over an established connection before that connection is terminated. The default value is 5. You configure this option on Receive connectors by using the *MaxProtocolErrors* parameter with the *Set-ReceiveConnector* cmdlet.

- **Tarpit Interval**   This option determines the delay that is used when SMTP communications patterns suggest a directory harvest attack or other unwelcome messages. Directory harvest attacks are attempts to determine valid email addresses for use with spam. You configure this option on Receive connectors by using the *TarpitInterval* parameter with the *Set-ReceiveConnector* cmdlet.

MORE INFO   **MESSAGE THROTTLING**

For more information on message throttling, consult the following TechNet article: *http://technet.microsoft.com/en-us/library/bb232205.aspx.*

Back Pressure

Back pressure monitors the Microsoft Exchange Transport service on Hub and Edge Transport servers, taking action when resource pressures build up as a method of ensuring availability. Back pressure works by preventing system resources from being overwhelmed by rejecting or limiting incoming connections until the pressure on system resources eases. Back pressure works in conjunction with message throttling. The difference is that back pressure only applies when the transport server's system resources are under pressure, whereas message throttling limits apply all the time.

> **MORE INFO**   **BACK PRESSURE**
>
> To learn more about back pressure, consult the following TechNet article: *http://technet. microsoft.com/en-us/library/bb201658.aspx*.

Message Queues and Shadow Redundancy

Shadow redundancy is a transport server feature that ensures that email messages are not lost in transit if a transport server fails. Shadow redundancy works by waiting until the transport server can verify that delivery has occurred to the next hop in a message's path before deleting the local copy. If the next hop delivery fails, the transport server resubmits the message to the next hop. Shadow redundancy is handled by the Shadow Redundancy Manager, which is responsible for keeping track of the shadow server for each primary message that the server is currently processing and the discard status to be sent to shadow servers. Including shadow redundancy in an Exchange design accomplishes the following goals:

- Ensures that as long as a redundant message path exists in a routing topology, message routing will occur in the event of transport server failure.

- Allows you to bring a Hub or Edge Transport server down for maintenance without having to worry about emptying queues or losing messages.

- Minimizes additional network traffic because it doesn't require duplicate messages to be transmitted to multiple servers. The only additional traffic is a discard status message.

- Reduces the necessity for storage hardware redundancy on transport system. Even if you don't have a redundant path, you can get a replacement transport server in place and the mail flow will resume without losing any messages. Whether this is an appropriate strategy depends on your SLA.

Shadow redundancy requires an extension of the SMTP service that is currently supported only by Exchange Server 2010 transport servers. During SMTP communication, a check is performed to determine whether the next hop server supports the shadow redundancy feature. In the event that the next hop server does not support shadow redundancy, the Shadow Redundancy Manager marks the message as delivered after it has been handed off to the next server and deletes it rather than waiting for confirmation from the next hop server that it has been successfully delivered to the next hop plus one server.

Shadow redundancy can be enabled or disabled on a per-organization level basis using the *Set-TransportConfig* cmdlet with the *ShadowRedundancyEnabled* parameter. For example, to enable shadow redundancy for all servers in the organization, use the following command:

```
Set-TransportConfig -ShadowRedundancyEnabled $true
```

> **MORE INFO**   **SHADOW REDUNDANCY**
>
> To learn more about shadow redundancy, consult the following TechNet article: *http://technet.microsoft.com/en-us/library/dd351027.aspx.*

Transport Storage Requirements

The amount of disk space required by a transport server depends on the number of messages sent and received each day, how long you keep transaction logs, and whether protocol logging has been set up. When including Hub Transport storage requirements in an Exchange design, you need to make an estimate of the number of messages that will queue on the server. Although a single server can queue up to 500,000 messages, unless a Hub Transport server routes messages directly to the Internet or a failure occurs, the average number of messages sitting in the queue is unlikely to be high. Your design should take into account failure scenarios, but you probably don't need to configure storage for a transport server so that it can cope with 500,000 queued messages, unless the server is likely to process that number of messages over a 24-hour period.

Your design needs to take into account how Hub Transport servers will respond in the event of some failure that prevents them from offloading messages to other transport servers.

When planning transport server storage requirements, take into account the following:

- If the average message size at an organization is 200 KB and 10,000 messages pass across the organization's main site every day, the queue database could grow to almost 2 GB if a failure occurs that stops messages being transmitted off the server for a 24-hour period.

- Message tracking logs consume roughly .5 KB per message sent or received. At a site that has 10,000 messages passing through each day, keeping message tracking logs for the default 7 days will consume another 35 MB or so of space.

- Agent, Protocol, and Connectivity logs record information about SMTP traffic. These logs vary in size depending on the size, amount, and kind of messages delivered by the transport server. Agent, Protocol, and Connectivity logs consume approximately 2 KB per message. At the theoretical site that processes 10,000 messages, that's another 20 MB a day.

- If you are using Database Availability Groups (DAGs), the transport dumpster can grow up to a default 18 MB for every mailbox database in a single Active Directory site. The Transport Dumpster holds a copy of messages sent to mailboxes that are part of a DAG and only deletes those messages when the message has successfully replicated to all members of the DAG. If a site hosts 200 Exchange mailboxes, it is theoretically possible that the combined transport dumpsters for those mailboxes will require approximately 3.6 GB of storage space.

You can modify the size of the Transport Dumpster and configure how long it retains messages on the General tab of the Transport Settings Properties dialog box, shown in Figure 1-4. You can access this dialog box by clicking the Global Settings tab when you have selected the Hub Transport node under Organization Configuration in Exchange Management Console. You can also configure the maximum dumpster size and retention time using the *Set-TransportConfig* cmdlet with the *MaxDumpsterSizePerDatabase* and *MaxDumpsterTime* parameters.

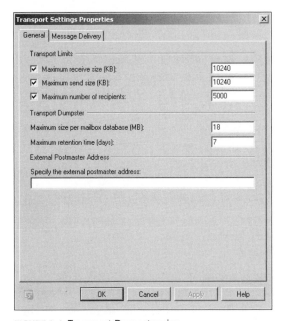

FIGURE 1-4 Transport Dumpster size

MORE INFO **CONFIGURE TRANSPORT DUMPSTER**

To learn about configuring transport dumpster settings and other transport settings, consult the following TechNet article: *http://technet.microsoft.com/en-us/library/bb676532.aspx.*

Planning Accepted and Remote Domains

Your Exchange organization can only accept messages for email domains that are configured as accepted domains. An accepted domain is also an email domain for which your organization is able to send email. For example, if your organization needs to accept email for addresses within the @tailspintoys.com and @wingtiptoys.com domains, you will need to include these domains as accepted domains within your Exchange design. If your recipients want to use the @adatum.com email domain when sending messages from Exchange, @adatum.com will need to be configured as an accepted domain.

Exchange Server 2010 supports three types of accepted domain:

- **Authoritative Domains**   This is the most obvious type of mail domain to include in your Exchange design because this is the domain you use for recipients who have mailboxes that are a part of your Exchange organization. The default authoritative domain for an Exchange organization is the fully qualified domain name (FQDN) of the forest root domain. This means that if the FQDN of your organization's forest root domain is contoso.internal, contoso.internal will be automatically configured as the default authoritative domain.

- **Internal Relay Domain**   You include this type of email domain in your design when Exchange will need to forward messages to another email system on the internal network. You use internal relay domains in your design if you need to route messages to a third-party email system or to another Exchange organization if your organization has multiple forests and is using the cross-forest topology model. Your design should include an internal relay domain if you've split your address space and some accounts in an email domain are hosted by Exchange and others by a third-party mail system.

- **External Relay Domain**   You include an external relay domain in your design if you need to configure your Exchange organization to accept email messages from external organizations so that they can be forwarded to another external organization. To have external relay domains function properly, Send connectors to the external domain must be configured on Edge Transport servers.

Remote domains allow you to control message formatting options for specific email address domains. They also allow you to configure whether external out-of-office messages will be sent to users in those domains. You include remote domains in your Exchange design when you want to control the types of messages and message formats that are sent to a specific external domain.

> ***MORE INFO*** **ACCEPTED DOMAINS**
>
> To learn more about accepted domains, consult the following TechNet article: *http://technet. microsoft.com/en-us/library/bb124423.aspx.*

Planning Send and Receive Connectors

Send and Receive connectors control how messages flow in, out, and through your Exchange organization. You include them in your Exchange design when you want to route messages between Hub Transport and Edge Transport servers when you don't have an edge subscription, or between transport servers and other messaging systems on the internal network or the Internet.

The difference between these connector types is as follows:

- A Receive connector allows a transport server to receive SMTP traffic from specific sources. This can include SMTP servers on the Internet, Edge Transport servers that aren't configured to use edge synchronization, third-party SMTP servers on the internal network, and SMTP mail clients.

- A Send connector transmits a message to a destination location using the SMTP protocol. Send connectors can be configured to send email directly to a destination SMTP server, or you can configure a Send connector to route outgoing messages through a smart host.

> **MORE INFO** **SMART HOST**
>
> A smart host is a server, usually hosted by an organization's ISP, that functions as a mail-relay between SMTP servers on the Internet and an organization's Edge Transport or Hub Transport server. You can find out more about smart hosts by reading the following TechNet article: *http://technet.microsoft.com/en-us/library/cc626187(WS.10).aspx.*

You don't need to plan Send connectors or Receive connectors for message transmission between Hub Transport servers that are in the same Exchange organization because Hub Transport servers that are members of the same Exchange organization are automatically configured to communicate with each other when you deploy Exchange. You also don't need to plan Send connectors or Receive connectors between Hub Transport and Edge Transport servers when you configure an edge subscription because the edge subscription process creates the necessary connectors between these servers.

You do need to plan Send and Receive connectors in the following circumstances:

- You need to configure communication with another messaging system hosted on your organization's internal network.

- You need to send messages through a smart host.

- You need to configure a secure connection with a partner organization that uses a technology such as mutually authenticated TLS.

- You want to route messages through Exchange Hosted Services as a method of using features such as hosted filtering, hosted archive, hosted encryption, and hosted continuity.

Planning Outbound Message Flow

For your Exchange organization to send messages out to hosts on the Internet, you need to have at least one SMTP Send connector that includes within its address space Internet SMTP domains. Depending on the size and structure of your organization, you may choose to deploy multiple Edge Transport servers with multiple SMTP Send connectors. You can also configure one SMTP Send connector to use multiple Edge Transport servers as a source server depending on your organizational needs.

Organizations that have multiple sites can choose to deploy an Edge Transport server at each site so that outbound messages from that site are routed directly to the Internet, rather than being routed across the internal network to be forwarded to the Internet from a single perimeter network. The Edge Transport servers at each site can either be configured with an edge subscription to their local parent site, or you can manually configure Send connectors on that local site's Hub and Edge Transport servers. You'll learn about setting up Edge Transport servers with and without subscriptions in Chapter 2.

Planning Inbound Message Flow

For your Exchange organization to accept incoming messages from the Internet, it is necessary for you to configure at least one SMTP Receive connector that will accept anonymous SMTP connections from SMTP servers on the Internet. You also need to configure a DNS Mail Exchange (MX) record to point to the server that hosts the SMTP Receive connector in your organization's externally resolvable DNS zone. This record allows SMTP servers on the Internet to determine the IP address of your organization's SMTP gateway.

If your organization has more than one location, you may choose to have multiple Edge Transport servers that process incoming email. For example, if your organization has offices in the Australian state capital cities of Brisbane, Sydney, and Melbourne, you might choose to deploy an Edge Transport server on each site's perimeter network. Whether this would lead to any efficiencies when you are using a single email domain namespace is questionable. If you create MX records with equal priorities that point to each of these Edge Transport servers, incoming messages will distributed across each Edge Transport server with no guarantee that email messages to users in the Sydney site will enter through the Sydney Edge Transport server. Messages will still need to be routed internally in most cases unless they are lucky enough to arrive at the correct site. If you configure the MX records with different priorities, only the MX record with the lowest priority will be used and inbound messages will only route to other servers in the event that the Edge Transport server associated with the lowest priority record is unavailable. Having Edge Transport servers at multiple sites is more beneficial for outbound traffic because these messages can be sent directly to Internet hosts without having to be routed internally.

You may also want to plan additional message connectors to meet specific business requirements. For example, your organization's external SMTP server needs to be able to accept messages from any SMTP server on the Internet. Historically the SMTP protocol does not require TLS, which means most organizations haven't configured it on their SMTP servers. If you required TLS on all incoming SMTP connections, you'd end up blocking messages from most organizations on the Internet. You do have the option, however, in conjunction with a partner organization, of configuring a special Receive connector that requires TLS encryption or authentication. This ensures that SMTP traffic that passes between your organization and the partner will be protected from interception as it passes across the public Internet. The majority of your incoming message traffic will not be protected, but message traffic to and from that particular partner will be.

Internal SMTP Relay

You include internal SMTP relay in your design when you need to configure your Exchange organization to route messages to recipients that are not hosted within the local Exchange organization, but may have mailboxes on a third-party messaging system or in another Active Directory forest located on your organization's internal network. This can either be in a shared address space scenario, in which multiple messaging systems host mailboxes in the same email address space, or the separate address space scenario, where Exchange accepts messages for an address space for which it doesn't host mailboxes and then routes those messages internally to another messaging system.

In both scenarios it is necessary to configure an Accepted domain as an internal relay domain and then configure a Send connector to route messages to SMTP servers of that separate—but internal—messaging system. For example, if you had two separate Active Directory forests, both of which were configured with Exchange and both of which used the contoso.com mail domain, you would configure one of those organizations to accept and route incoming messages to the other forest. The Send connector to the second forest's Exchange organization would only be utilized if the recipient mailbox wasn't hosted in the first forest that accepted the message from an SMTP server on the Internet.

> **MORE INFO** **ROUTING MESSAGES FOR SHARED ADDRESS SPACE**
>
> To learn more about routing messages to an internal shared address space, consult the following TechNet documentation: *http://technet.microsoft.com/en-us/library/bb676395.aspx.*

Planning DNS

Planning DNS for transport servers includes two main elements. The first is ensuring that your organization's Hub Transport and Edge Transport servers are able to resolve each other's names. The second is to ensure that your organization's external DNS servers respond if a mail server on the Internet performs a reverse lookup on the public IP address of your organization's Edge Transport servers.

Edge Transport DNS Resolution

Edge Transport servers need to be able to perform DNS resolution on Internet hosts, but also need to be able to resolve the addresses of Hub Transport servers to which they will route messages. When you are planning Edge Transport server deployment, you may need to configure different DNS server settings for the server's public and private network adapters, configuring the public adapter to use your ISP's DNS servers, and configuring the private network adapter to use your internal DNS servers. After you have done this, you can configure the Edge Transport server's properties by right-clicking the Edge Transport server in EMC and clicking Properties. Here you can specify external DNS lookup settings on the External DNS Lookups tab, as shown in Figure 1-5, or internal DNS lookup settings on the Internal DNS Lookups tab. You can configure Send and Receive connectors to use these internal and external DNS settings when performing name resolution during message transport.

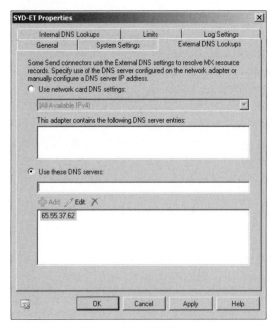

FIGURE 1-5 Configure external DNS lookup

Reverse Lookup Zones

Reverse lookup zones translate IP addresses to fully qualified domain names. You need to consider reverse lookup zones in your Exchange design because many organizations use reverse lookups as a method of filtering unsolicited commercial email, better known as spam. This process works by having an email gateway verify that the DNS domain name associated with the IP address of a remote SMTP server matches the mail domain of the email sent from that server. For example, if you did a DNS lookup on IP address 131.107.125.5 using the nslookup command-line utility, the DNS server would return the result mail.microsoft.com. If your email gateway received an incoming message from 131.107.125.5, it would match the sender's address against the DNS zone associated with that IP address.

Setting up local reverse lookup zones is straightforward and can be accomplished by performing the following general steps:

1. Open the DNS Manager console on a computer that hosts the DNS role service.

2. Right-click the Reverse Lookup Zones node and then click New Zone.

3. In the New Zone Wizard you specify what type of zone you want to create. In most cases this will be a primary zone.

4. Specify the DNS zone replication scope.

5. Specify whether you want to create an IPv4 or IPv6 reverse lookup zone:

   - If you want to create an IPv6 reverse lookup zone, you need to provide the IPv6 Address Prefix.

   - If you want to create an IPv4 reverse lookup zone, you can either provide the Network ID or the Reverse Lookup Zone Name, as shown in Figure 1-6. If you use the option to use the zone name, it needs to be in the format *z.y.x*.in-addr.apra where the IPv4 network that you are creating the zone for is in the format *x.y.z*.0. For example, network 131.107.125.0 would have the reverse lookup zone name 125.107.131.in-addr.apra.

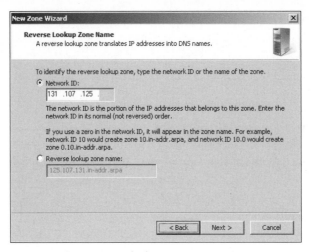

FIGURE 1-6 Create reverse lookup zone

6. Choose whether to allow secure dynamic updates only, no dynamic updates, or a mix of secure and nonsecure dynamic updates and then finish the wizard.

In most cases though, the public IP address that your organization's external mail gateway uses, which in a pure Exchange 2010 environment is an Edge Transport server, has been provided to your organization by an ISP. Reverse lookup zones are often managed by ISPs because reverse lookup zones are configured in such a way that the smallest reverse lookup zone is a class C address block. This means that you can't create a reverse lookup zone for the two or three public IP addresses that have been assigned to your organization. Instead you have to find which organization hosts the reverse lookup zone for the class C address block to which your organizations two or three public IP addresses belong. You'll then need to get the hosts of those zones to insert the appropriate reverse lookup record.

> **MORE INFO**   **CREATING REVERSE LOOKUP ZONES**
>
> To learn more about creating a reverse lookup zone on a computer running Windows Server 2008 R2, consult the following TechNet article: *http://technet.microsoft.com/en-us/library/dd894426(WS.10).aspx*.

Planning Transport Server Ports

Because you place Edge Transport servers on a perimeter network, there will be at least one firewall between any Edge Transport servers and the Hub Transport servers hosted in the adjacent Active Directory site. To support mail flow and edge synchronization between Edge Transport and Hub Transport servers, it is necessary to allow communication through specific network ports. Table 1-1 provides a list of the ports that need to be open between different components in an Exchange organization in the event that a firewall exists between them.

TABLE 1-1 Exchange Transport Roles and Required Ports

Exchange roles	Required ports
Hub Transport server to Hub Transport server	TCP port 25 (SMTP)
Hub Transport server to Edge Transport server	TCP port 25 (SMTP)
Edge Transport server to Hub Transport server	TCP port 25 (SMTP)
Edge Transport server to Edge Transport server	TCP port 25 (SMTP)
Mailbox server to Hub Transport server	TCP port 135 (RPC)
Hub Transport server to Mailbox server	TCP port 135 (RPC)
Edge subscription (EdgeSync) service from Hub Transport server to Edge Transport server	TCP port 50636
Active Directory Domain Controller from Hub Transport server	TCP and UDP port 389 (LDAP) TCP and UDP port 88 (Kerberos) TCP and UDP port 53 (DNS) TCP port 135 (RPC) TCP port 3268 (LDAP GC)
Hub Transport server to Active Directory Rights Management Services	TCP port 443 (HTTPS)
SMTP clients to Hub Transport server	TCP port 587 (SMTP) TCP port 25 (SMTP)

> **MORE INFO**   **TRANSPORT SERVER PORTS**
>
> To learn more information about which ports need to be open when firewalls exist between two servers, consult the following TechNet article: *http://technet.microsoft.com/en-us/library/bb331973.aspx*.

EXAM TIP

Be clear on the difference between a remote domain and a Send connector.

Objective Summary

- Ensure that at least one Hub Transport server is in each site that hosts a Mailbox server.
- Accepted domains determine the email domains for which the Exchange organization will process incoming messages. Authoritative domains are used when the Exchange organization hosts the mailbox. Internal relay domains are used in shared address space scenarios as well as when there is another messaging system on the internal network. External relay domains are used when accepted mail is to be processed and then relayed to an external organization.

- Remote domains allow you to control message formatting and distribution of out-of-office messages.

- Send connectors are used to forward outgoing SMTP traffic to a specific destination.

- Receive connectors are used to accept incoming SMTP traffic from a specific source.

- You can scale Hub Transport server performance by adding additional Hub Transport servers to sites.

Objective Review

Answer the following questions to test your knowledge of the information in this objective. You can find the answers to these questions and explanations of why each answer choice is correct or incorrect in the "Answers" section at the end of this chapter.

1. What type of accepted domain would you plan to use if you wanted your Exchange organization to route email messages accepted from hosts to a third-party messaging system hosted on your internal network? This email domain is not used by Exchange recipients.

    A. Authoritative domain

    B. Internal relay domain

    C. External relay domain

    D. Reverse lookup zone

2. You are in the process of designing an Exchange Server 2010 deployment. You will be using Edge Transport servers located on a perimeter network that will have edge subscriptions to Hub Transport servers located at your organization's main site. Which of the following ports need to be opened between the perimeter network and the main site internal network to support message transport and edge synchronization? (Choose all that apply.)

    A. TCP port 25

    B. TCP port 135

    C. TCP port 389

    D. TCP port 50636

3. Your organization has two separate Active Directory forests. You are planning to deploy an Exchange organization in each forest and want to use a shared address space so that recipients in both forests can use the @contoso.com email domain. Which of the following components will you need to configure in the Exchange organization that will be able to send and receive email from hosts on the Internet to ensure that recipients in the second Exchange organization receive messages? (Choose all that apply.)

   A. Internal relay domain

   B. Remote domain

   C. External relay domain

   D. Send connector

4. You want your Exchange design to use a different routing topology than the default Active Directory routing topology. Which of the following Exchange Management Shell (EMS) cmdlets would you use to set an Exchange-specific cost for an Active Directory IP site link?

   A. *Set-ADSite*

   B. *Set-ADSiteLink*

   C. *Get-ADSite*

   D. *Get-ADSiteLink*

5. Your organization does not use database availability groups. Which of the following features should you enable to ensure that email messages are not lost in transit in the event that a transport server fails?

   A. Remote domains

   B. Send connectors

   C. Transport dumpster

   D. Shadow redundancy

THOUGHT EXPERIMENT
Transport Server Design

In the following thought experiment, apply what you've learned about the "Designing message routing" objective to design a transport server infrastructure. You can find answers to these questions in the "Answers" section at the end of this chapter.

You are planning the transport server design for A. Datum Corporation. A. Datum has offices in the Australian state capital cities of Melbourne, Brisbane, Sydney, Adelaide, and Perth. A. Datum owns a subsidiary company Fabrikam, Inc. Fabrikam, Inc., has a separate Exchange organization located on their own network in the Northern Territory capital Darwin. While there is no direct connection between the Fabrikam network and the A. Datum network, you want to configure your Exchange organization to accept email for Fabrikam in the event that their Internet connection fails.

You are also concerned about the routing topology. You intend to deploy multiple Hub Transport servers in the Sydney branch office, but want to ensure that these servers are not overwhelmed by excessive traffic. The perimeter network at the Sydney office will also host the organization's Edge Transport server.

With these facts in mind, answer the following questions:

1. What kind of accepted domain should you configure for the fabrikam.com email domain?

2. Which transport server feature would you implement to ensure that a transport server is not overwhelmed by excessive message traffic?

3. Which Exchange Management Shell cmdlet can you use to configure the maximum connection rate per minute property to limit the number of inbound connections accepted per minute on the Edge Transport server hosted on the Sydney office's perimeter network?

4. Which Exchange Management Shell cmdlet should you use to configure the Sydney site as a hub site?

5. Which Exchange Management Shell cmdlet should you use to assign an Exchange cost to the Active Directory IP site links that connect the Melbourne and Brisbane sites to the Sydney site?

Objective 1.3: Design the Mailbox Server Role

Exchange Mailbox servers are big message storage servers. Out of all of the Exchange roles that you can deploy, the Exchange Mailbox server will utilize the most disk space. Most IT Professionals have heard of Moore's Law, which suggests that the number of transistors that can be placed on an integrated circuit doubles every two years. Although the growth isn't nearly as rapid, the amount of information transmitted by email across the world also doubles approximately every four years. This increase in information is reflected in most people's inboxes, and it is not unheard of in 2011 for some Exchange deployments to allow 50 GB mailbox quotas. This has become necessary because not only do people use Outlook to store email messages, but Outlook and Exchange mailboxes are also often used as informal document archives. In this objective you'll learn about planning database sizes, how to determine what sort of performance mailbox server storage will require, how to implement a multi-forest mailbox deployment, how to design a public folder infrastructure, and how to develop recipient and distribution group policies. In Chapter 2 you'll learn how to put these design decisions into operation.

> **This objective covers:**
> - Plan database sizing.
> - Storage performance requirements.
> - Multi-forest mailbox deployment.
> - Design public folders.
> - Develop recipient and distribution group policies.
> - Mailbox provisioning policies.

Plan Database Sizing

Exchange Server 2010 mailboxes and public folders are stored in databases hosted on Exchange mailbox servers. Databases are stored in Extensible Storage Engine format. Each database has an associated set of transaction logs that record changes made to the database. Transaction logs are primarily useful during database recovery and you will learn more about using them in this manner in Chapter 4.

By default, each database and its associated transaction logs are stored in the same folder. These folders are unique to each database, with each database's folder typically stored under the C:\Program Files\Microsoft\Exchange\Server\v14\Mailbox folder as shown in Figure 1-7. If you are deploying Exchange on standard disks that do not use RAID striping, you should consider placing the mailbox database and the transaction logs on separate disks. This has the benefit of improving performance and simplifying recovery. You have less reason to do this when you are using RAID striping because disk read and write operations are already optimized through the use of multiple drives and controllers.

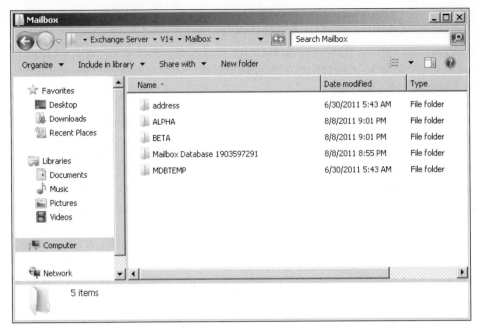

FIGURE 1-7 Database folders

The Standard edition of Exchange 2010 allows five databases per Mailbox server. One of these databases can be a public folder database. The Enterprise edition of Exchange 2010 allows 100 databases per Mailbox server. Only one of these databases can be a public folder database.

The following factors influence your plans when determining the size of mailbox databases:

- How many users will the mailbox database need to support?

- How large can mailbox databases grow? Even though most people won't reach their mailbox quota, you will need to plan the mailbox database size on the assumption that every mailbox will reach quota.

- What deleted item retention settings will you use? Deleted items consume database space in the same way that undeleted items do.

- Service Level Agreement (SLAs). Mailbox database size impacts recovery time, with larger mailbox databases meaning longer backup windows and longer recovery times. Backup and recovery can be more important to limiting mailbox database size than storage capacity.

The default database size limit for Exchange 2010 Service Pack 1 Standard edition is 1024 GB. If a mailbox database grows beyond this limit, the database automatically dismounts. You can modify the size limit of a database on the standard edition of Exchange 2010 by editing the registry. You can increase the database size limit to approximately 16 terabytes.

Although it is possible for mailbox databases on the Enterprise edition of Exchange 2010 to grow to 16 terabytes in size, Microsoft recommends that you keep mailbox databases to approximately 2 terabytes in size—where that size is 120 percent of calculated maximum database size—if you are using a high-availability configuration. For example, if every user has a 5-GB mailbox quota and you use the 120 percent of calculated maximum database size rule, you'd be able to provision just over 340 mailboxes per mailbox database using the 2-terabyte limit. If you aren't using a high-availability configuration, the recommended maximum database size is approximately 200 GB. This figure was arrived at based on backup and recovery times and the requirements of normal SLAs. Using Database Availability Groups gives you more flexibility in terms of recovery, allowing a substantially higher database size limit.

Determining mailbox database size is made more complicated by issues such as white space and database recoverable items. While an item deleted from a mailbox doesn't count towards a user's quota, the mailbox database still stores these items until the deleted item retention period expires. The amount of data consumed in this manner depends on the deleted item retention window. Microsoft provides the following formula for estimating how much storage is consumed in this manner:

Dumpster Size = (Daily Incoming/Outgoing Mail x Average Message Size x Deleted Item Retention Window) + (Mailbox Quota Size x 0.012) + (Mailbox Quota Size x 0.03)

When planning mailbox database storage requirements, you must also consider the content index. Each mailbox database has a content index that allows users to be able to quickly search through mail items. This index usually consumes approximately 10 percent of a mailbox database's size.

Plan Log Sizing

Transaction logs record every transaction performed by the Exchange database engine. Exchange writes each transaction to the log first and then those transactions are applied to the mailbox database later. Exchange Server 2010 transaction log files are 1 MB in size. Microsoft provides guidance that allows you to estimate the number of transaction logs that will be generated per mailbox per day assuming an average message that is 75 KB in size. A ballpark estimate is that for every five messages, Exchange generates one 1 MB transaction log file. Although you can enable circular logging, which overwrites transaction logs, Microsoft recommends you instead truncate transaction logs through regular backup. Products such as System Center Data Protection Manager 2012 allow you to perform backups every 15 minutes, truncating transaction logs regularly and minimizing the amount of transaction log data stored on the Exchange mailbox server.

Storage Performance Requirements

When planning storage for a mailbox server, you not only need to ensure that you dedicate enough space for the mailbox server, but you also need to ensure that the storage that you do use performs well enough to avoid being a bottleneck in the Exchange server's performance.

The basic principles of storage performance for mailbox servers are as follows:

- A larger number of users increases disk utilization.
- Users who send and receive more messages increase disk utilization.

Mailbox database performance is enhanced substantially through the use of server RAM for database caching. A user who sends and receives fifty 75-KB messages per day will utilize approximately 3 MB of RAM in the database cache. This user will also generate approximately 0.06 mailbox database I/O operations per second. A user who sends two hundred 75-KB messages per day will utilize approximately 12 MB of RAM in the database cache. This user will generate approximately 0.24 database I/O operations per second. When considering your mailbox server storage performance requirements, do not underestimate the impact of RAM. If the mailbox server has less RAM than is required to service each user's database cache needs, the number of database I/O operations per second will increase, reducing mailbox database performance.

The design of Exchange Server 2010 optimizes mailbox database I/O for standard hard disk drives. This means that you don't need specialized storage equipment to run an Exchange Mailbox server and that you'll have good performance even if you use "Just a Bunch of Disks" (JBOD), a technical way of describing standard, consumer-grade, hard-disk drives. Depending on your organization's requirements, you might choose to forego RAID 10 disk arrays in your storage design, relying less on redundant local storage and more on redundancy technologies such as Database Availability Groups. Of course it is always better to have a greater level of redundancy in any design. As any systems administrator knows, if something can go wrong, it will go wrong—usually at 4:50 P.M. on a Friday afternoon, right before you are about to go home for the weekend.

You can use the Exchange 2010 Mailbox Server Role Requirements Calculator, which you can download from Microsoft's website, to determine the precise storage and performance profile that will be necessary given your organization's needs. The tool is a spreadsheet that allows you to input information about your intended design. In general, though, Exchange 2010 is designed so that a 7200-RPM SATA disk will be easily able to handle the read and write traffic generated by a 2-terabyte mailbox database that hosts mailboxes that send and receive several hundred messages per day.

> **MORE INFO** **EXCHANGE 2010 MAILBOX SERVER ROLE REQUIREMENTS CALCULATOR**
>
> For more information about the Exchange 2010 Mailbox Server Role Requirements Calculator, consult this post on the Exchange team blog: *http://blogs.technet.com/b/exchange/archive/2009/11/09/3408737.aspx*.

When you are considering how to configure the disks used to host mailbox database and transaction logs, Microsoft recommends the following volume configurations:

- Use GUID partition table (GPT) rather than MBR in volume configuration. MBR is supported, but GPT is recommended.
- Only the NTFS file system is supported.
- Use an NTFS allocation unit of 64 KB for the volumes that host database files and log files.
- NTFS compression is not supported for database or log files.
- NTFS Encrypting File System is not supported for database or log files.
- BitLocker volume encryption is supported for volumes that host database files and log files.

Exchange supports the following storage architectures:

- **Direct-attached storage (DAS)**   Directly attached to the server, without a storage network. Includes SCSI and SATA drives.
- **Storage Area Network (SAN)**   Exchange supports the storage of mailbox databases on both iSCSI and Fibre Channel SANs.
- **Solid-state drive (SSD) flash disk**   Exchange can be deployed on a solid-state (SSD) flash disk.

Windows Server 2008 and Windows Server 2008 R2 support 512-byte sector disks. Only Windows Server 2008 R2 with Service Pack 1 and Exchange Server 2010 with Service Pack 1 support 512e disks. All copies of the database must reside on the same disk type, you can't have some copies of a database stored on a 512-byte sector disk and other copies stored on 512e. If your organization is not using a UPS, you should disable physical disk-write caching.

> **MORE INFO** **STORAGE CONFIGURATION**
>
> To learn more about Mailbox server storage options, consult the following TechNet links: *http://technet.microsoft.com/en-us/library/ee832792.aspx.*

Best practice for hosting mailbox database or log data is RAID 1 or RAID 10. Microsoft recommends that when you use RAID 5, you have a maximum of seven disks in the array. If you are using RAID 6, you should enable high-priority scrubbing and surface scanning.

> **MORE INFO** **MAILBOX STORAGE DESIGN**
>
> For more information about the influence of performance on mailbox storage design, consult the following TechNet article: *http://technet.microsoft.com/en-us/library/ee832791.aspx.*

Mailboxes in Multiple-Forest Topologies

As you learned earlier, if your organization uses more than one forest, you can deploy Exchange in either the cross-forest topology or the resource-forest topology. When you deploy Exchange in a cross-forest topology, each Active Directory forest has its own Exchange organization and hosts its own Exchange mailboxes. When you use a resource-forest topology, one forest hosts the Exchange organization and the other forest hosts the user accounts used by recipients. You can give these users in a resource-forest topology mailbox access by using linked mailboxes.

Linked mailboxes are mailboxes in the resource forest that are associated with an account hosted in a trusted Active Directory forest. The accounts in the Exchange forest are disabled for logon. The disabled user account in the Exchange forest is then associated with an enabled user account in the accounts forest. You can create the disabled account separately, or have it created automatically as a part of the linked mailbox creation process.

To create a linked mailbox using EMC, perform the following general steps:

1. Navigate to Recipient Configuration console tree and click New Mailbox in the Action pane.

2. On the Introduction page, select Linked Mailbox and click Next.

3. On the User Type page, click New User and then click Next. This will allow you to create the dummy user account in the resource forest.

4. On the User Information page, enter the details of the dummy user account. You can choose a special Organizational Unit for the account. The password that you specify on this page will be used to access the mailbox even though the user account cannot be used for computer logon in the resource forest. This password does not have to match the password of the user account in the account forest.

5. On the Mailbox Settings pace, specify the mailbox database, retention policy, and Exchange ActiveSync mailbox policy that will be associated with the account.

6. On the Master Account page, shown in Figure 1-8, click Browse to specify the trusted domain, specify an account to access the linked domain controller, specify a domain controller in the trusted domain, and specify the account in the account domain that will be the master account for the linked mailbox. Click Next, New, and then Finish to complete the creation of the linked mailbox.

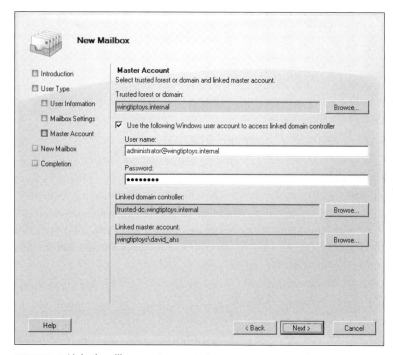

FIGURE 1-8 Linked mailbox master account

You can also create a linked mailbox from EMS by using the *New-Mailbox* cmdlet with the *LinkedMasterAccount* parameter. For example, to create a linked account for David Ahs in the local adatum.com forest when a trust has been established with the WingTipToys forest, use the following command:

```
New-Mailbox -Database "MBX-DB1" -Name "David Ahs" -LinkedDomainController
"DC01wingtiptoys" -LinkedMasterAccount wingtiptoys\david -OrganizationalUnit Users
-UserPrincipalName david@adatum.com -LinkedCredential:(Get-Credential wingtiptoys\Admin01)
```

A mail forest contact is a mail contact that is associated with a recipient object in another forest. Mail forests are present in cross-forest topology deployments and are usually created through Microsoft Identity Integration Server (MIIS) synchronization. Mail forest contacts can only be created through synchronization with other forests in a cross-forest deployment—you cannot modify or remove mail forest contacts using EMC or EMS.

MORE INFO **RESOURCE FOREST TOPOLOGY**

For more information about deploying Exchange Server 2010 in a Resource forest topology, consult the following TechNet article: *http://technet.microsoft.com/en-us/library/aa998031.aspx*.

EXAM TIP

Understand the process of linked mailbox creation and the role of the disabled account.

MORE INFO **CREATE A LINKED MAILBOX**

For more information about creating a linked mailbox, consult the following TechNet article: *http://technet.microsoft.com/en-us/library/bb123524.aspx*.

Recipient Policies

Recipient policies, also known as email address policies, allow you to configure email address formats for your organization. A single email address policy can define multiple address format variations. Email address policies allow you to generate addresses based on a person's first name, last name, middle initial, and accepted domains. You can only use accepted domains as the email domain suffix in an email address policy. You learned about accepted domains earlier in this chapter. The default email address policy for an organization involves the user's alias, the *at* symbol (@), and the default accepted domain.

You can use an email address policy to turn user name data into a variety of email addresses. By applying a policy, you could configure Exchange so that Kim Akers is given the following email addresses:

- k.akers@contoso.com
- kim.akers@contoso.com
- akers.kim@contoso.com
- akers.k@fabrikam.com

Although an email address policy can provision users with email addresses from multiple email domains, it's probably better to use separate policies when dealing with different email domains, which keeps things less complicated and more manageable. To create an email address policy using EMC, perform the following general steps:

1. Click the Organization Configuration\Hub Transport node and then click New E-mail Address Policy in the Actions pane.

2. On the Introduction page of the New E-mail Address Policy Wizard, enter a name for the policy, choose whether you want it to apply only to objects stored within a particular Active Directory container, and select the recipient types (mailbox users, mail-enabled users, and so on). Click Next.

3. On the Conditions page select which conditions will be used to limit the scope of the address policy. It is not necessary to limit the scope of the address policy—for example, if you want to apply the policy to all addresses in the organization. You can select from the following conditions:

   - **Recipient is in a State or Province**   Checks for a match against the State/Province attribute of the Active Directory account. This property is set on the Address tab of an account's properties in Active Directory Users and Computers.

   - **Recipient is in a Department**   Checks for a match against the Department attribute of the Active Directory account. This property is set on the Organization tab of an account's properties in Active Directory Users and Computers.

   - **Recipient is in a Company**   Checks for a match against the Company attribute of the Active Directory account. This property is set on the Organization tab of an account's properties in Active Directory Users and Computers.

   - **Custom Attribute equals Value**   It is also possible to configure up to 15 custom attributes for each account. The values of these attributes need to be set through Exchange management shell and aren't something that you can use Active Directory Users and Computers to configure.

> **MORE INFO**   **CONFIGURING CUSTOM ATTRIBUTES**
>
> To learn more about configuring custom attributes, consult the following TechNet article: *http://technet.microsoft.com/en-us/library/ee423541.aspx.*

4. On the E-Mail Addresses page, click Add. On the SMTP E-Mail Address page, shown in Figure 1-9, select the format that you want to use for the email address and then click OK. If you want to add more address formats, you can click Add again. If you have multiple addresses listed in the policy, you need to specify one format as the default reply-to address. Click Next.

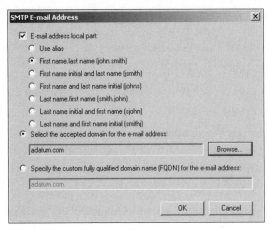

FIGURE 1-9 Email address format

5. On the Schedule page, select whether the policy is applied immediately, at a time in the future, or not applied at all.

You can apply multiple email address policies to a user. When you have multiple policies, you need to choose the order in which they apply. The reply-to address that is set in the policy with the highest priority is used as the default reply-to address. You can also manually configure a user's default reply-to address by editing the user's account properties directly. The default reply-to address set at this level overrides any set by policy.

You can use the following EMS cmdlets to manage email address policies:

- *New-EmailAddressPolicy* allows you to configure new address policies.
- *Get-EmailAddressPolicy* allows you to view the properties of existing policies.
- *Set-EmailAddressPolicy* allows you to modify the properties of existing policies.
- *Update-EmailAddressPolicy* allows you to apply policy changes to recipients within the scope of the policy. You must run this cmdlet after you create or modify an email address policy.
- *Remove-EmailAddressPolicy* allows you to remove existing policies, but will not remove email addresses from users that were created by those policies.

MORE INFO **RECIPIENT POLICIES**

For more information about email address policies, consult the following TechNet article: *http://technet.microsoft.com/en-us/library/bb232171.aspx.*

Distribution Group Policies

A distribution group is a collection of recipients, sometimes known as mailing lists. When a user sends a message to a distribution group, Exchange will forward that message to all members of the distribution group. Exchange Server 2010 supports three types of distribution groups:

- **Distribution groups**   A static group whose membership is managed manually.
- **Mail-enabled security groups**   Similar to a distribution group, except that security permissions can be assigned to a mail-enabled security group. This static group type also requires that membership be managed manually.
- **Dynamic distribution groups**   This group type has its membership generated automatically based on a query. For example, you might create a dynamic distribution group for everyone that works at a particular branch office according to their user account properties. When a person's account properties are updated to indicate that she works at that branch office, she will receive messages sent to that group. Group membership is calculated by a Hub Transport server when it receives a message addressed to the group.

> **MORE INFO**   **DISTRIBUTION GROUPS**
>
> For more information about distribution groups, consult the following TechNet article:
> *http://technet.microsoft.com/en-us/library/bb125256.aspx.*

Static Distribution Groups

Static distribution groups have several advantages over dynamic distribution groups. Static distribution groups allow you to define a membership where the objects in the group don't need to share a specific property. You can delegate management privileges of the distribution group to an ordinary user who can choose whom to add to the group. You can also configure group permissions so that users can add and remove themselves from the group as they choose. This functionality is very useful for things like project-based distribution groups. Mail-enabled security groups are also a type of static distribution group. If you are using the mail-enabled security group as a security group, remember that if you allow a non-administrative user to manage the group, you're also allowing that user to grant access to any resources to which the group has been assigned permissions.

To create a static distribution group using EMC, perform the following general steps:

1. Select the Recipient Configuration\Distribution Group node and then click New Distribution Group. This will launch the New Distribution Group Wizard.

2. Select whether you want to create a new distribution group or mail-enable an existing universal security group. If you want to mail-enable an existing universal security group, choose Existing Group, click Browse, and select the group. You can't mail-enable a security group with a domain local or global scope.

3. On the Group Information page, shown in Figure 1-10, choose between Distribution and Security. You can select an OU in which to place the group. You also need to provide a name, a pre-Windows 2000 name, and an alias name for the group. These can all be the same name. Then click Next, New, and then Finish.

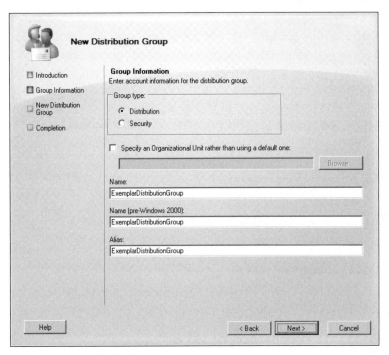

FIGURE 1-10 New distribution group

To create a new distribution group using EMS, use the *New-DistributionGroup* cmdlet. For example, to create a new mail-enabled security group named Alpha-Sec which will be stored in the Users container of the contoso.com domain, use the following cmdlet:

```
New-DistributionGroup -Name Alpha-Sec -OrganizationalUnit "Contoso.com/Users"
-SAMAccountName Alpha-Sec -Alias 'Alpha-Sec' -Type Security
```

The default manager of a distribution group is the user account that used to create the group. To delegate the ability to manage the group to another user, either use the *Set-DistributionGroup* cmdlet with the *ManagedBy* parameter, or navigate to the Group Information tab on the group's properties, shown in Figure 1-11, and click Add to specify a new group manager.

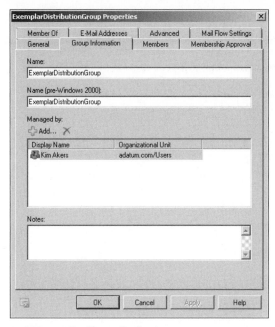

FIGURE 1-11 Configure distribution group manager

You can configure whether users are able to join the group themselves, whether they can join subject to approval, or if group members can only be added by the group managers on the Membership Approval tab, shown in Figure 1-12. You can also configure these settings using the *Set-DistributionGroup cmdlet* with the *MemberJoinRestriction* parameter using the options *Open, Closed*, or *ApprovalRequired*.

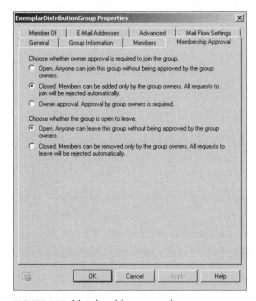

FIGURE 1-12 Membership approval

MORE INFO **CREATING STATIC DISTRIBUTION GROUPS**

For more information about creating static distribution groups, consult the following TechNet article: *http://technet.microsoft.com/en-us/library/bb124513.aspx*.

Dynamic Distribution Groups

Creating a dynamic distribution group involves creating a query that defines the membership of the group. This query runs each time a message is sent to the group. This means that the membership of the group is calculated each time the group receives a new message. For example, a dynamic distribution group might be defined by a query that locates all accountants in the Traralgon office. Each time a message is sent to the group, Exchange calculates which recipients are accountants located in the Traralgon office and forwards the message appropriately. To create a dynamic distribution group in EMC, perform the following general steps:

1. Select the Recipient Configuration\Distribution Group node and then click New Dynamic Distribution Group in the Actions pane.

2. On the Introduction page, specify an Organizational Unit container to host the group if you do not want the group account stored in the default container. Specify a group name and alias. Click Next.

3. On the Filter Settings page, choose whether you want to only include objects from a specific Active Directory Domain or OU. Also, choose whether you want to include all recipient types or if you want to restrict the group to one or more of the following: mailbox users, mail-enabled users, resource mailboxes, contacts, and mail-enabled groups.

4. On the Conditions page select which conditions will be used to limit the scope of the address list. You can choose to limit the scope based on recipient Active Directory attributes including State or Province, Department, Company, or a custom attribute value. Click Next, New, and then Finish.

You can use EMS to create more complicated dynamic distribution groups—such as creating a distribution group that only includes users who have mailboxes on a specific mailbox server—through the use of recipient filters and the *New-DynamicDistributionGroup* cmdlet. For example, to create a dynamic distribution group called SYD-MBX-Users that contains only those users who have mailboxes on server SYD-EX1, use the following command:

```
New-DynamicDistributionGroup -Name "SYD-MBX-Users" -OrganizationalUnit Users
-RecipientFilter {((RecipientType -eq 'UserMailbox' -and ServerName -eq 'SYD-EX1') -and
-not(Name -like 'SystemMailbox{*'))}
```

Public Folders

You need to include public folders in your design if you need to support clients that use Outlook 2003 or earlier. This is because these clients need to use public folders for performing free/busy searches and use them to obtain offline address books. A public folder database will be created on the first Exchange mailbox server that you deploy in your organization if you are deploying in a mixed environment, or indicate that you still need to support clients running Outlook 2003 or earlier.

Public folders almost always are inherited from a previous Exchange deployment. Organizations stick with them because of the effort involved in migrating to another solution. Microsoft recommends that organizations performing new deployments of Exchange use SharePoint rather than public folders. This is because the document management, authoring, and revisioning functionality of SharePoint better addresses how organizations interact with shared documents than Exchange public folder infrastructure does.

When designing public databases, consider the following:

- How large will your public folders be? As almost all organizations that use public folders with Exchange Server 2010 have used public folders with previous versions of Exchange. This means that you should be able to reasonably estimate the size of the necessary public folder databases. Unless you modify the registry, a public folder database cannot exceed 1024 GB in size on a computer running Exchange 2010 Standard edition.

- How often will public folders be accessed? The more often public folders are accessed, the greater the disk utilization.

- Do you need to support Outlook 2003? If your organization does not need to support Outlook 2003, you may wish to plan a migration of public folder content to SharePoint.

- If you want to support public folder replication as a way to make public folder content more failure tolerant, you will need to deploy a minimum of two public folder databases, each on a separate mailbox server.

You'll learn more about configuring public folders in Chapter 2.

Mailbox Provisioning Policies

Mailbox provisioning policies are a way of deciding where to place a specific Exchange mailbox. If you don't specify a mailbox database when provisioning a mailbox, the mailbox will be assigned automatically to an available mailbox database using a load-balanced approach. This can cause problems if you aren't careful—a new user's mailbox could be automatically deployed to a location that is geographically remote from where the user actually works.

Although placing a mailbox in the same Active Directory site as a user may be optimal from a performance standpoint because it allows high-speed access to a local Mailbox server, such a strategy might not be practical from an economic perspective. Mailbox servers cost money and you need to balance localized access performance with the economic realities of deploying multiple mailbox servers. If an organization has a large number of branch office sites with a relatively small number of employees, placing a Mailbox server at each site may not be viable from an administrative or economic standpoint. It may be cheaper to improve the connection to a central site than it is to provision that site with a local Mailbox server.

> **MORE INFO** **MAILBOX SERVERS DON'T NEED TO BE IN THE SAME SITE**
>
> All of the mailbox servers used by Microsoft's Australian and New Zealand offices are hosted in Singapore. From an end-user perspective, this works well without much in the way of appreciable lag. As long as you have a relatively high-bandwidth, low-latency connection to your mailbox server, it doesn't really matter if the mailbox server is in the same site or a different country.

When deciding where to place a mailbox, consider the following:

- Attempt to ensure that the mailbox is placed on a mailbox database that is either geographically close to the user or sufficiently provisioned with bandwidth that it does not cause the user performance problems.

- You can assign different quotas at the mailbox database and the individual mailbox level. Using a database-wide quota makes planning storage simpler than having a multitude of quotas applying to mailboxes hosted in the same database. If you need to use separate mailbox storage quotas in your organization, provision mailboxes to mailbox databases configured with appropriate quotas.

- If you use Exchange Online in conjunction with an on-premises deployment, it may make sense to place some mailboxes in the cloud rather than on a locally managed Exchange Mailbox server. This can be especially useful for remote sites with few users, though will require a cost benefit analysis to determine whether it is a more reasonable solution than hosting the mailbox at an on-premises location.

- Products such as Forefront Identity Manager (FIM) 2010 can be used to automate account and mailbox provisioning.

Your organization should also develop a mailbox deprovisioning policy. A mailbox deprovisioning policy details what steps should be taken in the event that a user leaves an organization. Although it might be tempting to simply delete the user mailbox after the user has left the building, compliance requirements often mean that the mailbox needs to be kept available in some manner for a certain period of time. How you design your deprovisioning policies will depend very much on your organizational needs and most organizations find a balance between deleting user mailboxes immediately and keeping zombie mailboxes on production servers for years after the employee has left the organization.

Objective Summary

- When determining how much storage space will be required by a mailbox database, take into account quotas as well as deleted item retention requirements.

- The amount of space required by transaction logs depends on average message size and how often the mailbox database is backed up.

- Although it is possible to have mailbox databases that are 16 terabytes in size, Microsoft recommends that mailbox databases do not exceed 2 terabytes in size on high-availability configurations and which do not exceed 200 GB in size for non-high-availability configurations.

- Use linked mailboxes to provide Exchange mailboxes to users with accounts in trusted forests.

- A maximum of five mailbox databases can be deployed on a mailbox server running the Standard edition of Exchange 2010. A maximum of 100 mailbox databases can be deployed on a mailbox server running the Enterprise edition of Exchange 2010. A maximum of one public folder database can be deployed per mailbox server.

- Recipient policies, also known as email address policies, determine the format of email addresses in the organization and the default reply-to address format.

- The membership of static distribution can be managed. Mail-enabled security groups must always use the universal scope. The membership of dynamic distribution groups is determined by a query.

Objective Review

Answer the following questions to test your knowledge of the information in this objective. You can find the answers to these questions and explanations of why each answer choice is correct or incorrect in the "Answers" section at the end of this chapter.

1. Your organization uses a resource-forest model, with two account forests and a single resource forest where you have deployed Exchange 2010. The account forests consist of multiple Active Directory domains. Which steps do you need to take to provision users in each account forests with mailboxes in the resource forest? (Choose two. Each answer forms part of a complete solution.)

    A. Ensure that there are forest trusts between the resource forest and the account forests.

    B. Install Exchange 2010 in the account forests.

    C. Create linked mailboxes in the resource forest.

    D. Create linked mailboxes in the account forests.

2. You have been asked by someone in management whether it is possible to configure a special address in Exchange so that people in the organization can send an email to that address and that email will be forwarded on to reach everyone who is currently a member of the Research department. The manager wants the mechanism by which this process works to be automatic. It should not require someone having to manually update the list of people who are in the Research department. The Human Resources department of your organization automatically populates the Department attribute for all Active Directory user accounts in your organization. Which of the following Exchange management shell commands would you use to meet management's goals?

    A. *New-Mailbox*

    B. *New-DistributionGroup*

    C. *Set-DistributionGroup*

    D. *New-DynamicDistributionGroup*

3. A mailbox database, hosted on a mailbox server running the standard edition of Exchange Server 2010 SP1, has dismounted because it has reached its maximum size. What steps can you take to increase the maximum size of the mailbox database beyond 1024 GB?

    A. Use the *New-MailboxDatabase* cmdlet.

    B. Use the *Get-MailboxDatabase* cmdlet.

    C. Edit the registry.

    D. Use the *Set-MailboxDatabase* cmdlet.

4. Your organization has three mailbox servers running Exchange Server 2010 SP1 Enterprise edition and two mailbox servers running Exchange Server 2010 SP1 Standard edition. What is the maximum number of Public Folder databases that you can deploy in this environment?

   A. 5

   B. 1

   C. 8

   D. 7

5. Your organization, currently known as Cohovineyard, is in the process of rebranding itself. An expensive consultant has decided that the name Cohowinery has more intrinsic synergy. You have obtained the appropriate rights to the cohowinery.com domain. You want to ensure that all users default reply-to address uses cohowinery.com rather than cohovineyard.com. Which of the following cmdlets should you use to accomplish this goal? (Choose three. Each answer forms part of a complete solution.)

   A. *New-AcceptedDomain*

   B. *Get-EmailAddressPolicy*

   C. *New-EmailAddressPolicy*

   D. *Update-EmailAddressPolicy*

THOUGHT EXPERIMENT
Recipient Policies, Distribution Groups

In the following thought experiment, apply what you've learned about the "Design the mailbox server role" objective to answer the following case study questions. You can find answers to these questions in the "Answers" section at the end of this chapter.

Your organization has two Active Directory forests, Contoso.com and Fabrikam.com. You have deployed Exchange Server 2010 in Contoso.com. A forest trust relationship exists between the Contoso.com and Fabrikam.com forests.

You want to help Simone from Accounts Receivable to set up a charity email list.

You have the following objectives:

- You need to be able to provide users who have accounts in the Fabrikam.com forest with email access in the Contoso.com Exchange organization.

- Users in the organization should use the *firstname.lastname*@contoso.com address format for their default reply-to address.

- Allow Simone from Accounts Receivable to manage the charity email list membership.

- Anyone in the organization should be able to join the charity email list subject to Simone's approval.

With this in mind, answer the following questions:

1. What kind of mailbox should you set up for users with accounts in the Fabrikam.com forest?

2. How can you ensure that all users in the organization will use the new default reply-to address format?

3. What steps should you take to create to support the charity email list?

4. What steps can you take to give Simone from Accounts Receivable the appropriate administrative privileges?

5. What approval setting should you configure for the group related to the charity email list?

Objective 1.4: Design Client Access

Client Access Servers (CAS) allow users to connect to their Exchange mailboxes, whether they are located on the same local area network or connecting remotely through Outlook Anywhere, VPN, Outlook Web App, or DirectAccess. When you are designing your organization's CAS deployment, you need to ensure that for every site with a mailbox server you have at least one CAS. In this objective, you'll learn about the factors you need to consider when creating a Client Access Server design for your organization. In Chapter 2 you'll learn about how to configure CAS to provide these services to users on your organization's network.

> **This objective covers:**
> - Plan Client Access Server location.
> - Design to support remote and local access.
> - Plan for supported Client Access Server services.
> - Plan for Autodiscover.
> - CAS support in multiple forest environments.

Planning Client Access Servers Location

The key fact that you need to remember when considering CAS placement is that you must place at least one CAS in every Active Directory site where there is a mailbox server. The greater the round-trip latency between the closest CAS and the mailbox server, the more degraded the experience is for clients accessing their mailboxes. You should also consider in your design the ability for CAS to function as proxies. This means that when a user who is in one site—for example, the Auckland site—is attempting to access his mailbox which is hosted on a mailbox server in a remote site such as the Wellington site, he will be able to use the CAS in the Auckland site to function as a proxy for the CAS in the Wellington site.

In earlier versions of Exchange, Outlook clients made a direct RPC connection to the mailbox server that hosted the appropriate mailbox. Exchange 2010 works differently in that the CAS functions as an intermediary, processing all client RPC requests. In an Exchange 2010 environment, the CAS interacts with the Mailbox server on behalf of the Outlook client. One of the most substantial benefits to this is that in the event of Mailbox server failure when Database Availability Groups are in use, the CAS automatically redirects clients to an available mailbox database.

CAS Proxying and Remote Access

The ability for one Exchange Server 2010 CAS to function as a proxy for another CAS will substantially influence your plans for an Exchange Server 2010 infrastructure. This is particularly useful when you have CAS and mailbox servers paired in sites that are not directly exposed to the Internet. For example, an organization may have CAS and Mailbox servers in the cities of Sydney and Melbourne, but only the Sydney CAS is exposed to the Internet. A user whose mailbox resides in the Melbourne site and who accesses OWA from the Internet would connect to the Sydney CAS. The Sydney CAS would then proxy that connection through to the CAS in the Melbourne site, rather than directly interacting with the mailbox server in the Melbourne site.

CAS Proxying not only works with traditional mailbox access through Outlook, but also works for access through Outlook Web App and Exchange ActiveSync. This technology allows you to provide access to Exchange for clients on the Internet by placing CAS on the perimeter network at a single site, knowing that CAS Proxying will ensure that those remote clients will be able to get access to the appropriate mailbox server.

Planning Client Access Server Services

When planning CAS deployment within your organization, you need to consider which services you want to offer. CAS provide the following services to an Exchange 2010 deployment:

- **Outlook Web App**   Allows clients to access mailboxes through their browser. Many organizations provide this service to allow clients a quick way of remotely accessing their mailboxes without having to use a dedicated client.
- **RPC Client Access**   Allows MAPI clients, such as Outlook 2010, to access mailboxes. This is the default way that Exchange mailboxes are accessed in most organizations through the CAS, primarily because organizations that are likely to use Exchange are also likely to use Outlook as their primary mail client.

- **POP3/IMAP4**   Allows clients that don't support MAPI, such as Windows Live Mail, to access mailboxes. As more and more clients support either MAPI or (in the case of mobile clients) ActiveSync, the use of POP3 and IMAP4 is decreasing on most organizational networks.

- **Outlook Anywhere**   Allows Outlook 2003 and later clients to access mailboxes through HTTPS. Outlook Anywhere can be used to allow remote mailbox access without granting DirectAccess or VPN access.

- **ActiveSync**   Allows mobile devices that use Exchange ActiveSync to synchronize mailbox information. This protocol is often used by consumer devices such as the iPad to access Exchange mailboxes.

- **Availability Service**   Provides clients with calendar free/busy information.

- **Exchange Web Services**   Allows programmatic access to Exchange functionality through XML/SOAP interface. Rarely used by most organizations for Client Access scenarios.

- **MailTips**   Provides users of Outlook 2010 and OWA with reminder information, such as whether the message recipient is out of office, or that they are sending to a distribution list.

- **Exchange Control Panel (ECP)**   A web-based interface that allows Exchange administrators to perform certain tasks such as performing searches of all organizational mailboxes for messages that meet a specific set of criteria.

- **Address Book Service**   Interface that allows address book queries.

- **Autodiscover**   Service that allows clients running Outlook 2007 and later and Windows Mobile 6.1 and later to be automatically configured based on user profile settings.

Most of these services are enabled by default. It is possible to disable them specifically on a per-CAS or per-user basis. Figure 1-13 shows these services disabled on a per-mailbox basis.

MORE INFO   **UNDERSTANDING CLIENT ACCESS SERVERS**

For more information about the functionality of Client Access Servers, consult the following TechNet article: *http://technet.microsoft.com/en-us/library/bb124915.aspx*.

Exchange Control Panel

Exchange Control Panel (ECP) is a web-based control panel that, when accessed by a user, allows the user to configure items such as vacation settings, inbox rules, group management, password change, email signature, and spelling options. Users with administrative privileges can also use ECP to configured users, groups, roles, and auditing settings as shown in Figure 1-14. Users that have been delegated the Discovery Management role can use ECP to perform multi-mailbox searches.

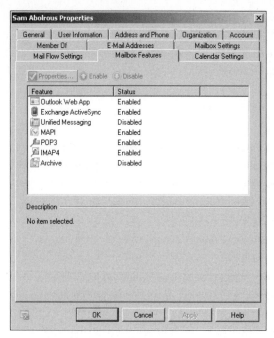

FIGURE 1-13 Client Access Server services

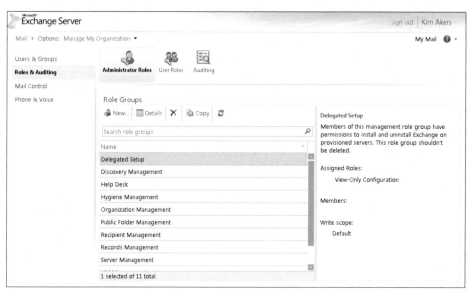

FIGURE 1-14 Exchange Control Panel

Exchange ActiveSync

Exchange ActiveSync allows the syncing of Exchange mailbox information—including messages, calendar, and contact data—to mobile devices such as phones and tablets. ActiveSync supports a technology known as DirectPush. DirectPush allows the mobile device to maintain a persistent connection to Exchange, meaning that new messages are received in real time rather than according to a scheduled polling interval.

Exchange ActiveSync Policies, applied through the ActiveSync process on compatible devices, allow you to control the security of mobile devices. For example, you can use an ActiveSync policy to control password policies, whether to allow the use of hardware such as cameras, Bluetooth, or removable storage usage; whether to support remote-device wipe; and which applications can be executed on the device.

You would plan the use of ActiveSync policies in your Exchange Server 2010 infrastructure if you had specific concerns around mobile device security. You will learn more about ActiveSync policies and how they can be used to improve information security in Chapter 3, "Designing and Deploying Security For the Exchange Organization."

Testing Client Access Server Performance

Administrators can use the Load Generator (LoadGen) tool to plan an Exchange Server 2010 deployment to determine how well a CAS infrastructure performs under a simulated client load. By using this tool you can assess whether you need more CAS, whether your planned deployment meets expectations, or whether you have overprovisioned the CAS role.

LoadGen is able to simulate the following types of client activity:

- Microsoft Office Outlook 2003 (online and cached)
- Outlook 2007 (online and cached)
- POP3
- IMAP4
- SMTP

- ActiveSync
- Outlook Web App

You can choose whether to simulate a single-protocol workload or combine client protocols to determine how well the CAS infrastructure deals with a multi-protocol workload. Using LoadGen you can also calculate client computer response time when CAS are under a specific load, estimate the number of users that each CAS will be able to provide services to concurrently, and identify hardware and design bottlenecks.

> **MORE INFO** **EXCHANGE PERFORMANCE AND SCALABILITY TOOLS**
>
> For more information on tools that you can use to test the performance and scalability of Exchange Server 2010, consult the following TechNet link: *http://technet.microsoft.com/en-us/library/dd335108.aspx*.

Client Access Server Hardware Requirements

Microsoft has done a substantial amount of research on Client Access Server capacity. You can reference this research in detail if you are interested in determining the relative weighting that you should give Client Access Server processor capacity in terms of the capacity of your organization's Mailbox server. A rough summary of Microsoft's finding is that you should deploy three Client Access Server processor cores in an Active Directory site for every four mailbox server cores, assuming cores of equal processing capacity. Exchange Client Access Servers will still function if you use a ratio that differs from this theoretically optimal one. The idea of this ratio is to give you an idea of what the optimal ratio is, so that you can figure out if the Client Access Server at a site might be a bottleneck in Exchange performance because it is under-resourced with processor capacity, or if you have overprovisioned the Client Access Server role with CPU capacity that will never be utilized.

> **MORE INFO** **RELATIVE COSTS OF EXCHANGE 2010 CLIENT ACCESS SERVER WORKLOADS**
>
> For more information about the relative performance costs of Client Access Server workloads, consult the following white paper on Microsoft's website: *http://technet.microsoft.com/en-us/library/ff803560.aspx*.

Planning Autodiscover

The Autodiscover service simplifies the process of configuring Outlook 2007, Outlook 2010, and mobile devices. Autodiscover allows the automatic provisioning of a user's profile given the user's email address and password. Rather than having to configure all necessary settings, the user simply enters her email address and password into the email client and all relevant mail server settings are automatically provided to the client through the Autodiscover service.

Planning Site Affinity for Autodiscover

If your organization has a number of clients that move between sites, you may wish to configure the Autodiscover service to use site affinity. When you configure the Autodiscover service to use site affinity on the Client Access Server, clients using Outlook 2007 or Outlook 2010 will be provisioned with Autodiscover information from the closest Active Directory site. In some organizations with geographically dispersed branch offices, this can substantially improve the performance of Autodiscover.

Planning Autodiscover for Internet Clients

You can configure Autodiscover so that remote clients on the Internet can automatically provision profile settings by entering their email address and password. For example, by using Autodiscover and using Outlook Anywhere, a user who is connected to the Internet can fully configure Outlook by entering his email address and password. The main requirement for Autodiscover for Internet clients is that you have an SSL certificate that is trusted by the client computer's operating system. If the majority of the clients that will use this service are using their own consumer devices, the simplest approach to ensuring that the SSL certificate is trusted by clients is to obtain the SSL certificate from a trusted third-party Certificate Authority.

Autodiscover in Multiple-Forest Environments

Autodiscover, when appropriately configured, supports cross-forest topologies. When Autodiscover is appropriately configured, a client that supports Autodiscover on a computer in another forest can be provisioned automatically by the local forest's Client Access Servers. For example, Contoso might have a cross-forest topology in which one Exchange organization is in Australia and another Exchange organization is in New Zealand. When Autodiscover is configured to support the multiple-forest environment, a user that logs on in the New Zealand forest—but who has been configured with a mailbox in the Australian Exchange organization—will be able to have those Australia-based profile settings automatically provided to her client by providing her email address and password.

> **MORE INFO** **AUTODISCOVER IN MULTIPLE FORESTS**
>
> For more information about configuring the Autodiscover service to support multiple-forest topologies, consult the following TechNet link: *http://technet.microsoft. com/en-us/library/aa996849.aspx.*

Planning Client Access Server Certificates

Server certificates, also commonly known as Secure Sockets Layer certificates, allow clients to establish a secure connection to a host that has a verified identity. This is very useful in CAS scenarios where a multitude of clients need to be able to use a CAS to securely access mailbox data through a variety of protocols.

Something that you must consider in your design is that unless you take specific steps to remedy the situation, Exchange defaults to using self-signed certificates created during the installation process. This is fine for communication between Exchange servers in the same organization because these servers trust these self-signed certificates. This is problematic for clients who are unlikely to trust these self-signed certificates without you performing remedial action. If a significant number of Exchange clients are going to be running computers that are not a part of your organization's domain, you should consider obtaining an SSL certificate from a trusted third-party Certificate Authority (CA). Although these trusted third-party CA certificates do have a fee associated with them, the cost of supporting the deployment of a certificate issued from an internal CA to clients that aren't members of a domain often exceeds the cost of obtaining the third-party certificate.

The key to planning the names assigned to certificates used by Client Access Servers is knowing the name that client will be using to access each required client protocol on the server. For example, you might be planning to have users connect to Outlook Web App using the address *https://owa.wingtiptoys.com,* to the POP3 server using POP.wingtiptoys.com, to Autodiscover using Autodiscover.wingtiptoys.com, and to IMAP4 using IMAP4.wingtiptoys.com. In this situation you need to ensure that the certificate you install supports all of these names. In this situation you can plan to take one of the following options:

- Obtain four separate certificates, one for each separate name. This is the traditional option, although it can be more cumbersome to implement.
- Obtain a single certificate that supports multiple subject alternative names (SANs). Getting a certificate that supports multiple SANs is usually the best option and almost all trusted third-party CAs will issue them more cheaply than they'll issue multiple

separate certificates. You have to perform a minor modification to a Windows Server 2008 R2 CA to configure them to support the issuance of certificates with multiple SANs.

- Obtain a certificate with a wildcard name. These certificates are also supported by most public CAs. In the example situation you would configure the certificate with the wildcard name *.wingtiptoys.com.

- Configure all services to use the same name, such as mail.wingtiptoys.com. This allows you to solve this problem by only needing to acquire a single certificate.

MORE INFO   **SSL FOR CLIENT ACCESS SERVERS**

For more information about preparing to use SSL certificates with Client Access Servers, consult the following TechNet document: *http://technet.microsoft.com/en-us/library/bb310795.aspx*.

EXAM TIP

Remember to place a CAS in the same site as your organization's Mailbox servers.

Objective Summary

- Include Outlook Anywhere in your design if you want to allow users remote access to Exchange without having to provision a VPN solution or DirectAccess. Outlook Anywhere is supported on clients running Outlook 2007 and Outlook 2010.

- ActiveSync allows supported mobile devices to access mailbox data.

- You can configure Autodiscover to automatically provision Outlook 2007 and Outlook 2010 clients. When properly set up and used in conjunction with Outlook Anywhere, Autodiscover can provision clients on the Internet.

- You can configure Autodiscover with ActiveSync to automatically provision ActiveSync clients based on email address and password.

- POP3 and IMAP4 can be enabled on CAS to support non-Outlook messaging clients that do not support ActiveSync or MAPI.

- Subject Alternative Name (SAN) certificates allow multiple FQDNs to be associated with a single certificate.

- The Load Generator (LoadGen) tool can be used to test a CAS against a simulated client workload.

- Exchange Control Panel allows administrators to perform discovery and RBAC tasks. It allows normal recipients to perform tasks such as password change, group creation, and rules management.

Objective Review

Answer the following questions to test your knowledge of the information in this objective. You can find the answers to these questions and explanations of why each answer choice is correct or incorrect in the "Answers" section at the end of this chapter.

1. You are in the process of evaluating a CAS deployment to determine whether it will be able to cope with a projected client load. Which of the following tools could you use to assist you in performing that evaluation?

   A. LoadGen

   B. Jetstress

   C. Exchange Best Practices Analyzer

   D. Exchange Remote Connectivity Analyzer

2. You are planning your organization's Exchange Server 2010 deployment. Your current plans involve placing two mailbox servers at the Sydney and Melbourne sites and one mailbox server at the Adelaide, Brisbane, and Darwin sites. What is the minimum number of Client Access Servers that you need to deploy to support this configuration?

   A. 1

   B. 4

   C. 5

   D. 7

3. Tailspin Toys has its main office in Auckland and branch offices in Christchurch, Wellington, and Dunedin. The Auckland site has two mailbox servers. What is the minimum number of Client Access Servers that need to be deployed to support this configuration?

   A. 1

   B. 2

   C. 4

   D. 8

4. What is the theoretical optimum ratio of Client Access Server processor cores to Mailbox server processor cores in a single Active Directory site?

   A. Three Client Access Server processor cores for every four Mailbox server processor cores

   B. Four Client Access Server processor cores for every three Mailbox server processor cores

   C. Two Client Access Server processor cores for every three Mailbox server processor cores

   D. Three Client Access Server processor cores for every four Mailbox server processor cores

5. You want to ensure that Outlook 2010 clients get Autodiscover information from the closest Active Directory site. Which of the following steps should you include in your Client Access Server deployment plan to accomplish this goal?

   A. Configure the Autodiscover Service for Internet Access.

   B. Configure the Autodiscover Service for Multiple Forests.

   C. Configure the Autodiscover Service to use Site Affinity.

   D. Configure Exchange ActiveSync Autodiscover Settings.

THOUGHT EXPERIMENT
Moving a Site from an Intranet to the Internet

In the following thought experiment, apply what you've learned about the "Design client access" objective to design a CAS implementation for Wingtip toys. You can find answers to these questions in the "Answers" section at the end of this chapter.

Wingtip Toys has its head office site in Auckland, New Zealand. There are branch office sites in the cities of Wellington, Dunedin, and Christchurch. You intend to deploy mailbox servers at each of these locations.

You want to support Outlook Web App, Outlook Anywhere, Autodiscover, IMAP4, ActiveSync, and MAPI.

You want to ensure that people working from home on their personal computers are able to securely access Outlook Web App.

You want to allow access to Exchange mailboxes for external clients running Outlook 2010 without having those clients use VPN or DirectAccess technologies.

With these factors in mind, answer the following questions:

1. In which sites must you deploy Client Access Servers?

2. How can you ensure that clients using Autodiscover are provisioned with profile information from the closest Active Directory site?

3. You want to minimize the number of certificates that you install on each CAS. What steps could you take to accomplish this goal?

4. What technology should you deploy to allow remote access to Exchange mailboxes for clients running Outlook 2010?

5. What type of Certificate Authority should you use to obtain the SSL certificate for the Client Access Server hosting Outlook Web App at the Auckland site?

Objective 1.5: Plan for Transition and Coexistence

One thing to keep in mind when planning for transition from Exchange 2003 or Exchange 2007 to Exchange 2010 or coexistence is that the term *upgrade* isn't entirely accurate. You can't perform an in-place upgrade from either Exchange 2003 or Exchange 2007 to Exchange 2010 in so far as it is not possible to directly upgrade a server running either of these products to Exchange 2010. An upgrade involves installing Exchange 2010 into your existing Exchange organization and then moving data and functionality across to the new Exchange 2010 servers. A migration involves moving from one messaging system to another. If you are performing a migration from Exchange 2003 or Exchange 2007, you install Exchange 2010 in a new Active Directory forest and then migrate data across.

> **This objective covers:**
> - Plan and investigate consolidation of Exchange servers.
> - Plan transition from Exchange 2003 to Exchange 2010.
> - Plan transition from Exchange 2007 to Exchange 2010.
> - Plan transition from mixed Exchange 2003 and Exchange 2007 environment to Exchange 2010.
> - Plan coexistence with third-party messaging systems.

Exchange Consolidation

As organizations are able to deploy more powerful hardware, they are able to consolidate their Exchange deployment onto fewer servers. For example, an organization that may have had 10 Exchange 2007 mailbox servers might, with the substantially better hardware that has become available in the intervening years, be able to service the same number of clients with fewer servers. Hardware improvements aside, Exchange Server 2010 has been engineered to provide better performance on the same hardware compared to previous versions of Exchange. When planning a transition from Exchange 2003 or Exchange 2007 to Exchange 2010, remember that you may not need to have as many Exchange 2010 servers as you had previously because of improvements in hardware an Exchange performance.

To determine the capacity of your new servers, Microsoft makes available two tools that you can use to perform a capacity analysis on your hardware. The drawback of these tools is that you have to actually have the hardware to test it against. The first tool, Exchange Server Jetstress 2010, allows you to perform I/O benchmarking against the storage on a mailbox server. The second tools, Exchange Server Load Generator 2010 (LoadGen) allows you to simulate a client workload against a test Exchange environment. You learned about LoadGen earlier in this chapter. Using these tools, you can make informed estimates about the capacity of the Exchange 2010 servers that you are going to deploy.

Upgrade Approaches

When you are developing your upgrade plan, you have to decide whether you are going to perform a single-phase upgrade or whether you are going to prepare a multiphase upgrade with coexistence. The differences between these two approaches are as follows:

- Single-phase upgrades involve replacing an existing messaging system with Exchange Server 2010. Single-phase upgrades minimize the coexistence period between the two systems and all required data and services are moved to Exchange 2010 as expeditiously as possible. These upgrades allow the transition to occur quickly, but the chance of problems arising is higher than when the transition occurs at a more measured pace.

- Multiphase upgrade with coexistence is a more measured approach to transitioning to Exchange Server 2010. This might involve upgrading one server at a time or one site at a time. This is often a more pragmatic approach for large sites where a quick transition of the existing infrastructure is infeasible because of the size of the migration. This involves planning for a period of interoperability. Although supporting interoperability is more complicated, the more measured approach allows each phase in the migration to be completed separately before moving on to the next phase.

When using a multiphase upgrade with coexistence strategy, you need to ensure that users that have mailboxes hosted on both the existing and the Exchange 2010 messaging system have access to the following:

- **Public folders**   If your Exchange 2003 or Exchange 2007 organization uses public folders, you will need to come up with a way of replicating public folder data between systems. As an alternative, you could migrate public folder data to SharePoint if you don't need to support Outlook 2003 clients.

- **E-mail message flow**   You need to keep this working transparently so that users of the old and new systems are able to send email to each other without having to know whether the destination mailbox is on the old or new system.

- **Global Address List (GAL)**   You need to ensure that users of both systems are able to efficiently locate addresses and address lists on both the old and new systems.

- **Calendar information**   Users in on both the old system and the new system need to be able to schedule meetings and view free/busy data of other people in the organization irrespective of which messaging system people's mailboxes reside on.

- **Administration tools**   Exchange administrators need to be able to quickly and efficiently manage servers running both the original messaging system and Exchange Server 2010.

Multiple Sites

Transitioning an organization that has a single site from Exchange 2003 or Exchange 2007 to Exchange 2010 is far simpler than transitioning an organization that has sites spread across geographically dispersed locations. When planning a transition from a previous version of Exchange to Exchange 2010, keep the following in mind:

- You must upgrade Internet-facing sites prior to upgrading internal sites. This restriction is due to Client Access Server proxying functionality.

- When upgrading a site, upgrade Exchange roles by introducing servers in the following manner:

    1. Client Access

    2. Hub Transport

    3. Mailbox

    4. Edge Transport

The Edge Transport server is only necessary if you are choosing to use an Edge Transport server rather than a third-party email gateway. Edge Transport servers are also only deployed on perimeter networks at Internet-facing sites, so you don't need to plan on deploying them at every site during a transition to Exchange 2010.

Exchange 2003 Upgrade or Coexistence

When planning an upgrade or coexistence scenario for an Exchange 2003 organization that you wish to transition to Exchange 2010, first ensure the following:

- Your Exchange 2003 organization is running in Native rather than Mixed mode.

- All servers running Exchange 2003 are upgraded to Exchange 2003 Service Pack 2.

- At least one global catalog server in each site is running at Windows Server 2003 Service Pack 2 or later.

- The computer that hosts the schema master role is running at Windows Server 2003 Service Pack 2 or later.

- The domain and forest functional level are configured at the Windows Server 2003 or higher level.

As you'll learn in Chapter 2, the requirements for Exchange Server 2010 SP1 are slightly different than those published for Exchange Server 2010 RTM, and that the 70-663 exam targets RTM rather than SP1. It is also worth checking with the relevant TechNet documentation that is linked to this and the next chapter to determine whether any other prerequisites have changed when Exchange Server 2010 Service Pack 2 is released. Chapter 2 will cover the process in more detail, but in general your plan should involve the following steps:

1. Upgrade any Internet-facing sites first.

2. Install the Client Access Server first. Configure clients to use the new Exchange 2010 Client Access Server as their connection point to both Exchange 2010 and Exchange 2003.

3. Install the Hub Transport role after the Client Access Server has been deployed. The first Hub Transport server deployment will involve you specifying an Exchange 2003 bridgehead server.

4. Deploy the Mailbox servers in the site.

5. Deploy the Edge Transport server and configure EdgeSync.

6. After you have performed steps 2 through 4 on all Internet-facing sites, perform steps 2 through 4 on all non-Internet-facing sites.

7. Begin migrating public folders and mailboxes from the Exchange 2003 servers to the Exchange 2010 servers. In multiple-site upgrades, you can begin moving mailboxes and public folders prior to upgrading additional sites if you so choose.

When planning a transition from Exchange 2003 to Exchange 2010, remember that the following Exchange 2003 features are not supported in Exchange 2010:

- **Novell GroupWise connector**   This connector allows coexistence between Novell GroupWise and an Exchange 2003 organization. If your organization requires the functionality this connector provides, it will be necessary to retain at least one server running Exchange 2003 in your environment until the functionality is no longer required or another solution becomes available.

- **NNTP**   Network News Transfer Protocol (NNTP) allows the use of newsgroup content. If it is necessary to retain NNTP functionality in your organization, either retain a server running Exchange 2003 or look for a third-party NNTP server solution.

- **Office Outlook Mobile Access**   The functionality that was provided by Office Outlook Mobile Access is now provided through ActiveSync.

- **Inter-Organization Replication Tool**   This tool allowed the exchange of meeting, appointment, and contact data between two different Exchange 2003 organizations. Exchange Server 2010 uses Microsoft Federation Gateway to provide this functionality.

Once you have moved all public folder and mailbox server data from Exchange 2003 to Exchange 2010, you can begin to decommission the existing Exchange 2003 infrastructure. Microsoft recommends that you remove Exchange 2003 in the following manner:

- Remove Exchange 2003 back-end servers first. You can remove back-end servers as soon as all the relevant data on the server has been migrated across to Exchange 2010.

- Remove the Exchange Server 2003 bridgehead server after you've removed the last mailbox server in a routing group.

- Remove the Exchange 2003 front-end servers last.

Exchange 2007 Upgrade or Coexistence

Exchange 2007 has a superficially similar structure to that of Exchange 2010 with both systems utilizing the Hub Transport, Edge Transport, Mailbox and Client Access Server roles. As is the case with an upgrade from Exchange 2003, you'll need to ensure that the global a catalog server in each site and the schema master is upgraded to the appropriate service pack level for the deployment of Exchange 2010 SP1. You also need to ensure that the forest functional level is set to Windows Server 2003. Finally, prior to attempting upgrade, ensure that all Exchange 2007 servers have Exchange 2007 Service Pack 2 installed. The specifics of upgrading Exchange 2007 to Exchange 2010 are covered in more detail by Chapter 2, but in general you need to perform the following steps:

1. In multi-site environments, upgrade any Internet-facing sites before upgrading any internal sites.

2. Deploy the Exchange 2010 Client Access Server first. After this is done, modify Autodiscover settings to point at the Exchange 2010 Client Access Server.

3. Install the Exchange Server 2010 Hub Transport server. During coexistence, you will have both Exchange Server 2010 and Exchange Server 2007 Hub Transport Servers in the same sites.

4. Install the Exchange Server 2010 Mailbox servers. You can begin migrating mailboxes and public folder data from Exchange Server 2007 Mailbox servers at this stage, or wait until several sites are upgraded fully before taking that step.

5. Install the Exchange Server 2010 Edge Transport Servers. Exchange Server 2010 Edge Transport servers can only synchronize with Exchange Server 2010 Hub Transport Servers.

6. Repeat steps 2 through 5 at all Internet-facing sites before performing steps 2 through 4 at all non-Internet-facing sites.

When planning an upgrade from Exchange 2007 to Exchange 2010, ensure that you account for the fact that the following Exchange 2007 features are not supported in Exchange 2010:

- **Single Copy Cluster**   Exchange 2007 high-availability features have been replaced in Exchange 2010 by Database Availability Groups. You'll learn more about Database Availability Groups in Chapter 4.

- **Local Continuous Replication** Exchange 2007 high-availability features have been replaced in Exchange 2010 by Database Availability Groups. You'll learn more about Database Availability Groups in Chapter 4.

- **Cluster Continuous Replication** Exchange 2007 high-availability features have been replaced in Exchange 2010 by Database Availability Groups. You'll learn more about Database Availability Groups in Chapter 4.

- **Standby Continuous Replication** Exchange 2007 high-availability features have been replaced in Exchange 2010 by Database Availability Groups. You'll learn more about Database Availability Groups in Chapter 4.

- **Microsoft Transport Suite for Lotus Domino** This tool allowed for interoperability between Exchange 2007 environments and Lotus Domino. It also provided tools that could be used to migrate users from Lotus Domino to Exchange Server 2007. If you need to retain interoperability with your organization's Lotus Domino messaging system, you'll need to retain at least one server running Exchange 2007 in your Exchange organization.

- **Programmatic Access to Exchange through ExOLEDB, WebDAV, or CDOEX (CDO for Exchange 2000 Server)** This functionality has been replaced by the Exchange Web Services (EWS) or EWS-Managed API. If you have not migrated the applications that use this technology to utilize the EWS-Managed API, you'll need to retain at least one server running Exchange 2007 in your Exchange organization.

After you have moved all data from your organization's Exchange 2007 Mailbox servers to the new Exchange 2010 Mailbox servers, you'll be able to begin removing the Exchange 2007 infrastructure. Remove Exchange 2007 servers in the following order:

1. Remove Mailbox servers first. You can decommission a mailbox server as soon as you have removed all mailbox and public folder data from it.

2. When all Exchange 2007 Mailbox servers at a site have been removed, you can remove any Exchange 2007 Hub Transport servers at that site.

3. Remove the Exchange 2007 Client Access Servers and Edge Transport servers.

MORE INFO **PLANNING EXCHANGE 2007 UPGRADE OR COEXISTENCE**

To learn more about the planning roadmap for Exchange 2007 upgrade or coexistence, consult the following TechNet article: *http://technet.microsoft.com/en-us/library/dd638158.aspx.*

Mixed Exchange 2003 and Exchange 2007 Environments

Planning to upgrade a mixed Exchange 2003 and Exchange 2007 environment is similar to upgrading from environments containing a single Exchange 2003 or Exchange 2007 organization. You'll need to upgrade Internet-facing sites first by introducing Client Access, Hub Transport, and then Mailbox servers. Introduce Edge Transport servers at this stage as appropriate. Move data from Exchange 2003 back-end and Exchange 2007 Mailbox servers to Exchange 2010. Begin decommissioning, removing the Exchange 2003 back-end servers, bridgehead servers, and then front-end servers. Then remove the Exchange 2007 Mailbox servers, Hub Transport servers, Client Access Servers, and then Edge Transport servers.

Exchange Server Deployment Assistant

The Exchange Server Deployment Assistant, also known as ExDeploy, which you learned about earlier in this chapter, is an excellent tool for generating checklists to assist you with transitioning your organization from Exchange 2003, Exchange 2007, or a mixed Exchange 2003 and Exchange 2007 environment to Exchange Server 2010. The tool is Silverlight-based and generates a transition checklist based on the answers you provide to a series of questions about your environment. The checklist for an Exchange 2003 to Exchange 2010 environment is shown in Figure 1-15.

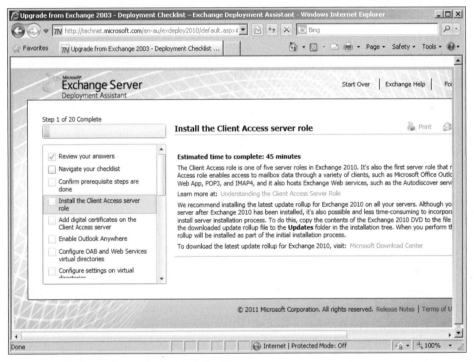

FIGURE 1-15 Exchange Server deployment checklist

You can use this automatically generated checklist as a guide in developing your plans to transition your organization from previous versions of Exchange. You can also use the checklist to verify each step of the transition process.

Coexistence with SMTP-Based Messaging Systems

Many organizations use messaging systems from multiple vendors. This is often the case
in environments that have substantial UNIX-based deployments where each team of
administrators is wary of using systems hosted on different platforms, though you may have
other technical and political reasons to maintain a multi-vendor messaging infrastructure.

In most cases the third-party messaging system will support SMTP traffic and it is
possible to get the both Exchange and the third-party messaging system to communicate by
configuring appropriate internal Send and Receive connectors.

Coexistence with non-SMTP Messaging Systems

Although almost all modern previous versions of Exchange did offer connector and migration
tools for third-party products such as Lotus Notes and Novell GroupWise, but these
connectors are not present in Exchange Server 2010. Exchange 2010 does support foreign
connectors for third-party messaging systems, but you need to obtain those connectors from
the vendor of the third-party messaging system or another third-party vendor who might
provide their own set of tools.

You can also use delivery agents and Foreign connectors to deliver messages to
third-party non-SMTP messaging systems. Although Foreign connectors are supported in
Exchange Server 2010, Microsoft recommends that you use Delivery Agents for coexistence
functionality. Delivery agents have the following benefits:

- Allows queue management for messages routed to foreign systems using standard
  queue management tasks
- Improved performance
- Can use the message representation and management features of Exchange
- Provides confirmation that messages have been delivered to the third-party system
- Allows administrators to track latency of message delivery to the foreign system

Global Address List Synchronization

In coexistence scenarios, it is often useful to include some sort of Global Address List scenario so that users of the Exchange messaging system are able to view and search addresses in the third-party messaging system. Similarly, users of the organization's third-party messaging system are likely to want to be able to search and view addresses of users with Exchange mailboxes. How effectively this can be done depends very much on the functionality available in the third-party messaging system. You have the following options when it comes to planning synchronization of Global Address lists between Exchange 2010 and third-party messaging systems:

- You may be able to use the GAL synchronization functionality available in Forefront Identity Manager 2010, though this is mostly used to support Exchange cross-forest topologies.

- The third-party vendor might provide a GAL synchronization tool that automatically synchronizes the third-party global address list with Exchange.

- You can create Lightweight Directory Access Protocol (LDAP) replication scripts. You can only do this if the third-party messaging system supports using LDAP queries to extract mailbox and contact information. These scripts will have to be run manually or be automated in some fashion.

EXAM TIP

Remember the order in which you need to introduce servers when planning an upgrade from Exchange 2003 or Exchange 2007 to Exchange 2010.

Objective Summary

- JetStress allows you to test how well a mailbox server handles simulated load. LoadGen allows you to simulate CAS load. Both tools can be used when determining whether it is feasible to consolidate existing servers.

- Single-phase upgrades minimize the coexistence periods. These are suitable for smaller organizations. Cutover to Exchange 2010 occurs rapidly organization-wide.

- Multiphase upgrades with coexistence have longer coexistence periods. This upgrade type is suitable for larger organizations. Parts of the organization are moved across to Exchange 2010 in stages, rather than all at once.

- If an organization needs to support Outlook 2003 clients, it will be necessary to retain a public folder infrastructure after the upgrade to Exchange 2010 is complete.

- When performing an upgrade, Internet-facing sites must be upgraded before sites that do not have a direct Internet connection.

- When upgrading from Exchange 2003, Exchange 2007, or a mixture of Exchange 2003 and Exchange 2007, introduce CAS to a site first, then Hub Transport, and then Mailbox servers. Add Edge Transport servers at Internet-facing sites as appropriate.

- Remove Exchange 2003 back-end servers first, but only after you have migrated all mailbox and public folder data from these servers.

- The Exchange Server Deployment Assistant can analyze a current environment to determine whether it meets the necessary infrastructure.

Objective Review

Answer the following questions to test your knowledge of the information in this objective. You can find the answers to these questions and explanations of why each answer choice is correct or incorrect in the "Answers" section at the end of this chapter.

1. You are in the process of planning a migration from Exchange Server 2003 to Exchange Server 2010. As part of your migration you want to consolidate your Exchange deployment onto fewer servers. You have purchased new hardware for an Exchange Server 2010 test deployment that reflects the hardware profile of the servers you will eventually deploy. In your new deployment, the Hub Transport, Mailbox, and Client Access Server roles will all be located on the same server. You need to determine how many client computers can use this server as part of your consolidation planning. Which of the following tools can you use to accomplish this goal?

   A. Exchange Server Load Generator 2010

   B. Exchange Server Jetstress 2010

   C. Exchange Remote Connectivity Analyzer

   D. Exchange Server Best Practices Analyzer

2. You are planning a transition from an environment running Exchange Server 2003 to Exchange Server 2010. You are planning on a coexistence period of approximately four months where both messaging systems must run side by side. Which of the following Exchange Server 2010 roles must you plan to install first?

   A. Hub Transport server

   B. Mailbox server

C. Client Access Server

D. Edge Transport server

3. You are planning the transition from Exchange Server 2003 to Exchange Server 2010. You will be deploying each Exchange Server 2010 role on a separate computer. You are working on the deployment order plan for each role. Which of the following Exchange Server 2010 roles would you deploy after all the others have been deployed?

   A. Mailbox server

   B. Client Access Server

   C. Hub Transport server

   D. Edge Transport server

4. You are planning a transition from an environment running Exchange Server 2007 to one running Exchange Server 2010. You expect the transition to take approximately three months. Your organization intends to keep using public folders, but you intend to use a third-party appliance as a mail gateway rather than an Edge Transport server. Which of the following Exchange Server 2010 roles must you deploy prior to starting to move mailboxes hosted on Exchange 2007 mailbox servers to Exchange 2010? (Choose all that apply.)

   A. Client Access Server

   B. Hub Transport server

   C. Mailbox server

   D. Edge Transport server

5. You are in the process of planning an upgrade of a mixed Exchange 2003 and Exchange 2007 environment to Exchange 2010. Which of the following tools can you use to analyze your organization's environment to determine whether the existing infrastructure is prepared for the deployment of Exchange Server 2010?

   A. Exchange Remote Connectivity Analyzer

   B. Exchange Best Practices Analyzer

   C. Exchange Pre-Deployment Analyzer

   D. Exchange Server Jetstress 2010

THOUGHT EXPERIMENT
Planning the Introduction of Exchange Server 2010 Where There Is an Existing Exchange Deployment

In the following thought experiment, apply what you've learned about the "Plan for transition and coexistence" objective to develop a design to meet an organization's needs. You can find answers to these questions in the "Answers" section at the end of this chapter.

Wingtip Toys and Tailspin Toys are in the process of merging. Each organization has its own Active Directory forest running at the Windows Server 2003 forest functional level. Wingtip Toys has an existing Exchange 2007 deployment. Tailspin Toys has an existing Exchange 2003 deployment. Wingtip Toys has only one Internet-facing site, which is located in Auckland, New Zealand. The other Wingtip Toys sites in Wellington, Dunedin, and Christchurch are all connected to the Auckland site via WAN links. Tailspin Toys has two Internet-facing sites in the cities of Melbourne and Sydney, Australia. The cities of Adelaide and Perth also have branch offices, and these are connected to the Internet-facing site through WAN links. You want to use Edge Transport servers for routing inbound and outbound messages. Each organization should retain its own Active Directory forest.

With this in mind, answer the following questions:

1. Which site or sites at Wingtip Toys should you plan to upgrade first?

2. Which site or sites at Tailspin Toys should you plan to upgrade first?

3. In which sites should you deploy Edge Transport servers?

4. Which multiple-forest topology should you use?

5. Which Microsoft product should you use to perform GAL synchronization between the Wingtip Toys and Tailspin Toys organizations?

6. Which server role will you introduce first at each organization and in which sites?

7. Which server role will you decommission first in the Wingtip Toys organization?

Chapter Summary

- Exchange Server 2010 can be installed in an on-premises, cloud, or coexistence configuration.

- SLA requirements determine parts of your Exchange design, primarily around high-availability features such as Database Availability Groups and Client Access Server Arrays.

- In multiple-forest environments, the resource-forest topology has Exchange deployed in one forest and accessed by users in other forests. The cross-forest topology has Exchange deployed in all forests and uses Forefront Identity Life Cycle Manager for GAL synchronization.

- Ensure that there is at least one Hub Transport server in every site where there is a Mailbox server on a per-forest basis.

- ActiveSync allows supported mobile devices to access mailbox data.

- You can configure Autodiscover to automatically provision Outlook 2007 and Outlook 2010 clients.

- The Load Generator (LoadGen) tool can be used to test a CAS against a simulated client workload.

- JetStress allows you to test how well a mailbox server handles simulated load. LoadGen allows you to simulate CAS load. Both tools can be used when determining whether it is feasible to consolidate existing servers.

- When performing an upgrade, Internet-facing sites must be upgraded before sites that do not have a direct Internet connection.

- When upgrading from previous versions of Exchange, introduce CAS to a site first, then Hub Transport, and then Mailbox servers. Add Edge Transport servers at Internet-facing sites as appropriate.

- The Exchange Server Deployment Assistant can analyze a current environment prior to the introduction of Exchange Server 2010.

Answers

This section contains the answers to the Object Reviews and the Thought Experiments.

Objective 1.1: Review

1. **Correct Answer:** D

    A. **Incorrect:** Active Directory Administrative Center allows administrators to perform simple tasks such as password reset and can search Active Directory for information. Although you can extend the tool with custom components, by default it cannot be used to view information about Active Directory site configuration.

    B. **Incorrect:** Active Directory Users and Computers can be used to view and manipulate user, computer, and group account information as well as manage organizational unit structure. You cannot use Active Directory Users and Computers to view or modify Active Directory site information.

    C. **Incorrect:** Active Directory Domains and Trusts can be used to view forest information as well as to establish trust relationships with other forests or Kerberos realms. You cannot use Active Directory Domains and Trusts to view or modify Active Directory site information.

    D. **Correct:** Active Directory Sites and Services can be used to verify current mappings between IP networks and specific Active Directory sites. You can also use this console to create mappings between IP networks and specific Active Directory sites.

2. **Correct Answers:** B and C

    A. **Incorrect:** Both the primary DNS suffix and the DNS domain name must be included on the *msDS-AllowedDNSSuffixes* Active Directory attribute if Exchange is to function in an environment with a disjointed namespace.

    B. **Correct:** To ensure that the Exchange servers can properly communicate with Active Directory, it is necessary to ensure that both the primary DNS suffix and the DNS domain name are included on the *msDS-AllowedDNSSuffixes* Active Directory attributed on the domain object container.

    C. **Correct:** To ensure that the Exchange servers and clients can properly communicate in the disjointed namespace environment, you need to include both the primary DNS suffix and the DNS domain name in the DNS suffix search list group policy item.

    D. **Incorrect:** You must include both the DNS domain name and the primary DNS suffix in the DNS suffix search list group policy item to ensure that the Exchange servers and clients can properly communicate in the disjointed namespace environment.

3. **Correct Answers:** A and D

   A. **Correct:** Tailspin Toys should use the cross-forest topology. This topology involves deploying Exchange in each forest and then using GAL synchronization to ensure that recipients from each forest are visible in every other forest.

   B. **Incorrect:** Tailspin Toys should not use the resource-forest topology because in this topology Exchange is only installed in one forest rather than all forests as suggested by the question text.

   C. **Incorrect:** Wingtip Toys should not use the cross-forest topology because Exchange should only be deployed in one forest at this organization.

   D. **Correct:** Wingtip Toys should use the resource-forest topology because in this topology Exchange is deployed in one forest and user accounts are stored in other forests.

4. **Correct Answer:** D

   A. **Incorrect:** System Center Configuration Manager 2012 can be used for application, software update, and operating system deployment. You cannot configure System Center Configuration Manager 2012 to measure service availability as part of monitoring compliance with an SLA.

   B. **Incorrect:** System Center Data Protection Manager 2012 can be used to back up and restore organizational data. You cannot configure System Center Data Protection Manager 2012 to measure service availability as part of monitoring compliance with an SLA.

   C. **Incorrect:** System Center Virtual Machine Manager 2012 allows you to manage large deployments of virtual machines. You cannot configure System Center Virtual Machine Manager 2012 to measure service availability as part of monitoring compliance with an SLA.

   D. **Correct:** System Center Operations Manager 2012 can be used to monitor service availability. System Center Operations Manager 2012 can raise alerts in the event that specific services or servers fail.

5. **Correct Answer:** C

   A. **Incorrect:** Forefront Threat Management Gateway 2010 is an advanced firewall product. You cannot use this product to support GAL synchronization in an Exchange cross-forest topology.

   B. **Incorrect:** Forefront Endpoint Protection 2012 is an anti-malware solution. You cannot use this product to support GAL synchronization in an Exchange cross-forest topology.

   C. **Correct:** Forefront Identity Life Cycle Manager 2010 can be used to implement GAL synchronization when Exchange Server 2010 is deployed in a cross-forest topology.

D. Incorrect: Forefront Unified Access Gateway 2010 allows you to provide access to internal resources for external clients. You cannot use this product to support GAL synchronization in an Exchange cross-forest topology.

Objective 1.1: Thought Experiment

1. You need to configure single sign-on prior to configuring directory synchronization.

2. You need to ensure that the domain that you are federating can be resolved by hosts on the Internet. You need to configure User Principle Names for all users. You need to deploy Active Directory Federation Services.

3. It will be necessary to deploy a computer to host the Directory Synchronization and an Exchange Server 2010 coexistence server.

Objective 1.2: Review

1. **Correct Answer:** B

   A. Incorrect: You use authoritative domains for email domains where the intended recipient has a mailbox hosted within the same Exchange organization, or where the email domain is split across Exchange and another messaging system.

   B. Correct: You would configure an Internal Relay domain to ensure that your Exchange organization would accept messages and then route them to a third-party messaging system hosted on your organization's internal network.

   C. Incorrect: You use an external relay domain when you want your Exchange organization to accept email messages and then route them to another messaging system.

   D. Incorrect: You use a reverse lookup zone to provide IP address to FQDN translation. This is created in DNS and is not something that you need to set up to ensure that your Exchange organization accepts messages and then routes them to a third-party messaging system hosted on the organization's internal network.

2. **Correct Answers:** A and D

   A. Correct: TCP port 25 is required for message transport between Edge Transport and Hub Transport servers.

   B. Incorrect: TCP port 135 is used for RPC communication between mailbox servers and Hub Transport servers. This port is not used for communication between Edge Transport servers and Hub Transport servers.

   C. Incorrect: TCP port 389 is used for LDAP communication between Hub Transport servers and Active Directory Domain Controllers. This port is not used for communication between Edge Transport servers and Hub Transport servers.

D. Correct: TCP port 50636 is used by the edge synchronization process to replicate configuration data from Hub Transport servers to Edge Transport servers.

3. **Correct Answers:** A and D

   A. Correct: You need to configure an internal relay domain and a Send connector when using a shared address space.

   B. Incorrect: You do not need to configure a remote domain when supporting a shared address space. Remote domains are used to configure message formatting options as well as whether out-of-office information is transmitted to remote recipients.

   C. Incorrect: You do not need to configure an external relay domain. External relay domains are used to route mail to organizations outside your internal network. In this case the organization is located on your internal network.

   D. Correct: You need to configure an internal relay domain and a Send connector when using a shared address space.

4. **Correct Answer:** B

   A. Incorrect: The *Set-ADSite* cmdlet is used to configure Active Directory site properties in Exchange. You cannot use this cmdlet to configure an Exchange specific cost for an Active Directory IP site link.

   B. Correct: You can use the *Set-ADSiteLink* cmdlet to configure an Exchange specific cost for an Active Directory IP site link.

   C. Incorrect: The *Get-ADSite* cmdlet provides information about Active Directory sites. You cannot use this cmdlet to configure an Exchange specific cost for an Active Directory IP site link.

   D. Incorrect: The *Get-ADSiteLink* cmdlet allows you to view the properties of Active Directory IP site links. You cannot use this cmdlet to configure an Exchange specific cost for an Active Directory IP site link.

5. **Correct Answer:** D

   A. Incorrect: Remote domains are used to control message formatting and out-of-office messages. You can't use remote domains as a redundancy technology.

   B. Incorrect: Send connectors are used to route messages to locations outside the Exchange organization. You can't use Send connectors as a redundancy technology.

   C. Incorrect: The transport dumpster is a redundancy feature that is used with database availability groups.

   D. Correct: Shadow redundancy is a transport server feature that ensures that email messages are not lost in transit if a transport server fails.

Objective 1.2: Thought Experiment

1. You should configure an external relay domain because the Fabrikam mail servers are not located on your organization's internal network.

2. You configure message throttling to ensure that a transport server is not overwhelmed by too much message traffic.

3. Use the *Set-Transport* cmdlet with the *MaxConnectionRatePerMinute* parameter to configure the maximum connection rate per minute for inbound connections.

4. Use the *Set-ADSite* cmdlet to configure the Sydney site as a hub site.

5. Use the *Set-ADSiteLink* cmdlet to configure Exchange costs for the Active Directory site links that connect the Melbourne and Brisbane sites to the Sydney site.

Objective 1.3: Review

1. **Correct Answers:** A and C

   A. **Correct:** You need to ensure that a trust relationship is established between the resource forest and the domains that host accounts in the account forests. The easiest way to accomplish this is to set up forest trusts, although in environments with more complex security needs you may configure more selective trusts.

   B. **Incorrect:** You do not need to install Exchange 2010 in the account forests to accomplish this goal. Exchange 2010 is installed in multiple forests.

   C. **Correct:** Linked mailboxes are created in the resource forest and linked to accounts in the account forests.

   D. **Incorrect:** You create linked mailboxes in the resource forest and not in the account forest.

2. **Correct Answer:** D

   A. **Incorrect:** The *New-Mailbox* cmdlet is used to create mailboxes. In this case, you want to create a group which uses a query against an Active Directory attribute to populate its membership.

   B. **Incorrect:** The *New-DistributionGroup* cmdlet allows you to create a new distribution group. Distribution groups have static memberships and require manual membership changes, which is not appropriate given management's requirements in this situation.

   C. **Incorrect:** The *Set-DistributionGroup* cmdlet is used to modify the properties of an existing distribution group. You cannot use the *Set-DistributionGroup* cmdlet to create a dynamic distribution group.

   D. **Correct:** Dynamic distribution groups can be configured using queries based on an Active Directory attribute, such as department membership. The membership of dynamic distribution groups is determined when the group is expanded on a Hub Transport server.

3. **Correct Answer:** C

   A. **Incorrect:** You cannot use the *New-MailboxDatabase* cmdlet to modify the default mailbox database maximum size limit on an Exchange Server 2010 SP1 mailbox server. You can only modify this limit by editing the registry.

   B. **Incorrect:** You cannot use the *Get-MailboxDatabase* cmdlet to modify the default mailbox database maximum size limit on an Exchange Server 2010 SP1 mailbox server. You can only modify this limit by editing the registry.

   C. **Correct:** The default maximum mailbox database size on an Exchange Server 2010 SP1 mailbox database server is 1024 GB. You can increase this size by editing the registry.

   D. **Incorrect:** You cannot use the *Set-MailboxDatabase* cmdlet to modify the default mailbox database maximum size limit on an Exchange Server 2010 SP1 mailbox server. You can only modify this limit by editing the registry.

4. **Correct Answer:** A

   A. **Correct:** Each Exchange Server 2010 SP1 mailbox server can only host one public folder database. This is irrespective of whether the server has an Enterprise or a Standard license. Five servers means a maximum of five public folder databases.

   B. **Incorrect:** Each Exchange mailbox server can only host one public folder database. Because there are only five mailbox servers, there is a maximum of five public folder databases.

   C. **Incorrect:** Each Exchange mailbox server can only host one public folder database. Because there are only five mailbox servers, there is a maximum of five public folder databases.

   D. **Incorrect:** Each Exchange mailbox server can only host one public folder database. Because there are only five mailbox servers, there is a maximum of five public folder databases.

5. **Correct Answers:** A, C, and D

   A. **Correct:** You use the *New-AcceptedDomain* cmdlet to create a new accepted domain. This will be necessary if you want to use the email domain cohowinery. com in an email address policy.

   B. **Incorrect:** *Get-EmailAddressPolicy* lists the properties of an email address policy. You can't use this cmdlet to create and apply a new email address policy.

   C. **Correct:** You use the *New-EmailAddressPolicy* to create a policy that will apply the cohowinery.com email domain in default reply-to addresses in the organization. It is also possible to modify the existing policy, but that option was not available.

   D. **Correct:** You use the *Update-EmailAddressPolicy* cmdlet to apply a new or modified email address policy.

Objective 1.3: Thought Experiment

1. You should set up linked mailboxes in the Contoso.com Exchange organization for users with accounts in the Fabrikam.com forest.

2. You can modify the existing email address policy or create a new email address policy.

3. You should create a static distribution group. This will allow you to delegate the appropriate administrative privileges to Simone from Accounts Receivable.

4. You should make Simone from Accounts Receivable the group owner, also known as the group manager.

5. Set the approval setting to Owner Approval. This will allow Simone from Accounts Receivable to approve membership.

Objective 1.4: Review

1. **Correct Answer:** A

   A. **Correct:** The LoadGen tool, also known as the Exchange Server Load Generator, allows you to test the adequacy of a CAS deployment for a specific number of clients.

   B. **Incorrect:** The Jetstress tool allows you to simulate mailbox database I/O and is suitable for testing mailbox server performance, but it does not allow you to simulate specific client load against a CAS deployment.

   C. **Incorrect:** The Exchange Best Practices Analyzer allows you to compare an Exchange deployment against best practices, but it does not allow you to simulate specific client load against a CAS deployment.

   D. **Incorrect:** The Remote Connectivity Analyzer allows you to verify that ActiveSync, Exchange Web Services, Outlook, and Internet Email work correctly, but it cannot be used to simulate specific client load against a CAS deployment.

2. **Correct Answer:** C

   A. **Incorrect:** It is necessary to have a Client Access Server in each site where there is a mailbox server. Deploying one Client Access Server would be insufficient when the proposed design has five sites with mailbox servers.

   B. **Incorrect:** It is necessary to have a Client Access Server in each site where there is a mailbox server. Deploying four Client Access Server would be insufficient when the proposed design has five sites with mailbox servers.

   C. **Correct:** It is necessary to have a Client Access Server in each site where there is a mailbox server. Because there are five sites, a minimum of five Client Access Servers are necessary.

D. **Incorrect:** It is necessary to have a Client Access Server in each site where there is a mailbox server. Although having seven Client Access Servers would provide redundancy in the event that a Client Access Server failed, five Client Access Servers is the minimum amount necessary.

3. **Correct Answer:** A

   A. **Correct:** The mailbox servers are only in a single site, so you only need to deploy a single Client Access Server to support this configuration.

   B. **Incorrect:** You only need to deploy a single Client Access Server to support this configuration.

   C. **Incorrect:** You only need to deploy a single Client Access Server to support this configuration.

   D. **Incorrect:** You only need to deploy a single Client Access Server to support this configuration.

4. **Correct Answer:** A

   A. **Correct:** Microsoft's theoretical optimum ratio is that there are three processor cores on a site's Client Access Servers for every four processor cores on a site's Mailbox servers.

   B. **Incorrect:** Microsoft's theoretical optimum ratio is that there are three processor cores on a site's Client Access Servers for every four processor cores on a site's Mailbox servers.

   C. **Incorrect:** Microsoft's theoretical optimum ratio is that there are three processor cores on a site's Client Access Servers for every four processor cores on a site's Mailbox servers.

   D. **Incorrect:** Microsoft's theoretical optimum ratio is that there are three processor cores on a site's Client Access Servers for every four processor cores on a site's Mailbox servers.

5. **Correct Answer:** C

   A. **Incorrect:** Configuring the Autodiscover service for Internet Access allows clients on external networks to be configured automatically through Autodiscover. Taking this step will not ensure that Outlook 2010 clients get Autodiscover information from the closest Active Directory site.

   B. **Incorrect:** Configuring the Autodiscover for multiple forests allows users running Outlook 2007 or Outlook 2010 in one forest to access Client Access Servers in a remote forest. Taking this step will not ensure that Outlook 2010 clients get Autodiscover information from the closest Active Directory site.

C. Correct: Configuring the Autodiscover service for Site Affinity ensures that Outlook 2007 and Outlook 2010 clients get Autodiscover information from the closest Active Directory site.

D. Incorrect: Configuring the Exchange ActiveSync Autodiscover settings allows automatic configuration of ActiveSync clients. Taking this step will not ensure that Outlook 2010 clients get Autodiscover information from the closest Active Directory site.

Objective 1.4: Thought Experiment

1. You must deploy Client Access Serves in the Auckland, Wellington, Dunedin, and Christchurch sites.

2. You can ensure that clients using Autodiscover are provisioned with profile information from the closest Active Directory site by configuring site affinity.

3. You can configure CAS to use the same name for all services, you can use certificates that support SANs, or you could configure the CAS with wildcard certificates.

4. You should deploy Outlook Anywhere because you want to allow remote access to Exchange mailboxes for clients running Outlook 2010 without configuring VPN or DirectAccess.

5. Because you need to support users accessing Outlook Web App from personal computers, you should use a trusted third-party CA, which will minimize the problems involved in getting clients to trust the certificates.

Objective 1.5: Review

1. **Correct Answer:** A

   A. Correct: The Exchange Server Load Generator 2010 allows you to test a simulated client workload against all aspects of an Exchange Server 2010 deployment. You can use this tool to determine how many clients a simulated Exchange Server 2010 deployment can comfortably handle.

   B. Incorrect: The Exchange Server Jetstress 2010 tool allows you to benchmark mailbox server storage, but does not allow you to test other aspects of an Exchange Server deployment.

   C. Incorrect: The Exchange Server Remote Connectivity Analyzer allows you to test client connectivity configuration, but does not allow you to test an Exchange server deployment against a simulated number of clients.

   D. Incorrect: The Exchange Server Best Practices Analyzer allows you to diagnose an existing deployment against Exchange best practices. You cannot use this tool to determine the capacity of an Exchange deployment.

2. **Correct Answer:** C

   A. **Incorrect:** You must install the Client Access Server role first when transitioning from Exchange 2003 to Exchange 2010. You install the Hub Transport server role after installing the Client Access Server role.

   B. **Incorrect:** You must install the Client Access Server role first when transitioning from Exchange 2003 to Exchange 2010. You install the Mailbox server role after you have installed the Client Access and Hub Transport server roles.

   C. **Correct:** You must install the Client Access Server role first when transitioning from Exchange 2003 to Exchange 2010.

   D. **Incorrect:** You must install the Client Access Server role first when transitioning from Exchange 2003 to Exchange 2010. You install the Edge Transport server role after you have installed the Client Access, Mailbox, and Hub Transport server roles.

3. **Correct Answer:** D

   A. **Incorrect:** When transitioning from an Exchange 2003 environment to an Exchange 2010 environment, the Edge Transport server role is installed after the other roles have been deployed.

   B. **Incorrect:** When transitioning from an Exchange 2003 environment to an Exchange 2010 environment, the Edge Transport server role is installed after the other roles have been deployed.

   C. **Incorrect:** When transitioning from an Exchange 2003 environment to an Exchange 2010 environment, the Edge Transport server role is installed after the other roles have been deployed.

   D. **Correct:** When transitioning from an Exchange 2003 environment to an Exchange 2010 environment, the Edge Transport server role is installed after the other roles have been deployed.

4. **Correct Answers:** A, B, and C

   A. **Correct:** You must plan to deploy the Client Access, Hub Transport, and Mailbox server roles before it is possible to migrate mailboxes from Exchange 2007 to Exchange 2010 Mailbox servers.

   B. **Correct:** You must plan to deploy the Client Access, Hub Transport, and Mailbox server roles before it is possible to migrate mailboxes from Exchange 2007 to Exchange 2010 Mailbox servers.

   C. **Correct:** You must plan to deploy the Client Access, Hub Transport, and Mailbox server roles before it is possible to migrate mailboxes from Exchange 2007 to Exchange 2010 Mailbox servers.

   D. **Incorrect:** The design will not use an Edge Transport server, so it is not necessary to deploy this role prior to migrating mailboxes from Exchange 2007.

5. **Correct Answer:** C

   A.   Incorrect: The Exchange Remote Connectivity Analyzer allows you to verify
   remote connectivity to a Client Access Server. You can't use this tool to determine
   whether Exchange 2003 and Exchange 2007 are ready for the deployment of
   Exchange 2010.

   B.   Incorrect: The Exchange Best Practices Analyzer allows you to examine your
   organization's environment to determine whether your Exchange configuration
   complies with best practices. You can't use this tool to determine whether
   Exchange 2003 and Exchange 2007 are ready for the deployment of Exchange
   2010.

   C.   Correct: The Exchange Pre-Deployment Analyzer can examine your organization's
   environment to determine whether Exchange 2003 and Exchange 2007 are ready
   for the upgrade or transition to Exchange 2010.

   D.   Incorrect: The Exchange Server Jetstress 2010 tool allows you to analyze mailbox
   server storage to assess performance characteristics under a specified load. You
   can't use this tool to determine whether Exchange 2003 and Exchange 2007 are
   ready for the deployment of Exchange 2010.

Objective 1.5: Thought Experiment

1. You should plan to upgrade the Auckland site at Wingtip Toys first because this site is
    Internet-facing.

2. You should plan to upgrade the Melbourne and Sydney Tailspin Toys sites first because
    these sites are Internet-facing.

3. You will need to deploy Edge Transport servers in the Melbourne, Sydney, and
    Auckland sites because these sites are Internet-facing.

4. You should use the cross-forest topology because both Wingtip Toys and Tailspin Toys
    will retain their own Exchange 2010 organizations.

5. You should use Forefront Identity Manger 2010 to perform GAL synchronization
    between the Wingtip Toys and Tailspin Toys Exchange organizations given that a trust
    exists between them.

6. You should deploy the Client Access Server role at the Melbourne, Sydney, and
    Auckland sites first.

7. You will decommission the Wingtip Toys back-end servers first.

Deploying the Exchange Server 2010 Infrastructure

It is commonly said that "No plan survives contact with reality." In Chapter 1, "Planning the Exchange Server 2010 Infrastructure," you learned how to plan the deployment of Exchange and specific Exchange Server 2010 roles. In this chapter you'll learn what steps to take to perform your planned deployment and verify that the infrastructure is performing as expected.

Objectives in this chapter:

- Objective 2.1: Prepare the infrastructure for Exchange Server 2010 deployment
- Objective 2.2: Deploy Edge transport server role
- Objective 2.3: Deploy client access server role
- Objective 2.4: Deploy hub transport server role
- Objective 2.5: Deploy mailbox server role
- Objective 2.6: Deploy server roles for coexistence and migration

Real World

An important part of the Exchange design and deployment process—especially when it comes to Exchange components such as transport rules—is explaining to the people who develop policy what the product is actually capable of doing. Although it might seem obvious to an Exchange administrator that the product can be configured to manage messages based on message content, such a thing isn't necessarily obvious to non-technical users. Unless policy makers—such as those who are members of the Human Resources department—are aware that you can configure Exchange to apply rules to take action on messages that meet specific criteria, these people are unlikely to develop policies that require operationalization through the application of transport rules. For an organization to be able to get the most out of their Exchange investment, many parts of the organization beyond the IT department need to be aware of what Exchange is capable of doing. If you, or someone else in the IT department, take the time to explain to non-technical policy makers what policy objectives can be accomplished using existing Exchange technologies, you substantially add value to your organization's investment in the product. You also accomplish the more useful objective of reinforcing the value of the IT department as you are demonstrating that you understand how to use technology to achieve organizational goals.

Objective 2.1: Prepare the Infrastructure for Exchange Server 2010 Deployment

Once you have a finalized plan for rolling out Exchange Server 2010 and that plan has met with approval, you need to begin preparations for deployment. Exchange Server 2010 is a complex application that integrates tightly into many important facets of your organization's infrastructure. This means that you need to make suitable preparations to that infrastructure, rather than just turning up at work one day, loading the Exchange installation media, and hoping for the best.

After your planning is complete, the first practical steps you need to take in deploying Exchange Server 2010 involve ensuring that Active Directory is properly prepared. If Active Directory Domain Services is not appropriately prepared, you may be unable to install Exchange Server 2010. Preparation is also important if you have an existing Exchange server deployment that you want to upgrade to Exchange Server 2010. In this section you learn about the steps that you need to take to properly prepare your organization's Active Directory infrastructure so that you can successfully deploy Exchange Server 2010.

This objective covers:

- Schema preparation requirements.
- Forest, Domain, and Active Directory readiness.
- Configuring Legacy Exchange permissions.
- Meeting domain controller versions and roles placement requirements.
- Preparing network services including directory synchronization.
- Organizing SMTP and Federation prerequisites.
- Preparing DNS for on-premises and/or cloud-based services.

Active Directory Functional Level Requirements

The first step you need to take when preparing to deploy Exchange is to ensure that domain and forest functional levels are set at or above the minimum required level. To deploy Exchange Server 2010, you must set the domain and forest functional level to the Windows Server 2003 functional level, the Windows Server 2008 functional level, or the Windows Server 2008 R2 functional level. Domain controller operation systems are the restricting factor on what domain functional level can be set. For example:

- To set a domain to the Windows Server 2003 functional level, all domain controllers in the domain must be running the Windows Server 2003, Windows Server 2008, or Windows Server 2008 R2 operating systems.
- To set a domain to the Windows Server 2008 functional level, all domain controllers in the domain must be running the Windows Server 2008 or Windows Server 2008 R2 operating systems.
- To set a domain to the Windows Server 2008 R2 functional level, all domain controllers must be running the Windows Server 2008 R2 operating system.

Although you might have domain controllers running the appropriate operating system, this doesn't mean that the domain functional level is set appropriately. Domain functional level is something that you must set manually. If your organization has been using Active Directory for some time, it is possible that although domain controllers were upgraded to newer operating systems over time, the domain functional level wasn't been modified.

The forest functional level that you can set is determined by the minimum domain functional level in the forest. To set a forest functional level, you can have a mix of domain functional levels in the forest, but the domain with the lowest functional level determines the highest forest functional level that can be set. For example:

- To set the forest functional level to Windows Server 2003, the minimum domain functional level in the forest must be Windows Server 2003.
- To set the Windows Server 2008 forest functional level, the minimum domain functional level in the forest must be Windows Server 2008.

- To set the Windows Server 2008 R2 forest functional level, the minimum domain functional level in the forest must be Windows Server 2008 R2.

You can view and manage the domain and forest level functional settings using the Active Directory Domains and Trusts console. To view the Domain and Forest functional level, right-click the domain in this console and then click Properties. The domain and forest functional levels will be shown on the General tab, as displayed in Figure 2-1.

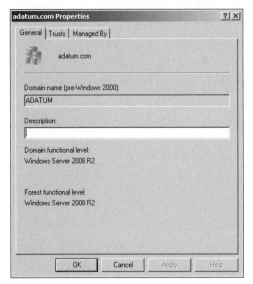

FIGURE 2-1 Forest and domain functional levels

Domain Controller Role Requirements

To deploy Exchange Server 2010, you must ensure that domain controllers that hold specific roles in the forest are running an operating system that meets the minimum requirement. Although the best way to future-proof a network is to ensure that all domain controllers that host Flexible Single Master Operations (FSMO) roles or function as Global Catalog servers are running the latest server operating system, this isn't always practical or possible:

- The domain controller that hosts the Schema Master role must be running the Windows Server 2003 operating system with Service Pack 2 or later.

- The domain controller that functions as a Global Catalog server at each site must be running the Windows Server 2003 operating system with Service Pack 2 or later.

Usually the computer that was the first domain controller in the forest hosts the Schema Master role. If you aren't sure which computer hosts the Schema Master role, you can run the following command from Windows PowerShell when the Active Directory module is loaded to locate the computer name:

```
Get-ADForest | FT SchemaMaster
```

Preparing Active Directory with an Existing Exchange Deployment

How you prepare Active Directory for the deployment of Exchange depends on whether you have an existing Exchange 2003 deployment. If you do have an existing Exchange Server 2003 deployment, you must prepare the legacy Exchange permissions prior to preparing the schema for Exchange Server 2010. Doing this ensures that the Exchange 2003 Recipient Update service functions correctly when the Active Directory schema is updated in preparation for the installation of Exchange Server 2010. If your organization only has an existing Exchange Server 2007 deployment or has no existing Exchange infrastructure, you do not need to perform this step.

To prepare the legacy Exchange permissions, it is necessary to run the following command with a user account that is a member of the Enterprise Admins group:

```
Setup /PrepareLegacyExchangePermissions
```

You can run this command without additional options in the same Active Directory site as the computer that holds the Schema Master role. When you do this, all domains in the forest are prepared for the deployment of Exchange Server 2010. You also have the option of running this command on a per-domain basis. When you do this you must run the command first in the forest root domain in the same site as the schema master. Then, when you run the command in other domains, that the account used to execute the command must be both a member of the Domain Admins group and must also have been delegated the Exchange Full Administrator permission in Exchange 2003.

> **MORE INFO** **PREPARE LEGACY EXCHANGE PERMISSIONS**
>
> To learn more about preparing legacy Exchange permissions prior to updating the Schema for the deployment of Exchange Server 2010, consult the following article on TechNet: *http://technet.microsoft.com/en-us/library/aa997914.aspx*.

Preparing the Active Directory Schema

The next step in preparing Active Directory for the deployment of Exchange—or the first step if your organization does not have an existing Exchange 2003 deployment—is preparing the schema. You can prepare the schema by running the following command from an elevated command prompt:

```
Setup /PrepareSchema
```

The command must be run under the following conditions:

- The user account used to execute the command must be a member of both the Enterprise Admins and Schema Admins security groups.
- The command must be executed on a computer that has a 64-bit operating system that is located in the same Active Directory site and domain as the domain controller that hosts the Schema Master role.
- The domain controller hosting the Schema Master role must be running Windows Server 2003 with Service Pack 2 or later, Windows Server 2008, or Windows Server 2008 R2.
- The forest functional level must be set to Windows Server 2003, Windows Server 2008, or Windows Server 2008 R2.
- At least one Global Catalog server in each site must be running Windows Server 2003 with Service Pack 2 or later, Windows Server 2008, or Windows Server 2008 R2.

As you learned earlier, you can locate the Schema Master by loading the Active Directory PowerShell module and running the *Get-ADForest* | *FT SchemaMaster* command. In most organizations, the first domain controller in the forest will hold the Schema Master role.

Changes in the schema need to replicate out across the organization before further steps in Active Directory preparation can be taken. You can use the following tools to monitor this replication:

- If your organization is using Windows Server 2003 domain controllers, use the Active Directory Replication Monitor (replmon.exe). This tool is included with the Windows Server 2003 support tools.
- If your organization is using Windows Server 2008 or Windows Server 2008 R2 domain controllers, use the repadmin.exe tool to monitor replication.

EXAM TIP

You don't have to run all of the commands listed for preparing schema and domains in this section manually—they execute automatically when you install Exchange Server 2010 for the first time in an organization. However, the 70-663 exam tests your knowledge of what steps need to happen and the order in which they have to happen, rather than just letting the installation wizard do it for you.

MORE INFO   ACTIVE DIRECTORY SCHEMA CHANGES

To learn more about the specifics of the changes made to the Active Directory schema by the *setup /PrepareSchema* command, consult the following document on MSDN: *http://msdn.microsoft.com/en-us/library/dd877014(EXCHG.140).aspx.*

Preparing Active Directory

After the alterations to the Active Directory schema have propagated across all sites in your organization, the next step is to run the *Setup /PrepareAD* command. You must run this command with a user account that is a member of the Enterprise Admins group. You must also run this command on a computer that is a member of the same domain and Active Directory site as the domain controller that holds the Schema Master role, which for most organizations means running the command on a computer in the forest root domain.

When running this command you must specify the name of the Exchange Server 2010 organization that you are going to create if there is no existing Exchange 2003 or Exchange 2007 organization. For example, to prepare Active Directory for a new Exchange organization named AdatumOrg, issue the following command:

```
Setup /PrepareAD /OrganizationName:AdatumOrg
```

When you run *Setup /PrepareAD*, the following changes occur:

- A check is performed to verify that the schema has been properly updated.
- If it does not already exist, the command creates a new Active Directory container called Microsoft Exchange.

- The command creates containers and objects under the following location: CN=<Organization Name>, CN=Microsoft Exchange, CN=Services, CN=Configuration, DC=<root domain>

- The command configures the default Accepted Domains setting based on the namespace of the forest root domain.

- The command applies appropriate permissions to the configuration partition.

- The command creates the Microsoft Exchange Security Groups OU in the forest root domain and populates this OU with the following groups:

  - Exchange Organization Administrators

  - Exchange Recipient Administrators

  - Exchange Servers

  - Exchange View-Only Administrators

  - Exchange Public Folder Administrators

  - ExchangeLegacyInterop

- The command prepares the root domain for the installation of Exchange. It is not necessary to run the *Setup /PrepareDomain* command against the domain in which you have run *Setup /PrepareAD*.

Preparing Domains

After the changes from the Setup /PrepareAD command have propagated across your organization's Active Directory forest, the domains need to be prepared for the installation of Exchange. This can be done in two ways, either by running a command to prepare all domains in the forest at once, or on a domain-by-domain basis.

To prepare all domains at once you can execute the *Setup /PrepareAllDomains* command with a user account that is a member of the Enterprise Admins group. Doing this will prepare all domains in the forest for the installation of Exchange Server 2010.

If, instead, you want to prepare each domain individually, you can run the *Setup /PrepareDomain* command in each domain. The account used to execute this command must be a member of the target domain's Domain Admins group. If you create a new domain after the execution of the *Setup /PrepareAD* command, you'll need to run *Setup /PrepareDomain* with a user account that is a member of both the Exchange Organization Administrators group and the Domain Admins group in this new domain.

> **MORE INFO**   **PREPARE ACTIVE DIRECTORY DOMAINS AND FORESTS**
>
> To learn more about preparing Active Directory domains for the introduction of Exchange Server 2010, consult the following TechNet article: *http://technet.microsoft.com/en-us/library/bb125224.aspx*.

Preparing Federation

Federation allows users who need to collaborate with third parties to share their calendar availability and contact information. You can only configure Exchange Federation after you have deployed Exchange Server 2010. Prior to configuring a federation trust you should take the following into account:

- The domain that you use to establish the federation trust must be able to be resolved by DNS clients on the Internet. You can use the domain that your organization uses for Internet email as the domain used to establish the federation trust.
- The Exchange server on which you are going to create the trust needs to be able to contact hosts on the Internet.
- If you are configuring federated delegation, you must use the same Microsoft Federation Gateway instance for setting up the federated trust. The two Microsoft Federation Gateway instances are the business instance and the consumer instance. When using self-signed certificates, Exchange Server 2010 with Service Pack 1 defaults to the business instance. Hosted versions of Exchange also use the business instance by default. Exchange organizations hosted by Microsoft Live@edu use the consumer instance by default. You should check with partner organizations to determine which Microsoft Federation Gateway instance they are using to ensure that you will be able to configure Federation appropriately. You can also determine which Microsoft Federation Gateway instance an organization is using by running the following command from Exchange Management Shell:

```
Get-FederationInformation -DomainName <Exchange domain namespace>
```

Create a Federation Trust

To create a federation trust a user account must have been delegated the Organization Management permission. To test an existing federation trust, a user account must have been delegated either the Organization Management, View-Only Organization Management, or Server Management permission

To create a federation trust, perform the following general steps:

1. Open Exchange Management Console and click the Organization Configuration node.

2. In the Actions pane, click New Federation Trust. This will launch the New Federation Trust Wizard. Click New.

3. The New Federation Trust Wizard will generate a new certificate and then contact the Microsoft Federation Gateway on the Internet, as shown in Figure 2-2.

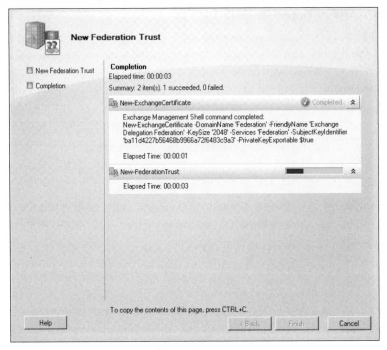

FIGURE 2-2 New Federation Trust Wizard

To use Exchange Management Shell to create a federation trust, you must perform the following steps:

1. Create a subject key identifier that will be used with the certificate. You can do this with the following Windows PowerShell code:

```
$ski = [System.Guid]::NewGuid().ToString("N")
```

2. Use the *New-ExchangeCertificate* cmdlet to create a new self-signed certificate. You can do this with the following Windows PowerShell code:

```
New-ExchangeCertificate -FriendlyName "Exchange Federation" -DomainName
$env:USERDNSDOMAIN -Services Federation -KeySize 4096 -PrivateKeyExportable $true
-SubjectKeyIdentifier $ski
```

3. Use the *New-FederationTrust* cmdlet in conjunction with the self-signed certificate to create the trust. You can do this with the following Windows PowerShell code:

```
Get-ExchangeCertificate | ?{$_.friendlyname -eq "Exchange Federation"} | New-
FederationTrust -Name "Microsoft Federation Gateway"
```

Create a Text (TXT) Record in DNS for Federation

After you have established the trust, you need to configure the federated organization identifier (OrgID) with the AccountNamespace domain and the other accepted mail domains that you want to use with federation. To do this you create a special type of record called a text (TXT) record in the DNS zone of each accepted domain you wish to include in the federation. The TXT record includes the federated domain proof encryption string. This string is generated when you run the *Get-FederatedDomainProof* cmdlet against each accepted domain. The DNS zones hosting the TXT records for federated delegation must be accessible to hosts on the Internet.

To create a TXT record in DNS to support federation, perform the following general steps:

1. Execute the *Get-FederatedDomainProof* cmdlet for each domain for which you want to support federation. This command will output a domain proof string. Copy this string.

2. In the DNS Manager console, select the forward lookup zone for which you are going to create the TXT record. Right-click this zone, click Other New Records, click Text, and then click Create Record. This will open the New Resource Record dialog box, as shown in Figure 2-3.

FIGURE 2-3 New TXT record

3. In the New Resource Record dialog box, leave the Record Name text box blank. Paste the federated domain proof string into the Text text box and then click OK.

You can use the *Set-FederatedOrganizationIdentifier* command to enable or disable federation by using the *$true* or *$false* options with the *Enabled* parameter. For example, to enable federation, use the following command:

```
Set-FederatedOrganizationIdentifier -Enabled $true
```

To disable federation, use the following command:

```
Set-FederatedOrganizationIdentifier -Enabled $false
```

> **MORE INFO** **CREATE A FEDERATION TRUST**
>
> To learn more about creating a federation trust, consult the following page on TechNet:
> *http://technet.microsoft.com/en-us/library/dd335198.aspx.*

Active Directory Synchronization

Active Directory synchronization allows you to configure synchronization between your local Active Directory environment and a cloud-hosted Exchange instance such as Office 365. Microsoft recommends that you configure single sign-on before you configure Active Directory synchronization. If you haven't configured single sign-on, passwords will not be synchronized from the local account database because the Active Directory synchronization tool does not synchronize passwords. Password synchronization occurs through Active Directory Federation Services when your domain is configured to use single sign-on.

At present, you cannot deactivate directory synchronization. Once you have activated directory synchronization, you are only able to edit synchronized objects using on-premises applications. Office 365 currently supports the synchronization of up to 10,000 objects. Organizations that need to synchronize more than 10,000 objects will need to contact Office 365 support.

You need to enable Active Directory synchronization on the hosted Exchange instance before installing the Directory Synchronization Tool. You can download the Directory Synchronization tool from the cloud provider. At present this tool can only be installed on computers running the 32-bit version of Windows Server 2003, Windows Server 2003 R2, or Windows Server 2008. A 64-bit version was made available in late 2011. The computer that you install the Directory Synchronization tool on must be a member of the forest in which Exchange is installed and cannot be configured as a domain controller.

The Microsoft Online Services Directory Synchronization Configuration Wizard creates a special account in the root domain called MSOL_AD_SYNC. The Directory Synchronization tool uses this account to read and synchronize local Active Directory information with the hosted Exchange instance. By default, synchronization occurs every three hours. You can force synchronization by running the *Start-OnlineCoexistenceSync* cmdlet.

> **MORE INFO** **ACTIVE DIRECTORY SYNCHRONIZATION TOOL**
>
> To learn more about preparing Active Directory synchronization between the local environment and a hosted Exchange instance, consult the following web page:
> *http://onlinehelp.microsoft.com/en-us/office365-enterprises/ff652545.aspx.*

Configuring DNS Support for SMTP

When preparing your organization's infrastructure for Exchange Server 2010 deployment, you need to ensure that the externally resolvable DNS zones for your organization have the appropriate Mail Exchanger (MX) records. MX records are used by external mail servers in the process of determining the address of SMTP servers for a domain. When deploying Exchange, you need to ensure that the MX records for the external DNZ zone that matches your mail domain point to the IP address or addresses of your organizations SMTP servers. In a traditional Exchange deployment, this might be the public IP address of the Edge Transport server located on your organization's perimeter network. In cloud-based deployments, it might be a public IP address associated with the cloud provider.

If your organization's external DNS zone is hosted by a third party, you will need to use those third-party tools to create and manage the MX records that point to the SMTP servers that receive external email. If your organization hosts the external DNS zone on a Windows Server 2003, Windows Server 2008, or Windows Server 2008 R2 DNS server, you can create an MX record by performing the following steps:

1. Ensure that a host record already exists in DNS that points to the SMTP server's IP address.

2. Right-click the appropriate forward lookup zone in DNS Manager and click New Mail Exchanger (MX). This will open the New Resource Record dialog box.

3. In the New Resource Record dialog box, shown in Figure 2-4, enter the fully qualified domain name (FQDN) of the SMTP server that will accept incoming email from external organizations.

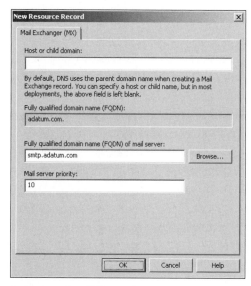

FIGURE 2-4 New MX record

The mail server priority number allows you to prioritize one SMTP server over another. MX records with lower-priority numbers are preferred over MX records with higher-priority numbers. You can create multiple MX records, allowing a backup SMTP server to be used in the event that a primary SMTP server goes down.

To verify that your organization's MX records are configured correctly, use the NSLOOKUP command-like utility with the querytype=mx parameter. For example, to locate the MX records for the adatum.com domain, issue the following command:

```
Nslookup -querytype=mx adatum.com
```

> **MORE INFO** **ADD AN MX RECORD TO A ZONE**
>
> To learn more about adding MX records to a zone, consult the following TechNet article: *http://technet.microsoft.com/en-us/library/cc816902(WS.10).aspx.*

Objective Summary

- The minimum forest functional level required for the deployment of Exchange Server 2010 is the Windows Server 2003 functional level.
- You need to run the *Setup /PrepareLegacyExchangePermissions* command if your organization has an existing Exchange Server 2003 deployment.
- You prepare the Active Directory Schema for the deployment of Exchange by running the *Setup /PrepareSchema* command.
- You prepare Active Directory for the deployment of Exchange by running the *Setup / PrepareAD* command.
- You prepare domains by running the *Setup /PrepareAllDomains* command.
- You can create a federation trust using the New Federation Trust Wizard. This creates a self-signed certificate and configures the federation trust relationship with the Microsoft Federation Gateway.
- You need to configure MX records in your organization's external DNS zone to point to SMTP servers that will accept messages from external hosts.

Objective Review

Answer the following questions to test your knowledge of the information in this objective. You can find the answers to these questions and explanations of why each answer choice is correct or incorrect in the "Answers" section at the end of this chapter.

1. You are preparing your organization's single-domain Active Directory forest for the introduction of Exchange Server 2010. All domain controllers in the organization are running Windows Server 2003 without any service packs applied. The Flexible Single Master Operations roles are spread across domain controllers so that no single domain controller hosts more than one FSMO role. Which of the following domain controllers must you upgrade to Windows Server 2003 Service Pack 2 or later prior to attempting to deploy Exchange Server 2010?

   A. Schema Master

   B. Domain Naming Master

   C. PDC Emulator

   D. Infrastructure Master

2. Which security groups must the user account used to run the *Setup /PrepareSchema* command be a member of? (Choose all that apply.)

   A. Schema Admins

   B. Enterprise Admins

   C. Domain Admins

   D. DNSAdmins

3. Under what conditions must you run the *Setup /PrepareLegacyExchangePermissions* command?

   A. Your organization's domain is configured to run at the Windows Server 2008 R2 forest functional level.

   B. Your organization has an existing Exchange Server 2007 deployment.

   C. Your organization has no existing Exchange deployment.

   D. Your organization has an existing Exchange Server 2003 deployment.

4. Your organization has an existing Exchange Server 2003 deployment. You want to prepare the Active Directory environment for the deployment of Exchange Server 2010. Which of the following commands should you run first?

   A. *Setup /PrepareAD*

   B. *Setup /PrepareSchema*

   C. *Setup /PrepareLegacyExchangePermissions*

   D. *Setup /PrepareAllDomains*

5. Which of the following types of DNS record must you create to support Exchange federated delegation?

   A. Public Key (KEY) record

   B. X.25 record

   C. Signature (SIG) record

   D. Text (TXT) record

THOUGHT EXPERIMENT
Preparing an Organization for the Deployment of Exchange Server 2010

In the following thought experiment, you will apply what you've learned about the prepare the infrastructure for Exchange Server 2010 deployment objective to predict how an organization should prepare for the deployment of Exchange Server 2010. You can find answers to these questions in the "Answers" section at the end of this chapter.

Contoso has a three-domain forest. The root domain has the name contoso.internal. The child domains are Australia.contoso.internal and NewZealand.contoso.internal. The computer that hosts the Schema Master role is located at the Melbourne site. The computer that hosts the Domain Naming Master role is located at the Auckland site. All domain controllers at Contoso are running Windows Server 2003 RTM and the forest functional level is set to Windows Server 2003. A single Global Catalog server is located at each site.

With this in mind, answer the following questions:

1. Which domain controllers should you update to Windows Server 2003 Service Pack 2?

2. Is it necessary to update the forest functional level prior to attempting to deploy Exchange Server 2010?

3. Which command should you run first: *Setup /PrepareAD*, *Setup /PrepareAll-Domains*, or *Setup /PrepareSchema*?

4. In which site and domain should you run this command?

5. Which command should you run next: *Setup /PrepareAD*, *Setup /PrepareAll-Domains*, or *Setup /PrepareSchema* after the changes caused by the running of the command in question two have propagated across the environment?

6. Which command should you run last: *Setup /PrepareAD*, *Setup /PrepareAll-Domains*, or *Setup /PrepareSchema*?

Objective 2.2: Deploy Edge Transport Server Role

As a component in an Exchange Server 2010 design, the Edge Transport role functions as a first port of call for inbound messages and a departure point for outbound messages. You primarily use this server role for the purpose of message sanitation. Message sanitation includes everything from ensuring that incoming spam doesn't reach user mailboxes to ensuring that sensitive information isn't transmitted to external third parties through email. Estimates suggest that up to 95 percent of email messages sent across the Internet are spam. Dealing with message sanitation on dedicated servers on the perimeter network ensures that Hub Transport servers on the organizational network do not become clogged processing traffic of dubious value.

> **This objective covers:**
> - Edge Transport role.
> - Edge Subscriptions.
> - Configure transport agents.
> - Third-party perimeter email gateway.
> - Configuring address rewriting.

Edge Transport Role

Edge Transport servers directly receive and send message traffic to other hosts on the Internet. Because they need to communicate directly with hosts on the public Internet, you place Edge Transport servers on perimeter networks rather than internal organizational networks. A perimeter network is a network located between two firewalls. The Internet firewall is configured to allow specific traffic through to the hosts on the perimeter network, but not to hosts on the internal network. The internal firewall is configured to allow specific traffic through to hosts on the internal network from hosts on the perimeter network. In theory, this dual firewall approach means that even if a host on the perimeter network is compromised by an outside attacker, hosts on the internal network will still be protected by the second firewall.

You install the Edge Transport role on stand-alone computers that are not members of an Active Directory domain. By using stand-alone computers running the Windows Server 2008 or Windows Server 2008 R2 operating system as hosts, you minimize the number of ports that need to be opened between the Edge Transport server and hosts on your organization's internal network. The stand-alone computer does not have a relationship with an Active Directory domain, which makes it more difficult for attackers to compromise Active Directory if they manage to compromise the Edge Transport server.

Edge Subscriptions

Edge subscriptions are the method that Microsoft recommends you use to configure Edge Transport servers in an Exchange Server 2010 deployment. Edge subscriptions allow transport server configuration data, such as transport rules, to replicate from Hub Transport servers on an organization's internal network out to Edge Transport servers that are located on perimeter networks. The EdgeSync process allows you to configure Edge Transport servers centrally rather than on an individual basis. If you have multiple Edge Transport servers in your Exchange deployment, edge subscriptions ensure that they share the same configuration. The other benefit of an edge subscription is that it sets up all the necessary connectors between the Edge Transport and the Hub Transport servers, meaning that you don't need to configure these connectors manually. When you create an edge subscription, a Send connector to route outbound messages to the Internet is also created. If you subscribe additional Edge Transport servers, they are added to this Send connector.

EXAM TIP

If outbound messages to the Internet must be routed through a smart host, you must manually modify the Send connector created by the edge subscription process with the details of that smart host.

EdgeSync replication occurs in only one direction, from Hub Transport servers out to Edge Transport servers. The unidirectional nature of the EdgeSync process ensures that an attacker cannot piggyback the replication process to attack the internal Exchange infrastructure in the event that they manage to compromise an Edge Transport server.

Edge subscriptions have the following limitations:

- An Edge Transport server can only be subscribed to one Active Directory site. Hub Transport servers in other sites will route messages addressed to hosts on the Internet to the site that has the edge subscription so that they can be then forwarded to the Edge Transport servers.

- An Edge subscription is unique to each Edge Transport server. If you add additional Edge Transport servers, you'll need to create a new edge subscription for each one.

- If you add additional Hub Transport servers to the subscribed Active Directory site, you will need to re-create existing edge subscriptions.

Edge subscriptions replicate data from Hub Transport servers and store it in an Active Directory Lightweight Directory Service (AD LDS) instance on the Edge Transport server. This data includes:

- **Recipients** This data replicates from the Hub Transport to the Edge Transport server every five minutes.

- **Safe Senders** This data replicates from the Hub Transport to the Edge Transport server every five minutes.

- **Send Connectors** This data replicates from the Hub Transport to the Edge Transport server every three minutes.

- **Hub Transport server addresses** This data replicates from the Hub Transport to the Edge Transport server every three minutes.

- **Accepted and remote domains** This data replicates from the Hub Transport to the Edge Transport server every three minutes.

The safe senders and recipient data is encrypted in such a way that this data cannot be extracted in the event that an attacker compromises the Edge Transport server.

You can use the following cmdlets from EMS to manage Edge Subscriptions:

- *New-EdgeSubscription* Use this cmdlet on an Edge Transport server to create a subscription file and on a Hub Transport server to import a subscription file.

- *Get-EdgeSubscription* Use this cmdlet to retrieve information on the list of existing Edge subscriptions.

- *Remove-EdgeSubscription* Use this cmdlet to cancel an existing Edge subscription.

- *Start-EdgeSynchronization* Use this cmdlet to trigger the EdgeSync process. This cmdlet can only be run on a Hub Transport server.

- *Test-EdgeSynchronization* Use this cmdlet to verify the synchronization status of all Edge Transport servers currently subscribed to the Hub Transport server's site.

- *New-EdgeSyncServiceConfig* Use this cmdlet to create EdgeSync synchronization service settings.

- *Get-EdgeSyncServiceConfig* Use this cmdlet to view EdgeSync synchronization service settings.

- *Set-EdgeSyncServiceConfig* Use this cmdlet to configure EdgeSync synchronization service settings.

To create an Edge subscription, perform the following general steps:

1. Verify that both the Edge Transport server and the Hub Transport server that you will configure the synchronization between can resolve each other's DNS names to IP addresses.

2. When logged on to the Edge Transport server, open EMS and run the command *New-EdgeSubscription -Filename:c:\edgesub.xml*.

3. Transfer the file edgesub.xml to the HubTransport server on which you will configure the synchronization within 1440 minutes.

4. When logged on to the Hub Transport server, open EMC. Select the Organization Configuration\Hub Transport node and then click the Edge Subscriptions tab. Click the New Edge Subscription in the Actions pane. This will open the New Edge Subscription Wizard. Specify the Active Directory site that hosts the Hub Transport server, select the subscription file, and select the Automatically Create A Send Connector For This Edge Subscription check box as shown in Figure 2-5. Click New to create the subscription.

FIGURE 2-5 New edge subscription

After you've subscribed an Edge Transport server to an Active Directory site, you'll need to create any additional Send connectors that use the Edge Transport server as a source server within the Exchange organization. When you do this, you specify the Edge Transport server or servers as the connector's source server, as shown in Figure 2-6. You need to create a custom Send connector in this manner for a specific address space when you configure an accepted domain as an external relay domain.

In some instances, such as a need to decommission an existing Edge Transport server, you may want to remove an edge subscription. Removing the subscription ensures that Hub Transport servers in the subscribed site no longer attempt to route messages to the Edge Transport server. When you remove an edge subscription from an Edge Transport server, all replicated data stored in Active Directory Lightweight Directory Services will be deleted. You can use EMC or the *Remove-EdgeSubscription* EMS cmdlet to remove an edge subscription.

> **MORE INFO** **UNDERSTANDING EDGE SUBSCRIPTIONS**
>
> To learn more about edge subscriptions, consult the following TechNet article: *http://technet.microsoft.com/en-us/library/aa997438.aspx.*

FIGURE 2-6 New Edge Transport Send connector

Direct Configuration

Although Microsoft recommends you use edge subscriptions between Edge Transport servers and Hub Transport servers, you can configure these servers to communicate with each other without them. Although this removes the benefit of being able to configure Edge Transport servers centrally, you can still configure them directly, either through EMC and EMS.

In the event that you don't have an edge subscription, you will need to manually establish mail flow between the Exchange organization and Edge Transport servers by creating and configuring Send connectors and Receive connectors on both the Edge Transport servers and the Hub Transport servers in your organization.

Prior to configuring the appropriate connectors, you need to perform the following tasks:

- Microsoft recommends that you protect communication between both servers using TLS. To do this, install an SSL certificate on both the Edge Transport server and the Hub Transport server. The FQDN configured for the SSL certificate for each server must use the FQDN used with the Receive connector on that server. It is possible to use the externally secured authentication method rather than TLS, but this requires you to set up a separate IPsec or VPN connection between the two servers.

- Create a user account within Active Directory for use by the Send connector on the Edge Transport server. You need to make this account a member of the Exchange Servers universal security group.

After you complete these tasks, you need to perform the following tasks on the Edge Transport server:

- Create a Send connector to route messages to the Internet.
- Create a Send connector to route messages to the Exchange organization. Configure this connector to use Basic authentication and Basic authentication requiring TLS. Use the user account that you created for this purpose when configuring authentication credentials.
- Create a Receive connector that will only receive messages from the Hub Transport servers in the Exchange organization. Configure this Receive connector to use Basic authentication over TLS.
- Create a Receive connector to accept messages from Internet hosts.

After you perform these steps, you need to create a Send connector for your organization's Hub Transport servers that is configured to send messages to the Edge Transport server on the perimeter network. This Send connector should be configured to use the IP address or FQDN of the Edge Transport server as a smart host. Set the authentication to Basic authentication over TLS. You don't need to configure Receive connectors on the Hub Transport server because the default ServerName connector—created when Exchange was installed—will accept messages from the Edge Transport server. You will learn more about creating Send connectors and Receive connectors later in this chapter.

> **MORE INFO** **CONNECT EDGE TRANSPORT WITHOUT EDGESYNC**
>
> To learn more about configuring mail flow between an Edge Transport server and a Hub Transport server without using EdgeSync, consult the following TechNet article: *http://technet.microsoft.com/en-us/library/bb232082.aspx*.

Clone Edge Transport Configuration

You should plan to deploy multiple Edge Transport servers if you need to guarantee that external email flow will still occur if an Edge Transport server fails. When you deploy multiple Edge Transport servers, you need to ensure that they have the same configuration. For example, if one Edge Transport server had an address rewriting rule and another does not, address entries on outbound mail might differ depending on which Edge Transport server processes the message. You can do this by cloning the Edge Transport server's configuration. You should plan to clone configurations even in situations where you're planning to use edge subscriptions. When deploying a second or third Edge Transport server in an environment where there is an existing EdgeSync subscription, you should import the cloned configuration prior to creating a new EdgeSync subscription for that server.

To clone an Edge Transport server, you need to perform the following general steps:

1. Install the Edge Transport role on the target server.

2. Open EMS on the original Edge Transport server. Run the ExportEdgeConfig.ps1 Windows PowerShell script. This script will generate an XML file. Transfer this file to the newly prepared Edge Transport server.

3. On the newly prepared Edge Transport server, open EMS and run the ImportEdge-Config.ps1 script. This will validate the contents of the XML file and will create an answer file that you can use to configure settings that are specific to the new Edge Transport server.

4. Edit the XML file in a text editor such as Notepad. Configure the new Source IP address for Send connectors and network bindings for each Receive connector. If the new Edge Transport server uses different data and log file paths, you'll need to modify these as well.

5. Run ImportEdgeConfig.ps1 script to import the cloned configuration.

Cloned configuration isn't necessary in the event that no direct customization of the original Edge Transport server configuration has occurred. For example, if you deploy an Edge Transport server, immediately create an EdgeSync subscription, and then deploy another Edge Transport server, configuration cloning will be unnecessary. If you are unsure as to whether the original Edge Transport server configuration has been modified, best practice is to clone the configuration prior to creating the new EdgeSync subscription. You'll learn more about making the Edge Transport server role highly available in Chapter 4, "Designing and Deploying Exchange Server 2010 Availability and Recovery."

> **MORE INFO** **EDGE TRANSPORT SERVER CLONED CONFIGURATION**
>
> To learn more about cloning Edge Transport server configuration, consult the following TechNet article: *http://technet.microsoft.com/en-us/library/aa998622.aspx*.

Configure Transport Agents

Transport agents allow the processing of email messages as they pass across a transport server through the transport pipeline. The transport agents that you need to be aware of for the 70-663 exam are the ones included with Exchange. Additional transport agents might also be added if you install custom applications designed to function with Exchange, such as a third-party anti-spam solution.

Edge Transport servers include the following transport agents by default:

- **Connection filtering agent** This agent manages the Edge Transport server's anti-spam routines.

- **Address Rewriting Inbound agent**   This agent is used to rewrite the email addresses of incoming messages.
- **Edge Rule agent**   This agent manages compliance transport rules.
- **Content Filter agent**   This agent examines inbound messages to determine whether they are spam.
- **Sender ID agent**   Another anti-spam related agent, this agent queries the sending server's DNS service to determine whether it is associated with the sender address in the message. Sender ID is primarily used to reduce the spoofing of a message's sender address.
- **Sender Filter agent**   This agent allows the filtering of messages based on sender email address or sender domain. For example, you can use it this agent in blocking email from a specific person or a specific organization.
- **Recipient Filter agent**   This anti-spam agent allows you to block messages based on recipient address.
- **Protocol Analysis agent**   This agent makes a record of the SMTP transmission that occurs between source and destination servers during message delivery.
- **Attachment Filtering agent**   This agent allows the filtering of attachments.
- **Address Rewriting Outbound agent**   This agent is used to rewrite the email addresses of outgoing messages.

You can use the *Get-TransportPipeline* cmdlet to view all currently enabled transport agents that have been triggered and the SMTP events with which they are associated. To view all transport agents and their status, run the *Get-TransportAgent* cmdlet. You can enable transport agents using the *Enable-TransportAgent* cmdlet. You can disable transport agents using the *Disable-TransportAgent* cmdlet.

> **MORE INFO**   **TRANSPORT AGENTS**
>
> To learn more about Transport Agents, consult the following TechNet article: *http://technet.microsoft.com/en-us/library/bb125012.aspx*.

Third-Party Email Gateways

In some organizations, it will be necessary to use a third-party email gateway in your Exchange Server 2010 design rather than an Exchange Server 2010 Edge Transport server. To use a third-party email gateway with an Exchange Server 2010 deployment, you need to configure a Send connector and a Receive connector between your organization's Hub Transport server and the third-party SMTP server that will process and route Internet email.

You can configure the following forms of authentication on the connection between the Hub Transport server and the third-party email gateway:

- **Basic authentication**   This form of authentication requires a user name and password. You can't use this form of authentication with Exchange Hosted Services. If you are using Basic authentication, as shown in Figure 2-7, you need to create a domain account that the third-party email gateway will use to authenticate prior to transmitting incoming email. If you are using Basic Authentication over TLS, you'll need to ensure that the target server is configured with an X.509 certificate that has the fully qualified domain name associated with the Receive connector.

- **Externally secured**   This method usually involves a technology like IPsec or a VPN, which will enable the connection between the Hub Transport server and the third-party email gateway to be both encrypted and authenticated. You need to secure this communications channel outside of Exchange.

- **Anonymous Relay**   Although this method is not recommended, if you do choose to allow connections without authentication, ensure that you configure the Receive connector to only accept connections from designated IP addresses. If you don't do this, your server may end up as an open relay and it won't be long before your Exchange infrastructure is used by spammers.

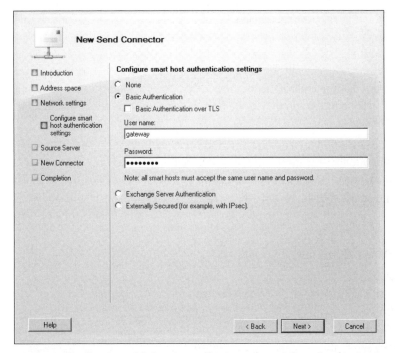

FIGURE 2-7 Configuring a third-party email gateway by creating a Send connector

When you configure a Receive connector for a third-party email gateway, all traffic from the IP address configured as the gateway endpoint will bypass anti-spam checks and message size limit checks. Traffic from properly configured third-party email gateways will be treated by the Hub Transport servers in your organization as though it originated from senders internal to your Exchange organization.

If your design involves eventually shifting from one external email gateway to another, you'll need to make sure that you either properly update the existing Send and Receive connectors, or create new Send and Receive connectors if the existing email gateway and its replacement will be functional at the same time.

> **MORE INFO** **EXTERNAL SMTP GATEWAYS**
>
> To learn more about configuring email to flow through an External SMTP gateway, consult the following TechNet article: *http://technet.microsoft.com/en-us/library/bb738161.aspx*.

Configure Address Rewriting

Address rewriting allows you to rearrange the format of email addresses as they pass across an Edge Transport server. You use address rewriting in your Exchange design when you want to ensure that inbound or outbound email address formats are consistent. For example, you might be using a cross-forest topology where each Active Directory forest has a separate Exchange organization, but you want your organization to use a single email domain name when communicating with the outside world. To accomplish this goal you could use address rewriting to ensure that the email messages that originate in each forest end up leaving your organization appearing as though they come from one mail system rather than multiple Exchange organizations.

Through address rewriting, you can rewrite individual addresses, single domains, or multiple domains. Perhaps the most common use of address rewriting is when organizations undergo name changes. You set up address rewriting so that all email to addresses that use the old company email domain are rewritten to use the new company email domain. Address rewriting is also often used during mergers and acquisitions, again to present a consistent and unified email address space.

To use address rewriting, enable the address rewriting agents. To enable both the inbound and outbound transport agents, execute the following EMS commands:

```
Enable-TransportAgent -Identity "Address Rewriting Inbound agent"
Enable-TransportAgent -Identity "Address Rewriting Outbound agent"
```

As of Exchange 2010 with service pack 1, you can only configure address rewriting through EMC. You can create address rewrite entries with the *New-AddressRewriteEntry* cmdlet. This can be done on the level of individual addresses. For example, to alter the address kim.akers@tailspintoys.com to akers.kim@wingtiptoys.com, use the following EMS command:

```
New-AddressRewriteEntry -name "Kim Akers" -Internal kim.akers@tailspintoys.com to
akers.kim@wingtiptoys.com
```

You can also configure address rewrite entries on the basis of email domain. To alter all email addresses from the cohowinery.com domain to the cohovineyard.com domain, use the following EMS command:

```
New-AddressRewriteEntry -Name "Winery to Vineyard" -InternalAddress cohowinery.com
-ExternalAddress cohovineyard.com
```

You can configure address rewrite entries to consolidate subdomain-based email domains. For example, to change all email addresses from subdomains, such as south.fabrikam.com and west.fabrikam.com, use the following EMS command:

```
New-AddressRewriteEntry -Name "All Fabrikam Subdomains" -InternalAddress *.fabrikam.com
-ExternalAddress fabrikam.com -OutboundOnly $true
```

To list the current set of address rewrite entries, use the *Get-AddressRewriteEntry* cmdlet. To change an existing address rewrite entry, use the *Set-AddressRewriteEntry* cmdlet. To remove an existing address rewrite entry, use the *Remove-AddressRewriteEntry* cmdlet.

> **MORE INFO   ADDRESS REWRITING**
>
> To learn more about address rewriting, consult the following TechNet article: *http://technet.microsoft.com/en-us/library/aa996806.aspx*.

EXAM TIP

Remember which EMS cmdlet you use to modify an existing address rewrite entry.

Objective Summary

- Edge subscriptions allow you to centralize the management of Edge Transport servers. When you create an edge subscription, the necessary Send and Receive connectors are created to allow routing of mail through the Edge Transport server to and from the Internet.

- If you add a Hub Transport server to the site where there is an existing edge subscription, you will need to re-create the edge subscription on each subscribed Edge Transport server.

- You need to create a new edge subscription to subscribe any new Edge Transport servers, but you do not need to recreate existing subscriptions when you add new Edge Transport servers.

- You can configure an Edge Transport server so that it can be used to route mail to and from an Exchange organization without an edge subscription, but this requires that you manually configure the appropriate Send and Receive connectors.

- Address rewriting, performed on an Edge Transport server, allows you to normalize email address formatting as messages are routed in and out of the organization. You must enable the address rewriting transport agents before you can use address rewriting.

Objective Review

Answer the following questions to test your knowledge of the information in this objective. You can find the answers to these questions and explanations of why each answer choice is correct or incorrect in the "Answers" section at the end of this chapter.

1. You want to ensure that all emails sent to users in your organization at your company's former email domain name, tailspintoys.com, are converted to your company's new email domain name, wingtiptoys.com, as they pass across your organization's Edge Transport server. The Edge Transport server is not currently configured to rewrite email addresses. Which of the following two EMS cmdlets must you use to meet your objective? (Choose two. Each answer forms part of a complete solution.)

   A. Enable-TransportAgent

   B. New-AddressRewriteEntry

   C. Set-AddressRewriteEntry

   D. Get-AddressRewriteEntry

2. Your organization has an existing Edge Transport server that is subscribed to the primary site through EdgeSync. The Edge Transport server is located on your organization's perimeter network. Your organization's primary site has one Hub Transport server. Your organization has a secondary site. This secondary site has a single Hub Transport server. You are working on a design proposal that includes adding an additional Edge Transport server on the perimeter network as well as an additional Hub Transport server to both the primary and secondary sites. How many new EdgeSync subscriptions will you need to create when all of these extra servers are deployed?

   A. 0

   B. 1

   C. 2

   D. 4

3. You have just deployed a new Edge Transport server on your organization's perimeter network. The new server has yet to process any messages routed to or received from hosts on the Internet. Given these conditions, which of the following Exchange Management Shell cmdlets can you use to determine which transport agents are active on the Edge Transport server?

   A. *Enable-TransportAgent*

   B. *Get-TransportAgentPipeline*

   C. *Get-TransportAgent*

   D. *Disable-TransportAgent*

4. You are planning the configuration of a Send connector to a third-party email gateway device. You want to use the externally secured smart host authentication setting. Which of the following technologies would you use to protect traffic between your Exchange organization and this third-party email gateway? (Choose all that apply.)

   A. Encrypting File System

   B. BitLocker

   C. IPsec

   D. Virtual Private Network

5. Your organization will not use edge subscriptions to connect an Edge Transport server located on the perimeter network with a Hub Transport server located in your organization's sole Active Directory site. You are in the process of creating an Active Directory user account that will be used by the Send connector on the Edge Transport server to authenticate with the Hub Transport server. Which security group must this user account be a member of to accomplish this goal?

   A. ExchangeLegacyInterop

   B. Exchange Servers

   C. Organization Management

   D. Server Management

In the following thought experiment, you will apply what you've learned about the objective "Deploy Edge Transport Server Role" to predict what steps to take to integrate an Edge Transport server into an Exchange design. You can find answers to these questions in the "Answers" section at the end of this chapter.

Contoso, Ltd., and Fabrikam, Inc., are going to merge into a new company named A. Datum Corporation. Both companies will move to a new headquarters location in Sydney, Australia and will be adopting Exchange Server 2010 as their messaging system. As a part of this move, you have been tasked with planning the deployment of an Edge Transport server. As a part of this implementation, management wants to ensure that recipients are still able to receive messages using their original @contoso.com and @fabrikam.com addresses, but that these be converted by some process to the new @adadum.com format.

With these facts in mind, answer the following questions:

1. Which operating systems can you install the Exchange Server 2010 Edge Transport server role on?

2. Which ports must you open on the firewall between the perimeter and internal networks to support an edge subscription?

3. Which domains should you configure as accepted domains at your organization?

4. Six months after the initial edge subscription is created, you plan to add another Hub Transport server to the Sydney Active Directory site. What step must you take on the Edge Transport server after the new server has been deployed?

5. Which EMS cmdlet do you use to configure an address rewrite entry to alter all existing @contoso.com and @fabrikam.com addresses into @adatum.com addresses?

Objective 2.3: Deploy Client Access Server Role

Client Access Servers (CAS) are the interface through which users interact with Exchange. When you deploy Exchange 2010 you need to ensure that there is a CAS in each site that hosts a mailbox server. In Exchange 2010 deployments, CAS provide support for RPC, Outlook Web App, Autodiscover, ActiveSync, Outlook Anywhere, POP3, IMAP4, and the Availability service.

This objective covers:

- Deploy CAS hardware and protocols.
- Deploy mobile messaging services and connectivity.
- Validate client connectivity.
- Validate client functionality.
- Autodiscover.
- Multi-site/domain/forest considerations.

Deploying the Client Access Role

The Client Access Server (CAS) role can be deployed on computers running Windows Server 2008 and Windows Server 2008 R2. You can co-locate the CAS role with the Hub Transport and Mailbox server roles. If you install Exchange 2010 with Service Pack One using the default settings, the CAS, Hub Transport, and Mailbox server roles will all be installed on the same server.

As you may recall from Chapter 1, "Planning the Exchange Server 2010 Infrastructure," you need to deploy a CAS at any site that hosts a mailbox server. Microsoft performance testing of CAS/Mailbox server combinations indicates that optimum performance is reached when you deploy the equivalent of three processor cores on the CAS servers for a site for every four processor cores that are present on the site's mailbox server. Although such precise processor allotment can be challenging on physical hardware, organizations increasingly deploy Exchange virtually, which gives administrators much more control over how processor resources are allocated.

The CAS role has the following prerequisites, which you can configure prior to installation, or, if you are using the Exchange 2010 SP1 setup wizard, have the setup routine install for you: RSAT Tools, .NET Framework 3.5.1, Web Server, Web Server Basic Authentication, Web Server Windows Authentication, Web Server Digest Authentication, IIS 6 Metabase Compatibility, Web Server .NET Extensibility, IIS 6 Management Console, Windows Process Activation Service Process Model, Web Server ISAPI Extensions, Web Server Dynamic Content Compression, .NET Framework HTTP Activation, and RPC over HTTP Proxy.

Requesting a CAS Certificate

As CAS are the Exchange component that clients are most likely to interact with, most organizations like to protect communication between the CAS and the client using digital certificates. In Chapter 1, you learned about the types of certificate you could use with a CAS. Your options include:

- Obtain a separate certificate for each name the server has.
- Obtain a single certificate that supports Subject Alternative Names.
- Obtain a wildcard certificate.
- Configure all services to use the same fully qualified domain name (FQDN).

You can create a certificate request for a CAS certificate using the New Exchange Certificate Wizard. Once the certificate request is completed, you can forward it for processing either to an internal or trusted third-party Certificate Authority. To run the New Exchange Certificate Wizard, perform the following steps:

1. Open Exchange Management Console, select the Server Configuration node. Click a server. In the Actions pane, click New Exchange Certificate.

2. On the Introduction page, enter a new display name for the certificate.

3. On the Domain Scope page, select the Enable Wildcard Certificate option if you need to support subdomains or want to use a wildcard certificate as a way of simplifying certificate names.

4. On the Exchange Configuration page, shown in Figure 2-8, use the arrows to expand each service for which you want to configure a certificate and provide the FQDN by which the service will be addressed.

5. On the Certificate Domains page, verify that all required certificate names are present. Click Add to add any additional Subject Alternative Names.

6. On the Organization And Location page, provide organizational information. Also specify the location where you want to save the certificate request file.

You can forward the certificate request file to an appropriate CA. When you have received a response, you can use the Complete Pending Request item—which becomes available when you select the certificate within EMC—to install the newly issued certificate. After you have installed the certificate, you can assign services to that certificate. To assign services, right-click the certificate and then click Assign Services To Certificate. Select the servers that you wish to assign services to and then, on the Assign Services To Certificate page (Figure 2-9), select the services that you want to utilize with the certificate.

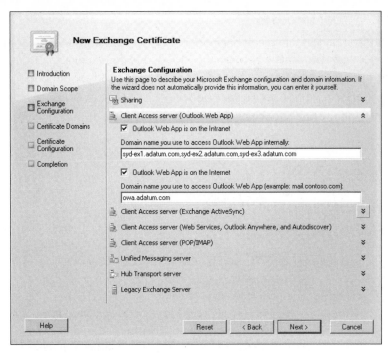

FIGURE 2-8 New Exchange certificate

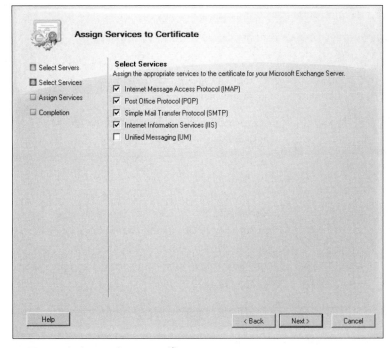

FIGURE 2-9 Assign services to certificate

You will learn more about provisioning CAS with certificates in Chapter 3, "Designing and Deploying Security for the Exchange Organization."

MORE INFO   **MANAGING SSL FOR A CAS**

To learn more about managing SSL for a CAS, consult the following TechNet article: *http://technet.microsoft.com/en-us/library/bb310795.aspx.*

Configuring Outlook Web App

Outlook Web App (OWA) is a web application that runs on CAS and allows users to replicate the Outlook 2010 experience through their browsers. This usage scenario is increasingly important as users access their Exchange mailboxes not only through traditional client operating systems running Outlook, but through third-party mobile and tablet operating systems. You can configure settings for all OWA users by editing the properties of the OWA virtual directory. You can do this in one of two ways: You can navigate to the Server Configuration\Client Access node of EMC, select the CAS server to configure, click the Outlook Web App tab, click the OWA site, and then click Properties in the Actions pane to bring up the dialog box shown in Figure 2-10. Or you can modify the properties of the OWA virtual directory using the *Set-OwaVirtualDirectory* cmdlet in EMS. You can also configure many OWA-based settings through OWA mailbox policies, allowing you to provide separate groups of users with different experiences. This objective concentrates on configuring CAS rather than recipients, so it concentrates on configuring OWA directly.

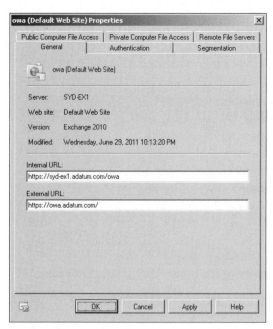

FIGURE 2-10 OWA virtual directory

Configuring Virtual Directories

You configure OWA primarily by configuring the OWA virtual directories. You do this either by using EMC to edit the virtual directory properties directly or by using the *Set-Owa-VirtualDirectory* cmdlet in EMS. If you want to configure specific SSL settings for an OWA virtual directory, you need to use the Internet Information Services (IIS) console, although assigning the certificate to IIS using the technique outlined earlier is adequate for most organizations:

- **General**   You can use this tab to configure the URL that users use to access OWA either from internal or external network locations.

- **Segmentation**   You can use this tab to configure which OWA features are available to users.

- **Public Computer File Access**   This tab allows you to control Direct File Access and WebReady Document Viewing settings for people that report that they are using a public computer during logon.

- **Private Computer File Access**   This tab allows you to control Direct File Access and WebReady Document Viewing settings for people that report that they are using a private computer during logon.

- **Remote File Servers**   You can use this tab to specify which remote file servers OWA users are able to access on your organization's internal network. Exchange only uses this list when a message has a link to a file stored on a SharePoint server or file server on an internal network.

- **Authentication**   You can use the Authentication tab, shown in Figure 2-11, to configure how users authenticate against OWA. You can choose between the standard authentication methods, which allow Basic Authentication, Digest Authentication, or Integrated Windows authentication. The default authentication method for Exchange 2010 SP1 is to use forms-based authentication with the *domain\user name* format. You can also choose to use User Principle Name (UPN) or User Name.

You can use the following commands to manage OWA virtual directories:

- **Get-OwaVirtualDirectory**   View the properties of an existing OWA virtual directory
- **New-OwaVirtualDirectory**   Create a new OWA virtual directory
- **Set-OwaVirtualDirectory**   Configure the properties of an OWA virtual directory
- **Remove-OwaVirtualDirectory**   Remove an existing OWA virtual directory

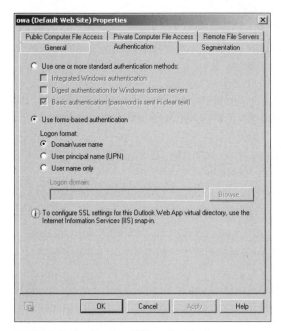

FIGURE 2-11 Configuring OWA authentication

WebReady Document Viewing and Direct File Access

WebReady document viewing allows users to view documents attached to their email through their browsers. This is useful in situations where users are accessing their messages through OWA on a device that doesn't support Microsoft Office or on which Microsoft Office is not installed. You can configure different settings depending on whether an OWA user reports that she is on a public computer or a private computer. It is usually good to have the same settings for both public and private computers because Exchange can't actually check and users will often indicate that they are coming from a private computer so that they can take advantage of the less-stringent security policies.

Direct File Access allows users access to linked email attachments stored on file shares or SharePoint servers. For example, rather than email a 20-MB PowerPoint file, which usually exceeds the incoming message size restrictions of most organizations, a user might choose to post the file on an organizational SharePoint site and include a link to that file in his email message. By configuring Direct File Access policies, you can choose whether you are going to allow users to access files without saving them, block users from accessing specific file types through OWA, configure behavior for unknown file types, and specify whether users must save certain file types locally before being able to open them.

You configure WebReady document viewing and Direct File Access by configuring the properties of the OWA virtual directory, as shown in Figure 2-12. You can also configure these settings on a per-user basis through OWA mailbox policies. You can configure the OWA virtual directory properties from EMS using the *Set-OwaVirtualDirectory cmdlet*.

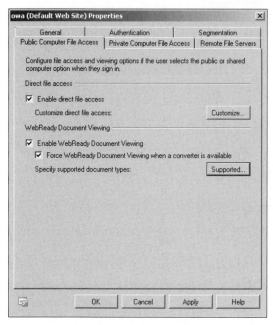

FIGURE 2-12 WebReady document viewing

> **MORE INFO** **CONFIGURING WEBREADY DOCUMENT VIEWING**
>
> To learn more about configuring WebReady document viewing, consult the following TechNet article: *http://technet.microsoft.com/en-us/library/aa995967.aspx*.

Managing OWA Advanced Features

OWA has several advanced features that you can manage by configuring the OWA virtual directory. You can configure these features from EMS using the *Set-OwaVirtualDirectory* cmdlet. You can also configure them through OWA mailbox policies, which allow you to apply different OWA settings to different users. OWA Advanced Features include the following:

- **Segmentation** Use segmentation to enable or disable certain OWA features including Calendar, Change Password, Contacts, E-Mail Signature, Journal, Junk E-Mail Filtering, Notes, Public Folders, Recover Deleted Items, S/MIME, Spelling Checker, Tasks, and Theme Selection. You can also configure these settings on the Segmentation tab of the OWA virtual directory, as shown in Figure 2-13. You will learn more about segmentation in Chapter 3.

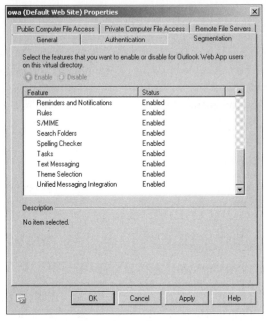

FIGURE 2-13 Segmentation settings

- **Gzip Compression Settings**   This feature improves performance over slow networks by compressing content at the server. The drawback of this feature is that it imposes a performance hit on the server.

- **Web Beacon and HTML Form Filtering**   This feature allows you to block items embedded in email messages that might be used to monitor when a message is opened or contain malicious code.

- **Address Lists**   You can use ADSI Edit, rather than the *Set-OwaVirtualDirectory* cmdlet, to control which address lists are available to OWA users.

- **Character Settings**   Allows you to control which character set is used for OWA.

- **Language Settings**   Language settings determine the language of the OWA sign-in page and error messages. The user can change this by altering the Regional Settings in OWA. To support labels such as To and From in languages other than English, it is necessary to install the appropriate language pack.

- **Custom Sign-In and Sign-Out Pages**   By editing specific files in the OWA directory you can modify the appearance of the OWA sign-in and sign-out pages.

- **OWA Themes**   By editing specific files, you can create new OWA themes that users can select as a way of enhancing their OWA experience.

MORE INFO **ADVANCED OWA FEATURES**

To learn more about Outlook Web App advanced features, consult the following TechNet document: *http://technet.microsoft.com/en-us/library/bb124348.aspx.*

Outlook Anywhere

When you enable Outlook Anywhere, clients on the Internet are able to access resources on the internal network without having to use a VPN or DirectAccess connection. The CAS that hosts Outlook Anywhere needs to be accessible to clients on the Internet. This generally means that it is placed on an organization's perimeter network and needs to be published through the external firewall. Before you can enable Outlook Anywhere you need to provision the CAS server with an SSL certificate, add the RPC over HTTP feature, and verify that the CAS server's external FQDN is resolvable by clients on the Internet.

To enable Outlook Anywhere, perform the following general steps:

1. Open Exchange Management Console. Select the Server Configuration \ Client Access node. Select the Client Access Server on which you wish to enable Outlook Anywhere. Click Enable Outlook Anywhere in the Actions pane.

2. On the Enable Outlook Anywhere Wizard page, shown in Figure 2-14, provide the external host name that clients use for access. Select which authentication method will be used and whether you want to allow SSL offloading. The Negotiate Ex authentication option is an authentication type that is reserved for a future Microsoft release and is not supported with Exchange Server 2010 SP1 on Windows Server 2008 R2 SP1.

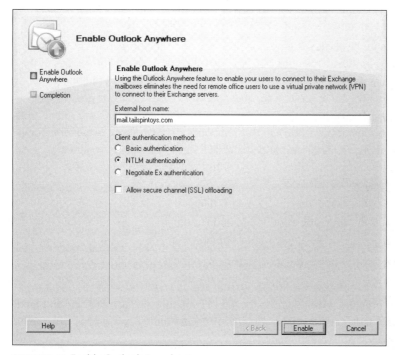

FIGURE 2-14 Enable Outlook Anywhere

You can enable Outlook Anywhere from EMS by using the *Enable-OutlookAnywhere* cmdlet. For example, to configure Outlook Anywhere on a server named SYD-CAS that has the external host name mail.tailspintoys.com and using NTLM for authentication, issue the following command:

```
Enable-OutlookAnywhere -Server 'SYD-CAS' -ExternalHostname 'mail.tailspintoys.com'
-DefaultAuthenticationMethod 'NTLM'
```

You can modify the configuration of Outlook Anywhere using the *Set-OutlookAnywhere* cmdlet, or by editing the properties of the CAS that hosts Outlook Anywhere when you have the Server Configuration \ Client Access node active in Exchange Management Console.

MORE INFO   **OUTLOOK ANYWHERE**

To learn more about managing Outlook Anywhere, consult the following TechNet document: *http://technet.microsoft.com/en-us/library/bb123513.aspx.*

ActiveSync

ActiveSync allows devices that are configured to use the ActiveSync protocol—which includes the majority of smartphone and tablet operating systems—to access Exchange 2010 mailboxes. ActiveSync is designed to work well across high-latency, low-bandwidth networks, which is the type of network often encountered by mobile device users.

You configure ActiveSync settings on a CAS by editing the properties of the ActiveSync virtual directory, as shown in Figure 2-15. You can also configure the properties of the ActiveSync virtual directory using the *Set-ActiveSyncVirtualDirectory* cmdlet. Default ActiveSync authentication is Basic Authentication, which uses clear text passwords. You can improve this by provisioning ActiveSync devices with client certificates and requiring those certificates for authentication. You can also configure the ActiveSync virtual directories to block or allow access to file servers and SharePoint sites on the internal network.

Autodiscover

The Autodiscover service allows you to automatically provision Outlook 2007, Outlook 2010, and ActiveSync clients with user profile configuration settings. Users simply provide their email addresses and passwords; Autodiscover provisions the client will all other necessary settings such incoming and outgoing server addresses and port and security settings.

To configure the Autodiscover service so that clients on the Internet can use it to automatically configure settings, you will need to configure an SSL certificate and bind it to IIS, as described earlier in this objective. Outlook checks the following URLs when attempting to use Autodiscover from the Internet:

- *http://autodiscover.<e-maildomain>/autodiscover/autodiscover.xml*
- *http://<e-maildomain>/autodiscover/autodiscover.xml*

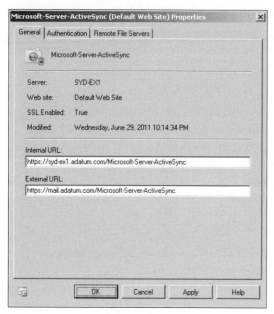

FIGURE 2-15 ActiveSync Virtual Directory properties

To configure the Autodiscover service to support Exchange in a multiple forest or resource forest topology, you need to update Active Directory so that users who are running Outlook 2007 or Outlook 2010 in one forest are able to access the CAS servers in the other forest. You do this by running the *Export-AutoDiscoverConfig* cmdlet in each forest that has CAS servers, targeting a domain controller in the other forest. For example:

- In a two-forest cross-forest topology that has Forest A and Forest B, you would need to run *Export-AutoDiscoverConfig* in Forest A targeting a Domain Controller in Forest B. Then you would need to run *Export-AutoDiscoverConfig* in Forest B targeting a Domain Controller in Forest A.

- If you were configuring a resource forest topology with three forests, where Exchange was installed in Forest A and where accounts were in Forest B and Forest C, you'd need to run *Export-AutoDiscoverConfig* twice in Forest A—the first time targeting a Domain Controller in Forest B and the second time targeting a Domain Controller in Forest C.

You can configure Autodiscover for site affinity, which means that Outlook 2007 and Outlook 2010 clients will seek Autodiscover information from the closest Active Directory site. You do this by configuring the *Set-ClientAccessServer* cmdlet. Using this command you separately configure each Active Directory site with the address of a CAS at that site.

You can use the *Set-ActiveSyncVirtualDirectory* cmdlet to configure the Autodiscover service to work with Exchange ActiveSync. For example, to configure server CAS-ALPHA that uses the external host name mail.contoso.com to support Autodiscover with ActiveSync, issue the following EMS command:

```
Set-ActiveSyncVirtualDirectory -Identity "CAS-ALPHA\Microsoft-Server-ActiveSync (Default
Web Site)" -ActiveSyncServer "https://mail.contoso.com/"
```

You use the *Enable-OutlookAnywhere* cmdlet to configure the Outlook Anywhere external host name for Autodiscover. For example, to configure the external host name of mail. contoso.com for Outlook Anywhere on server CAS-ALPHA, use the following EMS command:

```
Enable-OutlookAnywhere -Server CAS-ALPHA -ExternalHostname "mail.contoso.com"
-DefaultAuthenticationMethod "Basic" -SSLOffloading:$False
```

You can use the *Set-OABVirtualDirectory* cmdlet to configure Autodiscover with the URL for the offline address book. For example, to configure Autodiscover to use the OAB stored on CAS-ALPHA, which uses the external URL mail.contoso.com, use the following command:

```
Set-OABVirtualDirectory -identity "CAS-ALPHA\OAB (Default Web Site)" -externalurl
https://mail.contoso.com/OAB -RequireSSL:$true
```

> **MORE INFO**   **MANAGING AUTODISCOVER**
>
> To learn more about managing the Autodiscover service, consult the following TechNet article: *http://technet.microsoft.com/en-us/library/aa995956.aspx.*

Availability Service

The Availability service provides Outlook and OWA clients with information about the user's calendaring and meeting schedules. The service is installed by default with Exchange 2010 and uses the URL http://*servername*/EWS. The availability service allows Outlook and OWA clients to perform the following tasks:

- Access up-to-date free/busy information for Exchange 2010 mailboxes
- Access up-to-date free/busy information from other Exchange 2010 organizations with which there is a federated relationship
- Access free/busy information through public folders for users with mailboxes on previous versions of Exchange
- Show meeting time suggestions
- View recipient working hours

If your organization is using a trusted cross-forest topology, you don't have to use federation to provide shared calendaring data. You can configure cross-forest access to the Availability server using the *Add-ADPermission* and *Add-AvailabilityAddressSpace* cmdlets.

> **MORE INFO**   **AVAILABILITY SERVICE**
>
> To learn more about the Availability service, consult the following TechNet document: *http://technet.microsoft.com/en-us/library/bb232134.aspx.*

POP3 and IMAP4 Access

Some organizations provide POP3 and IMAP4 access to mailboxes for clients that don't support Outlook. Although these services are installed on CAS during deployment, the services themselves are set to the Manual startup type. If you want to allow clients to use these services, you'll need to reconfigure these services to use the Automatic startup type. You can do this from the Services console on the CAS.

After you have configured the services to start automatically, you can edit the service's properties through EMC. To do this, click the Server Configuration\Client Access node, click the server that you want to configure the service on, click the POP3 And IMAP4 tab, click the protocol you want to configure, and then click Properties on the Actions pane. From each protocol's dialog box, you can configure the following:

- Port and IP address bindings for unencrypted and SSL connections. The default ports for IMAP4 are 143 and 993. The default ports for POP3 are 110 and 995.
- Logon method, including plain text (basic), plain text (integrated Windows authentication), and Secure Logon (which requires an SSL certificate).
- Connection time out settings and connection limits.
- Message MIME format.

You can also configure settings for these services using the *Set-POPSettings* or *Set-IMAPSettings* cmdlets.

> **MORE INFO   POP3 AND IMAP4 ACCESS**
>
> To learn more about managing POP3 and IMAP4 access, consult the following TechNet document: *http://technet.microsoft.com/en-us/library/aa996347.aspx.*

Verifying Client Access Server Functionality

The CAS is the Exchange component that clients use to interact with Exchange, so you need to ensure that it is functioning properly. If a user or users are having problems interacting with Exchange, you should determine whether the CAS is functional before attempting more complicated troubleshooting steps. Microsoft provides several tools with which you can diagnose problems with the CAS. This includes the Exchange Remote Connectivity Analyzer, Exchange Server User Monitor, and a large number of feature-specific EMS cmdlets.

Exchange Remote Connectivity Analyzer

The Exchange Server Remote Connectivity Analyzer, shown in Figure 2-16, is an online web-based tool that allows you to verify the functionality of CAS from the perspective of a client on the Internet. You can access this tool by navigating to the URL *http://www.testexchange-connectivity.com*. You can use this tool to check the following CAS functionality:

- ActiveSync
- Autodiscover (Outlook and ActiveSync)
- Outlook Anywhere
- Inbound and Outbound SMTP
- Exchange Web Services

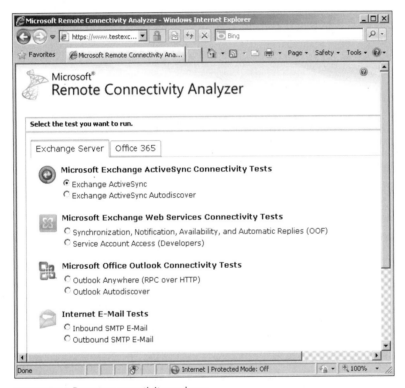

FIGURE 2-16 Remote connectivity analyzer

MORE INFO   REMOTE CONNECTIVITY ANALYZER

To learn more about Exchange Remote Connectivity Analyzer, consult the following TechNet article: *http://technet.microsoft.com/en-us/library/dd439364(EXCHG.80).aspx*.

Exchange Server User Monitor

The Exchange Server User Monitor (ExMon) allows you to view and analyze a specific user's Exchange usage and performance. This tool can be useful when evaluating the performance of a CAS and allows you to monitor the following:

- Client IP addresses
- Outlook version
- Outlook mode (Cached Exchange / Classic online)
- CPU usage
- Server-site processor latency
- Network bytes

> **MORE INFO** **EXCHANGE SERVER USER MONITOR**
>
> To learn more about Exchange Server User Monitor, consult the following TechNet website: *http://technet.microsoft.com/en-us/library/bb508855(EXCHG.65).aspx.*

Diagnosing CAS Functionality with EMS

You can use a number of EMS cmdlets to verify CAS functionality. You do this on the basis of a specific functionality—for example, testing whether ActiveSync works or whether OWA works, rather than testing everything at once. The commands that you can use to verify the functionality of specific CAS components include:

- **Test-ActiveSyncConnectivity**   This cmdlet allows you to test ActiveSync functionality against a specific mailbox.
- **Test-EcpConnectivity**   This cmdlet allows you to verify that Exchange Control Panel is functioning properly.
- **Test-ImapConnectivity**   This cmdlet allows you to check whether the IMAP4 service is working properly.
- **Test-OutlookConnectivity**   This cmdlet allows you to test end-to-end Outlook client connectivity including Outlook Anywhere (RPC/HTTP) and TCP-based.
- **Test-PopConnectivity**   Use this cmdlet to verify that the POP3 service is functioning correctly.
- **Test-SmtpConnectivity**   This cmdlet allows you to verify the SMTP functionality of a target Exchange server.
- **Test-OwaConnectivity**   This cmdlet allows an administrator to verify that OWA is functioning.

- **Test-WebServicesConnectivity** This cmdlet allows you to verify that Exchange Web Services is functioning properly.
- **Test-OutlookWebServices** This cmdlet allows you to verify that the Autodiscover service is functioning and configured properly on Client Access Servers. You can also use this cmdlet to test whether the Availability service is functioning correctly.

Objective Summary

- Optimum CAS performance involved deploying three processor cores on CAS for every four processor cores assigned to mailbox servers at a specific Active Directory site.
- When requesting a CAS certificate, you can request a wildcard certificate, a certificate that supports subject alternative names, or separate certificates for each URL used by the CAS.
- You should set an external URL for OWA if it is going to be accessed by clients across the Internet. You can configure OWA using the *Set-OwaVirtualDirectory* cmdlet.
- WebReady document viewing allows OWA users to view Microsoft Office documents on computers through the browser even if Microsoft Office is not locally installed.
- Outlook Anywhere allows clients on the Internet to access Exchange mailboxes using Outlook clients without having to establish a VPN or DirectAccess connection.
- ActiveSync allows mobile devices to synchronize messages, contacts, and calendaring data with Exchange.
- Autodiscover allows Outlook 2007, Outlook 2010, and compatible ActiveSync clients to be automatically provisioned with configuration settings.
- The Availability service provides Outlook and OWA clients with calendaring information.

Objective Review

Answer the following questions to test your knowledge of the information in this objective. You can find the answers to these questions and explanations of why each answer choice is correct or incorrect in the "Answers" section at the end of this chapter.

1. You are in the process of deploying Exchange Server 2010. You want to verify that the Autodiscover service is functioning properly on your organization's five newly deployed Client Access Servers. Which of the following Exchange Management Shell cmdlets could you use to accomplish this goal?

   A. Test-ActiveSyncConnectivity

   B. Test-OwaConnectivity

   C. Test-WebServicesConnectivity

   D. Test-OutlookWebServices

2. Prior to instructing your support staff to use Outlook Anywhere, you want to verify that the deployed technology works as expected. Which of the following Exchange Management Shell cmdlets could you use to verify this functionality?

   A. *Test-OwaConnectivity*

   B. *Test-OutlookWebServices*

   C. *Test-OutlookConnectivity*

   D. *Test-WebServicesConnectivity*

3. Which of the following tools can you use to test Autodiscover functionality for ActiveSync devices that are connecting remotely to your organization's CAS using the Internet?

   A. Exchange Server User Monitor

   B. Exchange Remote Connectivity Analyzer

   C. *Test-OutlookConnectivity* cmdlet

   D. *Test-OwaConnectivity* cmdlet

4. You want to prevent users in your organization from downloading Microsoft Office Word documents when they are connected to Outlook Web App from a public computer. Which of the following Exchange Management Shell cmdlets could you use to accomplish this goal?

   A. *Set-OwaVirtualDirectory*

   B. *Set-PublicFolder*

   C. *Set-ResourceConfig*

   D. *Set-OutlookAnywhere*

5. Your organization has deployed mailbox servers in five separate Active Directory sites. You are deploying Outlook Web App (OWA) on the Client Access Servers in these sites. Which of the following Exchange Management Shell cmdlets can you use to verify the functionality of OWA on these servers?

   A. *Test-PopConnectivity*

   B. *Test-OwaConnectivity*

   C. *Test-ActiveSyncConnectivity*

   D. *Test-OutlookConnectivity*

THOUGHT EXPERIMENT
Deploying Client Access at Contoso

In the following thought experiment, you will apply what you've learned in this objective to a CAS deployment scenario. You can find answers to these questions in the "Answers" section at the end of this chapter.

You will be deploying Exchange 2010 in your organization using a cross-forest topology, with both the Wingtip Toys and the Tailspin Toys forests having their own Exchange 2010 deployment.

You plan to decommission VPN access after Exchange 2010 is deployed.

You plan to have all Exchange 2010 server roles hosted on separate virtual machines.

You plan to allocate eight virtual processors to the mailbox server at each site.

With these facts in mind, answer the following questions:

1. What tool can you use to determine that ActiveSync and Autodiscover works for clients attempting to provision mobile devices using their email addresses and passwords from locations on the Internet?

2. What feature should you enable to allow Outlook 2010 clients on the Internet to access their mailboxes after the VPN is decommissioned?

3. Which EMS cmdlet would you run in both forests to ensure that Autodiscover works independently of which forest a user logs on to?

4. Which feature should you configure to ensure that people using OWA through public computers are unable to view Microsoft Office documents through a web browser?

5. To achieve optimum performance, how many virtual processors should you allocate to the CAS at each site?

Objective 2.4: Deploy Hub Transport Server Role

After you've decided where you want to deploy Hub Transport servers and your goals for your routing infrastructure, you need to operationalize your plans. This involves configuring components such as transport rules, accepted domains, remote domains, Send connectors, and Receive connectors to meet your original design objectives.

This objective covers:

- Deploy Hub Transport servers in multi-site and multi-forest environments.
- Configure transport rules.
- Accepted domains.
- Remote domains.
- Send and Receive connectors.
- Message and recipient limits.
- Deploy email relay.

Hub Transport Servers in Multi-Site and Multi-Forest Environments

You need to deploy at least one Hub Transport server in each Active Directory site that hosts an Exchange Mailbox server. Sites that host multiple domains that are part of the same forest and have a mailbox server require at least one Hub Transport server. For example, Contoso, Ltd uses three domains in the contoso.local forest at their Melbourne Active Directory site. This site has two Exchange Server 2010 mailbox servers, each of which is a member of a different domain. This site will require at least one Hub Transport server to service these mailbox servers because you only need one Hub Transport server per Active Directory site, irrespective of how many domains are present.

If your organization has multiple forests, you will still need to deploy one Hub Transport server per forest for every site that has a mailbox server. For example, let's say your organization has three separate Active Directory forests and uses a model where there is an Exchange organization in each forest. At the Melbourne single-branch office, you have deployed a mailbox server for each forest's Exchange organization. To support this configuration, you'll need to deploy three Hub Transport servers, one in each forest, even though they will all be at the same branch office site. You'll also need to set up appropriate Send connectors and Receive connectors to transmit messages between each Exchange organization's Hub Transport servers.

Configuring Accepted Domains

As you learned in Chapter 1, Exchange organization will only accept messages for email domains that are configured as accepted domains. You also learned that there are three types of accepted domains:

- **Authoritative domains** You use this email domain for recipients who have mailboxes that are part of your Exchange organization.

- **Internal Relay domain** This email domain is used by another messaging system internal to your organization. You configure an Internal Relay domain when you want to support a shared address space. When you configure an Internal Relay domain, you also need to configure a Send connector that uses a Hub Transport server as its source server.

- **External Relay domain** This email domain is used by another messaging system external to your organization, but for which your Exchange organization processes email. When you configure an External Relay domain, you also need to configure a Send connector that uses an Edge Transport server as its source server.

Microsoft recommends that you configure accepted domains for Edge Transport servers by using edge synchronization on the internal network. You configure the accepted domains centrally and allow those accepted domains to replicate out to Edge Transport servers through the edge subscription process.

To configure an accepted domain, perform the following general steps:

1. In Exchange Management console, navigate to the Organization Configuration\Hub Transport node. Click New Accepted Domain in the Actions pane.

2. On the New Accepted Domain page, enter a name for the domain and for the domain for which you will accept mail. and then choose between Authoritative Domain, Internal Relay Domain, and External Relay Domain, as shown in Figure 2-17. Click New and then click Finish.

You can also use the following EMS cmdlets to manage accepted domains:

- *New-AcceptedDomain* Use this cmdlet to create new accepted domains. Use the *DomainType* parameter to specify whether the domain functions as an authoritative, internal relay, or external relay domain.

- *Get-AcceptedDomain* Use this cmdlet to view the properties of existing accepted domains.

- *Set-AcceptedDomain* Use this cmdlet to modify the settings on an existing accepted domain.

- *Remove-AcceptedDomain* Use this cmdlet to delete an existing accepted domain.

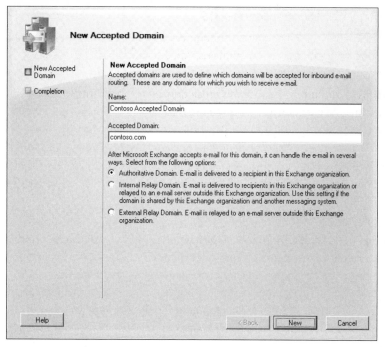

FIGURE 2-17 New Accepted Domain page

MORE INFO   **ACCEPTED DOMAINS**

To learn more about accepted domains, consult the following TechNet article:
http://technet.microsoft.com/en-us/library/bb124423.aspx.

Configuring Transport Rules

Transport rules allow you to apply messaging policies to email messages that pass across Hub Transport and Edge Transport servers. For example, you might need to ensure that email messages containing certain phrases—such as the name of a new product that has not been made public—cannot be sent outside your organization.

You can use transport rules to accomplish the following design objectives:

- Prevent problematic content, such as email messages containing expletives, from entering or leaving the organization.

- Filtering confidential information, such as social security numbers, to stop that information being transmitted outside the organization.

- Archiving or tracking messages sent to or received from designated individuals.

- Redirecting inbound and outbound messages that meet specific criteria for inspection before delivery.
- Adding legal disclaimers to messages as they leave the organization.

Transport rules are stored within Active Directory and replicated out to transport servers. This means that a rule configured on one transport server works on all transport servers.

Rules created on one Edge Transport server do not automatically replicate to other Edge Transport servers, even when those transport servers have edge subscriptions. You need to use the *Export-TransportRuleCollection* and *Import-TransportRuleCollection* cmdlets to migrate transport rules between Edge Transport servers. The advantage of using transport rules on agents is that they reduce the amount of message processing that needs to be done by Hub Transport servers on the internal network.

A transport rule has the following components:

- **Conditions** Use conditions to specify which messages to which the transport rule applies. Conditions involve one or more predicates. Predicates specify which part of the message the transport rule agent should examine. There are 42 available predicates including from, subject contains, and attachment size over for transport rules on Hub Transport servers. Thirteen predicates are available for transport rules on Edge Transport servers. Most predicates require you to specify a comparison operator like equals or contains. You can view a list of available predicates by using the *Get-TransportRulePredicate* cmdlet on a transport server.

- **Exceptions** Use exceptions to exempt messages that meet conditions from transport rules. For example you might create a transport rule that applies to all messages that contain the phrase "Project Alpha," but not want this rule to apply to messages sent by a specific person. Exceptions use the same predicates as conditions.

- **Actions** Actions determine what the rule actually does to the messages to which it applies. The 16 available actions include apply HTML disclaimer, blind copy to, and delete message available on Hub Transport servers. Thirteen actions are available on Edge Transport servers. You can view a list of available actions by using the *Get-TransportRuleAction* cmdlet.

To create transport rules, perform the following steps:

1. In EMC, select the Organization Configuration\Hub Transport node and then click New Transport Rule in the Actions pane. On an Edge Transport server, select the Edge Transport node and then click New Transport Rule.

2. On the Introduction page of the New Transport Rule Wizard, provide a name for the transport rule and then click Next.

3. On the Conditions page, shown in Figure 2-18, select and configure the transport rule conditions. You can configure as many conditions as necessary for each transport rule.

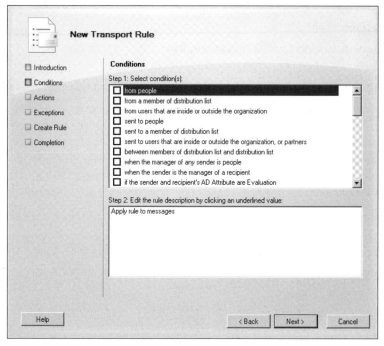

FIGURE 2-18 Transport rule conditions

4. On the Actions page, select what action you want the transport rule to take when the transport server encounters a message that meets the configured conditions.

5. On the Exceptions page, configure any exceptions that should apply to the rule.

6. On the Create Rule page, click New to create the rule. Click Finish to end the New Transport Rule Wizard.

You can manage transport rules by using the following EMS cmdlets:

- **Disable-TransportRule** Use this cmdlet to deactivate an existing transport rule without deleting that rule.

- **Enable-TransportRule** Use this cmdlet to activate a deactivated transport rule.

- **Get-TransportRule** Use this cmdlet to view existing transport rules.

- **New-TransportRule** Use this cmdlet to create a new transport rule.

- **Remove-TransportRule** Use this cmdlet to delete an existing transport rule.

- **Set-TransportRule** Use this cmdlet to modify an existing transport rule.

You'll learn more about designing transport rules for use with Active Directory Rights Management Services in Chapter 3. You'll learn about designing transport rules to meet compliance obligations in Chapter 5, "Designing and Deploying Messaging Compliance, System Monitoring, and Reporting."

Configuring Remote Domains

You use remote domains in your Exchange design to control the types of messages and
message formats that are sent to a specific external domain. You can also use remote
domains to control the external distribution of out-of-office messages as shown in
Figure 2-19. Remote domains allow you to configure the following settings generally or on a
per remote-domain basis:

- Allow automatic replies
- Allow automatic forward
- Allow delivery reports
- Allow non-delivery reports
- Display sender's name on messages
- Use message text line wrap at column
- Exchange rich-text format
- MIME character set
- Non-MIME character set

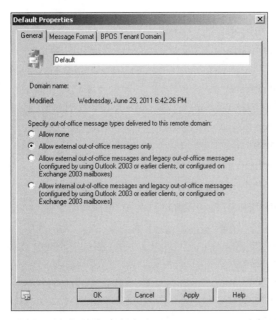

FIGURE 2-19 Remote domains

Exchange creates a default remote domain, represented by an asterisk (*) during deployment. The default remote domain settings influence all outgoing messages except those for which you configure specific remote domains. You can manage the properties of remote domains through the Organization Configuration\Hub Transport node in the EMC.

> **MORE INFO**   **REMOTE DOMAINS**
>
> To learn more about remote domains, consult the following TechNet article: *http://technet.microsoft.com/en-us/library/aa996309.aspx.*

Manage Send Connectors

Implicit and invisible Send connectors are created to route email across Hub Transport servers based on Active Directory site topology when you deploy Exchange. If you use an edge subscription to an Edge Transport server, an Internet Send connector is automatically created. In many cases, unless you have specific requirements, you may not need to plan the creation of Send connectors as a component in your Exchange Server 2010 design.

You can use the New Send Connector Wizard, available on the Actions page when you select the Organization Configuration\Hub Transport node of Exchange Management Console (EMC), to create a new Send connector, or you can use the *New-SendConnector* cmdlet to accomplish the same goal. When you use EMC, you need to choose a usage type for the connector. Usage type determines which default permissions are used with the connector. Usage type also determines the default smart host authentication mechanism.

The available usage types are as follows:

- **Custom**   Use this connector type in the following situations:
    - When a Hub Transport or Edge Transport server needs to send email to a third-party smart host.
    - When you are configuring a Send connector for an Edge Transport server that sends email to an external relay domain.
    - When an Edge Transport server that is not subscribed to a Hub Transport server sends email traffic to a Hub Transport server.
    - When you need to send messages from a Hub Transport server in one forest to a Hub Transport server in another forest when supporting a cross-forest deployment.
    - When you need to send messages from a Hub Transport server in one forest to an Exchange 2003 bridgehead server in another forest.
- **Internal**   Use this connector type when you need to configure an Edge Transport server to send email to an Exchange 2003 bridgehead server. This usage type is also used when you set up an edge subscription.
- **Internet**   Use this for transport servers that send email to the Internet.
- **Partner**   Use this type when you need to configure an Edge Transport server to send messages to a domain for which you have configured mutual TLS authentication.

When you are using a shared address space, Send connectors for internal relay domains need to be configured on Hub Transport servers rather than Edge Transport servers. If you configure a Send connector for a shared address space internal relay domain on an Edge Transport server, you'll trigger a routing loop. If you are configuring cross-forest connectors, you'll need to set up a special user account in each forest so that the connectors can perform authentication.

> **MORE INFO** **CROSS-FOREST CONNECTORS**
>
> To learn more about the steps involved in configuring cross-forest connectors, consult the following TechNet article: *http://technet.microsoft.com/en-us/library/bb123546.aspx*.

Consider the following when setting up Send connectors for internal and external relay domains:

- When configuring an accepted domain as an internal relay domain, you need to create a Send connector for that accepted domain's address space. When you configure this special Send Connector, use a smart host with the address of the other messaging system's SMTP server. Configure the source server on this connector as a Hub Transport server.

- When configuring an accepted domain as an external relay domain, you need to create a Send connector for that accepted domain's address space. When you configure this special Send connector, use a smart host with the address of the target domain's SMTP server. Configure the source server on this connector as the Edge Transport server. If you do not take these steps, a routing loop will occur.

To create a Send connector, perform the following general steps:

1. In Exchange Management Console, select the Organization Configuration\Hub Transport node and then click New Send Connector in the Actions pane. The New Send Connector Wizard opens.

2. On the Introduction page, enter a name for the Send connector and then choose a usage type.

3. On the Address Space page, click Add to add an Address space. For example, when creating a Send connector for the Contoso.com domain, enter **Contoso.com** in the address space text box. You can also select the Include All Subdomains option. In the case of Contoso.com, this would mean that email domains such as Australia.contoso.com and Fiji.contoso.com would be included.

4. On the Network Settings page, specify whether DNS will be used to route mail or mail will be routed through a particular smart host. You can specify the smart host address either by IP address or FQDN. You can also configure the Send connector to use External DNS Lookup settings when resolving external addresses when using the Send connector.

5. On the Source Server page, specify which transport servers are going to function as the sources for the connector. If you are configuring a Send connector that is going to be used on an Edge Transport server to route email to hosts on the Internet, specify the Edge Transport server as the source server. If you are creating an internal send connector to route email messages to an SMTP server on your organization's internal network, specify a Hub Transport server that is in the same Active Directory site as the target SMTP server. Click New and then click Finish to complete the creation of the connector.

You can also create Send connectors using the *New-SendConnector* EMS cmdlet.

***MORE INFO* SEND CONNECTORS**

For more information on Send connectors, consult the following TechNet article:
http://technet.microsoft.com/en-us/library/aa998662.aspx.

Manage Receive Connectors

Receive connectors are used to receive message traffic from hosts on the Internet or from hosts on the internal network. When you deploy Exchange, Hub Transport servers are automatically configured with Receive connectors that allow them to receive email messages from other Hub Transport servers in the same Exchange organization as well as SMTP connections for authenticated clients on the local area network.

Unlike Send connectors, which replicate out across all Hub Transport servers in the organization, Receive connectors are configured on a per-server basis. If you want to create a Receive connector on an Edge Transport server, you'll need to configure the server locally rather than using the edge subscription process.

When you create a Receive connector, you need to specify a unique combination of local IP address, port bindings, and remote IP address range. You also need to choose a Receive connector usage type. The difference between the usage types is as follows:

- **Internet**   Use this usage type when you create a Receive connector on an Edge Transport server or a Hub Transport server that will receive messages directly from SMTP servers on the Internet. This type is also used when you configure an Edge Transport server to receive incoming email from an Exchange 2003 bridgehead server.

- **Client**   This usage type is used on the automatic receive connectors that are created on Hub Transport server to support client email applications that use POP3 or IMAP4. This connector receives email on TCP port 587.

- **Internal**   Use this usage type if you want to configure a Hub Transport server to receive email from an Exchange 2003 bridgehead server. You also use this usage type when you manually configure an Edge Transport server to receive messages from Hub Transport servers. Also use this connector type when configuring a Hub Transport server to receive messages from a third-party message transfer agent (MTA).

- **Partner** Use this usage type when you want to configure a Receive connector to receive email from a partner organization where you have configured mutual TLS authentication.
- **Custom** Use this usage type in the following scenarios:
  - When you want to to receive messages from Hub Transport servers in another Exchange organization on the local network
  - When you want to receive messages from an Exchange 2003 bridgehead server in another Exchange organization on the local network
  - When you want to receive messages on an Edge Transport server from a third-party Mail Transfer Agent (MTA)
  - When you want to configure an Edge Transport server to receive email messages from an external relay domain
  - When you want to configure an Edge Transport or Hub Transport server to receive connections from Microsoft Exchange Hosted Services

To create a new Receive connector, perform the following general steps:

1. In Exchange Management Console, select the Organization Configuration\Server Configuration\Hub Transport node.

2. Select the Hub Transport server on which you wish to create the new Receive connector and then click New Receive Connector in the Actions pane. This will launch the New Receive Connector Wizard.

3. On the Introduction page, enter a name for the Receive connector and choose the intended use of the connector from the available usage types.

4. On the Local Network Settings page, click Add. Specify which IP addresses of the local server the Receive connector will listen for traffic on. The default is to listen on all network interfaces.

5. On the Remote Network Settings page, click Add to specify the IP address or IP address range of the remote servers that the Receive connector will accept traffic from. The default value is to accept traffic from all IP addresses. Click New to create the Receive connector and then click Finish.

You can also use the *New-ReceiveConnector* EMS cmdlet to create a new Receive connector.

MORE INFO   RECEIVE CONNECTORS

For more information on Receive connectors, consult the following TechNet article: *http://technet.microsoft.com/en-us/library/aa996395.aspx.*

Message Size Restrictions

You can limit the size of messages that transport servers process. You can create limits based on the total message size, or the size of individual components such as message header size, attachment size, or number of recipients. You can apply message size restrictions globally; on a per Hub Transport or Edge Transport server basis; to a specific connector, such as an Active Directory IP site link; or to a user object.

The following message size limits apply by default to an Exchange Server 2010 organization:

- **Maximum size for received messages** 10 MB. Configure this setting using the *Set-TransportConfig* EMS cmdlet with the *MaxReceiveSize* parameter. You can also configure this setting by selecting the Hub Transport node under Organization Configuration in EMC, selecting the Global Settings tab, clicking Transport Settings and then clicking Properties in the Actions pane. This will bring up the Transport Settings Properties dialog box, shown in Figure 2-20.

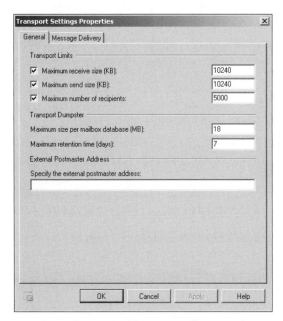

FIGURE 2-20 Transport settings properties

- **Maximum size for sent messages** 10 MB. Configure this setting using the *Set-TransportConfig* EMS cmdlet with the *MaxSendSize* parameter. This setting can also be configured on the Transport Settings Properties dialog box.

- **Maximum number of recipients per message** 5,000. Configure this setting using the *Set-TransportConfig* EMS cmdlet with the *MaxRecipientEnvelopeLimit* parameter. This setting can also be configured on the Transport Settings Properties dialog box.

- **Maximum attachment size in Transport rules** Not configured by default. Set a maximum attachment size using the *New-TransportRule* or *Set-TransportRule* cmdlet with the *AttachmentSizeOver* parameter.

- **Maximum header size through a Receive connector** 64 KB. Set a maximum header size using the *New-ReceiveConnector* or *Set-ReceiveConnector* cmdlet with the *MaxHeaderSize* parameter. You can also configure this setting in EMC by navigating to the Server Configuration\Hub Transport node and editing the properties of the Receive connector that you wish to configure.

- **Maximum message size through a Receive connector** 10 MB. Configure this setting using the *New-ReceiveConnector* or *Set-ReceiveConnector* cmdlet with the *MaxMessageSize* parameter.

- **Maximum recipients per Receive connector** 200 for Default Client Receive Connector, 5,000 for the Default Receive Connector on Hub Transport servers, 200 for the Default Receive connector on Edge Transport servers. Configure this setting using the *New-ReceiveConnector* or *Set-ReceiveConnector* cmdlet with the *MaxRecipients-PerMessage* parameter.

- **Maximum message size through a Send connector** 10 MB. Configure this setting using the *New-SendConnector* or *Set-SendConnector* cmdlet with the *MaxMessageSize* parameter.

To configure the maximum message size:

- For an Active Directory site link, use the *Set-ADSiteLink* cmdlet with the *MaxMessageSize* parameter.

- For a Routing Group connector, use the *Set-RoutingGroupConnector* cmdlet with the *MaxMessageSize* parameter.

- For a Delivery Agent connector, use the *New-DeliveryAgentConnector* or *Set-DeliveryAgentConnector* cmdlet with the *MaxMessageSize* parameter.

- For a foreign connector, use the *Set-ForeignConnector* cmdlet with the *MaxMessageSize* parameter.

To configure the maximum header size for messages in the pickup directory of a specific Hub Transport or Edge Transport server, use the *Set-TransportServer* cmdlet with the *PickupDirectoryMaxHeaderSize* parameter. To configure the maximum number of recipients per message for messages in the pickup directory, use the *Set-TransportServer* cmdlet with the *PickupDirectoryMaxRecipientsPerMessage* parameter.

MORE INFO **MESSAGE SIZE RESTRICTIONS**

For more information on understanding message size restrictions, consult the following TechNet article: *http://technet.microsoft.com/en-us/library/bb124345.aspx*.

Special Case Scenarios

Some Exchange designs need to account for special case scenarios. Some of these configurations, such as setting up a Hub Transport server to receive email messages from SMTP servers on the Internet, are not recommended but are theoretically possible. In this section you'll learn about three special case scenarios: Exchange Hosted Services, anonymous email relay, and direct Internet mail flow.

Internet Mail Flow Through Exchange Hosted Services

An increasing number of organizations are configuring Exchange so that they use both on-premises devices as well as a partial deployment through Exchange Hosted Services. Exchange Hosted Services offers the following services:

- **Hosted Filtering**   This service allows organizations to protect themselves from malware transmitted in email by having it sanitized in the cloud prior to reaching your local network.

- **Hosted Archive**   This service allows organizations to meet retention objectives by storing messages offsite in the cloud.

- **Hosted Encryption**   This service allows organizations to encrypt data as a method of preserving confidentiality.

- **Hosted Continuity**   This service allows organizations to ensure access to email during and after disaster occurrence.

You can configure Internet mail flow through Exchange Hosted Services to your organization by creating a Send connector and a Receive connector between your Hub Transport servers and the hosted Exchange Services server. Use the Custom usage type on both the Send connector and the Receive connector. You have to configure the Externally Secured authentication type for Exchange Hosted Services because the Basic authentication type is not supported. To set up this connection, you'll also need to configure an IPsec or VPN connection between your Hub Transport services and the Exchange Hosted Services servers in the cloud.

> **MORE INFO**   **MAIL FLOW AND EXCHANGE HOSTED SERVICES**
>
> To learn more about configuring Internet mail flow through Exchange Hosted Services, consult the following TechNet article: *http://technet.microsoft.com/en-us/library/bb738161.aspx*.

Deploying Email Relay

Anonymous relay allows a transport server to route messages for domains that aren't configured as accepted domains. It may be necessary to configure anonymous relay for some internal third-party email services, but in general enabling anonymous relay through a Send connector is considered to be a security risk. To configure anonymous relay, perform the following general steps:

1. Create a Receive connector using the Custom usage type. Use the IP address range 0.0.0.0 - 255.255.255.255 for the Remote Network Settings entry.

2. After you create the Receive connector, edit the properties of the connector. On the Permissions Groups tab, ensure that Anonymous Users is selected.

3. Use Exchange Management Shell to grant the relay permission on the connector. For example, to grant the relay permission on a Receive connector named AnonRelay, use the following command:

```
Get-ReceiveConnector "AnonRelay" | Add-ADPermission -User "NT AUTHORITY\ANONYMOUS
LOGON" -ExtendedRights "MS-Exch-SMTP-Accept-Any-Recipient"
```

MORE INFO   **ANONYMOUS RELAY ON A RECEIVE CONNECTOR**

For more information on setting up email relay, consult the following TechNet article: *http://technet.microsoft.com/en-us/library/bb232021.aspx.*

Direct Internet Mail Flow

Although it is not recommended, you can configure Hub Transport servers to accept email messages directly from hosts on the Internet. To do this, perform the following general steps:

- Create a Send connector that routes mail directly to the Internet from the Hub Transport server.

- Modify the default Receive connector so that it will accept mail from the Internet. To do this, edit the properties of the default Receive connector and on the Permissions tab ensure that the Anonymous Users group has access, as shown in Figure 2-21.

- Configure your organization's firewalls to ensure that the Hub Transport server can accept TCP port 25 traffic from hosts on the Internet. Also ensure that that the MX record associated with the DNS email domain points at the public IP address the Hub Transport server will receive email on.

MORE INFO   **DIRECT INTERNET MAIL FLOW**

To learn more about configuring direct Internet mail flow to a Hub Transport server, consult the following TechNet link: *http://technet.microsoft.com/en-us/library/bb738138.aspx.*

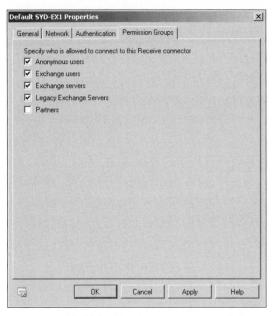

FIGURE 2-21 Modifying Receive connector permissions

EXAM TIP

Understand the types of connectors that you need to set up to support routing in a cross-forest Exchange topology.

Objective Summary

- Ensure that there is at least one Hub Transport server in every site where there is a mailbox server on a per-forest basis.

- Transport rules allow you to process messages according to the properties of those messages, such as sender, recipient, or message content.

- Remote domains allow you to control message formatting options as well as whether users in remote domains receive out-of-office messages.

- Send connectors provide a path for outgoing messages. You can configure Send connectors to route email through smart hosts and configure what type of authentication they use.

- Receive connectors accept incoming SMTP traffic. You can configure a Receive connector to accept messages from a specific source and configure the authentication that is required.

- You can configure message limits such as maximum message size and maximum number of recipients on a per Hub or Edge Transport server basis, on a per-connector basis, or on a per Active Directory IP site link basis.

Objective Review

Answer the following questions to test your knowledge of the information in this objective. You can find the answers to these questions and explanations of why each answer choice is correct or incorrect in the "Answers" section at the end of this chapter.

1. You are in the process of designing an Exchange Server 2010 deployment. You want to ensure that automatic replies and out-of-office messages will be transmitted to recipients in external organizations. Which of the following Exchange elements would you configure to accomplish this goal?

   A. Accepted domains

   B. Remote domains

   C. Send connectors

   D. Receive connectors

2. Which of the following Exchange components would you use to ensure that users in your organization are unable to send messages that mention the name of a new product to people outside the organization?

   A. Remote domains

   B. Send connectors

   C. Receive connectors

   D. Transport rules

3. Your organization has two Active Directory forests that spread across three branch sites. Each forest has two domains. Each forest will have its own Exchange 2010 organization. You intend to deploy a mailbox server for each organization in each branch site. What is the minimum number of Hub Transport servers that you need to deploy to support this configuration?

   A. 1

   B. 3.

   C. 6

   D. 12

4. You are the Exchange administrator for Contoso, Ltd. You want to configure your organization so that messages addressed to recipients in the adatum.com mail domain are routed to a third-party messaging system hosted on your organization's internal network. Which of the following steps do you need to take to accomplish this goal? (Choose two. Each answer forms part of a complete solution.)

   A. Configure adatum.com as an accepted internal relay domain.

   B. Configure adatum.com as an accepted external relay domain.

   C. Create a Send connector for the adatum.com domain and specify a Hub Transport server as the source server.

   D. Create a Send connector for the adatum.com domain and specify an Edge Transport server as the source server.

5. Which Exchange Management Shell cmdlet would you use to set the maximum size of a message attachment to 5 MB?

   A. *Set-TransportConfig*

   B. *New-TransportRule*

   C. *Set-TransportServer*

   D. *Set-ADSiteLink*

In the following thought experiment, you will apply what you've learned about the objective "Deploy Hub Transport Server Role" to determine how to best use the Hub Transport server role to meet Contoso, Ltd's needs. You can find answers to these questions in the "Answers" section at the end of this chapter.

Contoso has two Active Directory forests, Contoso.local and Contoso.internal. Each forest has an Exchange 2010 organization. The Contoso.local forest has Active Directory sites in the cities of Brisbane, Adelaide, and Perth. The Contoso.internal forest has Active Directory sites in Melbourne and Canberra. The Sydney location has computers and servers, some of which are members of the Contoso.local forest and others of which are members of the Contoso.internal forest.

Each branch office except Sydney will have one Exchange 2010 mailbox server. The Sydney branch office will have two mailbox servers. Each Sydney mailbox server will be a member of a different Exchange organization.

You plan to deploy an Edge Transport server on the Sydney branch office's perimeter network. You plan to subscribe this Edge Transport server to a Hub Transport server in the Contoso.local forest.

With this in mind, answer the following questions:

1. What is the total minimum number of Hub Transport servers that you need to deploy at all Contoso, Ltd., branch offices?

2. On which branch office's Hub Transport servers would you deploy the cross-forest connectors?

3. Which branch office's Hub Transport server should you configure with an edge subscription?

4. What kind of accepted domain would you configure for the Contoso.com email domain in the Contoso.local Exchange organization?

5. What address space would you configure for the cross-forest Send connectors that you deploy?

6. Which server should you configure as the source server for the cross-forest Send connector that you create in the Contoso.local Exchange organization?

Objective 2.5: Deploy Mailbox Server Role

After you've determined where you want to place your organization's mailbox servers, you need to actually get around to deploying the servers that will host them. After you deploy the mailbox servers, you have to configure the mailbox databases that will host mailboxes. It's always better to have configuration settings such as mailbox quotas and deleted item retention configured prior to deploying mailboxes rather than trying to apply policies after a substantial number of mailboxes are in use. In this section you'll learn about mailbox server deployment and mailbox database configuration as well as address list, offline address book, and public folder deployment.

> **This objective covers:**
> - Deploy mailbox servers.
> - Deploy mailbox databases.
> - Database configuration.
> - Mailbox provisioning and placement policies.
> - Deploy Address Lists and Offline Address Books.
> - Deploy Public Folders.
> - Validate Mailbox Server Access.

Deploy Mailbox Servers

Servers that host the Exchange Server 2010 Mailbox server role must be members of an Active Directory domain. You can co-locate the Mailbox server role on a computer that also hosts the Hub Transport and Client Access Server roles. When you do this, you need to ensure that you adequately provision the server with RAM to support this configuration. You can also use Database Availability Groups with mailbox servers that host these roles, which is different from Exchange 2007 where you couldn't deploy the clustered mailbox server role with the Hub Transport and Client Access Server roles. As you'll learn in Chapter 4, you don't need to do much in the way of special configuration to make an Exchange Server 2010 Mailbox server highly available.

You can deploy mailbox servers on traditional physical hosts, hosted as virtual machines, on a server with the Hyper-V role installed, or as virtual machines in a properly configured private or public cloud. For Exchange Server 2010 SP1, The host operating system can run Windows Server 2008 with Service Pack 2, or Windows Server 2008 R2.

The Mailbox role requires the following roles, role services, and features:

- RSAT Tools
- .NET Framework 3.5.1

- Web Server
- Web Server Basic Authentication
- Web Server Windows Authentication
- IIS 6 Metabase Compatibility
- Web Server .NET Extensibility
- IIS 6 Management Console
- Windows Process Activation Service Process Model

You also need to install the Microsoft Filter Pack to support the Mailbox server role. For Exchange 2010 RTM, you use the 2007 Office System Converter: Microsoft Filter Pack. For Exchange 2010 SP1 or later, you use the Microsoft Office 2010 filter packs. Filters are used by Exchange Search to index mail attachments on mailbox servers. These filter packs can be downloaded from Microsoft's website.

> **MORE INFO** **MICROSOFT OFFICE FILTER PACK**
>
> To learn more about Exchange Server SP1 and Microsoft Office Filter Pack 2010, consult the following post on the Exchange team blog: *http://blogs.technet.com/b/exchange/archive/2011/08/02/exchange-server-and-sp1-for-microsoft-office-filter-pack-2010.aspx.*

Deploy Mailbox Databases

A user must be assigned the Organization Management role to be able to create and manage mailbox or public folder databases in an organization-wide capacity. A user who has been assigned the Server Management role is able to create mailbox and public folder databases on the server where she has been delegated this permission. A server running the standard version of Exchange 2010 can support up to five mailbox databases, or four mailbox databases and one public folder database. A server running the Enterprise edition of Exchange 2010 can support 100 mailbox databases, or 99 mailbox databases and 1 public folder database.

Deploying a mailbox database involves providing the mailbox database with a name that is unique within the Exchange organization, specifying a path for the mailbox database file, and specifying a path for the transaction log files. If you are not using redundant storage, consider deploying transaction logs to folders on another hard disk, which will minimize the chance that you will lose both the database and the transaction logs in the event of disk failure.

To deploy a mailbox database, perform the following general steps:

1. Navigate to the Organization Configuration\Mailbox node in EMC.

2. In the Actions pane, click New Mailbox Database. This will launch the New Mailbox Database Wizard.

3. On the Introduction page, enter a name for the mailbox database. This name needs to be unique within your Exchange organization, not just unique on the mailbox server. Click Browse next to Server Name to specify the mailbox server on which you will place the new mailbox database. If you do not choose a server, the mailbox database will be placed on the first available mailbox server. Click Next.

4. On the Set Paths page, shown in Figure 2-22, specify the mailbox database file path and the log folder path. This is the path on the local mailbox server that you selected in step 3. By default, the database and log files are configured to use the same folder. By default, the mailbox database will be mounted after it is created. You can choose not to automatically mount a newly created mailbox database by clearing the Mount This Database check box on this page. Click Next, click New, and then click Finish.

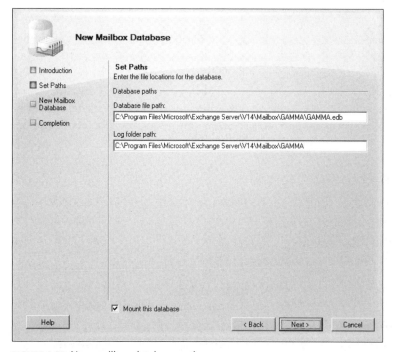

FIGURE 2-22 New mailbox database path

You can create a mailbox database from EMS using the *New-Mailbox* database cmdlet. For example, to create a mailbox database named SYD-MBX-DB using the folder c:\SYD-MBX-DB for both the database and log files on the server SYD-MBX, use the following command:

```
New-MailboxDatabase -Server 'SYD-MBX' -Name 'SYD-MBX-DB' -EdbFilePath 'C:\SYD-MBX-DB\
SYD-MBX-DB.edb' -LogFolderPath 'C:\SYD-MBX-DB'
```

To mount this database once it has been created, use the *Mount-Database* cmdlet as follows:

```
Mount-Database -Identity 'SYD-MBX-DB'
```

To dismount the database, use the *Dismount-Database* cmdlet. For example, to dismount the SYD-MBX-DB database, use the following command:

```
Dismount-Database -Identity 'SYD-MBX-DB'
```

To remove a mailbox database, either click the mailbox database in Exchange Management Console and then click Remove in the Actions pane, or use the *Remove-MailboxDatabase* cmdlet.

You can use EMC or EMS to change the mail database path as well as the path of the associated log files. When you move a database, the database will automatically dismount and will be unavailable to users. After the move is complete, the database will automatically remount. This will not occur if the database was in a dismounted state prior to initiating the move. You need to be logged on locally to the mailbox server to move the mailbox database. To move a mailbox database using EMC, perform the following general steps:

1. Select the mailbox database that you want to move on the Database Management tab when the Organization Configuration\Mailbox node is in focus.

2. Click Move Database Path on the Actions pane.

3. In the Move Database Path dialog box, enter the new path for the database file and log folder as shown in Figure 2-23. When prompted to allow a database dismount, click Yes. Click Finish when the move is complete.

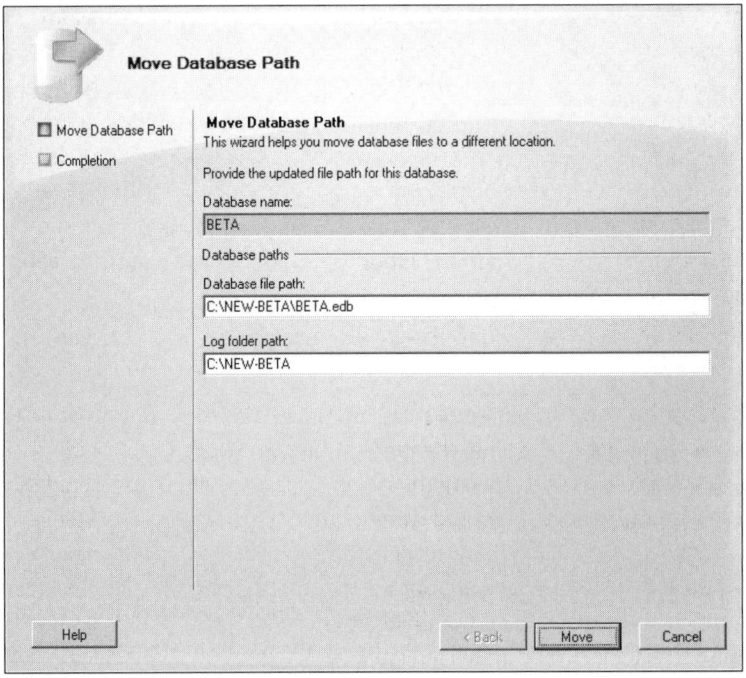

FIGURE 2-23 Move database path

You can also move mailbox databases and associated log file paths using the *Move-DatabasePath* cmdlet. For example, to move the mailbox database SYD-MBX-DB and its associated log files to the path e:\SYD-MBX-DB, use the following command:

```
Move-DatabasePath -Identity 'SYD-MBX-DB' -EdbFilePath 'E:\SYD-MBX-DB\SYD-MBX-DB.edb'
-LogFolderPath 'E:\SYD-MBX-DB'
```

> *MORE INFO*   **MANAGING MAILBOX DATABASES**
>
> To learn more about managing mailbox databases, consult the following article on TechNet: *http://technet.microsoft.com/en-us/library/dd351078.aspx*.

Database Configuration and Quota Policies

You can view the properties of a mailbox database navigating to the Organization Configuration\Mailbox node of EMC, clicking the Database Management Tab, selecting the database, and then clicking Properties in the Actions pane:

- The General tab provides you with information about the database path: when the database was last backed up, the server that hosts the mailbox database and, if the database is a member of a Database Availability Group (DAG), details of other DAG copies.

- The Maintenance tab allows you to specify a journal recipient for the mailbox database, the maintenance schedule, background database maintenance, whether the database is mounted at startup, whether the database can be overwritten by a restore, and whether circular logging is enabled. Circular logging allows Exchange to overwrite transaction log files when the data stored in the log files in written to the database. This reduces the storage requirements, but it also means that you'll only be able to recover to the last full backup. Best practice is to use backup for log truncation rather than circular logging. You'll learn more about recovery in Chapter 4. You'll learn more about journaling in Chapter 5.

- The Client Settings tab allows you to specify a default public folder database and offline address book.

- The Limits tab allows you to configure mailbox quota limits on a per mailbox-database basis. You can set the warning limit, the prohibit send limit, and the prohibit send and receive limit. You can also specify the warning message interval, deleted item settings, deleted mailbox settings, and whether to block the deletion of items until the database has been backed up. These settings are the most influential when it comes to estimating the database size. To work out the theoretical maximum (not including log file data), multiply the prohibit and send limit by the number of mailboxes hosted in the database. The limits tab is shown in Figure 2-24.

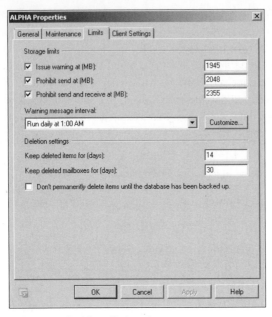

FIGURE 2-24 Database limits tab

You can also configure mailbox database properties using the *Set-MailboxDatabase* cmdlet. Some useful storage-related parameters that you can use in association with this cmdlet include:

- **DeletedItemRetention**   How long deleted items are retained before being purged
- **IssueWarningQuota**   Threshold value at which Exchange will issue a quota warning
- **MailboxRetention**   How long Exchange will retain deleted mailboxes
- **ProhibitSendQuota**   Threshold quota value where Exchange will block user from sending messages
- **ProhibitSendReceiveQuota**   Threshold quota value where Exchange will block user from sending or receiving messages
- **RetainDeletedItemsUntilBackup**   Determines whether Exchange will retain deleted items until a database backup occurs

Database Mailbox Provisioning Policies

If you create a new mailbox but don't specify which mailbox database the mailbox should be deployed to, a mailbox database will be selected in a load-balanced manner by the Mailbox Resources Management Agent. For example, if you run a script that creates 100 mailboxes without specifying a mailbox database, and your organization has four mailbox databases, the Mailbox Resources Management Agent will spread the new mailboxes equally across these mailbox databases, provisioning each mailbox database with approximately 25 new mailboxes.

In some cases you will want to exclude or suspend a particular mailbox database from the load balanced provisioning process. You can accomplish this using the *Set-MailboxDatabase* cmdlet with either the *IsExcludedFromProvisioning* or *IsSuspendedFromProvisioning* parameter. You use the *IsExcludedFromProvisioning* parameter when you want to permanently exclude a specific mailbox database from automatic provisioning. You can still manually add mailboxes to the database, but an excluded database won't be used by the Mailbox Resources Management Agent when no mailbox database is specified for a new mailbox. For example, to exclude mailbox database SYD-MBX-DB-ALPHA from provisioning, use the following command:

```
Set-MailboxDatabase -Identity SYD-MBX-DB-ALPHA -IsExcludedFromProvisioning:$true
```

If, instead of excluding, you want to temporarily suspend a specific mailbox database from provisioning, use the *IsSuspendedFromProvisioning* parameter. For example, to temporarily suspend mailbox database MEL-MBX-DB-ALPHA from provisioning, use the following command:

```
Set-MailboxDatabase -Identity SYD-MBX-DB-ALPHA -IsSuspendedFromProvisioning:$true
```

When you want to remove the suspension from the mailbox database, use the *$false* option with the *IsSuspendedFromProvisioning* parameter.

MORE INFO   SET-MAILBOXDATABASE

To learn more about the *Set-MailboxDatabase* cmdlet, consult the following TechNet article: *http://technet.microsoft.com/en-us/library/bb123971.aspx*.

Deploy Address Lists

Address lists are collections of Exchange objects. Address lists can include multiple object types, including users, contacts, groups, public folders, equipment mailboxes, and other items addressable within Exchange. You primarily use address lists to organize recipients in such a way that users within your organization can locate them more quickly. Address lists use queries based on object properties and hence are updated dynamically. For example, you can create an address list that includes all recipients that have the label Accountants associated with their Active Directory account's department attribute. Whenever a new user has his account configured with this attribute, he will be added to this address list. Whenever a user account is removed from Active Directory or the account's department attribute changes, the user will be removed from this particular address list.

Address lists are stored within Active Directory and are not directly available to offline users. It is possible to create Offline Address Books that provide address lists as they existed at the point in time when the offline address book was created. You'll learn more about Offline Address Books later in this chapter.

Address lists are available through the Address Book in Outlook 2007 and Outlook 2010. Exchange creates the following default address lists:

- **All Contacts**   This list contains all mail-enabled contacts in your Exchange organization.
- **All Groups**   This list contains all mail-enabled groups in your Exchange organization.
- **All Rooms**   This list contains all objects that have been designated as rooms within your Exchange organization.
- **All Users**   This list contains all mailbox users, mail-enabled users, room mailboxes, and equipment mailboxes in your organization. Mail-enabled users are users that have external email addresses. All Users is similar to All Contacts, except mail-enabled users have logon credentials.
- **Default Global Address List**   This list contains all recipients in the Exchange organization.
- **Public Folders**   This list contains all mail-enabled public folders.

In larger organizations users are likely to want to find people within specific departments rather than searching through every address in the organization in an attempt to locate the people to whom they want to send a message. To meet this goal, you can create custom address lists that hold only a specific subset of recipient objects, such as an address list that holds all the names of mailbox users at a specific site, or an address list that lists all room mailboxes in a particular building. Recipient objects can be members of multiple address lists.

You should carefully plan the deployment of address lists in your organization. Poorly planned address lists can annoy users more than they help them. When developing address lists, keep the following in mind:

- You should avoid creating so many address lists that users end up confused as to which list will hold the address they are looking for.
- Provide address lists with meaningful names. Users should be able to quickly identify what sort of recipients are contained within a list.
- Remind users that they can always use the GAL to find a user if they can't locate them in a specific address list.

To create an address list using EMC, perform the following steps:

1. Navigate to the Organization Configuration\Mailbox node and click New Address List in the Actions pane.

2. On the Introduction page, provide a name for the address list and a display name. You can also create the address list as a container so that it can hold other address lists. For example, you might create an address list container named Queensland and then create address lists under the Queensland container for different offices in that state. Click Next.

3. On the New Address List page, specify whether the list will only apply to objects within a particular OU or domain, or whether it will apply to objects throughout the organization. Choose what recipient types will be included. You can choose between the following:

   - Users with Exchange mailboxes
   - Users with external email addresses
   - Resource mailboxes
   - Contacts with external email addresses
   - Mail-enabled groups

4. On the conditions page select which conditions will be used to limit the scope of the address list. You can choose to limit the scope based on recipient Active Directory attributes including State or Province, Department, Company, or a custom attribute value. It is not necessary to limit the scope of the address list, for example if you've already chosen the address list to apply to all objects within a particular OU.

5. On the Schedule page, select whether you want to create the address list but not apply it to recipients, create the address list immediately, or have the address list created later at a specified time. You can also use this page to terminate any address list tasks that have taken more than a specified number of hours to complete. Click Next, click New, and when the address list is created, click Finish.

You can create address lists from EMS by using the *New-AddressList* cmdlet. For example, to create an address list named QueenslandAddresses that will include all mailbox users that have their *State/Province* attribute set to Queensland, use the following command:

```
New-AddressList -Name QueenslandAddresses -RecipientFilter {((RecipientType -eq
'UserMailbox') -and (StateOrProvince -eq 'Queensland'))}
```

Once you've created the address list, you need to apply it using the *Update-AddressList* cmdlet. You can also do this using the Apply Address List Wizard, available from the Actions pane in EMC.

EXAM TIP

Remember that specifying State or Province, Department, or Company conditions means that your address list will automatically exclude mail-enabled distribution groups. This is because these attributes are only applicable to mailboxes, mail users, and mail contacts.

MORE INFO ADDRESS LISTS

To learn more about address lists, consult the following TechNet web page:
http://technet.microsoft.com/en-us/library/bb232119.aspx.

Deploy Offline Address Books

An Offline Address Book (OAB) is a collection of address lists that can be used by a Microsoft Outlook user when they aren't connected to the Exchange organization. You can distribute OABs to users either through web-based distribution or public folder distribution.

Web-based distribution is suitable for clients using Outlook 2007 and Outlook 2010 functioning in Cached Exchange Mode, through a dial-up or cellular connection, or which are completely offline. If your organization only supports only clients running Outlook 2007 or Outlook 2010, you can rely solely on web-based distribution. Web-based distribution has the benefit of supporting more concurrent client connections as well as using less bandwidth than public folder distribution.

CAS distribute OABs through the OAB virtual directory. This virtual directory is created in the default website on the CAS. If you need to distribute OABs to clients outside the organizational network, you can use the *New-OABVirtualDirectory* cmdlet to create a new external website that will be accessible to these clients. When the OAB is generated, it replicates to all of the selected OAB virtual directories on CAS servers within the Exchange organization.

If your organization needs to support Outlook 2003 clients that are working offline or through low-bandwidth dialup or cellular connections, OABs will be distributed through public folders. The necessary public folder infrastructure will be created during the Exchange installation process if you indicate that you need to support Outlook 2003 clients, or if you are deploying Exchange in a mixed environment.

To create an OAB using EMC, perform the following general steps:

1. Select the Organization Configuration\Mailbox node and then click New Offline Address Book in the Actions pane.

2. On the Introduction page, shown in Figure 2-25, specify the OAB name, whether the default Global Address List will be included, and whether any other address lists will be included. You can also select a specific Mailbox server to perform OAB generation. When you have configured these settings, click Next.

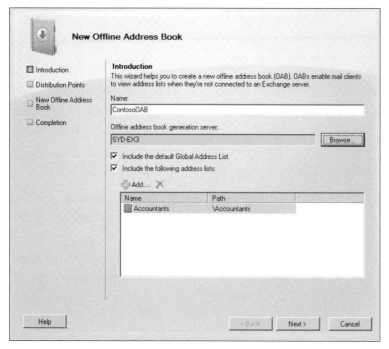

FIGURE 2-25 New OAB

3. On the Distribution points page, select Enable Web-Based Distribution and/or Enable Public Folder Distribution. If you choose to enable web-based distribution, click Add to select which Client Access Server OAB virtual directories you will use for distribution. Click Next, click New, and then click Finish.

You can use the *New-OfflineAddressBook* cmdlet to create an OAB. For example, to create an OAB named ContosoOAB that uses the default GAL and the Accountants address list and will be distributed from the CAS SYD-EX1 and generated on server SYD-MBX1, use the following command:

```
New-OfflineAddressBook –Name 'ContosoOAB' –Server 'SYD-MBX1' –AddressLists
'\Default Global Address List','\Accountants' –PublicFolderDistributionEnabled $false
–VirtualDirectories 'SYD-EX1\OAB (Default Web Site)'
```

> **MORE INFO** **OFFLINE ADDRESS BOOKS**
>
> For more information on OABs consult the following TechNet webpage:
> *http://technet.microsoft.com/en-us/library/bb232155.aspx.*

Deploy Public Folders

Public folder database are created by default in mixed environments, or if you specify that your Exchange organization needs to support Outlook 2003 or Microsoft Entourage the first time you deploy Exchange 2010. Public folders are required if these client programs are used for the purposes of supporting calendar free/busy information and OAB distribution.

Each Exchange mailbox server can host a maximum of one Public Folder database. You can create a public folder database using EMC by performing the following general steps:

1. Navigate to the Organization Configuration\Mailbox node and then click New Public Folder Database in the Actions pane.

2. On the Introduction page, enter a name for the public folder database. This name must be unique within the Exchange organization. Click Browse to specify the Mailbox server that will host the public folder database. Click Next.

3. On the Set Paths page, either accept the default database file and log folder path or specify an alternative. You can also use this page to choose whether you want the public folder database mounted after creation. Click Next, click New, and then click Finish.

You can create a public folder database from EMS by using the *New-PublicFolderDatabase* cmdlet. To create a public folder database named SYD-PF-DB, placing both the log files and the database file in the e:\SYD-PF-DB folder on server SYD-EX1, issue the following command:

```
New-PublicFolderDatabase -Server 'SYD-EX1' -Name 'SYD-PF-DB' -EdbFilePath 'E:\SYD-PF-DB\
SYD-PF-DB.edb' -LogFolderPath 'E:\SYD-PF-DB'
```

Prior to removing a public folder database, you need to remove any public folder replicas hosted in the database as well as remove all public folders in the database. After these items have been removed, you can use the *Remove-PublicFolderDatabase* cmdlet to remove the database, or you can remove the public folder database by selecting it when you have navigated to the Organization\Configuration node in EMC and clicking Remove in the Actions pane.

After you've created a public folder database, you can deploy public folders. To create a public folder using EMC, perform the following general steps:

1. Navigate to the Toolbox node and double-click the Public Folder Management Console item.

2. Click Default Public Folders. If you want to create a folder within an existing hierarchy, navigate to the folder that will serve as the parent of the folder that you want to create. Click New Pub Folder in the Actions pane.

3. In the New Public Folder Wizard, shown in Figure 2-26, enter the name of the public folder and then click New.

You can use the *New-PublicFolder* EMS cmdlet to create new public folders. For example, to create a new public folder called Accounting under the existing ContosoDocs folder on server syd-ex1.contoso.com, issue the following command:

```
New-PublicFolder -Name 'Accounting' -Path '\ContosoDocs' -Server 'syd-ex1.contoso.com'
```

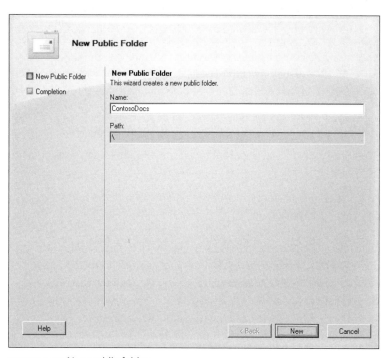

FIGURE 2-26 New public folder

> **MORE INFO** **PUBLIC FOLDERS**
>
> For more information about public folders, consult the following TechNet article:
> *http://technet.microsoft.com/en-us/library/bb397221.aspx.*

Configure Public Folder Replication

Public folder replication ensures that the public folder hierarchy and public folder content is regularly transmitted to other public folder databases in your organization. You can use public folder replication as a way of making public folder content highly available. You can't enroll public folder databases into Database Availability Groups (DAGS) in the same way that you can Exchange 2010 mailbox databases. Public folder content and public folder hierarchy replicate independently.

Each public folder database keeps a copy of the public folder hierarchy. Each public folder database also stores metadata about which public folder databases in the organization host local copies of specific public folders. Public folder hierarchy replication triggers automatically when the name of a public folder changes, a replica list is modified, a public folder is moved, or folder permissions are updated.

A content replica is a copy of a public folder hosted in another public folder database that includes all of that public folder's content. You can replicate content replicas selectively, duplicating the public folder and its contents on some, but not all, public folder databases within your organization. Unlike hierarchy replication, which triggers when there are specific changes, public folder content replication occurs on a schedule that is usually set at the database level.

To configure public folder replication, perform the following general steps:

1. Navigate to the Toolbox node of EMC and double-click the Public Folder Management Console item.

2. In the Public Folder Management Console, click the parent node of the folder for which you want to configure replication.

3. Select the folder that you want to replicate in the middle pane and then click Properties in the Actions pane.

4. On the Replication tab of the folder's properties, shown in Figure 2-27, click Add and then select the additional public folder databases to which you will replicate the public folder.

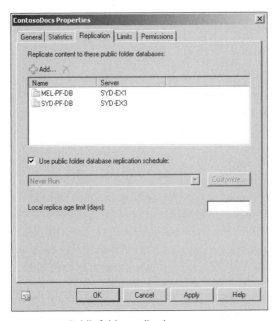

FIGURE 2-27 Public folder replication

You can use the *Set-PublicFolder* cmdlet with the *Replicas* parameter to specify which public folder databases are associated with a specific public folder. Be aware that this command can remove the current public folder databases if they are not included with the list. For example, if a public folder named ContosoDocs is already hosted by the public folder database MEL-PF-DB and you wanted to also have it replicate to the public folder database SYD-PF-DB, you would use the following command:

```
Set-PublicFolder -Identity '\ContosoDocs' -Replicas 'MEL-PF-DB','SYD-PF-DB'
```

By default, Exchange public folders replicate every 15 minutes. It is possible to configure replication at either the public folder database level or at the individual public folder level. Schedules configured at the public folder level override those configured at the public folder database level. You can configure the replication interval at the database level on the Replication tab of the public folder's database properties as shown in Figure 2-28. You can configure the replication interval at the public folder level on the public folder's Replication tab, which was shown earlier in Figure 2-27. From the drop-down list you can select Always Run, Never Run, Run Every Hour, Run Every 2 Hours, Run Every 4 Hours, or Use Custom Schedule. The custom schedule option allows you to configure replication to occur at specific times of the day.

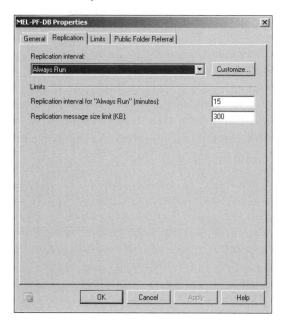

FIGURE 2-28 Public folder database replication

You can configure the public folder database replication interval using the *Set-Public-FolderDatabase* cmdlet with the *ReplicationPeriod* and *ReplicationSchedule* parameters. You can configure replication at the individual public folder level from EMS by using the *Set-PublicFolder* cmdlet with the *ReplicationSchedule* parameter.

You can use the *Suspend-PublicFolderReplication* cmdlet to suspend content replication. You can resume suspended content replication by using the *Resume-PublicFolderReplication* cmdlet. You can trigger public folder hierarchy replication using the *Update-PublicFolder-Hierarchy* cmdlet. You can force a particular public folder replica to update using the *Update-PublicFolder* cmdlet or by right-clicking the replica in the Public Folder Management Console and then selecting Update Content.

> **MORE INFO**   **PUBLIC FOLDER REPLICATION**
>
> For more information about public folder replication, consult the following TechNet article: *http://technet.microsoft.com/en-us/library/bb629523.aspx.*

Configure Public Folder Permissions

Public folder permissions determine what access rights a user has over a public folder or a public folder hierarchy. You assign public folder permissions by adding users to roles. The two types of roles are administrator roles and client access roles. The pre-defined client based public folder roles in Exchange 2010 are Owner, PublishingEditor, Editor, PublishingAuthor, Author, Non-EditingAuthor, Reviewer, and Contributor. The following list details the client access rights and the roles that are associated with those rights:

- **ReadItems**   The user is able to read items in the public folder. The Owner, PublishingEditor, Editor, PublishingAuthor, Author, Non-EditingAuthor, and Reviewer roles hold this right.

- **CreateItems**   The user is able to create items in the public folder and is also able to send email messages to the mail-enabled public folder. The Owner, PublishingEditor, Editor, PublishingAuthor, Author, Non-EditingAuthor, and Contributor roles hold this right.

- **EditOwnedItems**   The user is able to edit items that he or she owns in the public folder. The Owner, PublishingEditor, Editor, PublishingAuthor, and Author roles have this right.

- **DeleteOwnedItems**   The user is able to delete items that he or she owns in the public folder. The Owner, PublishingEditor, Editor, PublishingAuthor, and Author roles have this right.

- **EditAllItems**   The user is able to edit any item in the public folder. The Owner, PublishingEditor, and Editor roles have this right.

- **DeleteAllItems**   The user is able to delete any item in the public folder. The Owner, PublishingEditor, and PublishingAuthor roles have this right.

- **CreateSubfolders**   The user is able to create subfolders in the public folder. The Owner, PublishingEditor, and PublishingAuthor roles have this right.

- **FolderOwner**   The user is assigned ownership permission for the public folder, allowing him or her to view and move the public folder, create subfolders, and configure permissions on the folder. This permission does not allow the user to read, edit, delete, or create folder items. Only the Owner role has this right.

- **FolderContact**   The user is assigned as the contact for the public folder. Only the Owner role has this right.

- **FolderVisible**   The user is able to view the public folder, but can't read or edit items within the public folder. All roles have this right.

You can use the *Add-PublicFolderClientPermission* cmdlet to assign client permissions to a public folder. You do this on the basis of one of the client permission roles. For example, to assign the Kim_Akers user account the PublishingAuthor role on the Documents public folder, use the following command:

```
Add-PublicFolderClientPermission -Identity "\Documents" -AccessRights PublishingAuthor
-User Kim_Akers
```

You can grant administrators the right to manage public folders in two different ways. You can add a user to the Public Folder Management role group, either by adding her to the security group using Active Directory Users and Computers, or by using the *Add-RoleGroup-Member* cmdlet. You can also use the *Add-PublicFolderAdministrativePermission* cmdlet to assign the user permissions directly on specific public folders, rather than using the role group to assign permissions on an organization-wide basis. You can add the following permissions using the *Add-PublicFolderAdministrativePermission* cmdlet:

- **ModifyPublicFolderACL**   Modify the Client Access Server role permission on the public folder.

- **ModifyPublicFolderAdminACL**   Modify the administrator permissions on the public folder.

- **ModifyPublicFolderDeletedItemRetention**   Modify the deleted item retention attributes on the public folder.

- **ModifyPublicFolderExpiry**   Modify the expiration attributes of the public folder.

- **ModifyPublicFolderQuotas**   Modify the quota attributes of the public folder.

- **AdministerInformationStore**   Modify any public folder not defined previously.

- **AllExtendedRights**   Modify any public folder property.

For example, to grant the Kim_Akers user account administrative permissions over all public folders in the organization, use the following command:

```
Add-RoleGroupMember -Identity "Public Folder Management" -Member Kim_Akers
```

To grant the Kim_Akers user account administrative permissions over only the Documents public folder and all folders under that folder, use the following command:

```
Add-PublicFolderAdministrativePermission -Identity "\Documents" -User "Kim_Akers"
-AccessRights AllExtendedRights -InteritanceType SelfAndChildren
```

As the client and administrative permissions are separate from each other, you use different cmdlets to view those permissions. To view client permissions on a public folder, use the *Get-PublicFolderClientPermission* cmdlet. To view Administrative permissions on a public folder, use the *Get-PublicFolderAdministrativePermission* cmdlet.

> **MORE INFO** **PUBLIC FOLDER PERMISSIONS**
>
> For more information about public folder permissions, consult the following TechNet article: *http://technet.microsoft.com/en-us/library/ee633461.aspx*.

Validate Mailbox Server Access

The simplest way to check mailbox server access is to load up OWA in a browser and log on to a mailbox. In some situations, you might not have deployed a CAS server, or you might simply be interested in quickly checking whether mail flow is functioning properly. You can do this with the *Test-Mailflow* cmdlet.

For example, to test mail flow between mailbox servers SYD-EX1 and MEL-EX1, use the following command:

```
Test-Mailflow SYD-EX1 –TargetMailboxServer MEL-EX2
```

You can also test mail flow from a mailbox server to a specific Exchange mailbox. For example, to test mail flow from server SYD-EX1 to the kim_akers@contoso.com mailbox, use the following command:

```
Test-Mailflow SYD-EX1 –TargetEmailAddress kim_akers@contoso.com
```

You can test end-to-end Microsoft Outlook client connectivity without firing up Outlook by using the *Test-OutlookConnectivity* cmdlet. When you use this cmdlet, it also checks Outlook Anywhere (RPC/HTTP) and TCP-based connections. You can create a test user automatically by using the New-TestCasConnectivityUser.ps1 script located in the scripts folder. For example, to check Outlook connectivity using the HTTP protocol, issue the following command:

```
Test-OutlookConnectivity -Protocol:HTTP –GetDefaultsFromAutoDiscover:$true
```

> **MORE INFO** **TEST MAIL FLOW**
>
> For more information about testing mail flow, consult the following TechNet article: *http://technet.microsoft.com/en-us/library/aa995894.aspx*.

EXAM TIP

Remember the limit on the number of public folder databases that can be hosted on a single Exchange mailbox server.

Objective Summary

- Mailbox servers can be deployed on domain members that also host the Hub Transport and Client Access Server roles.

- You can temporarily suspend or exempt mailbox databases from being automatically provisioned with mailboxes using EMS.

- Address lists are used by clients to quickly locate recipient addresses. You can configure address lists based on filters to make it easier for users to locate addresses by category, rather than having to look through the entire Global Address List.

- Offline Address Books (OABs) allow users to view address lists when not connected to the Exchange infrastructure. OABs for Outlook 2003 clients are deployed through public folders. OABs for Outlook 2007 and Outlook 2010 clients are deployed through an IIS virtual directory on the CAS server.

- You can validate client connectivity using the *Test-MailFlow* and *Test-Outlook-Connectivity* cmdlets.

Objective Review

Answer the following questions to test your knowledge of the information in this objective. You can find the answers to these questions and explanations of why each answer choice is correct or incorrect in the "Answers" section at the end of this chapter.

1. Your organization has a large number of clients that still use Outlook 2003. Which of the following automatic distribution methods should you plan to use for Offline Address books (OABs)?

   A. Public Folders

   B. Web-based

   C. File share

   D. Distributed File System (DFS)

2. You have used the following EMS command to create a mailbox database:

   ```
   New-MailboxDatabase -Server 'MEL-MBX' -Name 'MEL-MBX-DB' -EdbFilePath 'C:\MEL-MBX-
   DB\MEL-MBX-DB.edb' -LogFolderPath 'C:\MEL-MBX-DB'
   ```

   You want to enable the mailbox database so that you can provision it with new mailboxes. You also want to configure the mailbox database with a warning quota of 5 GB. Which of the following commands would you use to accomplish this goal? (Coose two. Each answer forms part of a complete solution.)

   A. *New-MailboxDatabase -Server 'SYD-MBX' -Name 'SYD-MBX-DB' -EdbFilePath 'c:\ SYD-MBX-DB.edb' -LogFolderPath 'C:\MEL-MBX-DB'*

   B. *Set-MailboxDatabase -Identity SYD-MBX -IssueWarningQuota 5 GB*

C. *Mount-Database -Identity MEL-MBX*

D. *Set-MailboxDatabase -Identity MEL-MBX -IssueWarningQuota 5 GB*

3. You want to assign Kim Akers the PublishingEditor role on the Documents public folder. Which of the following EMS cmdlets would you use to accomplish this goal?

   A. *Add-PublicFolderAdministrativePermission*

   B. *Add-PublicFolderClientPermission*

   C. *Set-PublicFolder*

   D. *Set-MailPublicFolder*

4. You are about to add 200 mailboxes to your Exchange organization. You want these mailboxes to be evenly distributed across all but one of your organization's existing mailbox databases. You want to suspend one particular mailbox database, named MEL-MBX-DB, from the provisioning process so that it will not be allocated any of these new 200 mailboxes, but can be included in load-balanced mailbox provisioning in future. Which of the following EMS cmdlets could you use to accomplish this goal?

   A. *Set-MailboxDatabase -Identity MEL-MBX-DB -IsExcludedFromProvisioning:$true*

   B. *Set-MailboxDatabase -Identity MEL-MBX-DB -IsExcludedFromProvisioning:$false*

   C. *Set-MailboxDatabase -Identity MEL-MBX-DB -IsSuspendedFromProvisioning:$true*

   D. *Set-MailboxDatabase -Identity MEL-MBX-DB -IsSuspendedFromProvisioning:$false*

5. Which of the following EMS commands would you use to configure the mailbox database SYD-MBX-DB so that deleted items were retained for 21 days, a quota warning is issued at 4 GB, a user is prohibited from sending messages when they reach 5 GB and is prohibited from sending and receiving messages when the mailbox reaches 6 GB in size?

   A. *Set-MailboxDatabase -Identity 'SYD-MBX-DB' -ProhibitSendRecieveQuota 4GB -ProhibitSendQuota 5GB -IssueWarningQuota 6GB -DeletedItemRetention 21*

   B. *Set-MailboxDatabase -Identity 'SYD-MBX-DB' -IssueWarningQuota 4GB -Prohibit- SendQuota 5GB -ProhibitSendRecieveQuota 6GB -DeletedItemRetention 7*

   C. *Set-MailboxDatabase -Identity 'SYD-MBX-DB' -ProhibitSendRecieveQuota 4GB -ProhibitSendQuota 5GB -IssueWarningQuota 6GB -DeletedItemRetention 7*

   D. *Set-MailboxDatabase -Identity 'SYD-MBX-DB' -IssueWarningQuota 4GB -Prohibit- SendQuota 5GB -ProhibitSendRecieveQuota 6GB -DeletedItemRetention 21*

THOUGHT EXPERIMENT
Mailbox Servers, Mailbox and Public Folder Databases

In the following thought experiment, you will apply what you've learned about the deploy mailbox server role objective to answer question in a case study. You can find answers to these questions in the "Answers" section at the end of this chapter.

You are planning the deployment of Exchange Server 2010 at your company, which has offices in the Australian state capital cities of Brisbane, Melbourne, Sydney, Adelaide, and Perth. You are intending to deploy three mailbox servers. Two of these mailbox servers will be located in Melbourne and one will be located in Perth. You intend to provision each mailbox server with three mailbox databases and one public folder database.

All clients in your company will access Exchange using Outlook 2010.

With these facts in mind, answer the following questions:

1. Which EMS cmdlet can you use to verify that message flow is occurring properly between the mailbox servers located in Melbourne and the mailbox servers located in Perth?

2. What steps can you take to allow users in each state capital branch office to be easily able to locate the addresses of other users in that branch office?

3. You want to ensure that all users in the organization are unable to receive mail if they are storing more than 5 GB of data in their mailboxes. What type of quota would you configure to accomplish this goal?

4. What steps can you take to ensure that the mailbox databases hosted on the Perth server are not automatically provisioned with new mailboxes when a mailbox is created but a mailbox database is not specified?

5. Which method should you use to deploy OABs to clients?

Objective 2.6: Deploy Server Roles for Coexistence and Migration

When you discuss upgrading to Exchange Server 2010 from Exchange 2003 or Exchange 2007, it is important to remember that you don't actually upgrade a specific server, but that the upgrade is performed on the organization. You introduce new servers running the new version of Exchange to the existing organization, rather than (for example) directly upgrading an Exchange 2007 mailbox server so that it runs Exchange 2010. When you see the word *migration* in relation to Exchange, this means shifting to an entirely new organization with a new Active Directory forest, rather than introducing new servers into your existing Active Directory forest and moving data across to those servers.

> **This objective covers:**
>
> - Coexistence with and/or migration from Exchange 2003, 2007, 2010, cloud-based services, and third-party messaging systems.
> - Namespace coexistence.
> - Verifying Exchange deployment.
> - Transport rule coexistence.
> - Conversion from LDAP to OPATH filtering.
> - Routing group connector configuration.

Upgrading and Coexistence with Exchange 2003

Performing an upgrade from Exchange 2003 to Exchange 2010 usually involves a coexistence period where both the existing organization and the new organization must interoperate with each other. This coexistence period continues until all Exchange 2003 servers are removed from the environment. You learned about the general steps involved in introducing Exchange 2010 into an Exchange 2003 environment in Chapter 1. Later in this objective, you will learn how to configure Routing Group Connectors for an Exchange 2003 and Exchange 2010 coexistence deployment.

The first step in upgrading from Exchange 2003 to Exchange 2010 is to verify that your organization already meets the prerequisites in terms of having Global Catalog servers and the schema master running at the minimum appropriate level and that the Active Directory forest functional level is set to the appropriate level. These requirements are the same irrespective of whether you are performing a new Exchange 2010 deployment or upgrading from Exchange 2003.

After you've met that requirement, the first step in performing an upgrade from Exchange 2003 to Exchange 2010 is ensuring that your Exchange 2003 organization is running in native mode and that all your existing Exchange 2003 servers have been updated to run Exchange

2003 Service Pack 2. To configure an Exchange 2003 organization to function in native mode, perform the following steps:

1. On a server running Exchange 2003, open Exchange System Manager.

2. Right-click the organization and then select Properties.

3. On the General tab, under Change Operations Mode, click Change Mode. Click Yes when prompted if you are sure that you want to permanently switch the organization's mode to native mode.

If your organization is using a disjoint namespace, where the DNS name associated with hosts in your organization does not match the domain name associated with your clients, you'll need to configure the DNS suffix search list to include the DNS name as well as the domain name. This can be done by editing the Computer Configuration\Administrative Templates\Network\DNS Client\DNS Suffix Search List group policy item to include all DNS suffixes used at the organization.

As you may recall from earlier in the chapter, prior to installing the first Exchange 2010 server, you need to run the *Setup /PrepareLegacyExchangePermissions* command in the same Active Directory site as the computer that hosts the Schema Master role. Although if you run the installation routine directly from the install media, this step will be performed automatically, it is a good idea to run the step separately so that you can verify that everything has worked properly. It never hurts to take a slow and steady approach when it comes to updating a critical piece of IT infrastructure such as an organization's messaging system. Running *Setup /PrepareLegacyExchangePermissions* ensures that the Exchange 2003 recipient update service will function correctly after the Active Directory schema is updated.

After you've successfully run *Setup /PrepareLegacyExchangePermissions*, you can then run the *Setup /PrepareSchema* command on a computer on the same site as the Schema Master. Once that command completes, run the *Setup /PrepareAD* command in the same site as the Schema Master. You then have the choice of running the *Setup /PrepareAllDomains* command if you want to prepare all domains in the forest for the introduction of Exchange 2010, or just *Setup /PrepareDomain* if you want to prepare each domain on an individual basis. You learned about the permissions required to run these command earlier in the chapter.

When the environment has been prepared, you can install Exchange 2010. As you learned in Chapter 1, you need to deploy Exchange 2010 in a specific way when there is an existing Exchange deployment. You can use the ExDeploy web-based tool to generate a checklist of steps that you must complete when deploying Exchange 2010 in an Exchange 2003 environment. This boils down to the following general steps:

1. Install the Client Access Server role on an Internet-facing site.

2. Add necessary digital certificates to the Client Access Server.

3. Enable Outlook Anywhere if you will be using Outlook Anywhere to provision clients.

4. Configure the OAB Outlook Web App, and Exchange ActiveSync virtual directories on the Client Access Server.

5. Install the Hub Transport server role in the Internet-facing site. At this point, you'll specify a bridgehead server that you will use with a routing group connector. You'll learn more about this later in the objective.

6. Configure a legacy host name. Configure the Exchange 2003 infrastructure to use the legacy host names while the new Exchange 2010 infrastructure uses the existing host names.

> **MORE INFO** **CONFIGURE LEGACY HOST NAMES**
>
> To learn more about configuring legacy host names for Exchange 2003 Client Access, consult the following TechNet article: *http://technet.microsoft.com/en-us/library/ ee332348.aspx*.

7. Configure Exchange ActiveSync authentication.

8. Deploy the first Exchange Server 2010 Mailbox server.

9. Move the OAB generation server.

10. If you are going to use an Exchange 2010 Edge Transport server, deploy and configure this server.

11. Change incoming Internet mail flow from Exchange 2003 to Exchange 2010 by updating the appropriate DNS MX records.

After you have performed these steps, you can begin to deploy Client Access Servers, Hub Transport servers, and Mailbox servers in other sites in your organization. Always introduce the Client Access role first into a site, followed by the Hub Transport role, and then the Mailbox server role. After that's done, you can begin migrating mailboxes and public folders from Exchange 2003 to Exchange 2010 with the eventual aim of decommissioning the Exchange 2003 infrastructure.

> **MORE INFO** **UPGRADING FROM EXCHANGE 2003**
>
> To learn more about upgrading from Exchange 2003 to Exchange 2010, consult the following TechNet article: *http://technet.microsoft.com/en-us/library/ff805040.aspx*.

Upgrading and Coexistence with Exchange 2007

Installing Exchange 2010 in an environment that has Exchange 2007 is superficially similar to installing Exchange 2010 in an environment that has Exchange 2003 deployed. You need to make sure that your organization's Global Catalog servers and schema master are upgraded to the appropriate service pack level and the forest is set to the appropriate functional level. You then need to ensure that all of the Exchange 2007 servers are upgraded to Exchange Server 2007 Service Pack 2 prior to beginning your Exchange 2010 deployment.

After you have verified that this is done you need to prepare the environment. This involves running the Active Directory preparation commands:

- **Setup /PrepareSchema**   Run this command on the same site as the Schema Master.
- **Setup /PrepareAD**   Run this command on the same site as the Schema Master.
- **Setup /PrepareAllDomains**   Run this command to prepare all domains, or run *Setup /PrepareDomain* to prepare specific domains for the deployment of Exchange 2010.

The permissions required to run these commands are described earlier in this chapter. These commands will be run automatically if you just perform a direct installation from the media, but you are expected to know each of the separate commands for the 70-663 exam.

EXAM TIP

Remember that you don't have to run the *Setup /PrepareLegacyExchangePermissions* command for an environment that only has Exchange 2007. You only need to run that command if Exchange 2003 is present.

You need to deploy Exchange 2010 in Internet-facing sites prior to deploying in non-Internet-facing sites. The first Exchange component that you need to deploy is the Client Access Server. When configuring the first Exchange 2010 Client Access Server in an Exchange 2007 environment, you'll need to do the following:

- Enable Outlook Anywhere if your organization is going to use it to provision clients.
- Configure the virtual directories for the OAB, Exchange Web Services, Exchange ActiveSync, Outlook Web App, and Exchange Control Panel.
- Migrate Outlook Web App settings from Exchange 2007 to Exchange 2010 using the *Get-OwaVirtualDirectory* cmdlet against the Exchange 2007 CAS and using the *Set-Owa-VirtualDirectory* cmdlet against the Exchange 2010 CAS.
- Configure ActiveSync authentication settings. You can view existing Exchange 2007 authentication settings by running the *Get-ActiveSyncVirtualDirectory* cmdlet and configure the Exchange 2010 authentication settings by running the *Set-ActiveSync-VirtualDirectory* cmdlet.

After the first Exchange 2010 Client Access Server is deployed in the Internet-facing sites, deploy the Hub Transport and then the Mailbox Server roles. After these roles are successfully deployed, then deploy the Exchange 2010 Edge Transport server. Reconfigure incoming email to use the Exchange 2010 transport servers by modifying the appropriate DNS MX records.

At some point during the coexistence period you will need to do the following:

- Move the OAB generation server so that OAB generation occurs on servers running Exchange 2010.

- Configure web distribution for the OAB so that it is distributed from an Exchange 2010 Client Access Server.

- Create a legacy host name for your organization's Exchange 2007 CAS Server. Assign this name to the server and configure the Exchange 2010 CAS Server to use the original name. That way users who are used to accessing Outlook Web App using a specific URL won't need to use a new URL.

After all Internet-facing sites have been upgraded, you can introduce Exchange 2010 to all other sites as necessary. At each site, you'll need to always introduce the Client Access Server first, the Hub Transport server second, and then the Mailbox server last.

> **MORE INFO**   **UPGRADING FROM EXCHANGE 2007**
>
> To learn more about installing Exchange 2010 into an existing Exchange 2007 environment, consult the following TechNet document: *http://technet.microsoft.com/en-us/library/bb124350.aspx*.

Installing Exchange 2010 in a Mixed Exchange 2003 and Exchange 2007 Environment

Just as it is possible to upgrade environments running Exchange 2003 or Exchange 2007 to Exchange 2010, it is also possible to introduce Exchange 2010 to environments that have a mixture of Exchange 2003 and Exchange 2007 environments. This is most likely to occur when an organization decides to move to Exchange 2010 when they still haven't completed their move from Exchange 2003 to Exchange 2007. In general it would be simpler to reduce complexity by completing the upgrade to Exchange 2007 before upgrading again to Exchange 2010 with Service Pack 1. The main things to remember are:

- Ensure that the Schema Master is running Windows Server 2003 SP2 or higher.

- Ensure that at least one Global Catalog server in each site is running Windows Server 2003 SP2 or higher.

- Ensure that all Exchange 2003 servers are upgraded to Exchange 2003 Service Pack 2.

- Ensure that all Exchange 2007 servers are patched to Exchange 2007 Service Pack 2.

- Run *Setup /PrepareSchema* in the same site as the Schema Master.

- Run *Setup /PrepareAD* in the same site as the Schema Master.

- Run *Setup /PrepareAllDomains* in the forest root domain, or use *Setup /PrepareDomain* on a domain-by-domain basis.

- Upgrade the Internet-facing sites first.

- Introduce the Client Access Server role first. Prepare all virtual directories, SSL settings, and DNS names as appropriate.

- Introduce the Hub Transport server role.

- Introduce the Mailbox server role.

- Introduce the Edge Transport role if it is appropriate. Migrate mail flow to the Exchange 2010 Edge Transport role.

After you complete these steps, introduce Exchange 2010 to other sites, remembering the Client Access, Hub Transport, Mailbox server introduction order. When that is done, you should really start moving mailboxes and public folders off the Exchange 2003 and Exchange 2007 servers—you'd probably go crazy having to use three different sets of administrative tools to manage the three different Exchange technologies.

> **MORE INFO**   **INTRODUCING EXCHANGE INTO MIXED ENVIRONMENTS**
>
> To learn more about deploying Exchange 2010 in mixed environments, consult the following TechNet webpage: *http://technet.microsoft.com/en-us/library/ee681662.aspx.*

Validating Exchange Server Deployment

Today it is increasingly common that the deployment of servers and products such as Exchange is performed automatically, either through technologies such as System Center Virtual Machine Manager 2012, System Center Configuration Manager 2012, or System Center Orchestrator 2012. Although you can save substantial time and money by automating the Exchange deployment process, you should verify that the installation has been performed successfully. One of the simplest methods you can use to accomplish this goal is using the *Get-ExchangeServer* cmdlet. Using this command will provide you with information such as which roles are installed, the current version, Active Directory Site location, and edition information as shown in Figure 2-29. This command can be run remotely, so you can incorporate its output into your automatic deployment mechanisms as a way of verifying the deployment's success or failure.

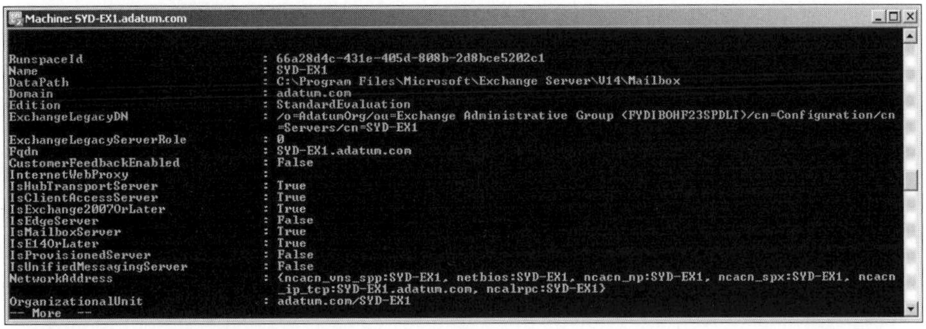

FIGURE 2-29 *Get-ExchangeServer*

Coexistence with Third-Party Email Systems

Most third-party email systems use SMTP. Coexistence with these messaging systems is a matter of configuring appropriate internal Send and Receive connectors. You configure the Send connector on one or more Hub Transport servers that are close on the network to the SMTP server of the third-party messaging system.

When configuring a Send connector to transmit email messages from a Hub Transport server to an internal third-party host that uses SMTP, you can either use the *New-Send-Connector* cmdlet or the New Send Connector Wizard in Exchange Management Console. To create a new Send connector using Exchange Management console, perform the following general steps:

1. Open Exchange Management console and click the Organization Configuration\Hub Transport node.

2. In the Actions pane, click New Send Connector. This will launch the New Send Connector Wizard.

3. On the Introduction page, shown in Figure 2-30, enter a name for the connector to the third-party email system. Ensure that the intended use is set to Custom and then click Next.

4. On the Address Space tab, click Add and then specify the address space—for example, **wingtiptoys.com**—and whether you want to include all subdomains. Click OK. You can configure multiple address spaces if the third-party messaging system uses more than one email domain.

5. On the Network Settings page, click Route Mail Through The Following Smart Hosts, click Add and specify the address of the third-party messaging system's SMTP server on your network.

6. If the third-party messaging system's SMTP server requires authentication, configure the authentication settings on the Configure Smart Host Authentication Settings page. You can configure Basic Authentication and Basic Authentication over TLS. Click Next.

7. On the Source Server page, add all the Hub Transport servers that you want to have participate in the Send connector. When you use multiple Hub Transport servers in a Send connector, Exchange routes messages to those server in a load-balanced manner for eventual forwarding to the destination SMTP server. Click Next, click New, and then click Finish.

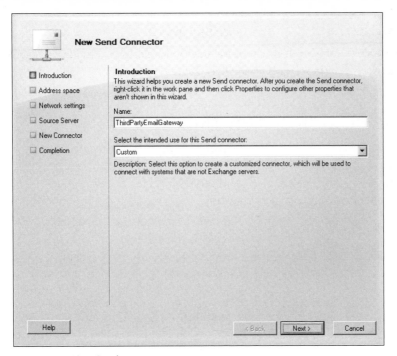

FIGURE 2-30 New Send connector

To receive email messages from the third-party messaging system on your local network, configure a Receive connector. You can do this using the *New-ReceiveConnector* cmdlet or by using the New Receive Connector Wizard. To create a new receive connector to receive email from the SMTP server of a third-party messaging system on your organization's internal network, using Exchange Management Console, perform the following steps:

1. Click the Server Configuration\Hub Transport node, select the Hub Transport server closest to the third-party messaging system's SMTP server on the network, and then click the New Receive Connector item in the Actions menu.

2. On the Introduction page of the New Receive Connector Wizard, enter a name for the Receive connector and set the use for this Receive connector to Custom.

3. On the Local Network Settings page, specify which IP address on which the Hub Transport server will listen for incoming traffic.

4. On the Remote Network Settings page, specify the IP address of the third-party messaging system's SMTP server as shown in Figure 2-31.

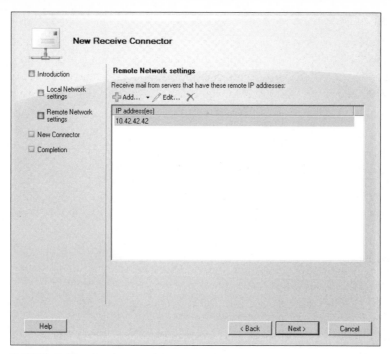

FIGURE 2-31 New Receive connector

5. Click Next, click New, and then click Finish to complete configuration of the Receive connector.

You'll also need to configure the appropriate plumbing on the third-party messaging system so that it will be able to receive and send messages to the Send and Receive connectors that you have configured in Exchange.

Migrating from a third-party email system to Exchange and configuring items such as address-list synchronization isn't something that is directly supported by Exchange, and as such it is unlikely to be tested on the 70-663 exam. Migration and synchronization tools are often available from third-party vendors.

MORE INFO **MIGRATION FROM THIRD-PARTY EMAIL SYSTEMS**

To learn about partners that provide tools to migrate to Exchange from non-Microsoft messaging platforms, consult the following TechNet link: *http://technet.microsoft.com/en-au/exchangelabshelp/ff633682*.

Foreign Connectors

Foreign connectors use a drop directory to send messages to a local messaging system that does not use SMTP as its primary transport mechanism. A common use for foreign connectors is third-party fax gateways. These gateways allow users to send an email that ends up forwarded as a fax. You can only install foreign connectors on Hub Transport servers. You can create a foreign connector using the *New-ForeignConnector* Exchange Management Shell cmdlet.

> **MORE INFO**   **FOREIGN CONNECTORS**
>
> To learn more about foreign connectors, consult the following TechNet article: *http://technet.microsoft.com/en-us/library/aa996779.aspx*.

Delivery Agents

Delivery agents are a new technology that, like foreign connectors, allow delivery of messages to third-party messaging systems that don't use the SMTP protocol. Delivery agents provide the following benefits over foreign connectors:

- They allow queue management of messages routed to third-party systems.
- Message delivery performance is improved.
- It is possible to verify the delivery of messages that use a delivery agent and track message delivery latency.

Delivery agents require that delivery agent software exist. The only delivery agent that ships with Exchange 2010 is the Text Messaging Delivery Agent connector. Although Microsoft provides information how delivery agent software can be created for third-party messaging systems, delivery agents are relatively new, which means that the availability of these agents can be problematic. If no delivery agent exists, you should use a foreign connector as a delivery system to a third-party messaging system that doesn't support SMTP.

> **MORE INFO**   **UNDERSTANDING DELIVERY AGENTS**
>
> To learn more about delivery agents, consult the following TechNet document: *http://technet.microsoft.com/en-us/library/dd638118.aspx*.

Transport Rule Coexistence

If your pre-upgrade Exchange 2007 organization extensively uses transport rules or journaling, you will need to make sure that these rules continue to function during the coexistence period, independent of whether an Exchange 2007 or an Exchange 2010 Hub Transport server processes a specific message. You will need to do this because substantial alterations were made to transport and journaling rules in Exchange 2010 and this can cause problems when managing these features in a mixed environment. The changes between Exchange 2007 transport rules and Exchange 2010 transport rules include the use of new predicates and actions and changes to where transport rules are stored within Active Directory. Exchange 2007 Hub Transport servers are unable to work with the new predicates and actions, meaning that problems can arise if you make changes to rules during the coexistence period.

When you perform an upgrade from Exchange 2007 to Exchange 2010, all existing transport rules and journal rules are migrated to Exchange 2010 format. This occurs automatically and does not require administrator intervention. After that initial process has occurred, if you make changes to existing rules, or create new rules, the modification or new rule will only exist in the location you created it. For example, if you modify an existing transport rule though Exchange Management Console on Exchange 2007, that modification will only replicate out to Exchange 2007 Hub Transport servers. If you modify an existing transport rule through Exchange Management Console on Exchange 2010, that modification will only replicate out to Exchange 2010 Hub Transport servers. In a coexistence scenario, you'll need to create and modify transport rules twice: once with the Exchange 2010 tools and once with the Exchange 2007 tools.

> **MORE INFO** **TRANSPORT RULE COEXISTENCE**
>
> To learn more about transport rules in Exchange 2007 coexistence scenarios, consult the following TechNet article: *http://technet.microsoft.com/en-us/library/dd346708.aspx*.

Converting LDAP to OPATH Filters

Exchange 2003 uses LDAP filtering syntax to create custom address lists, email address policies, distribution groups, and global address lists (GALs). In Exchange 2010, OPATH filtering syntax is used to create custom address lists, email address policies, distribution groups, and GALs. When you perform an upgrade from Exchange 2003 to Exchange 2010, the original LDAP syntax filters will be supported through the migration. However, if you want to modify the syntax filters, you need to upgrade the LDAP filters to the OPATH syntax. Exchange 2007 uses OPATH filtering syntax, so it is not necessary to upgrade LDAP filters if you are upgrading from Exchange 2007.

You can determine which email address policies require upgrading from LDAP to OPATH using the following command:

```
Get-EmailAddressPolicy | Format-List Name, *RecipientFilter*, ExchangeVersion
```

If the *RecipientFilter* attribute is empty, the *RecipientFilterType* attribute is equal to *"Legacy"*, or the value of the *ExchangeVersion* attribute equals "0.0 (6.5.6200.0), the object still uses LDAP filters and may need to be upgraded to OPATH.

When you upgrade from Exchange 2003 to Exchange 2010, the following objects will be migrated but will keep using the LDAP filter format:

- **E-mail Address Policies**   Default Policy
- **Address Lists**   All Contacts, All Groups, All Rooms, All Users, Default Global Address List, Public Folders

You only need to upgrade these to OPATH if you need to modify the object in Exchange 2010. You can upgrade the default email address policy after you have upgraded from Exchange 2003 to Exchange 2010 by issuing the following command:

```
Set-EmailAddressPolicy "Default Policy" -IncludedRecipients AllRecipients
```

To upgrade the All Users default address list, issue the following command:

```
Set-AddressList "All Users" -IncludedRecipients MailboxUsers
```

To upgrade the All Groups default address list, issue the following command:

```
Set-AddressList "All Groups" -IncludedRecipients MailGroups
```

To upgrade the All Contacts address list, issue the following command:

```
Set-AddressList "All Contacts" -IncludedRecipients Mailcontacts
```

Upgrading custom LDAP filters can be more challenging because you must first determine what the LDAP filter does. It can sometimes be easier to create a new filter than attempt to parse the syntax of an existing LDAP filter and convert it to OPATH format.

> **MORE INFO**   **UPGRADING CUSTOM LDAP FILTERS TO OPATH FILTERS**
>
> To learn more about converting custom LDAP filters to OPATH filters, consult the following TechNet article: *http://technet.microsoft.com/en-us/library/cc164375.aspx*.

Routing Group Connector Configuration

Exchange 2003 environments use routing groups as a way of defining a set of Exchange servers that are located on the same high-speed network. In theory Exchange 2003 routing groups should closely mirror an organization's Active Directory site configuration, though this is not always the case. Routing group connectors are used to facilitate mail flow between Exchange 2003 servers in separate routing groups. Routing group connectors are unidirectional, so it is necessary to establish one in each direction for bidirectional mail flow. You should ensure that every Exchange 2003 routing group has a least one connector to another routing group prior to introducing the first Exchange 2010 server.

Exchange 2010 doesn't use routing groups, but instead leverages the existing Active Directory site configuration. When you install Exchange 2010 in an Exchange 2003 environment, all Exchange 2010 servers are added to Exchange Routing Group (DWBGZMFD01QNBJR) within Exchange Administrative Group (FYDIBOHF23SPDLT). You should not move servers out of this group or rename the group. When you deploy the first Exchange 2010 server in the Exchange 2003 environment, you'll be asked to specify an Exchange 2003 server to function as a bridgehead server as a part of establishing a new routing group connector. You should select a bridgehead server in an Exchange 2003 routing group that has a large number of mailboxes.

You can modify the source and target servers on the routing group connector by using the *Set-RoutingGroupConnector* cmdlet in Exchange Management Shell. Microsoft recommends that you specify multiple source and target servers as a way of making the the routing group connector redundant. You can create additional routing group connectors between the Exchange Routing Group (DWBGZMFD01QNBJR) and other Exchange 2003 routing groups using the *New-RoutingGroupConnector* cmdlet. Using this cmdlet with the *BiDirectional* parameter will create both inbound and outbound connectors in a single operation. If you intend to create multiple routing group connectors between Exchange 2010 and Exchange 2003, you should disable Link State Updates. This is done by using the registry editor.

> **MORE INFO**   **ROUTING TOPOLOGY IN EXCHANGE 2003 COEXISTENCE SCENARIOS**
>
> To learn more about routing group connector configuration in Exchange 2003 coexistence scenarios, including how to disable link state updates, consult the following TechNet article: *http://technet.microsoft.com/en-us/library/dd638103.aspx.*

EXAM TIP

Remember that it is only necessary to run *Setup /PrepareLegacyExchangePermissions* if there is an existing Exchange 2003 deployment. If the existing deployment is Exchange 2007 only, you don't need to run this command.

Objective Summary

- Prior to upgrading to Exchange Server 2010 SP1, you must ensure that at least one Global Catalog server at each site is upgraded to Windows Server 2003 SP2 or higher and that the computer that hosts the Schema Master role is upgraded to Windows Server 2003 SP2 or higher. Any Exchange 2003 servers must have Exchange 2003 Service Pack 2 applied. Any Exchange 2007 servers are upgraded to Exchange 2007 Service Pack 2.

- You should upgrade Internet-facing sites before upgrading other sites.

- Install the CAS role, followed by the Hub Transport role, and then the Mailbox role. If an Edge Transport server is going to be used, install that last.

- You must run the *Setup /PrepareLegacyExchangePermissions* command if you are upgrading from Exchange 2003 to Exchange 2010.

- You can use the *Get-ExchangeServer* cmdlet to verify a deployment.

- Use a Delivery Agent connector if possible to connect Exchange to a non-SMTP third-party product. Use Foreign connectors if a non-SMTP third-party product does not have a delivery agent.

- In mixed Exchange 2007/Exchange 2010 environments, modification and creation of transport rules needs to occur on both the Exchange 2007 and Exchange 2010 servers.

- You will need to update Exchange 2003 LDAP filters to Exchange 2010 OPATH syntax if you want to modify those filters after the upgrade.

- You can add additional source and target servers to the routing group connector between the Exchange 2003 routing group and the Exchange 2010 routing group with the *Set-RoutingGroupConnector* cmdlet.

Objective Review

Answer the following questions to test your knowledge of the information in this objective. You can find the answers to these questions and explanations of why each answer choice is correct or incorrect in the "Answers" section at the end of this chapter.

1. You are planning to upgrade an Exchange 2003 organization to Exchange 2010 SP1. Which of the following steps must you take prior to beginning the upgrade? (Choose all that apply.)

   A. Ensure that at least one Global Catalog server in each site where you will deploy Exchange is running Windows Server 2003 SP2 or later.

   B. Ensure that the Exchange 2003 organization is running in Native mode.

   C. Ensure that the forest functional level is set to Windows Server 2008.

   D. Ensure that the computer that hosts the Schema Master role is running Windows Server 2003 SP2 or later.

2. You have performed an automatic deployment of servers running Exchange Server 2010 as a part of your organization's upgrade from Exchange Server 2007. Which of the following Exchange Management Shell cmdlets could you use to verify that the appropriate roles have been installed on these automatically deployed servers?

   A. *Connect-ExchangeServer*

   B. *Discover-ExchangeServer*

   C. *Get-ExchangeServer*

   D. *Set-ExchangeServer*

3. Your organization has deployed Exchange 2010 in its existing Exchange 2007 environment. You envision that the two systems will coexist for a period of 12 months. You determine that you need three new transport rules and that you need to modify two existing transport rules. The existing transport rules were created prior to the installation of the first Exchange 2010 server. Which of the following must you do to create these three new rules and modify the two existing rules? (Choose two. Each answer forms part of a complete solution.)

   A. Modify the existing rules using Exchange Management Console on both a server running Exchange 2007 and a server running Exchange 2010.

   B. Modify the existing rules using Exchange Management Console only on the server running Exchange 2010.

   C. Create the new rules using Exchange Management Console on both a server running Exchange 2007 and a server running Exchange 2010.

   D. Create the new rules using Exchange Management Console only on the server running Exchange 2010.

4. Your organization has been using Exchange 2003 for several years across five sites. Each site has its own routing group. The headquarters site has three Exchange 2003 servers named SYD-EX03-A, SYD-EX03-B, and SYD-EX03-C deployed. A branch office site has two Exchange 2003 servers named MEL-EX03-A and MEL-EX03-B. You introduce Exchange Server 2010 on a server named SYD-EX10-A at your organization's headquarters site. During setup you specify SYD-EX03-A as the bridgehead server. SYD-EX10-A hosts the Client Access, Hub Transport, and Mailbox server roles. Tomorrow you will install two servers, SYD-EX10-B and SYD-EX10-C, which will also hosts these Exchange 2010 roles. You want to ensure that the existing routing group connector does not fail if server SYD-EX10-A or SYD-EX03-A fails. Which of the following steps can you take to accomplish this goal?

   A. Use the *New-RoutingGroupConnector* cmdlet to create a new routing group connector that uses SYD-EX03-A and SYD-EX10-B.

   B. Use the *New-RoutingGroupConnector* cmdlet to create a new routing group connector that uses SYD-EX10-A and MEL-EX03-A.

   C. Use the *Set-RoutingGroupConnector* cmdlet to add SYD-EX03-B and SYD-EX10-B to the existing routing group connector.

   D. Use the *Set-RoutingGroupConnector* cmdlet to add MEL-EX10-A to the existing routing group connector.

5. Tailspin Toys has an Exchange 2003 deployment that you are in the process of upgrading to Exchange 2010. Wingtip Toys has an Exchange 2007 deployment that you are in the process of upgrading to 2010. You are concerned about being able to modify custom filters used to generate address lists after these upgrades have been completed. Which of the following steps will it be necessary to take to ensure that the custom filters used to generate address lists can be modified after the upgrade to Exchange 2010 has been completed?

   A. Upgrade custom OPATH filters to LDAP filters at Tailspin Toys.

   B. Upgrade custom LDAP filters to OPATH filters at Tailspin Toys.

   C. Upgrade custom OPATH filters to LDAP filters at Wingtip Toys.

   D. Upgrade custom LDAP filters to OPATH filters at Wingtip Toys.

THOUGHT EXPERIMENT
Exchange Coexistence and Migration

In the following thought experiment, you will apply what you've learned in this objective to answer questions about coexistence and migration. You can find answers to these questions in the "Answers" section at the end of this chapter.

Your organization's environment is configured as follows:

> *Melbourne:*
>
> > *One Exchange 2007 SP1 server hosting CAS, HT, and MBX roles*
>
> *Sydney:*
>
> > *Two Exchange 2007 SP1 servers hosting CAS, HT, and MBX roles*
> >
> > *third-party messaging system.*
>
> *Wangaratta:*
>
> > *One Exchange 2007 SP1 server hosting CAS, HT, and MBX roles*
> >
> > *One Exchange 2007 SP1 server hosting the ET role.*

The third-party messaging system at the Sydney site does not support SMTP and the vendor has not written delivery agent software.

You intend to deploy Exchange 2010, with a 10-month planned coexistence period.

With these facts in mind, answer the following questions:

1. Which step should you take before upgrading the Active Directory Schema?

2. Which site should you install the first Exchange 2010 server in?

3. Which role should be installed first?

4. Which role should be installed last at the Wangaratta site?

5. What type of connector should you create to communicate with the third-party messaging system at the Sydney site?

6. What special steps will you need to take if you need to modify any transport rules during the coexistence period?

Chapter Summary

- You need to run the *Setup /PrepareLegacyExchangePermissions* command if your organization has an existing Exchange Server 2003 deployment.

- You prepare the Active Directory Schema for the deployment of Exchange by running the *Setup /PrepareSchema* command, then the *Setup /PrepareAD* command, followed by the *Setup /PrepareAllDomains* command.

- Accepted domains determine the email domains for which the Exchange organization will process incoming messages.

- Remote domains allow you to control message formatting and distribution of out-of-office messages.

- Send connectors are used to forward outgoing SMTP traffic to a specific destination.

- Receive connectors are used to accept incoming SMTP traffic from a specific source.

- Address rewriting, performed on an Edge Transport server, allows you to normalize email address formatting as messages are routed in and out of the organization.

- Transport rules allow you to process messages according to the properties of those messages, such as sender, recipient, or message content.

- You can configure message limits such as maximum message size and maximum number of recipients on a per Hub or Edge Transport server basis, on a per-connector basis, or on a per Active Directory IP site link basis.

- Outlook Anywhere allows clients on the Internet to access Exchange mailboxes using Outlook clients without having to establish a VPN or DirectAccess connection.

- ActiveSync allows mobile devices to synchronize messages, contacts, and calendaring data with Exchange.

- Autodiscover allows Outlook 2007, Outlook 2010, and compatible ActiveSync clients to be automatically provisioned with configuration settings.

- The Availability service provides Outlook and OWA clients with calendaring information.

- Linked mailboxes provide Exchange mailboxes to users with accounts in trusted forests.

- Email address policies determine email address format.

- Address lists are used by clients to quickly locate recipient addresses. Offline Address Books (OABs) allow users to view address lists when not connected to the Exchange infrastructure. OABs for Outlook 2003 clients are deployed through public folders. OABs for Outlook 2007 and Outlook 2010 clients are deployed through an IIS virtual directory on the CAS.

- Upgrade Internet-facing sites before upgrading other sites.

- Install the CAS role, followed by the Hub Transport role, and then the Mailbox role. If an Edge Transport server is going to be used, install that last.

- Use a Delivery Agent connector if possible to connect Exchange to a non-SMTP third-party product. Use Foreign connectors if a non-SMTP third-party product does not have a Delivery Agent.

- Exchange 2010 filters use OPATH syntax.

- Add additional source and target servers routing group connectors with the *Set-RoutingGroupConnector* cmdlet.

Answers

This section contains the answers to the Object Reviews and the Thought Experiments.

Objective 2.1: Review

1. **Correct Answer:** A

   A. **Correct:** The schema master must be running Windows Server 2003 Service Pack 2 or later.

   B. **Incorrect:** Although it would be prudent to ensure that the computer that hosts the Domain Naming Master was updated to Windows Server 2003 Service Pack 2 or a later operating system, this is not a requirement to deploy Exchange Server 2010.

   C. **Incorrect:** Although it would be prudent to ensure that the computer that hosts the PDC Emulator role was updated to Windows Server 2003 Service Pack 2 or a later operating system, this is not a requirement to deploy Exchange Server 2010.

   D. **Incorrect:** Although it would be prudent to ensure that the computer that hosts the Infrastructure Master role was updated to Windows Server 2003 Service Pack 2 or a later operating system, this is not a requirement to deploy Exchange Server 2010.

2. **Correct Answers:** A and B

   A. **Correct:** The account used to run the *Setup /PrepareSchema* command must be a member of both the Enterprise Admins and Schema Admins security groups.

   B. **Correct:** The account used to run the *Setup /PrepareSchema* command must be a member of both the Enterprise Admins and Schema Admins security groups.

   C. **Incorrect:** The account used to run the *Setup /PrepareSchema* command does not need to be a member of the Domain Admins group.

   D. **Incorrect:** The account used to run the *Setup /PrepareSchema* command does not need to be a member of the DNSAdmins group.

3. **Correct Answer:** D

   A. **Incorrect:** Whether you run *Setup /PrepareLegacyExchangePermissions* depends on whether you have an existing Exchange Server 2003 deployment. Running this command is not dependent on the forest functional level.

   B. **Incorrect:** It is not necessary to run the *Setup /PrepareLegacyExchangePermissions* command if your organization has an existing Exchange Server 2007 deployment.

   C. **Incorrect:** It is not necessary to run the *Setup /PrepareLegacyExchangePermissions* command if your organization has no existing Exchange deployment.

   D. **Correct:** You must run the *Setup /PrepareLegacyExchangePermissions* command if your organization has an existing Exchange Server 2003 deployment.

4. **Correct Answer:** C

   A. **Incorrect:** You need to run *Setup /PrepareLegacyExchangePermissions* and then *Setup /PrepareSchema* before running *Setup /PrepareAD* if your organization has an existing Exchange Server 2003 deployment.

   B. **Incorrect:** You need to run *Setup /PrepareLegacyExchangePermissions* prior to running *Setup /PrepareSchema* if your organization has an existing Exchange Server 2003 deployment.

   C. **Correct:** If your organization has an existing Exchange Server 2003 deployment, the first command that you need to run when preparing the Active Directory environment is *Setup /PrepareLegacyExchangePermissions*. You would then follow this by running *Setup /PrepareSchema*, followed by *Setup /PrepareAD*, and finally *Setup /PrepareAllDomains*.

   D. **Incorrect:** You need to run *Setup /PrepareLegacyExchangePermissions*, then *Setup /PrepareSchema,* and then *Setup /PrepareAD* before running *Setup /PrepareAll-Domains* if your organization has an existing Exchange Server 2003 deployment.

5. **Correct Answer:** D

   A. **Incorrect:** A public key (KEY) record stores a public key related to a DNS domain name. This resource record is authenticated by a SIG resource record. Although a public key record does involve a cryptographic key in the same way that a TXT record does, you don't need to create a public key record to support Exchange federated delegation.

   B. **Incorrect:** X.25 records map a DNS name to a Public Switched Data Network address. You do not need to create X.25 records to support Exchange federated delegation.

   C. **Incorrect:** A Signature (SIG) record authenticates a record and binds it to the signer's DNS domain name. Although it can be used perform a similar cryptographic verification function to a TXT record, you do not need to create a SIG record to support Exchange federated delegation.

   D. **Correct:** You need to create a Text (TXT) record that includes the federated domain proof encryption string to support federated delegation in the zones for which you want to include in Exchange federated delegation.

Objective 2.1: Thought Experiment

1. You Should update the computer that holds the Schema Master role and the Global Catalog servers to Windows Server 2003 Service Pack 2.

2. Exchange Server 2010 requires that the forest functional level be set to a minimum of Windows Server 2003. Because the forest functional level is already set to Windows Server 2003, you don't need to raise the forest functional level higher.

3. You should run *Setup /PrepareSchema* first.

4. You should run the command *Setup /PrepareSchema* in the contoso.internal domain at the Melbourne site because this site and domain hosts the computer that holds the Schema Master role.

5. You should run the command *Setup /PrepareAD* after running *Setup /PrepareSchema*.

6. The final command that you should run, after running *Setup /PrepareSchema* and *Setup /PrepareAD*, is *Setup /PrepareAllDomains*.

Objective 2.2: Review

1. **Correct Answers:** A and B

   A. **Correct:** You must use the *Enable-TransportAgent* cmdlet to enable the address rewriting agent on the Edge Transport server.

   B. **Correct:** You must use the *New-AddressRewriteEntry* cmdlet to create the address rewrite entry.

   C. **Incorrect:** You use the *Set-AddressRewriteEntry* cmdlet to modify an existing address rewrite entry.

   D. **Incorrect:** You use the *Get-AddressRewriteEntry* cmdlet to view a list of existing address rewrites entries.

2. **Correct Answer:** C

   A. **Incorrect:** You need to create two EdgeSync subscriptions—a replacement for the existing subscription and a new one for the new Edge Transport server.

   B. **Incorrect:** You need to create two EdgeSync subscriptions—a replacement for the existing subscription and a new one for the new Edge Transport server.

   C. **Correct:** Each Edge Transport server must have a unique EdgeSync subscription to the primary site. If you add a Hub Transport server to a site that has an existing EdgeSync subscription, you must re-create that subscription to account for the new Hub Transport server. This means that you need to create two EdgeSync subscriptions—a replacement for the existing subscription and one for the new Edge Transport server.

   D. **Incorrect:** You need to create two EdgeSync subscriptions—a replacement for the existing subscription and a new one for the new Edge Transport server.

3. **Correct Answer:** C

   A. **Incorrect:** The *Enable-TransportAgent* cmdlet allows you to enable transport agents on an Edge Transport server. You cannot use this cmdlet to determine which transport agents are currently active on an Edge Transport server.

B. Incorrect: You can only use the *Get-TransportAgentPipeline* cmdlet to determine the status of messages in the event that the server has processed messages.

C. Correct: You can use the *Get-TransportAgent* cmdlet to determine which transport agents are enabled on an Edge Transports server even when the server has not processed messages.

D. Incorrect: The *Disable-TransportAgent* cmdlet allows you to disable transport agents on an Edge Transport server. You cannot use this cmdlet to determine which transport agents are currently active on an Edge Transport server.

4. **Correct Answers:** C and D

A. Incorrect: Encrypting File System is a technology used to protect files and folders stored on a local volume. You cannot use Encrypting File System to protect network traffic between an Exchange organization and a third-party email gateway.

B. Incorrect: BitLocker is a technology that allows you to fully encrypt a hard disk drive and ensure boot integrity protection. You cannot use BitLocker to protect network traffic between an Exchange organization and a third-party email gateway.

C. Correct: You can use IPsec to protect network traffic between an Exchange organization and a third-party email gateway when choosing to use the externally secured smart host authentication setting.

D. Correct: You can use a Virtual Private Network connection to protect network traffic between an Exchange organization and a third-party email gateway when choosing to use the externally secured smart host authentication setting.

5. **Correct Answer:** B

A. Incorrect: The ExchangeLegacyInterop group is used for interoperability with Exchange 2003 servers in the same forest. You do not add the user account that will be used to support connectivity with an Edge Transport server to this group.

B. Correct: You need to make this user account a member of the Exchange servers security group for this Send connector to work properly.

C. Incorrect: The Organization Management group has permission to manage Exchange objects and their properties. You do not add the user account that will be used to support connectivity with an Edge Transport server to this group.

D. Incorrect: The Server Management group has permission to manage all Exchange servers in the organization. You do not add the user account that will be used to support connectivity with an Edge Transport server to this group.

Objective 2.2: Thought Experiment

1. The Exchange Server 2010 Edge Transport server role can be installed on computers running the Windows Server 2008 and Windows Server 2008 R2 operating systems.

2. You need to open TCP port 25 for bidirectional SMTP communication between the Hub Transport server and the Edge Transport server. You need to open TCP port 50636 for unidirectional EdgeSync communication between the Hub Transport server and the Edge Transport server.

3. You need to configure the contoso.com, Fabrikam.com, and adatum.com domains as accepted domains because previous customers may still use these domains when sending email to recipients in the newly merged organization.

4. You need to re-create the edge subscription after you deploy the new Hub Transport server at the Sydney site. This will ensure that the Edge Transport server communicates with the newly deployed Hub Transport server.

5. You use the *New-AddressRewriteEntry* cmdlet to configure address rewrite entries. You need to create an address rewrite entry for both the contoso.com and the fabrikam.com email domains.

Objective 2.3: Review

1. **Correct Answer:** D

   A. **Incorrect:** *Test-ActiveSyncConnectivity* allows an administrator to test ActiveSync functionality against a mailbox. You cannot use this cmdlet to verify that Autodiscover is functioning properly.

   B. **Incorrect:** *Test-OwaConnectivity* allows an administrator to verify that OWA is functioning. You cannot use this cmdlet to verify that Autodiscover is functioning properly.

   C. **Incorrect:** *Test-WebServicesConnectivity* allows you to verify that Exchange Web Services is functioning properly. You cannot use this cmdlet to verify that Autodiscover is functioning properly.

   D. **Correct:** You can use the *Test-OutlookWebServices* cmdlet to verify that the Autodiscover service is functioning and configured properly on Client Access Servers.

2. **Correct Answer:** C

   A. **Incorrect:** The *Test-OwaConnectivity* cmdlet allows administrators to verify that Outlook Web App is functioning properly. This cmdlet cannot be used to verify the functionality of Outlook Anywhere.

B. **Incorrect:** The *Test-OutlookWebServices* cmdlet allows administrators to verify Autodiscover settings. This cmdlet cannot be used to verify the functionality of Outlook Anywhere.

C. **Correct:** The *Test-OutlookConnectivity* cmdlet allows administrators to verify the functionality of Outlook Anywhere.

D. **Incorrect:** The *Test-WebServicesConnectivity* cmdlet is used by administrators to verify the functionality of Exchange Web Services. This cmdlet cannot be used to verify the functionality of Outlook Anywhere.

3. **Correct Answer:** B

   A. **Incorrect:** The Exchange Server User Monitor allows you to view and analyze a specific user's Exchange usage and performance. You can't use this tool to remotely verify Autodiscover functionality for ActiveSync.

   B. **Correct:** You can use the Exchange Remote Connectivity Analyzer to remotely verify Exchange functionality including Autodiscover functionality for ActiveSync.

   C. **Incorrect:** *Test-OutlookConnectivity* allows you to test end-to-end Outlook client connectivity including Outlook Anywhere (RPC/HTTP) and TCP-based. You can't use this tool to remotely test Autodiscover for ActiveSync.

   D. **Incorrect:** *Test-OwaConnectivity* allows you to test Outlook Web App functionality. You can't use this tool to remotely test Autodiscover for ActiveSync.

4. **Correct Answer:** A

   A. **Correct:** You can use the *Set-OwaVirtualDirectory* cmdlet to prevent users on public computers from downloading and accessing attachments when connected to OWA.

   B. **Incorrect:** The *Set-PublicFolder* cmdlet allows you to configure public folder properties. You cannot use this cmdlet to prevent users from downloading and accessing attachments when connected to OWA from a public computer.

   C. **Incorrect:** The *Set-ResourceConfig* cmdlet allows you to set resource property schema and resource locations on the Resource Config Active Directory object. You cannot use this cmdlet to prevent users from downloading and accessing attachments when connected to OWA from a public computer.

   D. **Incorrect:** *Set-OutlookAnywhere* allows you to configure Outlook Anywhere settings. You cannot use this cmdlet to prevent users from downloading and accessing attachments when connected to OWA from a public computer.

5. **Correct Answer:** B

   A. **Incorrect:** Administrators use the *Test-PopConnectivity* cmdlet to verify that POP3 access to mailboxes functions on target Client Access Servers. This cmdlet cannot be used to verify the functionality of Outlook Web App.

B. **Correct:** Administrators can use the *Test-OwaConnectivity* cmdlet to verify that Outlook Web App is functioning properly on Client Access Servers.

C. **Incorrect:** Administrators use the *Test-ActiveSyncConnectivity* cmdlet to verify that the ActiveSync protocol is functioning properly. This cmdlet cannot be used to verify the functionality of Outlook Web App.

D. **Incorrect:** Administrators use the *Test-OutlookConnectivity* cmdlet to verify that services that support Outlook 2007 and Outlook 2010 clients, such as Outlook Anywhere, are functioning properly. This cmdlet cannot be used to verify the functionality of Outlook Web App.

Objective 2.3: Thought Experiment

1. You can use the Exchange Remote Connectivity Analyzer to determine that ActiveSync clients on the Internet are able to provision their messaging settings using Autodiscover on the Internet.

2. Enable Outlook Anywhere to grant Outlook 2010 clients access to mailboxes from external locations once the VPN is decommissioned.

3. You use the *Export-AutoDiscoverConfig* cmdlet in each forest to ensure that users can use Autodiscover independently of which forest they log on to.

4. You should configure WebReady document viewing to ensure that users of public computers can't view Microsoft Office documents through the browser when connected to OWA.

5. You should allocate six virtual processors to the CAS at each site. Microsoft advises that the best ratio of CAS processors to mailbox server processors is 3:4. Eight virtual processors allocated to mailbox servers suggests six virtual processors assigned to CAS.

Objective 2.4: Review

1. **Correct Answer:** B

   A. **Incorrect:** Accepted domains determine the email domains for which Exchange will accept messages. You cannot use accepted domains to configure whether external organizations will receive out-of-office messages or automatic replies.

   B. **Correct:** You would configure remote domains to ensure that automatic replies and out-of-office messages will be transmitted to recipients in external organizations.

   C. **Incorrect:** Although Send connectors do represent the outbound path that messages take, you cannot use Send connectors to configure whether external organizations will receive out-of-office messages or automatic replies.

D.   Incorrect: Receive connectors are used to configure Exchange to accept incoming email. You cannot use Receive connectors to configure whether external organizations will receive out-of-office messages or automatic replies.

2.   **Correct Answer:** D

   A.   Incorrect: Remote domains allow you to configure message formatting settings and whether out-of-office replies will be transmitted to external recipients. You cannot configure remote domains to check email messages for a specific word or phrase.

   B.   Incorrect: Send connectors are used to specify the path that outbound mail takes from your organization's servers. You cannot configure Send connectors to check email messages for a specific word or phrase.

   C.   Incorrect: Receive connectors are used to configure Exchange to accept incoming email. You cannot configure Receive connectors to check email messages for a specific word or phrase.

   D.   Correct: You can use transport rules to check the content of messages for a word or a phrase and to take an action, such as deleting the message, if that word or phrase is detected.

3.   **Correct Answer:** C

   A.   Incorrect: You need to deploy a minimum of six Hub Transport servers to support this configuration.

   B.   Incorrect: You need to deploy a minimum of six Hub Transport servers to support this configuration.

   C.   Correct: You need to deploy a Hub Transport server at each site where there is a mailbox server. Hub Transport servers cannot be shared across Exchange organizations. To service the two mailbox servers at each site, one in each different Exchange organization, you need to deploy two Hub Transport servers at each of the three sites.

   D.   Incorrect: You need to deploy a minimum of six Hub Transport servers to support this configuration.

4.   **Correct Answers:** A and C

   A.   Correct: You need to configure adatum.com as an accepted internal relay domain. You configure internal relay domains when you need to route messages to a separate messaging system that is located on your organization's internal network.

   B.   Incorrect: You should not configure an accepted external relay domain. You configure external relay domains when you need to route messages to an organization's messaging system when that system is located on an external network.

   C.   Correct: You should configure a Send connector that uses a Hub Transport server as the source server to route messages to the separate messaging system on the internal network.

D. Incorrect: You only use an Edge Transport server as a source server for a Send connector for accepted domains when those domains are external relay domains.

5. **Correct Answer:** B

   A. Incorrect: You can use the *Set-TransportConfig* cmdlet to configure the maximum size of a message, but you need to use a transport rule to limit the maximum size of an attachment.

   B. Correct: You can only use transport rules to control the size of attachments—the other cmdlet options only allow you to control overall maximum message size.

   C. Incorrect: Although you can use *Set-TransportServer* to configure the pickup directory maximum header size, you can't use this cmdlet to configure a maximum attachment size.

   D. Incorrect: Although you can configure a maximum message size for an Active Directory site link, you cannot configure a maximum attachment size for an Active Directory site link.

Objective 2.4: Thought Experiment

1. One for the branch offices in Melbourne, Adelaide, Canberra, Brisbane, and Perth. Two for Sydney as it requires one for each organization's mailbox server.

2. The Sydney office because this office will host Hub Transport servers from both Active Directory forests.

3. You would configure the Hub Transport server in the Sydney office that was a member of the Contoso.local forest with the edge subscription because this Hub Transport server is in the Active Directory site adjacent to the Sydney perimeter network.

4. You would configure the Contoso.com as an accepted internal relay domain.

5. You would configure the Contoso.com email domain as the Address Space value for the cross-forest Send connector.

6. You would configure the Sydney Hub Transport server as the source server for the cross-forest send connector that you create in the Contoso.local Exchange organization.

Objective 2.5: Review

1. **Correct Answer:** A

   A. Correct: Outlook 2003 clients require Offline Address Books (OABs) that are distributed through Public Folders. You can't distribute OABs to Outlook 2003 clients automatically using the web-based distribution method. This only works with clients running Outlook 2007 or Outlook 2010. You can't automatically distribute OABs using file shares or DFS.

B. Incorrect: You can't distribute OABs to Outlook 2003 clients automatically using the web-based distribution method. This only works with clients running Outlook 2007 or Outlook 2010.

C. Incorrect: You can't automatically distribute OABs using file shares or DFS.

D. Incorrect: You can't automatically distribute OABs using file shares or DFS.

2. **Correct Answers:** C and D

A. Incorrect: The *New-MailboxDatabase* cmdlet creates a new mailbox database. It can't be used to mount an existing mailbox database.

B. Incorrect: Although this cmdlet does configure a quota correctly, it does so for the incorrect mailbox database.

C. Correct: When you create a mailbox database using EMS, the database is not automatically mounted. A mailbox database must be mounted before you can provision it with mailboxes. You use the *Mount-Database -Identity MEL-MBX* command to mount a mailbox database.

D. Correct: You use the *Set-MailboxDatabase* cmdlet with the *IssueWarningQuota* parameter to configure a warning quota for a mailbox database.

3. **Correct Answer:** B

A. Incorrect: You use the *Add-PublicFolderAdministrativePermission* cmdlet to assign administrative, rather than client, permissions to public folders. Administrative permissions differ from client permissions and allow the delegated user to configure items such as public folder retention settings.

B. Correct: You use the *Add-PublicFolderClientPermission* cmdlet to assign public folder client permission. The PublishingEditor role is a client permission.

C. Incorrect: The *Set-PublicFolder* cmdlet allows you to configure items such as maximum item size, but does not allow you to set client or administrative permissions.

D. Incorrect: The *Set-MailPublicFolder* allows you to configure the settings such as maximum received item size for mail-enabled public folders, but does not allow you to configure client or administrative permissions.

4. **Correct Answer:** C

A. Incorrect: The *IsExcludedFromProvisioning* parameter is used to permanently exclude a mailbox database from the load-balanced mailbox provisioning process.

B. Incorrect: The *IsExcludedFromProvisioning* parameter is used to permanently exclude a mailbox database from the load-balanced mailbox provisioning process.

C. Correct: You use the *IsSuspendedFromProvisioning* parameter with the value *$true* to temporarily suspend a mailbox database from automatically being allocated new mailboxes in a load-balanced manner.

D. Incorrect: Using the *$false* option with the *IsSuspendedFromProvisioning* parameter allows a mailbox database that is suspended from provisioning to be used again in the provisioning process.

5. **Correct Answer:** D

   A. Incorrect: This answer sets the prohibit send and receive quota to 4 GB instead of 6 GB and the issue warning quota to 6 GB instead of 4 GB.

   B. Incorrect: This answer sets the deleted item retention value to 7 days instead of 21.

   C. Incorrect: This answer sets the prohibit send and receive quota to 4 GB instead of 6 GB and the issue warning quota to 6 GB instead of 4 GB. This answer also sets the deleted item retention value to 7 days instead of 21.

   D. Correct: Only this answer sets the warning quota to 4 GB, the prohibit send quota to 5 GB, the prohibit send and receive quota to 6 GB, and the deleted item retention to 21 days.

Objective 2.5: Thought Experiment

1. You can use the *Test-Mailflow* cmdlet to diagnose whether mail can be successfully sent from one mailbox server to another.

2. You should create an address list for each branch office. This will simplify the process of locating addresses.

3. You would configure a prohibit send and receive quota to accomplish the goal of blocking users from receiving email when they exceeded their mailbox quota.

4. Use the *Set-MailboxDatabase* cmdlet with the *IsExcludedFromProvisioning* parameter to configure the mailbox databases hosted on the Perth servers to be excluded from mailbox provisioning.

5. All clients are using Outlook 2010, so you should use the web-based method of OAB deployment.

Objective 2.6: Review

1. **Correct Answers:** A, B, and D

   A. Correct: A Global Catalog server at each site where you are going to deploy Exchange 2010 SP1 must be running at Windows Server 2003 SP2 or later. Note that Exchange 2010 SP1 has slightly different Active Directory environment requirements than Exchange 2010 RTM.

   B. Correct: The Exchange 2003 organization must be running in Native mode prior to introducing Exchange 2010 to the environment.

C. Incorrect: The forest functional level only needs to be set to Windows Server 2003 and does not need to be set to the Windows Server 2008 level.

D. Correct: The computer that hosts the Schema Master role must be set to Windows Server 2003 SP2 or later. Note that Exchange 2010 SP1 has slightly different Active Directory environment requirements than Exchange 2010 RTM.

2. **Correct Answer:** C

A. Incorrect: The *Connect-ExchangeServer* cmdlet allows you to discover the best Exchange servers to connect to automatically. You cannot use this cmdlet to verify that appropriate roles have been installed on a newly deployed Exchange server.

B. Incorrect: This command allows you to connect to the closest Exchange server. You cannot use this cmdlet to verify that appropriate roles have been installed on a newly deployed Exchange server.

C. Correct: You can use the *Get-ExchangeServer* cmdlet to verify that appropriate roles have been installed on a newly deployed Exchange server.

D. Incorrect: The *Set-ExchangeServer* cmdlet allows you to set attributes in Active Directory for a specified server. You cannot use this cmdlet to verify that appropriate roles have been installed on a newly deployed Exchange server.

3. **Correct Answers:** A and C

A. Correct: In Exchange 2007 and Exchange 2010 coexistence scenarios it is necessary to modify existing transport rules using Exchange 2010 and Exchange 2007 administration tools.

B. Incorrect: In Exchange 2007/Exchange 2010 coexistence scenarios, you must modify existing transport rules using both Exchange 2010 and Exchange 2007 administration tools rather than just the Exchange 2010 administration tools.

C. Correct: In Exchange 2007 and Exchange 2010 coexistence scenarios it is necessary to create new transport rules using Exchange 2010 and Exchange 2007 administration tools.

D. Incorrect: In Exchange 2007/Exchange 2010 coexistence scenarios, you must create transport rules using both Exchange 2010 and Exchange 2007 administration tools rather than just the Exchange 2010 administration tools.

4. **Correct Answer:** C

A. Incorrect: You should not create a new routing group connector—this will not ensure that the existing routing group connector does not fail if server SYD-EX10-A or SYD-EX03-A fails.

B. Incorrect: Adding a new routing group connector to the branch office site will not make the existing routing group connector at the headquarters site more reliable.

C. Correct: You can improve the redundancy of an existing routing group connector by adding additional source and target servers using the *Set-RoutingGroup-Connector* cmdlet.

D. Incorrect: There is no existing routing group connector between the headquarters site Exchange 2010 servers and the Exchange 2003 servers at the branch office.

5. **Correct Answer:** B

A. Incorrect: Exchange 2003 uses LDAP filters for custom address lists and requires them to be converted to OPATH filters, rather than the other way around.

B. Correct: Exchange 2003 uses LDAP filters for custom address lists. Although these address lists will migrate to Exchange 2010, you'll need to upgrade them to use OPATH filters if you want to modify them at some point in the future.

C. Incorrect: Exchange 2007 already uses OPATH filters on custom address lists. It is not necessary to upgrade these filters after transitioning to Exchange Server 2010.

D. Incorrect: Exchange 2007 already uses OPATH filters on custom address lists. It is not necessary to upgrade these filters after transitioning to Exchange Server 2010.

Objective 2.6: Thought Experiment

1. Upgrade all the Exchange 2007 servers to Exchange 2007 SP2.

2. You should install Exchange 2010 in the Wangaratta site. This site has an Edge Transport server and is therefore Internet-facing.

3. You should install the CAS server role first.

4. You should install the ET server role last at the Wangaratta site.

5. You should install a foreign connector because the third-party messaging system does not support SMTP and the vendor has not written delivery agent software.

6. You need to ensure that you update the rules using both the Exchange 2007 and Exchange 2010 administration tools.

Designing and Deploying Security for the Exchange Organization

S ecurity for a messaging system is important: Several organizations have had their email archives leaked over the Internet. Security isn't just about public relations—many businesses, such as those that handle medical records, have compliance responsibilities that mean that security isn't just an optional extra, but an organizational imperative. In this chapter you'll learn how to design and deploy messaging security within an Exchange organization, how to develop an appropriate Exchange privileges model, how to manage message hygiene, and how to ensure that client access is secure and that Exchange object permissions are configured appropriately.

Objectives in this chapter:

- Objective 3.1: Design and deploy messaging security
- Objective 3.2: Design and deploy Exchange permissions model
- Objective 3.3: Design and deploy message hygiene
- Objective 3.4: Design and deploy client access security
- Objective 3.5: Design and deploy Exchange object permissions

Real World

M ake sure that if you configure a system to sign and encrypt email at your organization, you configure the system so that at least one authorized administrator is able to perform certificate recovery. You would be surprised at how many people lose access to their public or private keys, or, in systems where a password needs to be entered to access the keys, simply end up forgetting their password. I've been guilty of this forgetfulness myself when using products that use the OpenPGP standard published in RFC 4880. When deploying this type of solution in your organization, ensure that you have some way of dealing with the problem of lost certificates and, if necessary, passwords. If you don't, people in your organization will inevitably lose access to any previously received secure messages because they lose access to their previous keys.

Objective 3.1: Design and Deploy Messaging Security

In many organizations, security is a reactive rather than a proactive process. In other words, security is something that people think about only after something has gone wrong, rather than before the problem occurs. In this objective, you will learn about factors to take into account when designing message security. This includes what to take into account when preparing a certificate request, the situations where secure relaying and mutual TLS is appropriate, the advantages of integrating information rights management into the messaging infrastructure, transport protection and decryption options, and planning Outlook Protection Rules.

This objective covers:
- Define message security requirements.
- Certificates.
- Secure relaying.
- Signing and/or encrypting with S/MIME.
- MTLS.
- Information Rights Management.
- Transport Protection and Decryption.
- Planning Outlook Protection Rules.

Define Message Security Requirements

The first step in designing and deploying message security is to determine exactly what your organization's message security requirements are. This involves making some type of determination about the necessity for confidentiality within your organization's messaging infrastructure. It might be desirable for all organizations to always use encrypted messages—in which the recipient can verify sender identity and that the message hasn't been tampered with—but this level of messaging security is often not necessary.

When defining your organization's message security requirements, you can split the requirements into several factors:

- **Protection of the message from interception** This type of protection ensures that if the message is intercepted by an unauthorized third party, that unauthorized third party is unable to access the message contents.

- **Protection of the message contents from alteration** This type of protection allows the recipient to be able to verify that the message wasn't tampered with in transit.

- **Verification of the sender's identification** This type of protection allows the recipient to verify the identity of the sender.

- **Protection from information leakage** This type of protection allows the sender to determine what actions the recipient can take with the information.

When defining your organization's message security requirements, you need to concentrate on what is desirable and necessary rather than what is technically possible. Depending on the type of business your organization is in—for example, if your organization handles medical records—you may have more or less stringent requirements.

An important additional consideration is to assess how message security requirements will be enforced on end users. For example, you might have a policy that all email that involves customer confidential information must be secured using S/MIME. Having a policy and the technology to comply with that policy doesn't ensure that the policy is actually followed. When determining messaging security requirements, you also have to consider how you will configure Exchange to enforce eventual policies.

Certificates

In Chapter 1, "Planning the Exchange Server 2010 Infrastructure," and Chapter 2, "Deploying the Exchange Server 2010 Infrastructure," you learned about what to consider when planning certificates for your Exchange 2010 deployment. This included information about what type of certificate to obtain and the type of Certificate Authority that you would obtain it from. The majority of certificates used internally by Exchange are actually self-signed, automatically trusted by all Exchange servers, and don't require any administrator intervention. You only need to think about certificates when you are interfacing with client computers or outside organizations.

When considering digital certificates as a method of securing your Exchange organization, you'll need to choose which of the following certificate properties are appropriate for your deployment:

- **Standard certificate**   This certificate has a single FQDN associated with the certificate—for example, mail.tailspintoys.com. Use this when your CAS uses the same name for all services.

- **Wildcard certificate**   This certificate allows all hosts within a domain using a wildcard. For example, a certificate requested for *.tailspintoys.com would be valid for all hosts that had the domain suffix tailspintoys.com. The advantage of this certificate is that if you want to add new names after the certificate has been obtained, you don't have to obtain a new certificate. Any host name that has the appropriate domain suffix can be used, so the certificate is less secure than a standard certificate or one that supports Subject Alternative Names.

- **Subject Alternative Names**   Multiple FQDNs are associated with a single certificate. Today this is the most common approach to provisioning a CAS certificate.

- **Trusted Third-Party Certificate Authority (CA)**   The benefit of using a certificate from a trusted third-party CA is that your certificates will be trusted by clients outside your organization. Trusted third-party CAs are a good place to source certificates, such as SSL certificates, that need to be trusted by people outside your organization.

- **Internal CA**   Internal CAs don't have any extra costs involved other than the cost of managing them. The drawback of an internal CA is that it can take some work to get external clients to trust the CA. It is also possible to get a trusted third-party CA to issue a signing certificate to an internal CA. This is usually expensive, but allows people outside the organization to trust the certificates issued by the CA without any additional special configuration.

> *MORE INFO*   **TLS CERTIFICATES**
>
> To learn more about TLS Certificates, consult the following TechNet document: *http://technet.microsoft.com/en-us/library/aa998840.aspx*.

Secure Relaying

When you set up anonymous relay, an SMTP server will accept and forward messages for email domains for which it is not authoritative. When the original RFCs for SMTP were published, anonymous relay of messages—also known as *open relay*—was encouraged to provide redundancy. If a message couldn't be delivered to a target SMTP server, it was delivered to a nearby SMTP server until the target came online. Anonymous relay was rarely problematic until people started to send unsolicited commercial email, colloquially known as spam. Spammers quickly found that they could use SMTP servers that allowed anonymous relay as a way of transmitting their unsolicited messages. Rather than let their SMTP servers be used as a vector for the transmission of spam, organizations configured their SMTP servers to only relay messages received from the Internet that were related to the domains for which the SMTP server was authoritative. Organizations that leave their SMTP servers as open relays today are likely to end up on block lists. You'll learn more about block lists later in this chapter.

Rather than be completely open like an anonymous relay, a secure relay is one in which you choose to relay messages for a specific partner organization. For example, you might configure your organization's Edge Transport server as a secure relay so that it transmits messages to the Internet on behalf of a partner organization. Several steps are involved in this process:

- Set up an externally secured connection between the partner SMTP server and the server that will host the secure relay.

- Create the Receive connector that will function as the secure relay on the server that will host the secure relay.

- Configure the newly created Receive connector with the relay permission for anonymous connections.

- Configure the newly created Receive connector to be externally secure.

When creating the new Receive connector, ensure that you specify either the IP address or the IP address range of your partner's SMTP server. This will ensure that the new Receive connector that you use for secure relay can coexist with other Receive connectors. Receive connectors cannot share the same local IP address, local port, or remote IP address settings.

Externally Secured Receive Connector

An externally secured Receive connector is one that uses another mechanism to secure the connection, rather than having authentication occur directly at the SMTP connector. Usually this mechanism is an IPsec connection, but could also be a specially configured VPN or DirectAccess connection. The key to understanding externally secured Receive connectors is knowing the process that secures the traffic between source and destination SMTP server is independent of Exchange. To externally secure a Receive connector, select the Externally Secured option on the Authentication tab of the Receive Connector Properties dialog box, shown in Figure 3-1. Then click the Permission Groups and enable Exchange servers. Use the *Set-ReceiveConnector* cmdlet to configure these options from EMS.

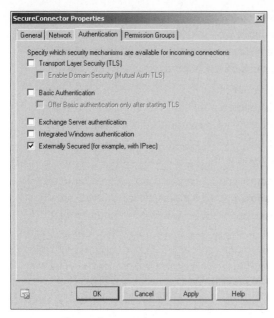

FIGURE 3-1 Externally secured connector

Anonymous Permissions on Receive Connector

For secure relay to work, you need to grant relay permissions to anonymous connections on the newly created Receive connector. In Exchange 2010 SP1, this task can only be performed from EMS by using the *Get-ReceiveConnector* and *Add-ADPermission* cmdlets and cannot be performed using EMC. For example, to grant relay permission for anonymous connections for the Receive connector named SecureConnector using EMS, issue the following command:

```
Get-ReceiveConnector "SecureConnector" | Add-ADPermission -User "NT AUTHORITY\ANONYMOUS
LOGON" -ExtendedRights "Ms-Exch-SMTP-Accept-Any-Recipient"
```

> **MORE INFO**   **ANONYMOUS RELAY AND RECEIVE CONNECTORS**
>
> To learn more about allowing anonymous relay on a Receive connector, consult the following TechNet document: *http://technet.microsoft.com/en-us/library/bb232021.aspx*.

Signing, Encrypting, and S/MIME

S/MIME (Secure/Multipurpose Internet Mail Extensions) allows messages to be digitally signed and, if necessary, encrypted. Digitally signing a message provides the recipient with a verification of the sender's identity. A digital signature can also provide proof that the message was not modified in transit. When encrypting a message, the intention of the sender is that the message can only be opened by the intended recipient. To do this the sender encrypts the message using the recipient's public key. Only a person who has access to the recipient's private key is able to decrypt the message. After the message is encrypted, not even the sender can read the message without access to the recipient's private key.

Integrating S/MIME with Exchange 2010 requires that your organization deploy a Public Key Infrastructure (PKI). A PKI includes CAs, registration authorities (RAs), and digital certificates. S/MIME requires that you deploy certificates to client computers. Using an enterprise CA simplifies this process. If you want to ensure that external recipients trust the certificates issued by this CA, the enterprise CA's certificate will need to be signed by a public CA.

A big drawback of using S/MIME is the complications involved when you want to encrypt messages to recipients outside the organization. This is because to encrypt a message to a recipient, you need access to that recipient's public certificate. This is straightforward when the recipient is within the same Exchange organization and the process can be made automatic. This is vastly more complicated when the recipient is in an external organization— in that case automation is not possible and certificates need to be exchanged manually. Most average users aren't up to swapping certificates with people outside the organization, so they tend simply not to use S/MIME to protect or sign messages to people outside the Exchange organization.

> **MORE INFO**   **OUTLOOK WEB APP AND S/MIME**
>
> To learn more about Outlook Web App and S/MIME, consult the following TechNet document: *http://technet.microsoft.com/en-us/library/bb738140.aspx*.

MTLS and Domain Security

Domain Security allows you to create secure message paths to business partners over the Internet. Messages sent across these secure paths from an authenticated sender will be flagged as "Domain Secured" by Outlook and OWA. Domain security uses MTLS (Mutual Transport Layer Security). In typical TLS scenarios, authentication only occurs in one direction, with the client validating the server's certificate. MTLS is bidirectional and has each server verifying the connection with the partner server by validating the partner server's certificate.

The key to getting MTLS to work is ensuring that the SMTP servers at each organization trust the CA that issued the SMTP server certificate. This certificate should be configured with all of the internal SMTP domains for which the SMTP server will accept messages. If your organization uses separate email domains like contoso.com and adatum.com, you'll need to acquire a certificate that supports Subject Alternative Names. MTLS can use existing external Send and Receive connectors.

After the certificate has been obtained and imported, you need to configure outbound and inbound domain security. This is done using the *Set-TransportConfig* cmdlet. For example, to configure outbound domain security for the tailspintoys.com domain, use the following command on an internal Exchange server:

```
Set-TransportConfig –TLSSendDomainSecureList tailspintoys.com
```

When you use this command, the existing *TSLSendDomainSecureList* is replaced by whatever is specified in the new command. If you want to add a secure domain, you'll need to include the old and the new domains in the list. For example, if you wanted to add wingtiptoys.com when you already have tailspintoys.com configured as a secure domain, use the following command:

```
Set-TransportConfig –TLSSendDomainSecureList tailspintoys.com,wingtiptoys.com
```

You can use the *Get-TransportConfig* cmdlet to view a list of domains for which outbound domain security is configured. To configure Send connectors to support outbound domain security, use the *Set-SendConnector* cmdlet with the *DomainSecureEnabled* parameter. For example, to configure the Internet Send connector to support outbound domain security, issue the following command:

```
Set-SendConnector Internet –DomainSecureEnabled:$true
```

You use the *Set-TransportConfig* cmdlet with the *TLSReceiveDomainSecureList* parameter to configure inbound domain security. For example, to configure the partner domain tailspintoys.com for inbound domain security, issue the following command on an internal Exchange server:

```
Set-TransportConfig –TLSReceiveDomainSecureList tailspintoys.com
```

As is the case with configuring the secure send domains, the receive domain secure list is replaced when you issue this command. If you have existing secure receive domains, you need to include them in the list with the new domain. After you have configured the receive domain secure list, use the *Set-ReceiveConnector* cmdlet to configure the appropriate Receive connector to support inbound domain security. If your organization has multiple Edge Transport servers, you'll need to do this on the appropriate Receive connector on each server. For example, to configure the Receive connector named Internet to support inbound domain security, issue the following command:

```
Set-ReceiveConnector Internet –DomainSecureEnabled $True –AuthMechanism TLS
```

MORE INFO **MTLS**

To learn more about MTLS, consult the following TechNet document: *http://technet. microsoft.com/en-us/library/bb123543.aspx.*

Information Rights Management (IRM)

Information Rights Management is about controlling the flow of sensitive information within the organization. In traditional messaging systems, a sender has no control over the content of a message after that message has been sent to a recipient. IRM allows a sender to place restrictions on what a recipient can do with a message. This can include prohibiting the recipient from copying the contents of the message or printing it, as well as blocking recipients from forwarding messages to unauthorized users.

Exchange 2010 allows organizations to use IRM features to apply persistent protection to messages and attachments. IRM uses the Active Directory Rights Management Services (AD RMS) role, so a server that has the AD RMS role installed and a service connection point configured must be present in the forest that hosts the Exchange organization.

IRM protection can be applied to messages in multiple ways:

- Automatically through transport rules based on the content and properties of messages
- Automatically through Outlook protection rules based on department, message scope, and recipient address
- Manually by users of Outlook 2007, Outlook 2010, OWA, and Exchange ActiveSync devices

Exchange 2010 ships with a single AD RMS template called Do Not Forward. When the Do Not Forward template is applied to a message, only the recipient addressed in the message is able to decrypt and view the message contents. The recipient of the message will be unable to forward that message, copy content from that message, or print the message. Most organizations will create additional RMS templates on the RMS server that meet their particular needs using the Do Not Forward template as a basis.

> **MORE INFO**   **IRM IN EXCHANGE 2010**
>
> To learn more about IRM in Exchange 2010, consult the following TechNet document: *http://technet.microsoft.com/en-us/library/dd638140.aspx.*

IRM is enabled by default for internal messages. This means that you can create transport protection rules and Microsoft Outlook protection rules to protect messages as long as you have deployed AD RMS in the Exchange organization's forest. You can disable IRM for internal messages by issuing the following command:

```
Set-IRMConfiguration -InternalLicensingEnabled:$false
```

You can enable IRM for internal messages by issuing the following command:

```
Set-IRMConfiguration -InternalLicensingEnabled:$true
```

To enable transport decryption, journal report decryption, IRM with OWA, and IRM for Exchange Search, you need to add the Federation mailbox—a system mailbox created by the Exchange 2010 setup process—to the AD RMS Super Users group.

ActiveSync with IRM

IRM functionality can be used with supported Exchange ActiveSync devices without administrators having to configure specific AD RMS permissions or sync the device to a computer to activate it for IRM. Support isn't restricted to devices running Windows Mobile or Windows Phone, but to those organizations that license the Exchange ActiveSync protocol. To support IRM, the device's mobile email application must support the RightsManagementInformation tag, as specified in Exchange ActiveSync version 14.1 or later. ActiveSync IRM functionality allows users to:

- Create IRM-protected messages.
- Read IRM-protected messages.
- Reply to and forward IRM-protected messages.

To use ActiveSync with IRM, your must have configured or have available the following infrastructure components:

- Your organization's CAS must be running Exchange 2010 SP1 or later.
- You must have deployed an AD RMS server.
- IRM must be enabled for internal messages. You learned how to enable IRM for internal messages earlier in this objective.
- IRM must be enabled in the Exchange ActiveSync Mailbox policy. To do this you need to perform the following steps:
  - Add the Federation mailbox to the AD RMS super users group.
  - Use the *Set-IRMConfiguration* cmdlet to enable IRM on the CAS.
  - Ensure that the Require Password and Require Encryption On Device items are set on the ActiveSync Mailbox policy, as shown in Figure 3-2. Also ensure that the Allow Non-provisionable Devices check box is cleared.

MORE INFO **ACTIVESYNC WITH IRM**

To learn more about using ActiveSync with IRM, consult the following TechNet document: *http://technet.microsoft.com/en-us/library/ff657743.aspx.*

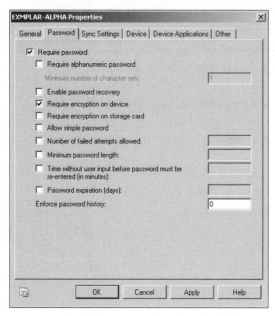

FIGURE 3-2 ActiveSync password settings for IRM

IRM in Multiple-Forest Environments

You can use IRM in cross-forest topologies, allowing you to have users in one organization use AD RMS templates when sending messages to users in another Exchange organization. To use IRM in cross-forest deployments, you must ensure that:

- The forests have an existing trust relationship.
- AD RMS clusters trust each other. They must also support users in other trusted forests.
- Exchange servers are given super-user authority for AD RMS clusters in the cross-forest topology.

To do this, perform the following general steps:

- Export trusted user domains from each AD RMS cluster. Import them to the RMS clusters in the other forests that comprise the cross-forest topology. Doing this will ensure that the AD RMS cluster in each forest is able to issue client licensor certificates and use licenses for users in all forests.
- Migrate the Federated Delivery mailbox account, with SID history, from each forest to the others, disabling the account in the target forests. You use the Active Directory Migration Tool to accomplish this task.
- Add the disabled Federated Delivery mailbox accounts from each forest in the cross-forest topology to the AD RMS server Super Users group on each forest's AD RMS cluster.

EXAM TIP

You cannot configure AD RMS between organizations that do not have a federated relationship.

Transport Protection and Decryption

Transport protection rules allow you to apply AD RMS templates to messages as they cross a transport server based on the properties of the message. Figure 3-3 shows a message where the Do Not Forward AD RMS template will be applied to any message that passes across the transport server that has the subject field or message body containing the words "Secret Project".

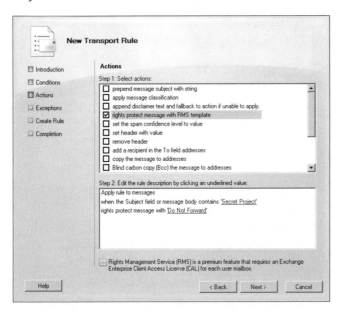

FIGURE 3-3 Transport protection

Transport decryption ensures that encrypted messages that pass across transport servers so that the transport rules agent can examine the message content and apply appropriate transport rules. This allows actions such as applying a disclaimer, or allowing antivirus scanners to verify that the message does not contain viruses or malware. When all necessary actions have been taken on the message, the message is re-encrypted with the same rights that applied to the message prior to decryption by the Decryption agent. The message is also flagged in such a way that it won't be decrypted again by any other Hub Transport servers in the organization.

You use the *Set-IRMConfiguration* cmdlet to configure transport decryption. Prior to configuring transport decryption, you need to add the Federation mailbox to the AD RMS cluster's super users group. When you enable transport decryption, you can choose between mandatory decryption and optional decryption. When you specify mandatory decryption, a message will be rejected if the transport agent is unable to decrypt it. If you specify optional decryption, a best-effort approach will be made to decrypt the message. If the decryption fails, the message is delivered as normal. For example, to configure mandatory transport decryption, issue the following EMS command:

```
Set-IRMConfiguration –TransportDecryptionSetting Mandatory
```

To disable transport decryption, issue the following EMS command:

```
Set-IRMConfiguration –TransportDecryptionSetting Disabled
```

> **MORE INFO**   **TRANSPORT DECRYPTION**
>
> To learn more about transport decryption, consult the following TechNet document: *http://technet.microsoft.com/en-us/library/dd638122.aspx*.

Outlook Protection Rule

Outlook protection rules function in a similar way to transport protection rules that automatically apply IRM protection to messages. The main difference is that the Outlook protection rule applies to messages at the client level rather than at the transport server level. The benefit of this is that IRM-protected messages are saved in an encrypted manner within Outlook's Sent Items folder, something that doesn't happen if the IRM protection is applied by a transport server.

Outlook protection rules work with clients running Office Outlook 2010 and OWA. Exchange distributes Outlook protection rules automatically to Exchange clients through Exchange Web Services. Outlook 2010 can only apply Outlook Protection rules if the appropriate AD RMS rights policy template is available to the client computer.

You can only use the following predicates when creating Outlook Protection Rules:

- **FromDepartment**   A query is used to check the sender's department attribute in Active Directory. The message will automatically be IRM protected if the sender's department matches a department specified in a rule.
- **SentTo**   Allows you to create an Outlook Protection Rule based on recipient.
- **SentToScope**   Allows you to specify whether a message should be protected based on whether the recipient is inside or outside the organization.

You create Outlook Protection Rules using the *New-OutlookProtectionRule* cmdlet in EMS. When creating a rule, you can specify whether a user is able to override the rule through the *UserCanOverride* parameter. For example, to apply the AD RMS template Template-WingTip to messages sent to the SMTP address specialprojects@wingtiptoys.com and to configure the rule so that it can't be overridden by the user, issue the following command:

```
New-OutlookProtectionRule –Name "Wingtip Projects" –SentTo specialprojects@wingtiptoys.com
–ApplyRightsProtectionTemplate "Template-Wingtip" –UserCanOverRide:$false
```

> **MORE INFO** **OUTLOOK PROTECTION RULES**
>
> To learn more about Outlook protection rules, consult the following TechNet document: *http://technet.microsoft.com/en-us/library/dd638178.aspx*.

EXAM TIP

Understand what steps are needed to configure domain security.

Objective Summary

- You can use externally secured Receive connectors to relay messages for partner organizations.
- In MTLS, both the sending and receiving SMTP servers authenticate the connection by checking each other's certificates.
- Domain security allows you to perform sender verification when messages are transmitted to partners across MTLS secured connections.
- You need to add the Federation mailbox to the AD RMS super users group to utilize many IRM features such as transport decryption and IRM with OWA.
- The default AD RMS template for Exchange is Do Not Forward.
- Transport protection rules can apply RMS templates to messages as they pass across transport servers.
- Enable transport decryption to ensure that transport rules apply to IRM-protected messages.
- Outlook Protection Rules allow IRM protection to be applied at the client level rather than at the transport server level.

Objective Review

Answer the following questions to test your knowledge of the information in this objective. You can find the answers to these questions and explanations of why each answer choice is correct or incorrect in the "Answers" section at the end of this chapter.

1. You have deployed Exchange 2010 in your organization and all clients are running Windows 7 with Office 2010 installed. You want users to be able to mark messages as Internal-Use-Only. The company's information security officer must be copied on all messages marked in this manner. Which of the following Exchange features would you use to accomplish this goal? (Choose two. Each answer forms part of a complete solution.)

   A. Message classification

   B. Outlook protection rule

   C. Moderated transport

   D. Transport rule

2. The majority of users in your organization use Outlook Web App to send and receive email messages. You want to ensure that users are able to encrypt the contents of their messages so that unauthorized third parties cannot view the message content. Additionally, message recipients should be able to verify the sender's identity. Which of the following technologies should you use to accomplish this goal?

   A. BitLocker to Go

   B. Encrypting File System certificates

   C. S/MIME certificates

   D. Transport Layer Security (TLS) certificates

3. You are in the process of deploying and configuring IRM in your Exchange 2010 organization. You want to use the following Exchange 2010 features: transport decryption, journal report decryption, IRM with OWA, and IRM for Exchange Search. Which of the following configuration steps do you need to take to accomplish this goal?

   A. Add the Federation mailbox to the Organization Management security group.

   B. Add the Federation mailbox to the Discovery Management security group.

   C. Add the Federation mailbox to the Records Management security group.

   D. Add the Federation mailbox to the AD RMS Super Users group.

4. You want to configure domain security for a partner organization fabrikam.com. You have obtained and installed the necessary TLS certificate on your organization's Edge Transport server. No other domains are configured for domain security. Which of the following cmdlets will you need to use to configure your Exchange organization to support domain security for the fabrikam.com domain? (Choose three. Each answer forms part of a complete solution.)

   A. *Set-TransportConfig*

   B. *Set-ReceiveConnector*

   C. *Set-SendConnector*

   D. *Set-AcceptedDomain*

5. You are in the process of creating a Receive connector that will be used for secure relay with a third-party organization. You have already configured an IPsec connection between the third-party organization's SMTP server and your organization's Edge Transport server and created a Receive connector that uses the partner organization's SMTP server's IP address as the remote server. Which of the following settings should you enable on the connector to ensure that you configure secure relay correctly? (Choose two. Each answer forms part of a complete solution.)

   A. Exchange Server authentication

   B. Externally Secured authentication

   C. Exchange Servers permissions group

   D. Anonymous users permissions group

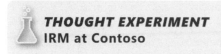

THOUGHT EXPERIMENT
IRM at Contoso

In the following thought experiment, you will apply what you've learned about the design and deploy messaging security objective to answer some questions about a hypothetical IRM deployment. You can find answers to these questions in the "Answers" section at the end of this chapter.

You are in the process of preparing for the deployment of IRM functionality at Contoso. The main objective of the deployment is to ensure that when someone in the finance department sends a message to anyone outside the organization, the Finance-IRM RMS template should apply to that message.

With these facts in mind, answer the following questions about deploying and configuring IRM:

1. Which role must you install on a server in the Active Directory forest before you can use IRM?

2. How can you ensure that messages that are sent to the special projects distribution list are encrypted in the sender's Sent Items folder?

3. Which group must you add the Federated mailbox to if you want to support the goal of using IRM with OWA?

4. Which predicates would you use when creating an Outlook protection rule to meet the needs of the records department?

Objective 3.2: Design and Deploy Exchange Permissions Model

Getting the privilege structure for Exchange administrators rights is as important as getting the physical and software infrastructure right. In many organizations, Exchange administrators are delegated privileges that they don't need and won't use. When designing your organization's Exchange deployment, you want to ensure that the IT professionals that manage Exchange only have those privileges necessary to complete their job role. In this objective, you will learn about role-based access control, a technology that allows you to partition administrative privileges across Exchange objects including servers and mailbox databases. You'll learn what tasks can be accomplished using Exchange Control Panel, how to remotely manage Exchange, and how to implement split permissions.

Role-Based Access Control

Role-based access control (RBAC) is a more sophisticated approach to the assignment of administrative privileges. Rather than the traditional approach where you had a specific security group that had specific privileges over the entire Exchange organization, RBAC uses the principle of granularity. With RBAC:

- You define what can be done by collecting together Windows PowerShell cmdlets and their parameters.
- You define where it can be done by collecting together Exchange objects, such as mailbox databases or mailbox servers.

A substantial difference is that rather than assigning an administrator or help desk staff member to a group that has more administrative privileges than they need, you can instead create your own custom administrative group that has only those privileges that you want to delegate.

Ultimately assigning privileges is still a matter of adding user accounts with Exchange mailboxes to groups, but the big difference is in the ability to actually create the group and define what it can do and where it can do it. The most difficult aspect of understanding RBAC is the terminology. Understanding RBAC involves understanding the following concepts:

- Management role entry
- Management role
- Management role group
- Management role assignment
- Management role scope

> **MORE INFO**   **ROLE-BASED ACCESS CONTROL**
>
> To learn more about RBAC, consult the following TechNet document: *http://technet.microsoft.com/en-us/library/dd298183.aspx*.

Management Roles and Management Role Entries

A management role is a collection of management role entries. A management role entry is an EMS cmdlet and a set of parameters that can be used with that cmdlet. For example, *Set-IRMConfiguration* and the *TransportDecryptionSetting* parameter could make up a role entry. Although there are other parameters for this cmdlet, when creating a role entry you specify only those parameters which you want to include. This allows you to be very specific when assigning administrative permissions.

Exchange Server 2010 includes more than 70 built-in management roles, so chances are that a management role already exists that collects the management role entries that you're interested in delegating. It is important to remember that you can't modify any of the built-in management roles, although you can create a duplicate of that role and then modify which management role entries are associated with the role.

You create management roles using the *New-ManagementRole* cmdlet. When creating a new management role, you need to specify a parent management role. By default, the newly created management role will inherit the same permissions and role entries assigned to the parent role. For example, to create a new management role based on the Databases role, issue the following command:

```
New-ManagementRole -Name CustomDatabase -Parent Databases
```

> **MORE INFO**   **MANAGEMENT ROLES**
>
> To learn more about management roles, consult the following TechNet document: *http://technet.microsoft.com/en-us/library/dd298116.aspx*.

Built-in Role Groups

Exchange 2010 includes 11 built-in role groups. You should note that these built-in role groups are set to use the default organization-wide scope. You can modify built-in role groups, but best practice is to create a duplicate of the role group and then modify it as necessary when creating custom role groups. The built-in role groups, shown in Figure 3-4, are as follows:

- **Organization Management**   Mailboxes that hold this role have access to the entire Exchange organization and can perform almost all tasks except for mailbox searches and management of unscoped top-level management roles.

- **View-Only Organization Management**   Mailboxes that hold this role can view the properties of all objects in the Exchange organization.

- **Recipient Management**   Mailboxes that hold this role are able to create or modify recipients within the Exchange organization.

- **UM Management**   Mailboxes that hold this role can managed Unified Messaging (UM) server configuration, UM properties on mailboxes, UM prompts, and UM auto attendant configuration.

- **Help Desk**   Mailboxes that hold this role can perform limited recipient management tasks. These involve being able to perform any task that users can perform themselves, such as modifying an OWA display name.

- **Hygiene Management**   Mailboxes that hold this role are able to configure antivirus and anti-spam functionality for Exchange Server 2010.

- **Records Management**   Mailboxes that hold this role are able to configure compliance features such as retention policy tags, message classification, and transport rules.

- **Discovery Management**   Mailboxes that hold this role are able to perform mailbox searches and can also configure legal holds.

- **Public Folder Management**   Mailboxes that hold this role are able to manage public folders and public folder databases.

- **Server Management**   Mailboxes that hold this role are able to view and configure all Exchange Server 2010 servers in the organization.

- **Delegated Setup**   Mailboxes that hold this role are able to deploy Exchange Server 2010, but have no permission to manage the server after it is deployed.

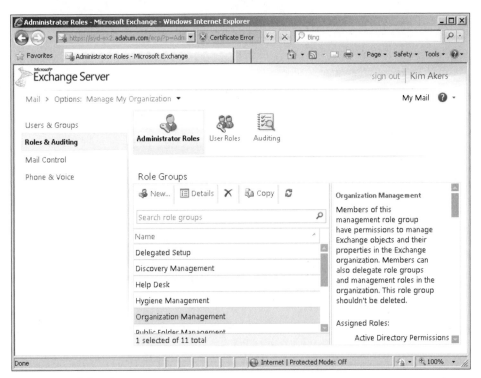

FIGURE 3-4 Built-in role groups

MORE INFO   BUILT-IN ROLE GROUPS

To learn more about built-in role groups, consult the following TechNet document: *http://technet.microsoft.com/en-us/library/dd351266.aspx.*

Custom Management Role Groups

A management role group is a universal security group that has Exchange mailboxes as members. You use management role assignments to connect management role groups to management roles. You create custom management role groups using the *New-RoleGroup* cmdlet. When doing this you should specify which roles are associated with the group, what the scope of the groups is, who manages the group, and what the group membership is. For example, to create a new management role group called Australia Recipients that has the Mail Recipients, Distribution Groups, and Move Mailboxes roles over the Australia Users scope; is managed by Mick; and has Ian, Ken, and Rooslan as members; issue the following command:

```
New-RoleGroup -Name "Australia Recipients" -Roles "Mail Recipients", "Distribution
Groups", "Move Mailboxes" -CustomRecipientWriteScope "Australia Users", -ManagedBy
"Mick" -Members "Ian", "Ken", "Rooslan"
```

Linked role groups are used in resource-forest scenarios. Linked role groups work by creating a link between a management role group in the forest that hosts Exchange and a universal security group in the trusted accounts forest.

Members of the Organization Management role group are able to modify the membership of role groups. If you want to allow a user who isn't a member of the Organization Management role group to modify the membership of a role group, configure the *ManagedBy* property on that role group. You can accomplish this with the *Set-RoleGroup* EMS cmdlet.

MORE INFO   MANAGEMENT ROLE GROUPS

To learn more about management role groups, consult the following TechNet document: *http://technet.microsoft.com/en-us/library/dd638105.aspx.*

Management Role Scopes

Management role scopes are a collection of objects within Exchange. You use management role scopes to limit where an administrator can use particular administrative privileges. Management scopes can be one of the following:

- **Exclusive scope**   Exclusive scopes allow you to deny access to objects contained within the scope if users aren't assigned a role associated with that exclusive scope. For example, you might have a scope that includes all mailboxes in the Sydney office. You may create an exclusive scope that is for the mailboxes of the management team in the Sydney office. Only users assigned to a role associated with the exclusive scope would be able to perform tasks against the mailboxes of the management team in the Sydney office, even if they were assigned to a role associated with all the mailboxes in the Sydney office.

- **Regular scope**   Regular scopes aren't exclusive. Regular scopes are collections of objects that can be managed by users assigned to a role associated with that scope. For example, you might have a scope that includes all mailboxes in the Sydney office and another scope that includes all mailboxes hosted in Australia. Because none of these is an exclusive scope, a user assigned to a role associated with the "all mailboxes in Australia" scope would be able to manage mailboxes in the Sydney office.

A role can have all or some of the following scope types:

- **Recipient read scope**   This specifies which recipient objects users assigned the management role are allowed to view from Active Directory.
- **Recipient write scope**   This specifies which recipient objects users assigned the management role scope are allowed to modify in Active Directory.
- **Configuration read scope**   This specifies which objects users assigned the management role are able to view from Active Directory.
- **Configuration write scope**   This specifies which objects users assigned the management role are able to modify in Active Directory.

Implicit scopes are the built-in scopes that apply to management roles. All of the parent and child management roles within the same role type share the same implicit scopes. Implicit scopes apply to the built-in management role as well as any custom management roles. Exchange 2010 has the following built-in implicit scopes:

- **Organization**   If present in the write scope, the role can create or modify recipient objects across the entire Exchange organization. If present in the read scope, the role can view any recipient object across the entire Exchange organization.
- **MyGAL**   When present with the write scope, the role can create or modify the properties of any recipient within the current user's GAL When present in the read scope, the role can view the properties of any recipient within the current user's GAL.
- **Self**   When present in the write scope, the role can modify the properties of the current user mailbox. When present in the read scope, the role can view the properties of the current user mailbox.
- **MyDistributionGroups**   When present in the write scope, the role can create or modify distribution list objects owned by the current user. When present in the read scope, the role can view the properties of distribution list objects owned by the current user.
- **OrganizationConfig**   If OrganizationConfig is present in the role's write scope, role holders can create or modify any server or database object in the Exchange organization. If OrganizationConfig is present in the role's read scope, role holders can view the properties of any server of database configuration object in the Exchange organization.

Custom scopes allow you to be more specific about the types of objects that you delegate privileges over. Custom scopes allow you to delegate rights over a particular OU, a specific type of recipient, or other collection of Exchange objects. Exchange 2010 allows you to create the following types of custom scopes:

- **OU Scope**   This scope allows users assigned the role the ability to modify recipient objects within a specific Organizational Unit.
- **Recipient filter scope**   This scope allows users assigned the role the ability to modify recipient objects based on recipient properties such as department, location, and manager.
- **Configuration scope**   This scope allows users assigned the role the ability to modify specific servers based either on lists or server filterable properties such as Active Directory site or role. Exchange 2010 with Service Pack 1 allows configuration scopes to include specific mailbox databases either as lists or through filterable database properties.

You can create scopes with the *New-ManagementScope* cmdlet. For example, to create a new management scope named Sydney-Mailbox-Servers that includes only the servers SYDMBX1, SYDMBX2, and SYDMBX3, issue the following command:

```
New-ManagementScope -Name "Sydney-Mailbox-Servers" -ServerList SYDMBX1, SYDMBX2, SYDMBX3
```

> **MORE INFO**   **MANAGEMENT ROLE SCOPES**
>
> To learn more about management role scopes, consult the following TechNet document: *http://technet.microsoft.com/en-us/library/dd335146.aspx.*

Management Role Assignments

Management role assignments connect a management role to a role group. This is already done for all of the default role groups and in most cases the defaults will work for any organization. Role assignments can also assign a role to a user account or a role assignment policy. Each time you assign a role to a unique role group, role assignment policy, or individual user account, a new role assignment is created. You create management role assignments using the *New-ManagementRoleAssignment* cmdlet. For example, to assign the Mail Recipients role for the Sydney Recipients scope to the SydMailAdmins security group, use the following cmdlet:

```
New-ManagementRoleAssignment -Name "Sydney Recipient Management" -SecurityGroup
"SydMailAdmins" -Role "Mail Recipients" -CustomRecipientWriteScope "Sydney Recipients"
```

> **MORE INFO**   **MANAGEMENT ROLE ASSIGNMENTS**
>
> To learn more about management role assignments, consult the following TechNet document: *http://technet.microsoft.com/en-us/library/dd335131.aspx.*

Exchange Control Panel

Exchange Control Panel (ECP), shown in Figure 3-5, is a web-based control panel that allows users and Exchange administrators to manage certain aspects of Exchange. When used from a typical user account, ECP can be used to perform tasks such as modify settings, create inbox rules, and set automatic replies.

FIGURE 3-5 Exchange Control Panel

Administrators can use ECP to perform RBAC tasks. This includes the creation of new role groups, the modification of scopes, modification of role groups, and modification of role group membership.

ECP only displays functionality that an administrator has been delegated. For example, a user with the Discovery role will only be able to see discovery-related tasks. ECP allows administrators to manage and edit RBAC roles, something that cannot be accomplished through EMC. While you can add users to role using Active Directory Users and Computers, you can't associate a scope with a role group using this tool. This can only be done from EMS or through EMC.

> **MORE INFO**   **EXCHANGE CONTROL PANEL**
>
> To learn more about ECP, consult the following TechNet document: *http://technet. microsoft.com/en-us/library/dd876904.aspx*.

Split Permissions Model

The split permissions model allows organizations to separate the management of Exchange Server 2010 objects and Active Directory objects. This way an organization can have two different groups of administrators: Exchange administrators who manage Exchange servers and recipients, and Active Directory administrators who manage domains, users, group policy, and other Active Directory items. The split permissions model allows you to make a distinction between creating security principles—such as user accounts—in Active Directory, and the configuration of those objects for use with the messaging system. The Exchange Server 2010 Service Pack 1 setup wizard allows you to apply the Active Directory split permissions model during Exchange Setup, as shown in Figure 3-6.

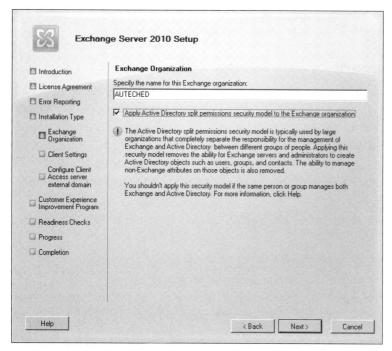

FIGURE 3-6 Configuring split permissions

Exchange 2010 SP1 defaults to a shared permissions model, which is the traditional model for managing Exchange 2010, but it is possible to instead use split permissions. The two types of split permissions model are:

- **Active Directory split permissions** The permission to create security principles in the Active Directory domain partition are completely separate from any Exchange user, service, or server. Creation of Active Directory security principles must be performed using Active Directory management tools such as Active Directory Users and Computers.

- **RBAC split permissions**   Permissions to create security principles in the Active Directory domain partition are controlled through Role Based Access Control. Only those that are members of the appropriate role group can create security principles. Exchange servers and services can create security principles under this model.

If you choose Active Directory split permissions, you can only change to shared permissions or RBAC split permissions by rerunning Setup and disabling Active Directory split permissions. The permissions model chosen applies to the entire Exchange organization.

> *MORE INFO*   **SPLIT PERMISSIONS**
>
> To learn more about split permissions, consult the following TechNet document: *http://technet.microsoft.com/en-us/library/dd638106.aspx*.

Objective Summary

- Management roles are collections of role entries. A role entry is an EMS cmdlet and a set of parameters. There are more than 70 built-in management roles. You can modify the default management roles.

- Management role groups are security groups that have members. These groups have been assigned management roles and management scopes. Most organizations will only use the built in role groups and will not fully take advantage of the options available in RBAC.

- Management role scopes define which objects a management role might be granted privileges over.

- Management role assignments assign management roles and scopes to universal security groups.

- Exchange Control Panel (ECP) allows you to perform some administrative tasks through a web interface. You can perform RBAC administration tasks through this control panel.

- With Exchange 2010 Service Pack 1 you can use split permissions. Exchange defaults to using shared permissions unless you explicitly choose otherwise.

- Active Directory split permissions limit the creation of Active Directory security principles to the Active Directory tools. It is not possible to create Active Directory security principles using the Exchange administration tools.

- RBAC split permissions mean that Active Directory domain permissions are controlled through role-based access control. Users with the appropriate permissions can create Active Directory security principles using Exchange administration tools.

Objective Review

Answer the following questions to test your knowledge of the information in this objective. You can find the answers to these questions and explanations of why each answer choice is correct or incorrect in the "Answers" section at the end of this chapter.

1. Your organization has a single-forest spread with country-based domains in Australia, New Zealand, and Tonga. You have deployed Mailbox servers in each of these countries. Each location has a compliance officer. The compliance officer for each country should only have access to the Exchange servers in that country. You are preparing the appropriate settings for the compliance officer in Tonga. Which of the following steps should you take to accomplish this goal? (Choose three. Each answer forms part of a complete solution.)

   A. Create a custom role group based on the Records Management built-in role group.

   B. Create a custom management scope. Assign this scope to the custom role group.

   C. Add the compliance officer for Tonga to the custom role group.

   D. Modify the Records Management built-in role group.

2. Your organization has a single-forest spread with country-based domains in Australia, New Zealand, and Tonga. You have deployed Exchange servers in each of these countries. You want to allow local administrators in each country to be able to perform Exchange server management tasks on these servers. You only want to provide these administrators with the minimum privileges necessary to perform their tasks. When creating the configuration for the New Zealand offices, which of the following steps should you take to accomplish this task? (Choose two. Each answer forms part of a complete solution.)

   A. Create a custom role group based off the Server Management role group.

   B. Create a custom role group based off the Organization Management role group.

   C. Create a custom scope that includes all servers located in New Zealand.

   D. Create a custom scope that includes all servers located in New Zealand, Tonga, and Australia.

3. What type of custom scope would you create if you wanted to create a scope that was limited to specific mailbox databases?

   A. OU scope

   B. Recipient filter scope

   C. Configuration scope

   D. Organization scope

4. You are in the process of designing an Exchange 2010 permissions model. You want to use a permissions model that blocks the creation of Active Directory security principles from Exchange Management Console and Exchange Management Shell. Which of the following permissions models should you choose?

   A. Active Directory split permissions

   B. Shared permissions

   C. RBAC split permissions

   D. Mixed mode

THOUGHT EXPERIMENT
Designing an Exchange Permissions Model

In the following thought experiment, you will apply what you've learned about the design and deploy Exchange permissions model objective to determine which built-in role groups to use when designing your organization's Exchange administration model. You can find answers to these questions in the "Answers" section at the end of this chapter.

Ian's team should be responsible for creating recipients, but should not have the ability to manage Exchange servers.

Sam's team should be able to configure servers, but not manage recipients.

Kim's team should be responsible for configuring antivirus and anti-spam functionality.

Ken's team should be able to view the properties of all objects in the Exchange organization.

Answer the following questions:

1. To which role should you add Ian's team?

2. To which role should you add Kim's team?

3. To which role should you add Sam's team?

4. To which role should you add Ken's team?

Objective 3.3: Design and Deploy Message Hygiene

The real cost of spam to your organization isn't just in bandwidth bits, processor cycles, and storage bytes. The biggest cost of spam to your organization is in the collective minutes lost to employees across the organization when they have to deal with the distracting task of determining whether a particular message is relevant to their job or a waste of time. It might take a recipient only two seconds to assess whether a message is from a spammer, but when you multiply that figure by a couple of messages per day across every employee in your organization, it's easy to calculate hours of lost productivity. In this chapter you'll learn about configuring Exchange 2010's anti-spam and antivirus features, including connection, attachment, recipient, sender, and content filtering rules. You'll also learn about safelist aggregation, block list, phishing and spam confidence levels, and sender reputation levels.

This objective covers:

- Identifying, planning, and designing anti-spam and antivirus solutions for the messaging deployment.
- Defining connection, attachment, recipient, sender, and content filtering rules.
- Safelist aggregation and block lists.
- Phishing confidence level (PCL).
- Spam confidence level (SCL).
- Sender reputation level (SRL).

Antivirus Features

Even though most organizations run anti-malware scanners on client desktops, a good defense-in-depth strategy also involves running anti-malware software on Exchange Edge Transport, Hub Transport, and Mailbox servers. Microsoft provides an evaluation version of Forefront Protection 2010 for Exchange server with the Exchange 2010 installation media. Although there are other third-party anti-malware solutions for Exchange Server 2010, third-party products are rarely mentioned on Microsoft certification exams.

You can install Forefront Protection 2010 for Exchange server on servers hosting the Edge Transport, Hub Transport, and Mailbox server role. Installing the product on all these servers at once, although providing the highest level of protection, is excessive. This is especially so when client computers have their own separate anti-malware software installed. Organizations that use Edge Transport servers often deploy a product such as Forefront on the Edge Transport server to protect recipients from malware contained in inbound messages. Some organizations also configure protection on mailbox servers as a way of ensuring that these servers do not become infected if a client computer ends up compromised by malware despite its own local protection.

Anti-Spam Features

Exchange 2010 has a number of anti-spam technologies that are designed to reduce the number of spam messages that end up reaching a user's mailbox. When you are designing an anti-spam solution for your organization's Exchange environment, you have to ensure that you don't make your anti-spam settings so restrictive that legitimate messages are unable to reach their intended recipients.

Safelist Aggregation

Safelist aggregation is an anti-spam feature that uses both Outlook and Exchange. It collects information from the Safe Recipients Lists, Safe Senders Lists, Blocked Senders Lists, and Outlook user's contact data and forwards that data to the anti-spam agents on the Edge Transport server. The main difference with Safelist aggregation is that it uses intelligence about senders that has been gathered by the end users in your organization. Sometimes end users can be better at determining which messages are legitimate and which messages are spam than Exchange's anti-spam heuristics.

When safelist aggregation is enabled in an organization, the Content Filter will pass email messages designated as safe to mailboxes without processing. Safelist aggregation also works as a per-recipient Blocked Sender list, allowing the Edge Transport server to block a message from a sender to one recipient, but not to another depending on individual block list and safelist configuration.

Safelist aggregation uses each user's safelist collection. A safelist collection is made up of up to 1024 unique addresses that are drawn from the following items within Outlook:

- Safe senders and safe recipients
- Blocked senders
- Safe domain
- External contacts

Safelist aggregation is enabled by default in Exchange 2010. Safelist aggregation data is transmitted out to the Edge Transport server using the EdgeSync process. You can force an update of safelist aggregation data using the *Update-SafeList* cmdlet.

> **MORE INFO**   **SAFELIST AGGREGATION**
>
> To learn more about safelist aggregation, consult the following TechNet document: *http://technet.microsoft.com/en-us/library/bb125168.aspx.*

Sender ID

Sender ID is designed to combat spoofing, a practice where a sender attempts to impersonate a particular sender and domain as a way of circumventing anti-spam functionality. The Sender ID agent on an Edge Transport server queries the DNS zone associated with the sender's SMTP server to verify that the sending server's SMTP address is authorized to send messages for the sender's email domain.

Sender ID relies upon DNS administrators populating DNS zone data with Sender Policy Framework (SPF) records. SPF records specify which SMTP servers are authorized to send messages from that domain. The Sender ID evaluation process calculates a Sender ID status value for the message. This status value is used when calculating the Spam Confidence Level (SCL) rating associated with the message. You'll learn about SCL ratings later in this objective. The possible Sender ID status values are:

- **Pass**   The IP address and the Purported Responsible Address (PRA) pass the Sender ID check.
- **Neutral**   Published Sender ID data is inconclusive.
- **Soft fail**   The IP address for the PRA was not found in the list of authorized addresses.
- **Fail**   The IP address is not permitted, the sending domain does not exist, or no PRA is found in the incoming mail.
- **None**   The sender's DNS zone does not contain SPD data.
- **TempError**   A temporary DNS failure occurred.
- **PermError**   The DNS record is invalid.

You can configure how the Edge Transport server processes messages that are identified as spoofed or where the DNS server can't be reached by configuring an action on the Action tab of the Sender ID Properties dialog box, shown in Figure 3-7.

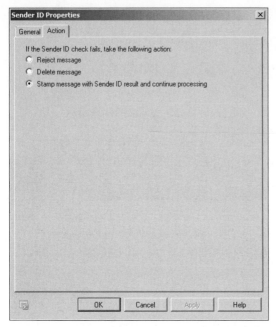

FIGURE 3-7 Sender ID properties

You can use the *Set-SenderIDConfig* cmdlet to configure Sender ID to ignore certain domains or specific recipients. For example, to configure Sender ID to not check messages from the address k.akers@tailspintoys.com, you would issue the following command:

```
Set-SenderIDConfig –BypassedRecipients k.akers@tailspintoys.com
```

To configure Sender ID to not process messages from the wingtiptoys.com mail domain, issue the following command:

```
Set-SenderIDConfig –BypassedSenderDomains wingtiptoys.com
```

> **MORE INFO** **SENDER ID**
>
> To learn more about Sender ID, consult the following TechNet document: *http://technet. microsoft.com/en-us/library/aa996295.aspx.*

Block Lists

IP block lists work off the simple principle of blocking incoming messages from a list of IP addresses. You can populate the list of IP addresses on the Blocked Addresses tab of the IP Block List Properties dialog box, shown in Figure 3-8. You can use the *Add-IPBlockListEntry* cmdlet to add IP addresses or IP address ranges to the block list.

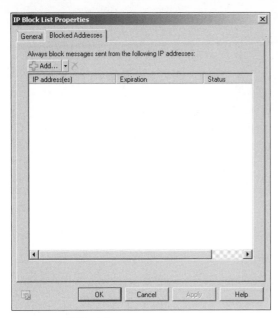

FIGURE 3-8 IP block list

The drawback of IP block lists is that the majority of spam today is launched through botnets installed on computers infected with malware, rather than from dedicated spammer SMTP servers. This means that in most cases you won't get spam from the same IP address twice and that a manually maintained IP block list will be an ineffective shield against spam.

A solution to this is to use what is known as an IP block list provider, who will provide you with regularly updated lists of addresses to block. This allows you to automate the process of blocking IP addresses that have been reported as sending spam. You can manage block list providers on the Providers tab of the IP Block List Providers Properties dialog box shown in Figure 3-9. You can use the Exceptions tab to specify recipient addresses within your organization that should be exempt from the block list. For example, if Don Hall needs to receive messages even if they come from blocked sites, you can add his email address on the Exceptions tab to accomplish this goal.

Allow lists work similarly to block lists, except that an SMTP server with IP address on an allow list will not have the messages blocked, even if the IP address is also on a block list. You can configure an IP allow list provider to provide you with updated information on SMTP servers that are known to be valid in the same way that you would configure a block list provider to keep you apprised of SMTP server IP addresses that are known sources of spam. You can use the *Add-IPAllowListEntry* cmdlet to add entries to the IP Allow list. You can also do this by editing the properties of the IP Allow list on the Edge Transport server.

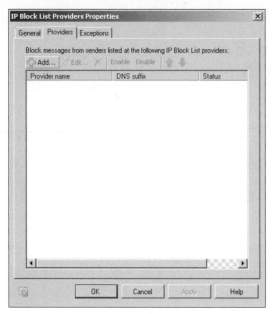

FIGURE 3-9 Block list providers

Sender Reputation Level

Sender reputation is a technology that runs on Edge Transport servers that analyzes and blocks messages based on message and sender characteristics. By default, sender reputation is disabled for internal messages. Sender reputation also uses existing data stored about the sender. If a sender sends multiple messages that are characterized as likely spam, their reputation score will increase the chance that they will be blocked, even if normally the messages by themselves would not be enough to trigger an anti-spam block.

Sender reputation uses a Sender Reputation Level (SRL) figure, calculated using the following statistics:

- **HELO/EHLO analysis** Checks whether the HELO/EHLO information is consistent and matches the originating IP address as determined by the Connection Filter agent. Inconsistencies in the HELO/EHLO information increase the probability that messages from this sender are spam.

- **Reverse DNS lookup** Checks whether the IP address from which the sender transmitted the message matches the DNS name associated with the HELO/EHLO

SMTP traffic. When there is no match, the message is judged to have a higher probability of being spam.

- **Analysis of sender's SCL ratings** The Content Filter assigns a Spam Confidence Level rating to each incoming message. If a sender is consistently transmitting messages that the Content Filter assigns a high probability of being spam, that will negatively impact the sender's reputation level.

- **Sender open proxy test** A check is performed to see whether the SMTP address that transmitted the message fails an open proxy test. If the sender's SMTP server is found to be an open proxy, the message is judged to have a higher probability of being spam.

By performing an analysis of each of these factors, the SRL is calculated. This is a number between 0 and 9 where 0 has been assessed of having minimal probability of coming from a spammer and 9 is assessed as almost certainty that the sender is a spammer. You configure the level at which a sender's messages will be blocked by configuring the Sender Reputation Level Block Threshold slider on the Sender Reputation Properties dialog box, shown in Figure 3-10. Using this dialog box, you can place a sender on the block list for a specific period of time, the default being 24 hours. You can configure SRL configuration properties from EMS using the *Set-SenderReputationConfig* cmdlet.

MORE INFO **SENDER REPUTATION**

To learn more about sender reputation, consult the following TechNet document: *http://technet.microsoft.com/en-us/library/bb124512.aspx.*

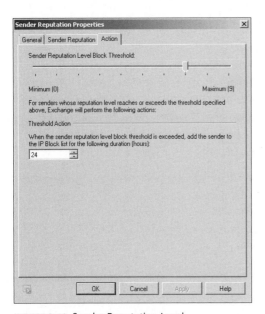

FIGURE 3-10 Sender Reputation Level

Phishing Confidence Level

Phishing is an attack in which a recipient is lured to a false website, usually in the hope that the recipient will provide important credentials such as logon information to an online banking website or provide credit card details. The content filtering agent generates a Phishing Confidence Level (PCL) rating for each inbound message that passes across an Edge Transport server. PCL values range in value from 1 to 8. The content filter stamps the message with the PCL rating and one of the following values:

- **Neutral** The message content has been assessed as unlikely to be phishing related. This value is assigned to messages with a PCL rating of 1 to 3.

- **Suspicious** The message content is likely to be phishing related. This value is assigned to messages with a PCL rating of 4 through 8.

The Edge Transport server takes no action on these messages based on the PCL rating. Instead, the values determine what steps the Outlook client takes.

Spam Confidence Level

The Content Filter agent uses a heuristic algorithm known as Microsoft SmartScreen to analyze the content of a message and to generate a Spam Confidence Level (SCL) value for that message. On the Content Filtering Properties dialog box, shown in Figure 3-11, you can configure what happens to a message depending on what SCL rating it generates. You can configure the following options:

- **SCL delete threshold** If a message has an SCL at or above this value, it is deleted by the Edge Transport server.

- **SCL reject threshold** If a message has an SCL at or above this value, but below the SCL delete threshold, it is rejected. When a message is rejected, Exchange forwards a non-delivery report (NDR) to the sender.

- **SCL quarantine threshold** If a message has an SCL at or above this value, but below the SCL reject threshold, it is forwarded to the quarantine mailbox.

If you choose to use a quarantine mailbox, someone in the organization should be tasked with regularly checking the mailbox for messages that have been incorrectly categorized as spam. If your organization doesn't have the resources to perform this sort of regular maintenance, you should not select the quarantine option.

> *MORE INFO* **SPAM CONFIDENCE LEVEL**
>
> To learn more about Spam Confidence Level, consult the following TechNet document: *http://technet.microsoft.com/en-us/library/aa995744.aspx.*

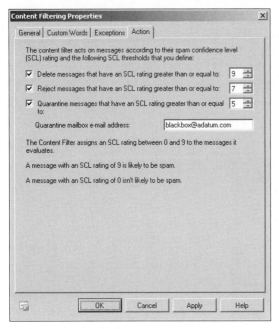

FIGURE 3-11 Spam Confidence Level

Content Filtering

On top of the heuristics that analyze a message to determine whether it contains spam content, you can configure content filtering to perform the following tasks:

- Exempt recipients on the basis of email address.
- Always allow messages that contain specific phrases.
- Block messages that contain specific phrases.

You can configure which words ensure that a message is always allowed and which words ensure that a message is always blocked on the Custom Words tab of the Content Filtering Properties dialog box as shown in Figure 3-12. You configure which email recipients are always exempted from content filtering on the Exceptions tab of this dialog box.

> **MORE INFO**   **CONTENT FILTERING**
>
> To learn more about content filtering, consult the following TechNet document: *http://technet.microsoft.com/en-us/library/bb124739.aspx.*

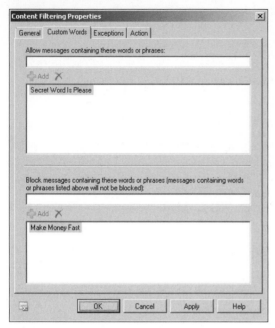

FIGURE 3-12 Content filtering

Attachment Filtering

Attachment filtering allows you to control the attachments that users in your organization are able to receive. When the attachment filter encounters an attachment on the list of blocked attachments, it takes one of the following actions:

- **Strip**   This is the default value. The attachment is stripped from the message, but the message itself is delivered to the recipient.
- **Reject**   The message is rejected. The sender is issued an NDR.
- **Silent Delete**   The message is rejected. No notification is provided.

You perform attachment filtering management tasks from EMS; you cannot perform them in EMC as of Exchange 2010 Service Pack 1. You configure the filtering action using the *Set-AttachmentFilterListConfig* cmdlet with the *Action* parameter.

To enable the Attachment Filter agent, issue the following command:

```
Enable-TransportAgent –Identity "Attachment Filtering agent"
```

You add attachment filter entries using the *Add-AttachmentFilterEntry* cmdlet. For example, to filter all JPEG files using an attachment filter, you can use the following MIME content type filter:

```
Add-AttachmentFilterEntry –Name image/jpeg –Type ContentType
```

To filter all email attachments with a specific extension—for example, all attachments with the .com extension—issue the following command:

```
Add-AttachmentFilterEntry –Name *.COM –Type FileName
```

To view all currently filtered attachment types, issue the following command:

```
Get-AttachmentFilterEntry
```

MORE INFO **ATTACHMENT FILTERING**

To learn more about attachment filtering, consult the following TechNet document: *http://technet.microsoft.com/en-us/library/bb124399.aspx.*

Recipient Filtering

Recipient filtering allows you to block messages sent to recipients that do not exist within the directory, or to specific recipients. You can use recipient filtering to block senders from outside the organization from sending messages to internal distribution lists. Figure 3-13 shows the Blocked Recipients tab of a Recipient Filtering agent.

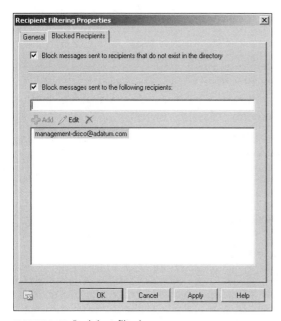

FIGURE 3-13 Recipient filtering

You configure recipient filtering with the *Set-RecipientFilterConfig* cmdlet. For example, to configure the Recipient Filter agent to block messages sent to recipients that are not in Active Directory, issue the following command:

```
Set-RecipientFilterConfig –RecipientValidationEnabled $true
```

Objective Summary

- Safelist aggregation takes user data about senders and recipients and uses this to block or allow incoming messages.
- Sender ID allows the validity of SMTP servers to be determined through a query of the DNS zone associated with the sender's email domain.
- Block and allow lists allow you to permit or deny messages based on the IP address of the SMTP server from which they were transmitted.
- Sender Reputation Level (SRL) is used to generate time-limited blocks on senders who send messages that are identified by the content filter as likely to be spam.
- Phishing Confidence Level (PCL) is a value that represents the likelihood that a message is phishing related.
- Spam Confidence Level (SCL) is a value that represents the likelihood that a message is spam.
- Content filtering allows you to block or allow messages based on certain phrases or words contained within the message.
- Attachment filtering allows you to configure attachments of certain file types to be automatically stripped from messages before they reach recipients.
- Recipient filtering allows you to block messages from outside the organization being sent to users who are not listed within the directory or to block messages being sent to particular addresses, such as distribution groups.

Objective Review

Answer the following questions to test your knowledge of the information in this objective. You can find the answers to these questions and explanations of why each answer choice is correct or incorrect in the "Answers" section at the end of this chapter.

1. You have just created three distribution lists for inter-office group communication. These groups should be of a freeform nature and should not require any sort of message submission approval process. You want to make sure that people outside the organization are unable to send messages to this list, even if they guess the list's address. Which of the following Exchange 2010 features should you configure to accomplish this goal?

   A. Recipient filtering

   B. Content filtering

    C. Moderated transport

    D. Transport rule

2. Which of the following cmdlets would you use if you wanted to configure Sender ID not to process incoming messages from the wingtiptoys.com domain?

    A. *Set-AcceptedDomain*

    B. *Set-SenderIDConfig*

    C. *Set-IPAllowListConfig*

    D. *Set-TransportRule*

3. Which of the following EMS cmdlets can you use to configure an Edge Transport server to block messages for 48 hours for a sender whose Sender Reputation Level exceeds a value of 6?

    A. *Set-IPAllowListConfig*

    B. *Set-TransportRule*

    C. *Set-SenderReputationConfig*

    D. *Set-SenderIDConfig*

4. You want to ensure that messages that contain a specific passphrase are always delivered to recipients in your organization, even if they would normally be rejected as spam. Which of the following anti-spam agents would you configure to accomplish this goal?

    A. Sender ID

    B. Sender reputation

    C. Recipient filtering

    D. Content filtering

THOUGHT EXPERIMENT
Improving Message Hygiene

In the following thought experiment, you will apply what you've learned about the design and deploy message hygiene objective to design a message hygiene solution. You can find answers to these questions in the "Answers" section at the end of this chapter.

You are planning a message hygiene strategy at Contoso. Your design should meet the following goals:

All messages that include the phrase Special Project should automatically bypass the spam filter.

All messages from SMTP servers associated with three specific IP addresses should be blocked.

Your anti-spam solution should recognize messages that use Sender Policy Framework (SPF).

External senders should not be able to send messages to critical distribution groups.

With this information in mind, answer the following questions:

1. Which anti-spam agent should you configure to ensure that messages with the passphrase automatically bypass the spam filter?

2. Which anti-spam agent should you configure to block messages from SMTP servers at specific IP addresses?

3. Which anti-spam agent should you configure to ensure that messages from SMTP servers registered with SPF records in DNS are recognized?

4. Which anti-spam agent should you configure to ensure that messages from senders outside the organization can't be sent to critical distribution groups?

Objective 3.4: Design and Deploy Client Access Security

Client Access security isn't just about ensuring that users are able to access their mailboxes in a secure manner, but also about ensuring that unauthorized third parties aren't able to access the mailboxes of users in your organization. In this chapter you will learn how to ensure that clients are accessing their Exchange mailboxes in a secure manner through ActiveSync, Outlook, third-party messaging clients, and Outlook Web App.

This objective covers:

- ActiveSync policies.
- OWA Authentication protocols.
- OWA segmentatiot.

ActiveSync Policies

ActiveSync policies give you control over the mobile devices that sync with Exchange. ActiveSync policies are increasingly important as more and more organizational data is stored on mobile devices, which are much easier to lose than items such as laptop computers.

It is important to recognize when designing ActiveSync policies that not all mobile devices that use ActiveSync support every ActiveSync policy item. For example, devices running Windows Phone 7 support fewer ActiveSync policy items than devices running Windows Mobile 6.5. When planning ActiveSync policies, you should ensure that the mobile devices used by people in your organization support policy features. Because people in your organization are likely to use a variety of mobile phones, this can be problematic. ActiveSync requires a minimum of Windows Mobile 5.0 with the Messaging and Security Feature Pack.

You can configure the following items in ActiveSync mailbox policies:

- **Allow Bluetooth** Determines whether phones allow Bluetooth connection. Can be set to Disable, HandsFree only, and Allow. Requires Enterprise CAL.
- **Allow Browser** Determines whether the mobile version of Internet Explorer can be used on the phone. Does not restrict third-party mobile browsers. Requires Enterprise CAL.
- **Allow Camera** Determines whether a mobile phone camera is enabled or disabled. Requires Enterprise CAL.
- **Allow Consumer Mail** Determines whether a user can configure a personal email account separate from the Exchange account. Requires Enterprise CAL.

- **Allow Desktop Sync** Determines whether the mobile device can synchronize with a computer using a cable, Bluetooth, or IrDA connection. Requires Enterprise CAL. Less frequently used with today's mobile devices, which can sync directly with Exchange.

- **Allow HTML E-mail** Determines whether messages synchronized to the phone can be in HTML format. If disabled, HTML format email is converted to plain text.

- **Allow Internet Sharing** Determines whether the mobile device can be used for Internet tethering. Requires Enterprise CAL.

- **Allow IRM over Exchange ActiveSync** Determines whether the mobile device can read items protected by IRM.

- **Allow IrDA** Determines whether infrared connections area allowed to the mobile device. Requires Enterprise CAL.

- **Allow Mobile OTA Updates** Determines whether software updates can be deployed to the mobile device through ActiveSync.

- **Allow non-provisionable devices** Determines whether devices that are not fully ActiveSync compliant can connect to Exchange through ActiveSync.

- **Allow POPIMAPEmail** Specifies whether users can configure POP3 or IMAP4 email accounts on the mobile device.

- **Allow Remote Desktop** Determines whether the mobile device can initiate remote desktop connections. Requires Enterprise CAL.

- **Allow simple password** Disables the use of basic mobile device passwords such as ABCD.

- **Allow S/MIME encryption algorithm negotiation** Determines whether the messaging application can negotiate the encryption algorithm if a recipient's certificate does not support the specified encryption algorithm.

- **Allow S/MIME software certificates** Determines whether S/MIME certificates can be used with the mobile device.

- **Allow storage card** Determines whether mobile device data can be stored on an added storage card.

- **Allow text messaging** Determines whether the mobile device can be used to send and receive text messages. Requires Enterprise CAL.

- **Allow unsigned applications** Determines whether applications that are not digitally signed by trusted Certificate Authorities can be deployed on the mobile device. Requires Enterprise CAL.

- **Allow unsigned installation packages** Determines whether an installation package that is not digitally signed by a trusted Certificate Authority can be run on the mobile device. Requires Enterprise CAL.

- **Allow Wi-Fi** Determines whether the mobile device can be used with Wi-Fi access points. Requires Enterprise CAL.

- **Alphanumeric password required** Determines whether the password must contain both numeric and non-numeric characters.

- **Approved Application List** Specifies a list of application that can be run on the mobile device. Requires Enterprise CAL.

- **Attachments enabled** Determines whether attachments can be downloaded to the mobile device through ActiveSync.

- **Device encryption enabled** Encrypts the mobile phone storage so that data cannot be recovered if the phone falls into the hands of unauthorized third parties.

- **Password enabled** Enables the mobile device password.

- **Password expiration** Configures an mobile device password expiration policy.

- **Password history** Configures how many passwords are remembered. Users cannot set a password that they have used before if the password is remembered.

- **Policy refresh interval** Determines how often the OWA mailbox policy refreshes.

- **Maximum attachment size** Specifies the maximum attachment size automatically downloaded to the mobile device.

- **Maximum calendar age filter** Specifies the maximum age of calendar items that can be synchronized with the mobile device.

- **Maximum failed password attempts** Specifies how many incorrect passwords can be entered before the mobile device triggers a wipe of all stored data.

- **Maximum inactivity time lock** Specifies how much time can elapse before the mobile device locks its screen, requiring a password to be reentered.

- **Minimum password length** Specifies minimum password length.

- **Maximum e-mail age filter** Specifies the maximum age of email messages that will be synced with the mobile device.

- **Maximum HTML e-mail body truncation size** Specifies maximum size of email messages before they will be truncated.

- **Minimum device password complex characters** Specifies minimum number of complex characters required in a mobile device password.

- **Maximum e-mail body truncation size** Specifies the maximum size of email messages before they are truncated.

- **Mobile OTA Update Mode** Used in multi-tenant deployments and not available for on-premises deployment. Determines the way that OTA (over the air) updates work.

- **Password recovery** Enables a mobile device recovery password to be stored with the user's Exchange mailbox, allowing recovery in the event that the mobile device password is lost.

- **Require Device Encryption** Specifies whether encryption is required. If set to true, the mobile device must support encryption to sync with Exchange.

- **Require encrypted S/MIME messages** Specifies whether S/MIME messages must be encrypted when used with the mobile device.
- **Require encryption S/MIME algorithm** Specifies which encryption algorithm must be used when encrypting messages using S/MIME.
- **Require manual synchronization while roaming** Specifies whether synchronization only occurs manually when the mobile device is roaming.
- **Require signed S/MIME algorithm** Specifies algorithm used to sign protected S/MIME messages.
- **Require signed S/MIME messages** Specifies whether the mobile device must send signed S/MIME messages.
- **Require storage card encryption** Specifies whether any additional storage cards must be encrypted.
- **Unapproved InROM application list** Specifies which applications cannot be run in ROM. Requires Enterprise CAL.

You can configure ActiveSync policies either through EMC in the Organization\Client Access node or through EMS using the *Set-ActiveSyncMailboxPolicy* cmdlet.

MORE INFO **ACTIVESYNC POLICIES**

To learn more about ActiveSync policies, consult the following TechNet document: *http://technet.microsoft.com/en-us/library/bb123484.aspx.*

OWA Authentication

OWA provides several different authentication options. This is necessary because OWA will be accessed by a variety of operating systems and browsers and Exchange administrators cannot assume that each client will be using Internet Explorer 9 on a Windows 7 computer. You configure OWA authentication on the Authentication tab of the OWA virtual directory properties as shown in Figure 3-14.

OWA supports the following authentication options:

- **Forms-Based Authentication** The default method of OWA authentication. Allows a single sign-on page. If you configure the authentication mode for both OWA and Exchange Control Panel to Forms-Based Authentication, it is possible to perform single sign-in and use both web applications. You can configure Forms-Based Authentication to use the Domain\username, User Principle Name, or user name only, while specifying a domain login formats.
- **Basic Authentication** A simple authentication method that is defined in the HTTP specification. The user's sign-in name and password are encoded and then sent to the CAS. Basic authentication does not support single sign-on. Basic authentication is supported by all web browsers.

- **Digest Authentication** This authentication method transmits passwords across the network using a hash value. Digest authentication can only be used for users who have an account stored in Active Directory, which is unproblematic in most Exchange 2010 scenarios.

- **Integrated Windows Authentication** Integrated Windows Authentication requires that the user has an Active Directory account, which is unproblematic in most Exchange 2010 scenarios. The drawback of Integrated Windows Authentication is that it requires a computer running a Windows operating system and the Internet Explorer browser. In organizations that need to support multiple desktop and tablet operating systems, Integrated Windows Authentication can be problematic.

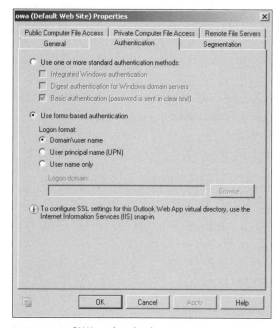

FIGURE 3-14 OWA authentication

You can configure OWA to require smart cards for authentication by performing the following general steps:

- Use IIS Manager to configure the OWA virtual directory to require client certificates as shown in Figure 3-15.

- Configure the OWA virtual directory to have no authentication method by choosing the Use One Or More Standard Authentication Methods but by not selecting any of the available authentication methods.

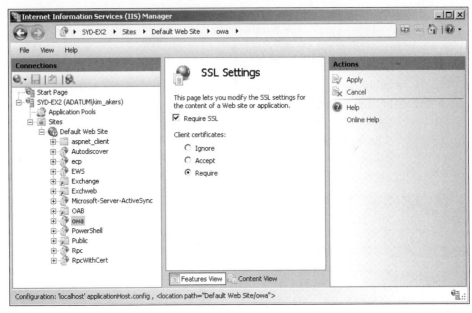

FIGURE 3-15 Certificate-based authentication

> ***MORE INFO*** **OWA AUTHENTICATION ALTERNATIVES**
>
> To learn more about OWA authentication alternatives, consult the following TechNet document: *http://technet.microsoft.com/en-us/library/bb430796.aspx*.

OWA Segmentation

OWA segmentation settings allow Exchange administrators to specify which features will be available to users when they connect to their mailboxes through a web browser. You can configure OWA segmentation on the OWA virtual directory level, as shown in Figure 3-16, or you can configure OWA segmentation through an OWA mailbox policy.

Using OWA Mailbox Policies to control segmentation settings is more likely to produce consistent results—otherwise you'll need to ensure that each OWA virtual directory on each CAS has precisely the same settings. You should also be aware that disabling a feature on the OWA virtual directory overrides enabling it within an OWA mailbox policy. For example, if an OWA mailbox policy that applies to Rooslan has the Calendar item enabled, but the Calendar item is disabled on the OWA virtual directory, Rooslan will be unable to access the Calendar on OWA. Of course if the calendar is disabled in the OWA mailbox policy that applies to Rooslan but is enabled on the OWA virtual directory, Rooslan still will be unable to access the Calendar when he connects to OWA.

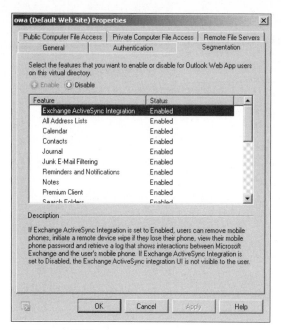

FIGURE 3-16 OWA segmentation

Both the OWA virtual directory and OWA mailbox policies have the same 22 segmentation settings:

- **All Address Lists**   Allows users to view all address lists. If disabled, allows users to view the default global address list.

- **Calendar**   Allows users to manage Calendar items. If this setting is disabled, users cannot view the calendar in OWA, but it is still available through Outlook.

- **Change Password**   Allows users to change their password.

- **Contacts**   Allows users to manage their contacts. If this setting is disabled, the user can still use contacts through Outlook.

- **E-Mail Signature**   Allows users to configure an email signature.

- **Exchange ActiveSync Integration**   Allows users to manage mobile phones linked to their Exchange mailbox. For example, a user can trigger a remote device wipe or access the mobile device password using this OWA functionality.

- **Instant Messaging**   Allows use of an instant messaging client in OWA. Not available in the light version of OWA.

- **Journal**   Allows users to view the Journal folder using OWA.

- **Junk E-mail Filtering**   Allows users to control mailbox junk email settings from OWA.

- **Notes**   Provides view-only access to Notes.

- **Premium Client**   Allows access to the standard OWA client. If this setting is disabled, users are only able to access the light version of OWA.

- **Public Folders**   Allows users to browse items in public folders through OWA.
- **Recover Deleted Items**   Allows users to view, recover, or permanently delete items in the Deleted Items folder.
- **Reminders and Notifications**   Allows users to be prompted with reminders for calendar items and tasks. Not available in the light version of OWA.
- **Rules**   Allows users to manage mailbox rules in OWA.
- **S/MIME**   Allows users to read S/MIME-encrypted messages. Also allows them to compose and digitally sign messages with S/MIME certificates.
- **Search Folders**   Allows users to use Search Folders with OWA.
- **Spelling Checker**   Allows users to run a spell check through OWA. Not available in the light version of the client.
- **Tasks**   Allows users to manage Tasks.
- **Text Messaging**   Allows users to send text messages through OWA to mobile phones.
- **Theme Selection**   Allows users to change themes. OWA themes are only available with Exchange 2010 SP1 and later.
- **Unified Messaging Integration**   If Unified Messaging is deployed, allows users to modify their UM settings through OWA.

You can configure the OWA virtual directory on a CAS using the *Set-OwaVirtualDirectory* cmdlet. For example, to disable the Calendar item on a CAS named SYD-CAS, issue the following command:

```
Set-OwaVirtualDirectory -Identity "SYD-CAS\owa (default web site)" -CalendarEnabled
$false
```

When configuring segmentation by altering the virtual directory, changes take effect after 60 minutes of user inactivity in OWA when there is a currently active session, or when a new logon occurs. If you want to force OWA segmentation changes made at the virtual directory level, issue the *iisreset /noforce* command on the CAS.

In general, the same syntax applies when managing OWA mailbox policies using the *Set-OwaMailboxPolicy* cmdlet. If you wanted to disable the Calendar item in the default OWA mailbox policy, you would issue the following command:

```
Set-OwaMailboxPolicy -Identity Default -CalendarEnabled $false
```

> **MORE INFO**   **OWA SEGMENTATION**
>
> To learn more about OWA segmentation, consult the following TechNet document: *http://technet.microsoft.com/en-us/library/bb123962.aspx.*

Objective Summary

- ActiveSync mailbox policies control mobile device features and security.
- OWA uses forms based authentication by default.
- Forms based authentication allows for single sign-on to OWA and ECP.
- OWA segmentation allows you to control access to OWA features.
- OWA segmentation can be configured on the OWA virtual directory level, or through OWA mailbox policies.
- A feature disabled on the OWA virtual directory cannot be enabled through an OWA mailbox policy.

Objective Review

Answer the following questions to test your knowledge of the information in this objective. You can find the answers to these questions and explanations of why each answer choice is correct or incorrect in the "Answers" section at the end of this chapter.

1. Users in your organization primarily access messages using Outlook Web App (OWA). You want to configure so that users are restricted to specific features depending on their departmental affiliation. Specifically:

   - Users in the Sales team should be unable to access the spelling checker, but should have access to the Tasks function.
   - Users in the Management team should be unable to change their passwords, but should have access to the Tasks function.
   - Users in all other teams should be blocked from using the Tasks and Notes functionality.

   Which of the following steps should you take to accomplish this goal? (Choose two. Each answer forms part of a complete solution.)

   A. Modify the Default Outlook Web App mailbox policy.

   B. Create one custom Outlook Web App mailbox policy. Apply this policy to the Sales team users and the Management team users.

   C. Create two custom Outlook Web App mailbox policies. Apply one policy to the Sales team users. Apply the second to the Management team users.

   D. Create two custom Exchange ActiveSync mailbox policies. Apply one policy to the Sales team users. Apply the second to the Management team users.

2. Your organization is in the process of upgrading from Exchange 2003 to Exchange 2010. You are planning a coexistence period of six months. In the past, a substantial number of users at the Adelaide site remotely accessed messages using the IMAP4 protocol. The Adelaide site still has Exchange 2003 front-end and back-end servers deployed. You have placed a CAS on the perimeter network at the Internet-facing Melbourne site and deployed a CAS in the Adelaide site. You need to ensure that communication between the perimeter network CAS and the Adelaide back-end server is encrypted. Which of the following authentication and encryption technologies can you use to accomplish this goal? (Choose two. Each answer forms part of a complete solution.)

   A. IPsec

   B. SSL

   C. Basic Authentication

   D. Integrated Windows Authentication

3. Which of the following authentication methods should you include in your design if you want to support single sign-on for OWA and Exchange Control Panel?

   A. Integrated Windows Authentication

   B. Digest Authentication

   C. Basic Authentication

   D. Forms-Based Authentication

4. You are planning an ActiveSync mailbox policy for a group of executives who will be accessing their Exchange mailboxes remotely through mobile devices. For security reasons you want to ensure that the executives' mobile devices will be wiped if they enter an incorrect password five times and that their mobile devices are password-locked if they do not interact with it for three minutes. Which of the following ActiveSync mailbox policy items should you configure to accomplish this goal? (Choose two. Each answer forms part of a complete solution.)

   A. Allow IRM Over Exchange ActiveSync

   B. Maximum Failed Password Attempts

   C. Maximum Inactivity Time Lock

   D. Password Recovery

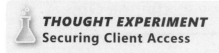

THOUGHT EXPERIMENT
Securing Client Access

In the following thought experiment, you will apply what you've learned about the design and deploy client access security objective to design an ActiveSync mailbox policy. You can find answers to these questions in the "Answers" section at the end of this chapter.

Users must be able to log onto OWA to receive a code to unlock their device if they forget their password.

It should not be possible for unauthorized third parties to recover data from devices if they are lost.

Users should change their mobile device passwords every 28 days.

Users should be unable to use any of their last five passwords.

With this information in mind, answer the following questions:

1. What option should you configure to ensure that users change their passwords every four weeks?

2. What option should you enable to ensure that data cannot be recovered from the device if it is mounted on a computer without authorization?

3. What option should you enable to ensure that users can unlock their devices if they forget their passwords?

4. What option should you configure to ensure that mobile device users don't use any of their last five passwords?

Objective 3.5: Design and Deploy Exchange Object Permissions

IT professionals aren't the only people who require access to Exchange objects such as mailboxes, distribution groups, and public folders. Often there are good reasons to allow regular users access to these objects and during the Exchange design and deployment phase you'll need to provision access to these object by users who are not members of the IT team. In this objective you'll learn how to configure public folder security, configure mailbox permissions and access, and configure appropriate security settings for distribution groups.

> **This objective covers:**
> - Public folder security.
> - Mailbox permissions.
> - Distribution group security.
> - Per-mailbox client access.

Public Folder Security

Exchange 2010 includes eight built-in public folder roles that are useful for granting clients access rights to public folders and the contents they host. You grant permissions to end users by assigning them to one of these eight roles. To understand what privileges the roles confer, you need to understand the following client user access rights that are associated with the roles:

- **ReadItems** The user can read items in the public folder.
- **CreateItems** The user can post items to the public folder.
- **EditOwnedItems** The user can edit items that he or she owns in the public folder.
- **DeleteOwnedItems** The user can delete items that he or she owns in the public folder.
- **EditAllItems** The user can edit any items in the public folder regardless of ownership.
- **DeleteAllItems** The user can delete any items in the public folder regardless of ownership.
- **CreateSubfolders** The user can create subfolders in the public folder.
- **FolderOwner** The user can view, move, and create subfolders in the public folder.

- **FolderContact** The user is the contact for the public folder.
- **FolderVisible** The user can view the public folder, but does not have access to items within the folder.

The roles collect these rights together, with each role having a different set of rights. The roles and their associated rights are as follows:

- **Owner** Holds the following roles: CreateItems, ReadItems, CreateSubfolders, FolderOwner, Folder Contact, EditOwnedItems, EditAllItems, DeleteOwnedItems, DeleteAllItems, and FolderVisible
- **PublishingEditor** Holds the following roles: CreateItems, ReadItems, CreateSubfolders, EditOwnedItems, EditAllItems, DeleteOwnedItems, DeleteAllItems, and FolderVisible
- **Editor** Holds the following roles: CreateItems, ReadItems, EditOwnedItems, EditAllItems, DeleteOwnedItems, DeleteAllItems, and FolderVisible
- **PublishingAuthor** Holds the following roles: CreateItems, ReadItems, CreateSubfolders, EditOwnedItems, DeleteOwnedItems, DeleteAllItems, and FolderVisible
- **Author** Holds the following roles: CreateItems, ReadItems, EditOwnedItems, DeleteOwnedItems, and FolderVisible
- **Non-EditingAuthor** Holds the following roles: CreateItems, ReadItems, and FolderVisible
- **Reviewer** Holds the following roles: ReadItems and FolderVisible
- **Contributor** Holds the following roles: CreateItems and FolderVisible

You can assign client permissions to a public folder using the *Add-PublicFolderClient-Permission* cmdlet. For example, to configure Ken with the PublishingEditor permission on the Ideas folder, issue the following command:

```
Add-PublicFolderClientPermission –Identity "\Ideas" –AccessRights PublishingEditor –User
Ken
```

Administrators who are added to the Public Folder Management role group have the ability to create and manage top-level public folders. This includes the ability to assign roles to other users. You can use the *Add-RoleGroupMember* cmdlet to add a user to the Public Folder Management role group.

MORE INFO **PUBLIC FOLDER PERMISSIONS**

To learn more about public folder permissions, consult the following TechNet document: *http://technet.microsoft.com/en-us/library/ee633461.aspx*.

Mailbox Permissions

You can grant three primary types of access to an Exchange user's mailbox: Receive As, Send As, and Full Access. Each permission works in the following way:

- **Full Access**   When a user is granted Full Access permission to a mailbox, the user can open and read the contents of that mailbox. In Exchange 2010 SP1, Outlook 2007 and Outlook 2010 clients will automatically map to any mailbox for which the user has been granted Full Access permission. A user who has been granted Full Access permission cannot send mail as that mailbox. Use the *Add-MailboxPermission* cmdlet to grant the Full Access right. For example, to grant user Oksana Full Access permission to Rooslan's mailbox, issue the following command:

```
Add-MailboxPermission Rooslan -User Oksana -AccessRights FullAccess
```

- **Receive As**   This permission is granted on a mailbox database. It allows a user to log onto all mailboxes hosted on that database, but does not allow the user granted this permission the ability to send mail from any of those mailboxes. This permission is often granted during legal review. You use the *Add-ADPermission* cmdlet to assign the Receive As permission on a mailbox database. For example, to grant Oksana the Receive As right for the mailbox database SYD-DB1, issue the following command:

```
Add-ADPermission -Identity SYD-DB1 -User Oksana -ExtendedRights Receive-As
```

- **Send As**   The Send As permissions allow you to configure a mailbox so that another user can use that mailbox to send messages as though that user were the mailbox owner. For example, you might grant user Ian the ability to send messages as Ken. Giving the right to send messages as a mailbox does not confer any other rights on that mailbox. Additionally, a user can't send messages on behalf of a mailbox if that mailbox is hidden from address lists. You use the *Add-ADPermission* cmdlet to configure the Send As permission. For example, to give Ian the ability to send messages as Ken, use the following command:

```
Add-ADPermission Ken -User Ian -Extendedrights "Send As"
```

> *MORE INFO*   **MAILBOX PERMISSIONS**
>
> To learn more about mailbox permissions, consult the following TechNet document: *http://technet.microsoft.com/en-us/library/aa996343.aspx.*

Distribution Group Security

Distribution groups are widely used in Exchange organizations to facilitate communication. Regular users can create distribution groups using Outlook. Users can manage the groups they create. They can also manage groups when they are configured as the group manager.

Configuring Distribution Group Ownership

You configure distribution group ownership on the Group Information tab. By default, the user that created the group is configured as a group manager. Group ownership allows a user to configure group settings. Figure 3-17 shows Kim Akers as the group member of a distribution group. You can click Add user to add additional group managers.

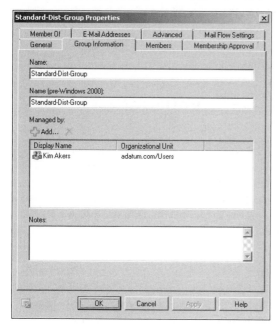

FIGURE 3-17 Group manager

You can use the *Set-DistributionGroup* cmdlet to configure a group manager. For example, to grant Kim Akers management of the Ideas distribution group, use the following command:

```
Set-DistributionGroup -Identity Ideas -ManagedBy 'Kim Akers'
```

Configuring Group Membership Approval

Three options are available when it comes to how users can join normal distribution groups. The memb'ership of dynamic distribution groups is governed by the query that defines the group membership. You configure the following group joining options on the Membership Approval tab of the group's properties:

- **Open** When the group is configured with this setting, any user can join the group without being approved by the group owners.
- **Closed** When the group is configured with this setting, only the group owners can add members to the groups. Requests to join will be automatically rejected.
- **Owner Approval** When the group is configured with this setting, Exchange forwards group join requests to the owner for approval.

You can also configure the following group leaving options on this tab:

- **Open**   When the group leave option is set to open, users can remove themselves.
- **Closed**   When the group leave option is set to closed, users can't leave unless they are removed by a group owner.

You can configure membership approval settings from EMS using the *Set-DistributionGroup* cmdlet with the *MemberJoinRestriction* and *MemberDepartRestriction* cmdlets.

Distribution Group Mail Flow Settings

The Mail Flow settings tab of a distribution group's properties allows you to configure group Message Size Restrictions, Message Delivery Restrictions, and Message Moderation. These mail flow settings work in the following way:

- **Message Size Restriction**   Allows you to specify a maximum message size that can be sent to the group. Messages that exceed this size will be dropped.
- **Message Delivery Restrictions**   Allows you to configure who can send messages to the group. The default is all senders, but you can configure this setting so that only users on a specific list can send messages to the group. You can also configure the group to automatically reject messages from specific senders.
- **Message Moderation**   The message moderation settings, shown in Figure 3-18, allow you to configure whether messages sent to the group must be approved by a moderator, who that moderator is, which users are exempt from moderation, and moderation notification settings.

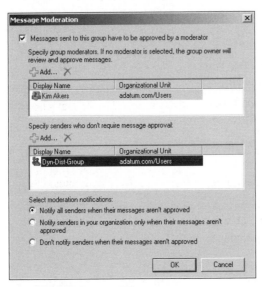

FIGURE 3-18 Message moderation settings

Block Creation of Distribution Groups

By default, all users in an Exchange organization have the ability to create and manage
distribution groups using their Outlook or OWA client. Users are only able to manage
distribution groups that they have been granted management rights over, which is usually
only those distribution groups that they have created. An organization can restrict this right
in two ways:

- Create a new assignment policy. Assign this policy to the users who you do not want to
  grant the privilege of creating or managing distribution groups.
- Remove the My Distribution Groups and the My Distribution Group Membership roles
  from the default management role assignment policy.

Objective Summary

- You configure public folder roles to determine what actions users can take on items
  within public folders.
- Users with Full Access permissions on a mailbox can access mailbox contents, but
  cannot send on that mailbox's behalf.
- Users with Send As permissions on a mailbox can send on that mailbox's behalf, but
  can't access mailbox contents.
- Membership approval settings can be used to restrict who can join a distribution
  group.
- Mail flow settings allow you to configure message size restrictions, message delivery
  restrictions, and message moderation settings.
- You can restrict users from being able to create groups by creating a new assignment
  policy or by modifying the default management role assignment.

Objective Review

Answer the following questions to test your knowledge of the information in this objective. You can find the answers to these questions and explanations of why each answer choice is correct or incorrect in the "Answers" section at the end of this chapter.

1. Your organization has branch offices in Queensland and Tasmania. You want to prohibit employees in the Tasmanian office from being able to create distribution groups. Employees in the Queensland office should be able to create distribution groups and manage the membership of those distribution groups. Which of the following steps should you take to accomplish this goal? (Choose two. Each answer forms part of a complete solution.)

   A. Modify the Distribution Groups built-in management role.

   B. Assign the role assignment policy to the users in the Queensland branch office.

   C. Create a role assignment policy.

   D. Assign the role assignment policy to the users in the Tasmanian branch office.

2. You want to give departmental administrative assistants the ability to send messages on behalf of departmental managers. Which of the following EMS cmdlets would you use to accomplish this goal?

   A. *Add-ADPermission*

   B. *Set-Mailbox*

   C. *Add-MailboxFolderPermission*

   D. *Add-MailboxPermission*

3. You want to give a departmental administrative assistant permission to access the contents of a departmental manager's mailbox, but not give the assistant the ability to send email messages on behalf of the departmental manager. Which of the following EMS cmdlets would you use to accomplish this goal?

   A. *Add-ADPermission*

   B. *Set-Mailbox*

   C. *Add-MailboxFolderPermission*

   D. *Add-MailboxPermission*

4. Don Hall creates a new distribution group. Which of the following steps should you take to ensure that Kim Akers, not Don Hall, is responsible for approving messages sent to the distribution group?

   A. Configure mail flow settings.

   B. Configure membership approval settings.

   C. Configure group information settings.

   D. Configure advanced settings.

THOUGHT EXPERIMENT
Determining Appropriate Public Folder Roles

In the following thought experiment, you will apply what you've learned about the design and deploy Exchange object permissions objective to design an appropriate public folder role allocation given specific information. You can find answers to these questions in the "Answers" section at the end of this chapter.

You are planning the appropriate public folder roles for several public folders at your organization. The users listed here have the following needs:

Kim needs to be able to edit and delete any items in the public folder irrespective of who created the item.

Don should be able to delete all items in the folder, but should not be able to edit items that he didn't create.

Ken should be able to create, edit, and delete his own items, but not delete items created by other people.

Ian should be able to read items, but not edit or delete items.

You don't want to assign any users the Owner role.

With this in mind, answer the following questions:

1. Which role should you assign to Kim?
2. Which role should you assign to Don?
3. Which role should you assign to Ken?
4. Which role should you assign to Ian?

Chapter Summary

- Externally secured receive connectors allow safe relay of messages for partner organizations.

- Domain security allows you to perform sender verification when messages are transmitted to partners across MTLS secured connections.

- Add the Federation mailbox to the AD RMS super users group to utilize many IRM features such as transport decryption and IRM with OWA.

- The default AD RMS template for Exchange is Do Not Forward.

- Management roles are collections of role entries. A role entry is an EMS cmdlet and a set of parameters.

- Management role groups are security groups that have members. These groups have been assigned management roles and management scopes.

- Management role scopes define which objects a management role might be granted privileges over.

- Management role assignments assign management roles and scopes to universal security groups.

- Active Directory split permissions limit the creation of Active Directory security principles to the Active Directory tools. It is not possible to create Active Directory security principles using the Exchange administration tools.

- RBAC split permissions mean that Active Directory domain permissions are controlled through role-based access control. Users with the appropriate permissions can create Active Directory security principles using Exchange administration tools.

- Safelist aggregation takes user data about senders and recipients and uses this to block or allow incoming messages.

- Sender ID allows the validity of SMTP servers to be determined through a query of the DNS zone associated with the sender's email domain.

- Block and allow lists allow you to permit or deny messages based on the IP address of the SMTP server from which the they were transmitted.

- Spam Confidence Level (SCL) is a value that represents the likelihood that a message is spam.

- Content filtering allows you to block or allow messages based on certain phrases or words contained within the message.

- ActiveSync mailbox policies control mobile device features and security.

- OWA uses Forms-Based Authentication by default, which allows for single sign-on to OWA and ECP.

- OWA segmentation allows you to control access to OWA features.

- You configure public folder roles to determine what actions users can take on items within public folders.

- Users with Full Access permissions on a mailbox can access mailbox contents, but cannot send on that mailbox's behalf.

- Users with Send As permissions on a mailbox can send on that mailbox's behalf, but can't access mailbox contents.

Answers

This section contains the answers to the Object Reviews and the Thought Experiments.

Objective 3.1: Review

1. **Correct Answers:** A and D

    A. **Correct:** Message classifications allow users to manually select a classification to apply to a message. This will allow users to mark messages as Internal-Use-Only

    B. **Incorrect:** Outlook protection rules are automatically applied to messages, rather than allowing a user to choose to manually apply the classification. Outlook protection rules are usually used with Rights Management Services.

    C. **Incorrect:** Moderated transport requires an approval process before a message is transmitted to its eventual destination. In this case no approval is required.

    D. **Correct:** Transport rules allow actions, such as forwarding a copy to a specific mailbox, to be performed against messages that meet certain criteria, such as having a specific classification.

2. **Correct Answer:** C

    A. **Incorrect:** BitLocker To Go is a full-volume encryption technology that is used with removable devices on computers running Windows 7 and Windows Server 2008 R2. BitLocker To Go cannot be used to encrypt or digitally sign messages.

    B. **Incorrect:** Encrypting File System (EFS) is a file-level encryption technology. Although it is possible to attach EFS encrypted files to a message sent through OWA, this file will automatically be decrypted during the attachment process. EFS cannot be used to encrypt message contents. It is also not possible to use EFS to digitally sign files.

    C. **Correct:** S/MIME allows users to encrypt and sign email messages. This allows the sender's identity to be verified by the recipient. S/MIME also allows the sender to encrypt the message using the recipient's public certificate, meaning that only the recipient, who holds a corresponding private certificate, is able to view the contents of the message.

    D. **Incorrect:** TLS Encryption can provide an encrypted tunnel for message transmission, but does not encrypt the message itself or provide a sender verification mechanism.

3. **Correct Answer:** D

    A. **Incorrect:** Members of the organization management group have permissions to manage Exchange objects and their properties in the Exchange organization. To enable the required features, you need to add the Federation mailbox to the AD RMS Super Users group.

B. **Incorrect:** Members of the Discover Management role group can perform searches of mailboxes in the Exchange organization. To enable the required features, you need to add the Federation mailbox to the AD RMS Super Users group.

C. **Incorrect:** Members of the Records Management security group can configure compliance features such as message classifications and retention policy tags. To enable the required features, you need to add the Federation mailbox to the AD RMS Super Users group.

D. **Correct:** To enable transport decryption, journal report decryption, IRM with OWA, and IRM for Exchange Search, it is necessary to add the Federation mailbox to the AD RMS Super Users group.

4. **Correct Answers:** A, B, and C

A. **Correct:** You use the *Set-TransportConfig* cmdlet to configure the receive domain secure list and the send domain secure list from inside your Exchange organization.

B. **Correct:** You use the *Set-ReceiveConnector* cmdlet to enable domain security on a specific Receive connector.

C. **Correct:** You use the *Set-SendConnector* cmdlet to enable domain security on a specific Send connector.

D. **Incorrect:** The *Set-AcceptedDomain* allows you to configure the properties of an accepted domain. This command is not related to configuring domain security.

5. **Correct Answers:** B and C

A. **Incorrect:** You shouldn't configure Exchange Server authentication when configuring external secure relay for a third-party organization. This type of authentication is often used with internal Receive connectors.

B. **Correct:** When configuring secure relay, you configure externally secured authentication such as IPsec.

C. **Correct:** When configuring secure relay, you configure the Exchange Servers permissions group.

D. **Incorrect:** Although you do allow anonymous relay, when configuring secure relay you do not enable the Anonymous users permissions group.

Objective 3.1: Thought Experiment

1. You need to install the Active Directory Rights Management Services role on a server in the forest before you can use IRM.

2. You can ensure that messages that are sent to the special projects distribution list are encrypted in the sender's Sent Items folder by configuring an Outlook Protection Rule.

3. To use IRM with OWA, you need to add the Federation mailbox to the AD RMS Super Users group.

4. You would use the *FromDepartment* and *SentToScope* predicates to ensure that the Finance-IRM RMS template should apply to all messages sent by people in the Finance department to anyone outside the organization.

Objective 3.2: Review

1. **Correct Answers:** A, B, and C

   A. **Correct:** Because you want the compliance officer to perform Records Management–related activities, you should create a custom role group using the Records Management built-in role group as a template.

   B. **Correct:** By creating a custom management scope, you can limit the compliance officer's access to the servers in Tonga.

   C. **Correct:** Adding the compliance officer to Tonga to the custom role group will give the compliance officer the requisite permissions to accomplish Records Management–related tasks only over servers listed in the custom management scope.

   D. **Incorrect:** If you modify the scope of the Records Management role group, it can only be used over specific objects. Creating copies of this role group, each with a different scope, accomplishes your goal.

2. **Correct Answers:** A and C

   A. **Correct:** You should create a custom role group based off the Server Management role group. This will provide the appropriate privileges, but you will be able to use the appropriate scope with this role group.

   B. **Incorrect:** A custom role group based off the Organization Management role group will provide the local administrators with too many privileges. Given the described situation, you should create a custom role group based off the Server Management role group.

   C. **Correct:** You should create a custom scope that includes all servers located in New Zealand. You can then use this scope with the custom role group, allowing administrators in New Zealand to manage the Exchange servers in that country's offices.

   D. **Incorrect:** You should not create a custom scope that includes all servers located in New Zealand, Tonga, and Australia. In this instance you are only interested in delegating permissions over the New Zealand Exchange servers.

3. **Correct Answer:** C

   A. **Incorrect:** Servers can be members of specific OUs, but you can't make mailbox databases members of OUs. You'll need to use a configuration scope to have a scope that includes specific mailbox databases.

B. **Incorrect:** Recipient filter scopes allow you to target recipients, not configuration items such as servers and mailbox databases.

C. **Correct:** With Exchange Server 2010 SP1, configuration scopes can include specific mailbox databases.

D. **Incorrect:** Organization is not an option for custom scopes, but is a built-in scope.

4. **Correct Answer:** A

A. **Correct:** The Active Directory split permissions model blocks the creation of security principles in the Active Directory partition from Exchange tools.

B. **Incorrect:** The shared permissions model is the default permissions model and was the only one available in Exchange 2010 at release. Under the shared permissions model you can create security principles in the Active Directory partition using Exchange administration tools.

C. **Incorrect:** The RBAC permissions model allows administrators who have been assigned the appropriate role to be able to create security principles in the Active Directory partition using Exchange administration tools.

D. **Incorrect:** Mixed mode and Native mode are Exchange 2003 settings and are not related to whether you can restrict the creation of Active Directory security principles to Active Directory–specific tools.

Objective 3.2: Thought Experiment

1. You should add Ian's team to the Recipient Management role. This will allow them to create recipients, but will not allow them to manage.

2. Kim's team should be added to the Hygiene Management role, which will allow them to configure anti-spam and antivirus functionality.

3. Sam's team should be added to the Server Management role, which will allow them to manage servers but not recipients.

4. You should add Ken's team to the View-Only organization management role, which will allow them to view the properties of all objects within the Exchange organization.

Objective 3.3: Review

1. **Correct Answer:** A

A. **Correct:** You can use recipient filtering to block incoming messages from outside the organization addressed to specific mailboxes or distribution lists.

B. **Incorrect:** Content filtering screens message content. You should use recipient filtering to block incoming messages from outside the organization addressed to specific mailboxes or distribution lists.

C.   Incorrect: You should not use moderated transport, which would require a moderator to approve messages sent to the distribution lists. The question scenario states that this type of approval process should not be implemented.

D.   Incorrect: You should not use a transport rule. Although you can configure a transport rule to block specific external addresses from sending messages to specific internal addresses, you need to provide those external addresses. This would be problematic given the number of possible external addresses. Recipient filtering allows you to do this in a blanket fashion and is more appropriate for this scenario.

2.   Correct Answer: B

A.   Incorrect: You can't use the *Set-AcceptedDomain* cmdlet to configure Sender ID not to process incoming messages from a specific email domain. You use *Set-SenderIDConfig* to accomplish this task.

B.   Correct: You use the *Set-SenderIDConfig* cmdlet to configure Sender ID not to process incoming messages from a specific mail domain.

C.   Incorrect: You can't use the *Set-IPAllowListConfig* cmdlet to configure Sender ID not to process incoming messages from a specific email domain. You use *Set-SenderIDConfig* to accomplish this task.

D.   Incorrect: You can't use the *Set-TransportRule* cmdlet to configure Sender ID not to process incoming messages from a specific email domain. You use *Set-SenderIDConfig* to accomplish this task.

3.   Correct Answer: C

A.   Incorrect: The *Set-IPAllowListConfig* cmdlet allows you to modify the IP Allow List configuration on an Edge Transport server. You cannot use this cmdlet to configure an Edge Transport server to block messages for 48 hours for a sender with a Sender Reputation Level exceeding 6.

B.   Incorrect: The *Set-TransportRule* cmdlet allows you to configure transport rules. You cannot use this cmdlet to configure an Edge Transport server to block messages for 48 hours for a sender with a Sender Reputation Level exceeding 6.

C.   Correct: You use the *Set-SenderReputationConfig* cmdlet to configure Sender Reputation Level settings on an Edge Transport server.

D.   Incorrect: The *Set-SenderIDConfig* cmdlet allows you to modify the sender ID configuration settings on an Edge Transport server. You cannot use this cmdlet to configure an Edge Transport server to block messages for 48 hours for a sender with a Sender Reputation Level exceeding 6.

4. **Correct Answer:** D

    A. **Incorrect:** The Sender ID agent performs a check to see whether the DNS zone of the sender's mail domain has authorized the sending SMTP server. You can't use this agent to recognize a passphrase to always allow a message to be delivered to recipients.

    B. **Incorrect:** Sender reputation assesses the likelihood that a sender is a spammer and blocks the sender if it decides, on balance of probability, that is the case. You can't use this agent to recognize a passphrase to always allow a message to be delivered to recipients.

    C. **Incorrect:** Recipient filtering allows you to block messages sent to specific recipients. You can't use this agent to recognize a passphrase to always allow a message to be delivered to recipients.

    D. **Correct:** You can use the Content Filtering anti-spam agent to ensure that messages that contain a specific passphrase are always delivered to recipients within your organization.

Objective 3.3: Thought Experiment

1. You configure the Content Filtering agent to provide words or phrases that automatically exempt a message from the spam filter.

2. You should configure the IP Block List to block SMTP servers at specific IP addresses.

3. You should configure Sender ID to ensure that messages that use SPF are recognized.

4. You should configure Recipient Filtering to block external users from sending messages to critical distribution groups.

Objective 3.4: Review

1. **Correct Answers:** A and C

    A. **Correct:** You should modify the default Outlook Web App mailbox policy and configure it so that users are blocked from using the Tasks and Notes functionality.

    B. **Incorrect:** You will need two Outlook Web App mailbox policies rather than one because the Sales and Management teams have different segmentation requirements.

    C. **Correct:** You will need two Outlook Web App mailbox policies: one to provide the appropriate segmentation settings for the Sales team and one to provide the appropriate segmentation settings for the Management team.

    D. **Incorrect:** You do not use Exchange ActiveSync mailbox policies to configure Outlook Web App settings.

2. **Correct Answers:** A and C

   A. **Correct:** You should secure traffic between the perimeter network CAS and the Adelaide back-end server using IPsec. SSL is not supported in this scenario.

   B. **Incorrect:** SSL is not supported in a CAS-to-Exchange 2003 back-end server when the POP3 or IMAP4 protocols are being used.

   C. **Correct:** You must use basic authentication in this scenario. Other forms of authentication are not supported in this coexistence configuration.

   D. **Incorrect:** You must use basic authentication in this scenario. Other forms of authentication are not supported in this coexistence configuration.

3. **Correct Answer:** D

   A. **Incorrect:** Integrated Windows Authentication does not support single-sign on for OWA and ECP.

   B. **Incorrect:** Digest Authentication does not support single sign-on for OWA and ECP.

   C. **Incorrect:** Basic Authentication does not support single sign-on for OWA and ECP.

   D. **Correct:** Forms-Based Authentication is the only authentication method that supports single sign-on for OWA and ECP.

4. **Correct Answers:** B and C

   A. **Incorrect:** Allow IRM Over Exchange ActiveSync allows the use of IRM protected content on mobile devices.

   B. **Correct:** By configuring the Maximum Failed Password Attempts item, you can ensure that the mobile device will be wiped if five incorrect passwords are entered sequentially.

   C. **Correct:** By configuring the Maximum Inactivity Time Lock Item, you can ensure that the mobile device will password-lock if someone does not interact with the mobile device after a period of three minutes.

   D. **Incorrect:** Password Recovery allows users to enter a recovery password that they can obtain through OWA if they forget the password of their mobile device.

Objective 3.4: Thought Experiment

1. Configure the password expiration setting to ensure that passwords expire every 28 days.

2. You should require device encryption. This will ensure that users who gain access to the device storage are unable to recover data.

3. You should enable the Password Recovery option.

4. Configure the Password History option to ensure that users don't use any of their last five passwords.

Objective 3.5: Review

1. **Correct Answers:** C and D

   A. **Incorrect:** You cannot modify built-in roles; hence, you cannot modify the Distribution Groups built-in management role.

   B. **Incorrect:** You should not assign the role assignment policy to the users in the Queensland branch office because you want them to retain the default ability to create distribution groups and manage the membership of those distribution groups.

   C. **Correct:** Role assignment policies allow you to control what a user is able to do with their mailbox. You can use a role assignment policy to limit users from creating distribution groups.

   D. **Correct:** Because you want to block the users in the Tasmanian branch office from being able to create distribution groups, you should assign the role assignment policy to these users.

2. **Correct Answer:** A

   A. **Correct:** You use the *Add-ADPermission* cmdlet to grant the Send As permission on a mailbox.

   B. **Incorrect:** The *Set-Mailbox* cmdlet is used to configure the properties of a mailbox, but cannot be used to grant the Send As permission on a mailbox.

   C. **Incorrect:** The *Add-MailboxFolderPermission* cmdlet allows you to configure folder-level permissions on folders within a user's mailbox. You can't use this cmdlet to grant the Send As permission on a mailbox.

   D. **Incorrect:** The *Add-MailboxPermission* cmdlet can be used to grant Full Access to a mailbox, but cannot be used to grant the Send As permission on a mailbox.

3. **Correct Answer:** D

   A. **Incorrect:** You use the *Add-ADPermission* cmdlet to grant the Send As permission on a mailbox, but you can't use this cmdlet to grant Full Access to a mailbox.

   B. **Incorrect:** The *Set-Mailbox* cmdlet allows you to configure the settings of a mailbox, but does not allow you to configure permissions associated with a mailbox.

C. **Incorrect:** The *Add-MailboxFolderPermission* cmdlet allows you to configure folder level permissions on a user's mailbox. This cmdlet can't be used to grant the Full Access permission on a mailbox.

D. **Correct:** You use the *Add-MailboxPermission* cmdlet to grant the Full Access permission on a mailbox. The Full Access permission does not confer the right to send messages on behalf of that mailbox.

4. **Correct Answer:** A

A. **Correct:** You can configure message moderation settings on the Mail Flow settings tab. You can use these settings to configure a user account that is not the group creator to be the moderator for the group.

B. **Incorrect:** Membership approval settings allow you to control who can join and leave the group. You can't use membership approval settings to control message approval.

C. **Incorrect:** You can configure group manager settings on the Group Information tab. Although a Group Manager can function as a group moderator, you still have to configure message moderation settings on the Mail Flow settings tab.

D. **Incorrect:** The Advanced settings tab of a group allows you to configure items such as the expansion server, whether the group is hidden from Exchange address lists, and whether out-of-office messages generated are sent back to the message originator. You can't configure message moderation settings through the Advanced settings tab.

Objective 3.5: Thought Experiment

1. Kim needs the EditAllItems and DeleteAllItems access rights. The Owner role and the PublishingEditor role have these rights. You don't want to assign anyone the Owner role; this leaves the PublishingEditor role.

2. Don needs to have the DeleteAllItems access right, but not have the EditAllItems access right. This means that he should be assigned the PublishingAuthor role as the Editor and PublishingEditor role, allow editing of other user's items.

3. Ken needs to have the CreateItems, EditOwnedItems, and DeleteOwnedItems access right. This means he should be assigned the Author role.

4. Ian needs the ReadItems access right. This means that he should be assigned the Reviewer role.

Designing and Deploying Exchange Server 2010 Availability and Recovery

Fifteen years ago, most organizations were able to function perfectly fine without a functioning messaging system. Today when messaging systems collapse, many organizations fall into a state of catatonia. Keeping Exchange running is perhaps the most important part of the process of Exchange administration. Doing this involves ensuring that each of Exchange's constituent components stays running as well as ensuring that the infrastructure that Exchange relies on stays functional. In this chapter you'll learn what design steps you can take to keep your Exchange 2010 infrastructure recoverable and highly available.

Objectives in this chapter:

- Objective 4.1: Design and deploy high availability and disaster recovery for Exchange dependencies
- Objective 4.2: Design and deploy high availability and disaster recovery for CAS role
- Objective 4.3: Design and deploy high availability and disaster recovery for mailbox server role
- Objective 4.4: Design and deploy high availability and disaster recovery for hub transport role
- Objective 4.5: Design and deploy high availability and disaster recovery for Edge transport server role

Real World

When you start working at a new place, it's worth taking some time to figure out how the previous person in your position actually configured things. When I started at one place, I visually inspected servers, noticing that the servers that hosted the messaging system had what looked like a RAID array. A colleague who had also just joined the firm was responsible for managing these servers. Unfortunately for my colleague, a developer rather than a systems administrator had built the servers. This became apparent when one of the disks on one of the messaging systems failed. It turns out that the developer hadn't actually configured the RAID array when building the server. Instead, the developer had used the disks in a traditional, non-redundant way. Needless to say that made the job of recovering the server substantially more involved than it should have been. The lesson learned was that you should always check a server very carefully when it becomes your responsibility—you can never be sure that the people who were previously responsible for it configured it in an intelligent manner.

Objective 4.1: Design and Deploy High Availability and Disaster Recovery for Exchange Dependencies

To butcher an aphorism, no network application is an island. Exchange 2010 is dependent on the functionality on critical infrastructure services in your organization working in a reliable manner. In this objective you'll learn what design steps you can take to ensure that the infrastructure that supports Exchange is as fault tolerant as your Exchange design itself.

This objective covers:

- Active Directory.
- DNS.
- Storage.
- Site.
- Updates.

Active Directory Redundancy and Recovery

Exchange requires writable domain controllers and each site with an Exchange deployment requires a global catalog server. You can make Active Directory domain controllers and global catalog servers highly available by deploying two or more at a site. If one server fails, the other can take up the slack until the original failed server is returned to service. The standard edition and the Enterprise edition of Windows Server 2008 and Windows Server 2008 R2 include licenses to run virtualized instances of the operating system on the same hardware. When developing an Active Directory redundancy strategy, consider deploying the redundant domain controller as a virtual machine. Just ensure that you host this redundant domain controller and Global Catalog server on a separate physical server. Like all Exchange roles, Active Directory domain controllers can be deployed virtually.

Exchange requires writable domain controllers, which limits the utility of Read Only Domain Controllers (RODCs). When planning your organization's Active Directory infrastructure, you need to remember that although an RODC is useful in most circumstances, the deployment of RODC does not support Exchange. It is possible to configure an RODC as a Global Catalog server, but a Global Catalog server hosted on an RODC does not support Exchange Server 2010.

EXAM TIP

Remember that in terms of Exchange deployment, RODCs with the Global Catalog role don't count as having a Global Catalog server at the site.

MORE INFO PLANNING EXCHANGE ACTIVE DIRECTORY ACCESS

To learn more about Active Directory access to Exchange, consult the following TechNet document: *http://technet.microsoft.com/en-us/library/aa998561.aspx*.

Active Directory Recovery

As long as you have more than one domain controller in a domain, Active Directory is highly available. The only time you have to worry about recovering Active Directory is if an important object is deleted. In that case, you can recover the item by rebooting a domain controller into Directory Services Restore Mode (DSRM). If your organization has raised the forest functional level to Windows Server 2008 R2 or higher, you can enable the Active Directory Recycle Bin feature. The Active Directory Recycle Bin feature allows for the recovery of deleted Active Directory objects without the complexity of restarting a domain controller in DSRM.

One issue you may encounter when you restore deleted objects is that some Exchange attributes must be unique across the forest, but that the tools you use to restore Active Directory objects do not check for this uniqueness. When it comes to recovering deleted Exchange-related Active Directory objects, Microsoft recommends you do the following:

- If an Exchange configuration object has been deleted using the Exchange management tools (EMS or EMC), you should not restore the object. You should instead re-create the object using the Exchange management tools.

- If an Exchange configuration object has been deleted using tools other than the Exchange management tools, you should recover those objects as soon as possible, either using Directory Services Restore Mode or Active Directory Recycle Bin.

- If you recover deleted Exchange recipients, check for errors relating to those recovered objects. If you have changed Exchange policies or other recipient configuration items, you will need to reapply current policies to the recovered objects.

When deploying Active Directory in a highly available configuration to support Exchange, remember that Exchange only uses writable Domain Controllers. If you are deploying Exchange in a site that has a Read Only Domain Controller, you'll need to also deploy two writable domain controllers if you want to ensure that the domain controller deployment is highly available. This also applies to Global Catalog servers. RODCs that are also configured as Global Catalog servers are not used by Exchange—you need to configure the Global Catalog role on a writable Domain Controller.

> **MORE INFO   ACTIVE DIRECTORY DOMAIN SERVICES BACKUP AND RECOVERY**
>
> To learn more about AD DS backup and recovery, consult the following TechNet document: *http://technet.microsoft.com/en-us/library/cc771290(WS.10).aspx.*

DNS

DNS is an integral component of Active Directory. This makes it an integral part of the network infrastructure, so you need to ensure that Exchange functions properly. The key to making DNS highly available is ensuring that DNS zone data is available to clients. This means replicating DNS zone data so that it is available in more than one place. Windows Server 2008 and 2008 R2 DNS servers support the following methods of replicating zone data between DNS servers:

- **Active Directory Integrated Zone**   This type of zone is used to replicate data between DNS servers that also function as domain controllers. When you use this type of zone, any writable domain controller that hosts the DNS role can process updates to an Active Directory integrated zone. You can configure Active Directory Integrated Zones to replicate zone data to all domain controllers in a domain, in the forest, or those domain controllers which are enrolled in a custom Active Directory partition. Although RODCs can host Active Directory integrated zones, updates to those zones must be processed by a writable domain controller.

- **Standard Primary and Secondary Zones**   This type of zone has one server that can process updates (known as a primary server) and subordinate DNS servers (known as secondary servers) that hold read only copies of the DNS zone data. Clients can query either the primary or the secondary servers to obtain DNS information, but the primary server itself is a single point of failure. If the server that hosts the primary zone goes off-line, processing updates to the zone will not be possible until you deploy a replacement for the primary.

You also need to ensure that you set Exchange server IP address configuration to use both a preferred and an alternate DNS server. These should be set to separate servers so that in the event that one DNS server fails, servers running Exchange can interact with another DNS server.

An Active Directory domain controller configured with a DNS server and an Active Directory Integrated DNS zone provides a highly available name resolution infrastructure, so you don't need to utilize other high-availability technologies such as Network Load Balancing. Although RODCs can host copies of Active Directory Integrated Zones, they cannot directly process updates to those zones.

To assist with site and server failover, DNS Time To Live (TTL) records should be configured with a maximum value of 5 minutes. You can do this on the Start of Authority (SOA) tab of the zone's records as shown in Figure 4-1. You should do this for the zone that hosts all Exchange client services records including those related to Outlook Web App, Exchange Web Services, ActiveSync, SMTP, POP3, IMAP4 and RPC Client Access addresses. Having low TTL values on DNS records will ensure that clients regularly check and receive updated address information during failover events.

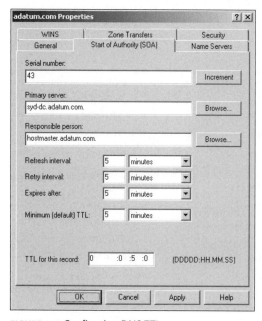

FIGURE 4-1 Configuring DNS TTL

Storage

When designing your Exchange and supporting infrastructure deployment, you should consider using redundant storage to minimize the chance that the failure of a hard disk drive will result in the loss of data. The following types of RAID are commonly used with server volumes:

- **RAID 0** Also known as disk striping. Provides good performance but is not fault tolerant.
- **RAID 1** Also known as disk mirroring. Uses disk pairing as a fault tolerance method. Each disk in a RAID 1 set has a duplicate. If the original fails, the duplicate can be used without loss of data. RAID 1 requires a minimum of two disks.
- **RAID 5** Also known as disk striping with parity. This method provides good performance by splitting disk parity data across multiple disks. If a disk fails, data is not lost; however when the disk is replaced, the data on it will need to be rebuilt by the RAID 5 process and this takes time. RAID 5 requires a minimum of three disks.
- **RAID 10** Also known as RAID 1+0, is a stripe of mirrored disks. It provides storage redundancy and performance, but also requires a minimum of four disks.

Site

To make sites highly available, you need to ensure that there is more than one connection to another location. The most common failure that sites encounter is with the connection to other sites. Traditionally these have been through dedicated lines, though today site-to-site connections are more likely to be through persistent VPN connections. You can reduce the chance that a site is unavailable by configuring a mesh topology rather than a hub and spoke topology. This topology means that if a site link fails, a site will be able to communicate with all other sites through redundant paths. If an entire site fails, only that site is lost. In hub and spoke topologies, if the primary hub site fails, none of the other sites can communicate with each other.

Updates

Windows Server Update Services is a role available to computers running Windows Server 2008 and Windows Server 2008 R2 that allows you to manage the distribution of software updates. This is substantially better than allowing computers to poll the Microsoft Update site on the Internet and to download and apply updates automatically. If you allow a computer to automatically download and install updates, you will have no control over the update process. Unfortunately that often means that you will not find out that an update causes a problem with a specific software configuration until after the update has installed.

WSUS allows you to control the approval of updates, meaning that they will only deploy to the computers in your organization when you are certain of their impact on existing configurations.

Having an update approval process allows you to create a test group of computers to which you can deploy the updates. After you have determined that the update is safe and does not cause unexpected configuration problems, you can deploy the update more widely across your organization.

WSUS allows you to place computers in groups, allowing you to stagger the deployment of updates. For example, you could create the following WSUS groups:

- All Exchange servers at a specific site
- All of the mailbox servers in the organization
- All of the mailbox server at a specific site

When you choose to deploy an update using WSUS, you choose which group or groups will be able to receive the update. The next time a computer performs an update check and finds an update that has been approved for installation, that update will be downloaded and installed.

The main limitations of WSUS are:

- **No scheduled update installation**   Update installation can't be scheduled to occur at a specific time, which makes WSUS difficult to use with a solution like Exchange or other mission-critical network infrastructure. Generally you want to be able to control precisely when a computer deploys an update so that you can be sure that servers do not restart to complete update installation at an inopportune moment.

- **No auditing facility to verify update compliance**   WSUS includes basic reporting functionality, but does not query computers to determine whether they have specific updates installed.

MORE INFO   **WINDOWS SERVER UPDATE SERVICES**

To learn more about WSUS, consult the following TechNet document: *http://technet. microsoft.com/en-us/windowsserver/bb332157.aspx*.

System Center Configuration Manager

System Center Configuration Manager 2012 offers advanced configuration management for Windows-based deployments, including the deployment of applications and the monitoring of server configuration baselines. From the perspective of this objective, you can use System Center Configuration Manager to perform advanced update deployment tasks. The benefits of System Center Configuration Manager over WSUS include:

- Allows you to configure maintenance windows that ensure that update installation only occurs at specified times. You can configure separate maintenance windows for separate collections of computers. You can use maintenance windows to ensure that you won't end up with all of your organization's critical servers rebooting at the same time.

- Computers can belong to multiple collections, allowing updates to be better targeted across the organization.

- Configuration baseline reports allow administrators to identify servers that are suffering from configuration drift from established baselines.

The drawback of System Center Configuration Manager is that it is more expensive than the freely available WSUS and requires a certain amount of supporting infrastructure to deploy. The product is less suitable for small organizations that may be better able to handle software update deployment issues simply because a smaller number of servers are easier to update manually.

Deploying Updates to DAG members

Microsoft recommends that you used a strategy other than automatic deployment when it comes to deploying updates to Exchange servers that are members of a DAG. You should manually deploy updates to Exchange servers that are members of a DAG because prior to the installation of the update, you should put the mailbox server into maintenance mode. The general process for installing updates follows these steps:

1. Run the StartDagServerMaintenance.ps1 script on the DAG member. This places the DAG member into maintenance mode.

2. Install the updates.

3. Run the StopDagServerMaintenance.ps1 script on the DAG member to bring it out of maintenance mode and back into production.

4. Perform the optional step of running the ReistributeActiveDatabases.ps1 script to rebalance the DAG. This will balance active mailbox database copy distribution.

You can use System Center Orchestrator to automate this process. Orchestrator provides a drag-and-drop interface for automating systems administration tasks such as running scripts and specific commands such as those required to run the update. If your organization is licensed for Orchestrator, this type of runbook automation can substantially improve the efficiency of update deployment.

Change Management

Change management is a way of formalizing the process of altering system configuration. Different organizations have different change management processes, and you should develop a change management process. For example, some organizations require multiple levels of sign-off before a software update can be deployed onto a production server. These organizations tend to be large and change management processes are typically more formalized as the number of potential people or customers influenced by the change grows. The benefit of this approach, as bureaucratically tedious as it may be, is that it ensures accountability for configuration changes. If something goes horribly wrong, determining what changes, if any, were made prior to faults occurring is relatively straightforward.

Other organizations have a far more ad hoc approach to change management, often deploying updates and making changes to server configuration without any form of approval process or documentation. The drawback of this approach is that it might be difficult to determine which member of staff was responsible for a specific problem occurring, though in many small- to medium-size organizations only one person is responsible for specific servers and thus apportioning blame for outages is simpler.

Backup and Recovery Objectives

Different organizations will have different backup and recovery objectives. In general you'll learn more about planning and meeting compliance obligations in Chapter 5, "Designing and Deploying Messaging Compliance, System Monitoring, and Reporting." Understanding backup and recovery objectives means understanding the following concepts:

- **Recovery Time Objective (RTO)**   The amount of time that is available to perform the recovery. When calculating what is possible, you need to consider how long the recovery will take. One reason that many organizations limit the size of mailbox databases isn't that they've reached the maximum size limit, but that the larger a mailbox database gets, the longer it takes to recover it from backup.

- **Recovery Point Objective (RPO)**   The amount of data that can be lost, measured in time. For example you might configure backups using a product such as System Center Data Protection Manager 2012, which allows you to take a backup of a mailbox server every 30 minutes. In this case your RPO would be 30 minutes because the maximum amount of data that would be lost if backups are taken every 30 minutes is 30 minutes of data.

Objective Summary

- Active Directory Domain Controllers and Global Catalog servers can be made highly available by deploying more than one in an Active Directory site.
- RODCs and RODCs with the Global Catalog role installed are not directly utilized by Exchange and should not be included when ensuring that the infrastructure that supports Exchange is highly available.
- Site resiliency can be improved by using a mesh network topology rather than a hub and spoke topology.
- Updates should be deployed manually on DAG members using scripts that put a DAG member into maintenance mode for update deployment.
- You can use WSUS and System Center Configuration Manager to deploy updates automatically to Exchange servers.

Objective Review

Answer the following questions to test your knowledge of the information in this objective. You can find the answers to these questions and explanations of why each answer choice is correct or incorrect in the "Answers" section at the end of this chapter.

1. Your organization has five branch offices. Each branch office has a single Read Only Domain Controller. Universal Group Membership Caching is enabled on each RODC and each RODC functions as a DNS server. Each DNS zone is an Active Directory Integrated Zone. You are planning on deploying Exchange Server 2010 at these sites. What steps should you take to ensure that the appropriate Active Directory and DNS infrastructure at these sites is redundant while maintaining security?

    A. Enable the Global Catalog role on each RODC at the branch office sites.

    B. Add a second RODC at each branch office site. Enable the Global Catalog and DNS roles on these servers.

    C. Add a writable domain controller to each branch office site. Enable the Global Catalog and DNS roles on these servers.

    D. Add two writable domain controllers to each branch office site. Enable the Global Catalog and DNS roles on these servers.

2. All of your organization's domain controllers are deployed traditionally on physical hardware. You want to ensure that these domain controllers will not need to be recovered from backup in the event that a single disk that hosts the operating system fails. You also want to minimize the number of disks required to implement this goal. Which of the following redundant disk technologies would you choose to accomplish this?

    A. RAID 0

    B. RAID 1

C. RAID 5

D. RAID 10

3. You want to ensure that any DNS server at your organization's primary site can process zone updates. You want at least three servers to function as DNS servers at your primary site. You want to minimize the amount of maintenance necessary to maintain the configuration. Which of the following configurations should you use? (Choose two. Each answer forms part of a complete solution.)

A. Configure three servers as Domain Controllers with the DNS role installed.

B. Configure three servers as Read Only Domain Controllers with the DNS role installed.

C. Configure the DNS zone as a Stub zone.

D. Configure the DNS zone as an Active Directory Integrated Zone.

4. You want to automate the deployment of software updates to computers that host infrastructure roles that will support your organization's Exchange Server 2010 deployment. Which of the following products can you use to accomplish this goal? (Choose all that apply.)

A. Microsoft Security Baseline Analyzer

B. System Center Operations Manager 2012

C. System Center Configuration Manager 2012

D. Windows Server Update Services 3.0 SP2

5. Which of the following scripts must you run when manually applying updates to mailbox servers that are members of a DAG? (Choose two. Each answer forms part of a complete solution.)

A. StartDagServerMaintenance.ps1

B. CheckDatabaseRedundancy.ps1

C. StopDagServerMaintenance.ps1

D. RedistributeActiveDatabases.ps1

THOUGHT EXPERIMENT
Exchange and Update Management

In the following thought experiment, you will apply what you've learned about the objective "Design and deploy high availability and disaster recovery for Exchange dependencies" to design an update management strategy for an Exchange organization. You can find answers to these questions in the "Answers" section at the end of this chapter.

You are planning an update solution for your organization's infrastructure servers and Exchange servers.

Your update solution should have the following characteristics:

An Exchange server can be a member of more than one group or collection.

You should be able to determine whether the Exchange server has all appropriate updates deployed even if you deploy those updates manually.

With these facts in mind, answer the following questions:

1. Which solution should you configure for managing software updates for your organization's Exchange server?

2. What is the name of the script that you use to place a DAG member into maintenance mode?

3. What is the name of the script that you use to bring a DAG member out of maintenance mode and to resume normal functionality?

4. What steps can you take to ensure that all of your organization's Domain Controllers, DNS Servers, and DHCP servers don't reboot at the same time to install and update?

Objective 4.2: Design and Deploy High Availability and Disaster Recovery for CAS Role

The primary method of making CAS highly available is by deploying CAS arrays. CAS arrays are site-local, network-load-balanced front ends that allow you to scale client access and ensure client mailbox access in the event of server failure.

This objective covers:

- Back up and recover CAS.
- Deploy CAS arrays.
- Design multi-site CAS deployment.
- Plan CAS site failover.

Back Up CAS

How you back up a CAS depends on your organization's data protection strategy. If your organization uses a product such as System Center Data Protection Manager 2012 and you have the capacity, you can configure backup so you can perform a bare metal recovery of a server within a 15-minute RPO. If your organization doesn't use an enterprise backup solution, or your SLA doesn't mandate that you back up CAS in such a way that they can be restored through bare metal recovery, most organizations will be able to recover CAS within the RTO by performing an operating system reinstallation and Exchange recovery. When developing a CAS backup strategy, consider the following points:

- The majority of CAS configuration files are stored within Active Directory and are associated with the CAS computer's account.

- Back up IIS configuration if you make changes to it. You can do this directly through IIS or by taking a system state backup.

- Back up the configuration files stored in the c:\program files\microsoft\Exchange\ Server\V14\ClientAccess path, which hosts any customizations you've made to the CAS configuration, including any modifications made to the appearance of OWA. This folder also hosts the configuration of the PRC Client Access Service, ECP, Availability Service, Autodiscover Service, ActiveSync, POP3, and IMAP4 settings.

- Back up SSL certificates. The simplest way of doing this is to export all SLL certificates and store them in a secure location. SSL certificates will also be backed up as part of a system state backup.

- If the server is a member of a CAS array, it may be necessary to back up the system state data of the host server because this holds the NLB configuration. Otherwise you'll need to rejoin a restored server to the NLB cluster manually.

The key to understanding backup of CAS components is that you only need to back up CAS configuration data when you make a change—it isn't something that you need to on a regular basis. Organizations that have not modified CAS server configuration other than through procuring SSL certificates may consider a no-backup strategy. As long as SSL certificates are stored in a secure location, it is relatively straightforward to recover a CAS using the operating system reinstall and Exchange recovery method and still meet RTO.

Recover CAS

How you recover a CAS depends on the backup technologies you utilized to protect Exchange. The strategy that you use to recover a CAS server that's protected by backup snapshots every 15 minutes through System Center Data Protection Manager 2012 is going to be different than the strategy that you use if you've just backed up the server's SSL certificates and stored them in a secure location. When it comes to restoration, you have several options, including:

- If you are using a backup product that allows you to perform bare metal recovery, you should recover the CAS in that manner, which will be faster than operating system reinstall and Exchange recovery. You should only do this if the backup that you are restoring from is relatively recent. Recovering from an old backup and then figuring out what might have changed in the intervening period is likely to take more time than the operating system reinstall and Exchange recovery method.

- Operating system reinstall and Exchange recovery. This is the recovery version more likely to be covered on the 70-663 exam and covered in the next part of this objective. It involves replacing the operating system and then installing Exchange in recovery mode.

Exchange 2010 uses a different full server recovery process than previous versions of Exchange. The key to understanding this process is that most of the Exchange configuration data for a particular Exchange data is stored within Active Directory and is associated with that server's computer account. When you perform a recovery installation, the installation process extracts that configuration data from Active Directory and uses it in setting up the replacement for the failed server.

The full operating system reinstall and Exchange recovery technique that you use to recover a CAS is the same general technique as you use to recover the Hub Transport and Mailbox server roles. Prior to attempting to recover a CAS using this technique, you must ensure that the following prerequisites are met:

- The replacement server must be running the same operating system as the failed server. You can't recover a failed CAS that was running on the Windows Server 2008 operating system using Windows Server 2008 R2. Similarly, you can't recover a failed CAS that was running on Windows Server 2008 R2 using Windows Server 2008. This applies equally to the next version of the Windows server operating system, due for release in 2012.

- You must configure the replacement server with the same name as the failed server. If the failed CAS had the name SYD-CAS1, the server that you are going to perform recovery to must also have the name SYD-CAS1.

- The replacement server must have a similar volume configuration to the failed server.

- The replacement server should have similar or better performance characteristics than the failed server.

After you have procured and configured the server that will function as the replacement for the failed CAS server, you need to perform the following steps:

- Within Active Directory, you need to reset the computer account of the server for which you will be performing full server recovery. Be careful to reset and not delete the computer account!

- Install the operating system on the replacement server. Configure the server with the same name as the failed server.

- Join the replacement server to the same domain.

- Install the necessary CAS server prerequisite components. If you are recovering a server that will host additional Exchange roles, ensure that you install the appropriate prerequisite components as well.

- Log on to the server using an account that has the right to install Exchange 2010, open a command prompt, navigate to the location that hosts the Exchange Server 2010 SP1 (or later) installation files and issue the following command:

```
Setup /m:RecoverServer
```

After the setup process is complete, you may need to take the following steps before returning the CAS to production:

- Restore the failed CAS IIS configuration if you made any changes to the default configuration.

- Reinstall any certificates used for Secure Sockets Layer communication.

- Restore any CAS virtual directory and OWA customizations.

- Rejoin the CAS to any CAS arrays to which it was a member.

Deploy CAS Arrays

A Client Access array, also known as a CAS array, is a collection of load-balanced Client Access Servers. CAS arrays allow you to make client access highly available. If one CAS in the array fails, clients who access CAS services through the address of the array are automatically redirected to a functioning node in the array. CAS arrays use network load balancing as the basis of their high availability. You can use a dedicated hardware network load-balancing solution or the built-in Windows Network Load Balancing feature.

CAS array deployments are constrained in the following ways:

- You can only deploy one Client Access Server per Active Directory site.

- CAS arrays can only contain CAS that are located in the same site.

- If you are using Windows Network Load Balancing, you can't deploy a CAS array on a server if the server is a member of a Database Availability Group.

- If you are using Windows Network Load Balancing, you can only have a maximum of eight CAS in the array.

To deploy a CAS, perform the following general steps:

1. Configure a load-balancing solution for the CAS at a specific site. You can use a hardware NLB solution or Windows NLB. When creating the NLB solution, ensure that you configure the array to load balance TCP port 135, TCP, and UDP ports 6005 through 65535.

2. Configure a new DNS record that points to the virtual IP address that you will use with the CAS array. This IP address needs to be in the range defined for the Active Directory site.

3. Create the CAS array using the *New-ClientAccessArray* cmdlet. For example, for a CAS array that uses the DNS name canberracas.contoso.com, located in the Canberra site, issue the following command:

```
New-ClientAccessArray -Name 'Canberra Array' -FQDN 'canberracas.contoso.com' -Site
'Canberra'
```

4. Bind mailbox databases in the site to the CAS array using the *Set-MailboxDatabase* cmdlet. For example, to bind the mailbox database CBR-MBX-1 to the CAS array created in the previous step, issue the following command:

```
Set-MailboxDatabase CBR-MBX-1 -RpcClientAccessServer 'canberracas.contoso.com'
```

Design Multi-Site CAS Deployment

When considering high availability of CAS arrays remember that unlike database availability groups, you can only have one CAS array per Active Directory site and a CAS array cannot span multiple Active Directory sites. For example, if your organization has mailbox servers in the cities of Adelaide and Melbourne that are members of the same Database Availability Group (DAG) and you wanted to make Client Access highly available, you'll need to deploy two CAS servers in each site and you'll also need two CAS arrays even though you have only one Database Availability Group. It is also important to remember that each CAS array's FQDN must be unique.

> **MORE INFO**   **MULTI-SITE CAS DEPLOYMENT**
>
> To learn more about multi-site CAS deployment, consult the following TechNet document:
> *http://technet.microsoft.com/en-us/magazine/ff626260.aspx.*

CAS Site Failover

CAS during site failover involves altering the mapping of DNS records for service endpoints such as OWA, Autodiscover, and RPC client access from IP addresses in the original site to IP addresses in the failover site. After this change has been made, clients will automatically connect to new service endpoints after one of the following has occurred:

- They will attempt to connect to the endpoints in the original site until the TTL on the DNS records expires. If you set the TTL on the zones to five minutes, this will take a maximum of five minutes to occur. When the TTL expires, clients will connect to endpoints in the failover site.

- Clients can run the *ipconfig /flushdns* command. This will expunge the original DNS records and the client will use the revised records.

In most cases the five-minute TTL on DNS record will mean that the situation is resolved quickly after the changes are made to the DNS zone. You can automate the process of updating DNS records using scripts or System Center Orchestrator runbooks.

> **MORE INFO** **CAS SITE FAILOVER**
>
> To learn more about CAS site failover, consult the following TechNet document:
> *http://technet.microsoft.com/en-us/library/dd351049.aspx.*

Objective Summary

- You should back up IIS configuration whenever you make changes to that configuration.

- You should back up the configuration files stored in the ClientAccess folder path because this hosts any customizations you've made to the CAS configuration.

- You should export and store any certificates used by CAS services.

- The operating system reinstall and Exchange recovery method involves deploying a new server with the same name and operating system as the failed server, resetting the failed server's Active Directory account, joining that server to the same domain, and then running Setup /m:RecoverServer. This will restore the CAS and most of its configuration data.

- Restore any configuration changes made after recovery has occurred, including importing any necessary certificates.

- You can only have one CAS array per site.

- CAS arrays cannot span multiple sites.

- You can initiate CAS failover by updating service records to point at the failover site.

Objective Review

Answer the following questions to test your knowledge of the information in this objective. You can find the answers to these questions and explanations of why each answer choice is correct or incorrect in the "Answers" section at the end of this chapter.

1. You are configuring the TTL value for DNS records related to services such as ActiveSync related to CAS. Which of the following TTL figures should you configure at the DNS zone level?

    A. 60 minutes

    B. 30 minutes

    C. 5 minutes

    D. 300 minutes

2. Your organization has 12 large sites spread across Australia, New Zealand, and Southeast Asia. Each of these large sites has two mailbox servers. You have configured three Database Availability Groups. You have enrolled each mailbox server in one of these groups. You want to ensure that client access at each of your organization's sites is highly available. What is the minimum number of CAS arrays that you would deploy to accomplish this goal?

    A. 4

    B. 6

    C. 12

    D. 1

3. You are considering the deployment of a CAS array at your organization's headquarters site. You will be using Windows Network Load Balancing as your NLB solution. Which of the following servers can be members of the CAS array? (Choose all that apply.)

    A. Mailbox server with Hub Transport and Client Access Server roles installed. Not a DAG member.

    B. Hub Transport Server with the Client Access Server role installed.

    C. Client Access Server.

    D. Mailbox server with Client Access Server role installed. Member of a DAG.

4. Which of the following steps should you take before running the *New-ClientAccess-Array* cmdlet?

    A. Configure DNS round robin.

    B. Configure a Database Availability Group.

C. Configure network load balancing.

   D. Configure failover clustering.

5. Your organization has two mailbox servers each at its Copenhagen, Stockholm, Moscow, and London offices. The round-trip delay between these sites is under 200 milliseconds (ms). All six mailbox servers are members of the same DAG. You want to deploy a minimum number of CAS servers to support highly available client access in your organization. How many CAS servers will be necessary to accomplish this goal?

   A. 2

   B. 4

   C. 6

   D. 12

THOUGHT EXPERIMENT
Recovering a Failed Exchange CAS

In the following thought experiment, you will apply what you've learned about the objective "Design and deploy high availability and disaster recovery for CAS role" to explain how recover a failed server that has the CAS role installed. You can find answers to these questions in the "Answers" section at the end of this chapter.

There are five CAS at your organization's Australian division. Each server is configured so that the CAS role is the only role that it hosts. Each server's hardware configuration includes a single hard disk drive. Each server uses Windows Server 2008 as the host operating system.

One of these servers, named ADL-CAS-A, fails. You replace the failed hard disk drive and prepare to recover the server.

With this in mind, answer the following questions:

1. What operating system should you install on the replacement hardware?

2. What name should you give the new computer?

3. What step should you take in configuring Active Directory prior to joining the newly installed computer to the domain?

4. What command should you run to begin Exchange setup?

Objective 4.3: Design and Deploy High Availability and Disaster Recovery for Mailbox Server Role

Database Availability Groups in Exchange Server 2010 make the process of protecting mailboxes simple. If an organization has more than one mailbox server, those mailbox servers can be enrolled in a Database Availability Group ensuring that each subscribed mailbox database will be available to users in the event that one of the mailbox servers fails. Deploying Database Availability Groups will drastically reduce the amount of money and time an organization needs to spend concerning itself with the data protection infrastructure required to protect mailbox server and public folder databases.

> **This objective covers:**
> - Back up and recover mailbox servers.
> - Design Database Availability Groups.
> - Design and deploy Public Folder replication.
> - Repair mailbox databases.

Back Up Mailbox Servers

The introduction of Database Availability Groups (DAGs) in Exchange Server 2010 changed the calculus of backup operations. With a DAGs you can use built-in replication to protect you from loss of mailbox database data. If you've configured a DAG and a mailbox server fails completely, clients just fail over to another node in the DAG. This new technology has a direct impact on your backup design. If you have a three-node DAG where one copy is lagged, you don't need to perform frequent backups—backups only become necessary for compliance purposes and for restoring data deleted beyond what is stored on the lagged copy.

When designing your mailbox server backup plan, consider the following:

- If your organization uses Database Availability Groups and does not use public folders, you will only need to perform backups for retention and compliance purposes. In this situation backups are not used for server recovery, but are only used to recover data that is not available through the lagged DAG copy. In the event of full server recovery, Mailbox databases are synchronized from other members of the DAG rather than being recovered from backup.

- Public Folder replication makes public folders highly available.

- Single Item Recovery ensures that all deleted and modified items are preserved for 14 days. Users are unable to hard-delete items. Administrators with the appropriate permissions can restore these items to the user's mailbox within this period. Single item recovery is not enabled by default and must be enabled on a per-mailbox basis, though you can use the following command to enable it for all mailboxes:

```
Get-Mailbox | where {$_.SingleItemRecoveryEnabled –eq $false} | Set-Mailbox
-SingleItemRecoveryEnabled $true
```

- Mailbox retention means that deleted mailboxes will remain within the mailbox database as a disconnected mailbox until the deleted mailbox retention setting is reached. This is 30 days by default. This means that it is possible to recover deleted mailboxes within a 30-day default window without having to restore from backup. Mailbox retention is configured on the Limits tab of a mailbox database's properties as shown in Figure 4-2.

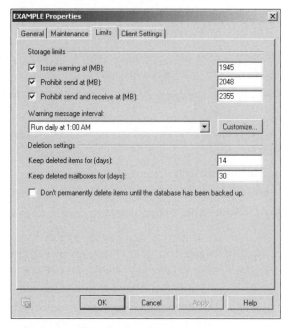

FIGURE 4-2 Mailbox database limits

- If your organization uses an enterprise-level backup product such as System Center Data Protection Manager, you can configure backup in such a way that you can perform bare metal recovery.

Recover Mailbox Servers

As with other Exchange roles such as the CAS and Hub Transport server roles, you have a couple of options when it comes to recovering an Exchange 2010 mailbox server:

- If you are using a backup product that allows you to perform bare metal recovery, you should recover the mailbox server in that manner. You should only do this if the backup that you are restoring from is relatively recent.

- Perform full operating system reinstall and then Exchange recovery.

The full operating system reinstall and Exchange recovery technique that you use to recover a mailbox server is the same general technique as you use to recover the Hub Transport and CAS roles. Prior to attempting to recover a mailbox server using this technique, you must ensure that the following prerequisites are met:

- The replacement server must be running the same operating system as the failed server.
- You must configure the replacement server with the same name as the failed server.
- The replacement server must have a similar volume configuration to the failed server.
- The replacement server should have similar or better performance characteristics than the failed server.

When you have procured and configured the server that will function as the replacement for the failed mailbox server, you need to perform the following steps:

- Within Active Directory, you need to reset the computer account of the server for which you will be performing full server recovery.
- Install the operating system on the replacement server. Configure the server with the same name as the failed server.
- Join the replacement server to the same domain.
- Install the necessary mailbox server prerequisite components. If you are recovering a server that will host additional Exchange roles, ensure that you install the appropriate prerequisite components as well.
- Log on to the server using an account that has the right to install Exchange 2010, open a command prompt, navigate to the location that hosts the Exchange Server 2010 SP1 (or later) installation files, and issue the following command:

```
Setup /m:RecoverServer
```

After the setup process has completed, you'll need to take the following steps before returning the Mailbox server to production:

- If the mailbox server is not a member of a DAG, you'll need to restore the mailbox databases to their original locations from backup. This can be done using Windows Server Backup. You may choose to perform a dial-tone recovery as a method of restoring service.
- If the mailbox server is a member of a DAG, you can configure the mailbox database copies to repopulate from the data stored in the Active mailbox database copy.

Recover Mailbox Databases and Data

As server hardware becomes more reliable, full server recovery becomes an increasingly edge case scenario. In some cases though no matter what preparation you take, you need to restore data from backup. The traditional recovery scenarios are as follows:

- **Database restore** You need to perform a database restore when a database is lost completely and you don't have a mechanism such as a DAG as a way to recover that database. You can restore the database from backup and then replay transaction logs to return the database to a point in time prior to the loss of the database. If your organization's mailbox database is very large, recovery can take a substantial amount of time and you may need to consider performing a dial-tone recovery to enable users to send and receive messages during the recovery process.

- **Recovery database** Recovery databases are useful in the event that you need to be able to recover specific data from within the database, such as a mailbox or an individual message, without recovering the mailbox database in its entirety. If you have enabled single-item recovery in your organization, administrators will be able to recover most deleted items without having to use a recovery database, as long as the item was deleted in the last 14 days.

- **Database portability** Database portability allows you to restore databases on different mailbox servers to the ones that originally hosted them. Database portability allows you to restore and mount a database on any Mailbox server within the organization.

- **Dial-tone recovery** Dial-tone recovery is a strategy that allows users whose mailboxes are situated on a mailbox that is being restored to still send and receive email messages. You allow a dial-tone recovery by creating an empty database for the mailboxes that were hosted in the database that failed. After the dial-tone database is online, you can restore the original data to a recovery database. When you have done this, you can then merge that data into the dial-tone database.

Design Database Availability Groups

Database Availability Groups (DAGs) is a high-availability technology that allows collections of up to 16 Exchange Server 2010 mailbox servers to perform automatic mailbox database failover in the event that a database, server, or network failure occurs. DAGs do not require storage area networks or complex cluster configuration. You can scale DAG membership incrementally, creating a DAG with two servers as members and then eventually growing that membership to 16 servers as required. Dag members must run one of the following operating systems:

- The enterprise or datacenter edition of Windows Server 2008 with Service Pack 2
- The enterprise or datacenter edition of Windows Server 2008 R2

The enterprise or datacenter editions are needed because the Windows Failover Clustering feature is required to support DAGs. When you add a server to a DAG, this feature is automatically enabled and configured. You also need to ensure that DAG members are all running the same operating system. You can't mix and match Windows Server 2008 with Windows Server 2008 R2.

DAGs have the following additional requirements:

- Each DAG member must have the same number of network adapters.
- Each DAG member must have no more than one MAPI network. MAPI networks are used to communicate with other Exchange servers and directory servers. If DAG members only have one network adapter, the MAPI network will be used as the replication network. This occurs automatically, but you can specifically enable a network for replication on the DAG network properties as shown in Figure 4-3.

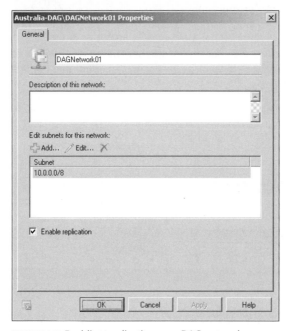

FIGURE 4-3 Enabling replication on a DAG network

- Each DAG member can only have a single MAPI network.
- You can add additional replication networks as needed. If you configure separate replication networks and MAPI networks, you must ensure that there is no direct routing that will allow heartbeat traffic from the replication network on one DAG member to be sent to the MAPI network on another DAG member server.
- IPv6 is only supported on DAG network if IPv4 is also used. DAG networks are currently not supported in a pure IPv6 environment.
- Client-facing DNS records should have a Time to Live (TTL) of five minutes. This will reduce client downtime during failover events.

Because you can have multiple DAGs in a forest, the name of the DAG must be unique throughout the organization. A DAG name can be up to 15 characters in length. You can assign an IPv4 or IPv6 address to the DAG when creating it through EMS with the *New-DatabaseAvailabilityGroup* cmdlet. When you create a DAG using EMC, the default is for the DAG to be assigned an IP address from a DHCP server and for the resulting name and address to be registered automatically.

To create a DAG, perform the following general steps:

1. Click the Organization Configuration\Mailbox node in EMC.

2. Click New Database Availability Group in the Actions pane.

3. On the New Database Availability Group page, shown in Figure 4-4, enter the name of the DAG, the name of the witness server, and the name of the witness directory on the witness server. You'll learn more about witness servers later in this objective. Click New to create the DAG.

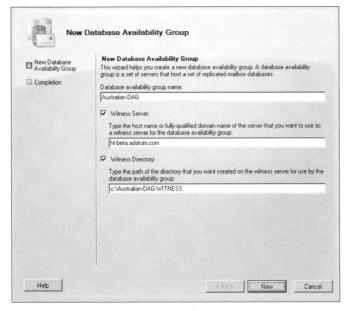

FIGURE 4-4 New Database Availability Group

You create DAGs from EMS using the *New-DatabaseAvailabilityGroup* cmdlet. For example, to create a new DAG called Australian-DAG that uses the witness server ht-beta.adatum.com, the witness directory c:\Australian-DAG-WITNESS, and the virtual IP address 192.168.15.100, use the following EMS command:

```
New-DatabaseAvailabilityGroup -Name Australian-DAG -DatabaseAvailabilityGroupIpAddresses
192.168.15.100 -WitnessServer 'ht-beta.adatum.com' -WitnessDirectory 'c:\Australian-DAG-
WITNESS'
```

To add one or more mailbox servers to a DAG, perform the following general steps:

1. Click the Organization Configuration\Mailbox node in EMC.

2. Click the Database Availability Groups tab. Click the DAG to which you want to add a mailbox server. On the Actions pane, click Managed Database Availability Group.

3. In the Manage Database Availability Group Membership dialog box, click Add.

4. Select the mailbox server that you wish to add to the DAG and then click OK.

5. Repeat step 4 to add any additional mailbox servers to the DAG.

6. The target servers will be configured with the failover clustering feature and added to the DAG.

You can also use the *Add-DatabaseAvailabilityGroupsServer* cmdlet to add a specific mailbox server to an existing DAG. You can use the *Remove-DatabaseAvailabilityGroupServer* cmdlet to remove a specific mailbox server from an existing DAG. For example, to add the server MEL-EX1 to DAG Australia-DAG, issue the following command:

```
Add-DatabaseAvailabilityGroupServer –Identity Australia-DAG –MailboxServer MEL-EX1
```

After you have added mailbox servers to the DAG, you can begin configuring mailbox database copies. Mailbox database copies are copies of an existing mailbox database that Exchange Server 2010 keeps up to date through continuous replication. Mailbox copies must meet the following criteria:

- You can only create mailbox database copies of mailbox databases already present You on mailbox servers that are members of the same DAG.

- can only create mailbox database copies of mailbox databases where the active copy of the mailbox database is mounted.

- You can only create a mailbox database if the source copy of the database does not have circular logging enabled. After the copy is created, you can re-enable circular logging on the source mailbox data.

- You cannot deploy more than one instance of a mailbox database copy on a single DAG member

- All mailbox database copies must use the same relative path.

To create a mailbox database copy, perform the following general steps:

1. Click the Organization Configuration\Mailbox node.

2. Click the Database Management tab and then click the mailbox database for which you want to create a copy.

3. On the Actions pane, click Add Mailbox Database Copy.

4. In the Add Mailbox Database Copy dialog box, click Browse to select the DAG member that will host the new copy.

5. Choose an Activation Preference number. You will learn more about activation preferences later in this objective. Click Add, click Finish, and then click Close to dismiss the wizard.

You can use the *Add-MailboxDatabaseCopy* cmdlet to add mailbox database copies. You use the *RemoveMailboxDatabaseCopy* cmdlet. For example, to add a mailbox database copy of an existing mailbox database named SYD-MBX1 with an activation preference of 5 to DAG member MEL-EX2, use the following EMS command:

```
Add-MailboxDatabaseCopy –Identity SYD-MBX1 –MailboxServer MEL-EX2 –ActivationPreference 5
```

> **MORE INFO** **DATABASE AVAILABILITY GROUPS**
>
> To learn more about DAGs, consult the following TechNet document: *http://technet. microsoft.com/en-us/library/dd979799.aspx.*

Continuous Replication

In Exchange 2010 RTM, continuous replication works by shipping copies of transaction log files that are generated by the active mailbox database to the mailbox servers that host the passive mailbox database copies. With the release of service pack 1, this form of replication becomes known as continuous replication - file mode. Exchange Server 2010 SP1 also introduces continuous replication - block mode. In block mode, when each update is written to the active mailbox database copy's active log buffer, the update is also shipped to a log buffer on every passive mailbox database copy in the DAG. When the log buffer fills, each database copy builds, verifies, and creates the next log file. If a failure occurs on the active mailbox database copy, the passive copies will be more up to date than they would be if they were relying upon just the shipping of transaction log files.

> **MORE INFO** **CONTINUOUS REPLICATION – BLOCK MODE**
>
> To learn more about continuous replication – block mode, consult the following TechNet document: *http://technet.microsoft.com/en-us/library/ff625233.aspx.*

Witness Server Resiliency

Witness servers allow DAGs with even numbers of servers to avoid *split-brain* syndrome. Split-brain syndrome occurs when DAG members are unable to communicate with each other but are otherwise fully functional. You can avoid split-brain syndrome by always requiring that a majority of DAG members (including the witness server when there are an even number of DAG members) be available and interacting for the DAG to be operational.

Witness servers are usually Hub Transport servers that do not have the Mailbox server role installed. It is possible to configure other servers to function as DAG witness servers, but Microsoft does not recommend that you pursue this course of action. Witness servers must have the following properties:

- DAGs with odd numbers of members do not use witness servers. Only DAGs with even numbers of members need witness servers.
- The witness server cannot be a member of a DAG.

- A single server can function as the witness server for multiple DAGs.
- Each DAG must have a unique witness directory.
- The witness server must be a member of the same Active Directory forest as the DAG.
- If the witness server does not have Exchange Server 2010 installed, you will need to add the Exchange Trusted Subsystem universal security group to the local Administrators group on the witness server.
- If a witness server is not specified during DAG creation, the witness server will automatically locate an available Hub Transport server on which to install the Mailbox server role. If this server also hosts the Mailbox server role, you will not be able to enroll it in the DAG at a later point in time.

You can configure an alternate witness server on the DAG Properties page shown in Figure 4-5. In Exchange 2010 RTM it was only possible to configure the alternate witness server properties from EMS. The alternate witness server is used in the event that the primary witness server is unavailable.

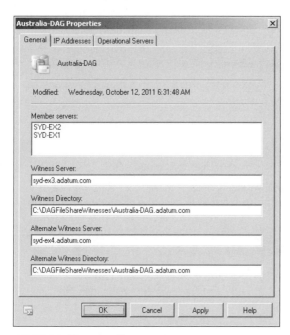

FIGURE 4-5 Alternate witness server

Activation Preference and Auto Activation

Active Manager is an Exchange component that is responsible for managing switchovers and failovers. Active Manager runs on all servers that are members of a DAG. Active Manager works by detecting a failure in a local resource and then triggering the failover process. Active Manager is responsible for informing CAS servers of which DAG member is hosting the active copy of a specific mailbox database. Active Manager works transparently and does not require direct configuration.

A mailbox database copy's activation preference number indicates the preferred order in which a passive mailbox database copy will activate if the active mailbox database copy fails. You can configure this setting by editing the mailbox database copy's properties as shown in Figure 4-6 or by using the *Set-MailboxDatabaseCopy* cmdlet with the *ActivationPreference* parameter.

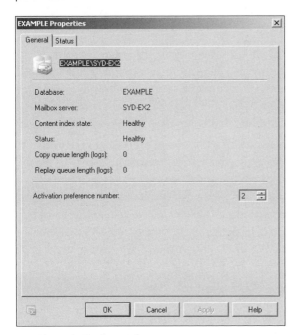

FIGURE 4-6 Activation preference

In some cases you may wish to block a specific passive mailbox database copy from becoming activated automatically during failover. To ensure that a passive mailbox database copies on a specific mailbox server do not become activated, you configure the copies to be suspended from activation. You can accomplish this by using the *Set-MailboxServer* cmdlet with the *DatabaseCopyAutoActivationPolicy* parameter set to *Blocked*. You can also configure the *DatabaseCopyAutoActivationPolicy* parameter to *IntrasiteOnly*, in which case database copies can only be activated by servers in the same site. This is a method of preventing cross-site failover or activation.

You can use the *Suspend-MailboxDatabaseCopy* cmdlet to suspend activation for a specific mailbox database copy. For example, to suspend activation of a mailbox database copy named SYD-MBX1 hosted on server MEL-EX1, issue the following command:

```
Suspend-MailboxDatabaseCopy –Identity SYD-MBX1\MEL-EX1 –ActivationOnly
```

You can use the *Resume-MailboxDatabaseCopy* cmdlet to resume a mailbox database for activation.

> **MORE INFO** **ACTIVATION POLICIES**
>
> To learn more about configuring activation policies, consult the following TechNet document: *http://technet.microsoft.com/en-us/library/dd298046.aspx*.

Datacenter Activation Coordination

Datacenter Activation Coordination (DAC) mode is a setting that you can configure for a DAG. DAC mode is disabled by default. Microsoft recommends that you enable it for all DAGs in your organization that have two or more members and use continuous replication. DAC mode is designed to control the startup database mount behavior during catastrophic failure events, such as the complete failure of a datacenter that brings down multiple DAG members.

For example, let's say a DAG is configured with three DAG members in each site, with a witness server in the first site. The first site fails completely. In this situation the second site normally couldn't activate because quorum can't be established. You can get around this limitation with DAC. You can enable DAC mode using the *Set-DatabaseAvailabiltyGroup* cmdlet with the *DatacenterActivationMode* parameter. After you enable DAC mode, you'll be able to activate the second site even though the majority of DAG nodes remain unavailable. Exchange 2010 SP1 supports two member DAGs where each member is in a separate site.

> **MORE INFO** **DATACENTER ACTIVATION COORDINATION**
>
> To learn more about DAC, consult the following TechNet document: *http://technet. microsoft.com/en-us/library/dd979790.aspx*.

Lagged Mailbox Database Copies

Typical mailbox database copies are up-to-the-moment replicas of the active mailbox database. A lagged mailbox database copy is a mailbox database copy that represents the state of the active mailbox database as it was up to 14 days previously. For example, you might configure a DAG with three mailbox servers. The first server hosts the active copy of a mailbox database, the second server hosts a passive copy that is an up-to-the-moment replica of the active copy. The third mailbox server hosts a lagged copy that is configured with a 14-day lag time. A message that arrives in a mailbox hosted in the active mailbox database copy will not be present in the same mailbox on the lagged copy until 14 days later. Lagged mailbox database copies are primarily useful for mailbox restoration scenarios. If the active mailbox database copy is found to host corrupt data, it may be possible to recover that data in an uncorrupted state from the lagged database copy without having to restore from backup.

When configuring a lagged mailbox database copy, you need to consider the two following settings:

- **Replay Lag Time** This setting determines the amount of time that Exchange waits to replay the active mailbox database copy's logs against the passive copy. The replay lag timer begins counting when the log file successfully replicates to the passive copy. Maximum replay lag time is 14 days.

- **Truncation Lag Time** This setting determines the amount of time that transaction logs are kept after the log has been replayed against the lagged mailbox database copy. The truncation lag timer begins counting when the log file has been applied. Delaying the truncation of log files will allow you to recover from failures that impact on the log files for the active mailbox database. The maximum allowable setting for truncation lag time is 14 days.

You can create a lagged mailbox copy using the *Add-MailboxDatabaseCopy* cmdlet with the *ReplayLagTime* and *TruncationLagTime* parameters. You can modify replay lag time and truncation lag time using the *Set-MailboxDatabaseCopy* cmdlet. For example, to add a 10-day lagged copy of the mailbox database SYD-MBX1 to DAG member MEL-EX3 with a truncation lag time of 12 days, issue the following command:

```
Add-MailboxDatabaseCopy -Identity SYD-MBX1 -MailboxServer MEL-EX3 -ReplayLagTime
10.00:00:00 -TruncationLagTime 12.00:00:00
```

To activate a lagged mailbox database copy, perform the following general steps:

1. Suspend replication for the lagged copy that you intend to activate using the *Suspend-MailboxDatabaseCopy* cmdlet.

2. Determine which log files you need to replay to meet your recovery objective. Do this based on log file date stamps. All log files created after this recovery objective point should be moved to an alternate directory until recovery is completed.

3. Delete the checkpoint (.chk) file for the lagged database copy.

4. Use eseutil.exe to replay log files against the database to bring it up to the desired point in time. When log replay completes, the database will be in a clean shutdown state and you can copy it and use it for recovery purposes.

5. You can resume replication of the database using the *Resume-MailboxDatabaseCopy* cmdlet.

> **MORE INFO** **LAGGED MAILBOX DATABASE COPIES**
>
> To learn more about activating lagged mailbox database copies, consult the following TechNet document: *http://technet.microsoft.com/en-us/library/dd979786.aspx*.

Design and Deploy DAGs Across Multiple Locations

It is possible to configure a single DAG across multiple locations as long as there is not a round-trip delay of more than 500 ms between any two potential DAG nodes. This applies right across the DAG, so even though one node might be able to communicate with all the other nodes with a round-trip delay of less than 500 ms, all nodes in the potential DAG must meet this benchmark.

EXAM TIP

In Exchange 2010 RTM the round-trip delay limitation was 250 milliseconds. The acceptable delay was increased to 500 milliseconds with the release of Exchange 2010 Service Pack 1.

An Exchange server can only be a member of a single DAG. You can have multiple DAGs within a single Exchange organization. All members of a DAG must be members of the same Exchange organization. This means that if you have a cross-forest topology, each DAG can only include mailbox servers that are members of the same Active Directory forest.

> **MORE INFO   DAG NETWORK REQUIREMENTS**
>
> To learn more about designing DAGs across multiple networks, consult the following TechNet document: *http://technet.microsoft.com/en-us/library/dd638104.aspx#NR*.

DAG Backup

You can use Windows Server Backup to back up volumes that host active mailbox database copies. You cannot use Windows Server Backup to back up volumes that host passive mailbox database copies. To back up a passive mailbox database copy and lagged mailbox database copies, you need to use System Center Data Protection Manager (DPM) or a third-party, Exchange-aware, VSS-based backup product.

Although you can back up passive mailbox database copies using DPM or a third-party, Exchange-aware, VSS-based backup product, the Microsoft Exchange Replication service VSS writer doesn't support direct restore scenarios. Instead you can restore the passive mailbox database copy to an alternate location, suspend replication on the current passive copy, and copy the database and log files from the alternate location over the current passive copy.

> **MORE INFO   DAG BACKUP**
>
> To learn more about DAG Backup, consult the following TechNet document: *http://technet. microsoft.com/en-us/library/dd876874.aspx*.

Design and Deploy Public Folder Replication

Public folder databases can't utilize DAG technology. To make public folders highly available, you need to configure public folder replication. Public folder replication allows the synchronization of both the public folder structure and public folder content from one public folder database to another.

The public folder hierarchy replicates independently of the synchronization of public folder content. Each public folder database hosts a copy of the public folder hierarchy. Each public folder database also stores information about which public folder databases store content replicas. A content replica is a synchronized copy of a public folder and its content. You can choose which public folder databases in your organization will host specific content replicas. Public folder replicates synchronize according to a schedule that you usually configure on the host public folder database.

To configure a public folder hosted on one mailbox server to replicate to a public folder database hosted on another mailbox server within the same Exchange organization, perform the following general steps:

1. Click the Toolbox node of EMC. Open the Public Folder Management Console.

2. In the Public Folder Management Console, click the parent node of the folder that you wish to synchronize to another public folder database.

3. In the center pane, right-click the folder that you wish to synchronize and then click Properties.

4. Click the Replication tab and then click Add. In the Select Public Folder Database dialog box, click the public folder databases that you want to include in the replication scope for the public folder.

You can configure the replication scope of a public folder using the *Set-PublicFolder* cmdlet with the *Replicas* parameter. When using the *Replicas* parameter, you must specify the current public folder databases as well as the additional public folder databases. For example, the Ideas public folder is currently hosted on a public folder database named SYD-PFDB. To configure this folder so that it also replicates to the public folder database named MEL-PFDB, issue the following command:

```
Set-PublicFolder –Identity '\Ideas' –Replicas 'SYD-PFDB','MEL-PFDB'
```

You can suspend content replication using the *Suspend-PublicFolderReplication* cmdlet. Suspending public folder replication only applies to the replication of public folder content and does not apply to the replication of public folder hierarchy data. The *Update-PublicFolder* cmdlet allows you to force synchronization of a specific public folder replica.

Public folders do not support continuous replication. The default synchronization period for public folder content is every 15 minutes. You can configure custom public folder synchronization by choosing one of the following options:

- **Always Run** Synchronization occurs every 15 minutes.

- **Never Run**   No synchronization occurs.
- **Run Every Hour**   Synchronization occurs every 60 minutes.
- **Run Every 2 Hours**   Synchronization occurs every 120 minutes.
- **Run Every 4 Hours**   Synchronization occurs every 240 minutes.
- **Use Custom Schedule**   Synchronization occurs every 15 minutes between blocked-out hours. For example, every 15 minutes between 10 P.M. and 6 A.M. on weekdays.

Public folder database replication can be configured using the *Set-PublicFolder-Database* cmdlet with the *ReplicationPeriod* and *ReplicationSchedule* parameters. With the *ReplicationSchedule* parameter, you can configure specific replication times or choose the *Always* option. You can configure public folder replica synchronization, which overrides the settings applied at the public folder database level, using the *Set-PublicFolder* cmdlet.

MORE INFO   **PUBLIC FOLDER REPLICATION**

To learn more about public folder replication, consult the following TechNet document: *http://technet.microsoft.com/en-us/library/bb629523.aspx*.

EXAM TIP

Remember that you can't add a public folder to a DAG, and that you have to use public folder replication to make public folders highly available.

Repair Mailbox Databases

Sometimes mailbox databases become corrupt because of disk error issues. If your organization doesn't use DAGs, or if you haven't configured lagged database copies, you may want to attempt to repair database corruption before attempting to restore from backup. The tools that you can use include the following:

- **ESEUtil**   A command-line tool that allows you to repair, view, and modify Exchange databases at the page level. Microsoft recommends that you have 120 percent of the size of the database you are intending to repair free before commencing ESEUtil operations. The most common command-line switches used with ESEUtil are:
  - **/p**   Allows you to repair a corrupt offline database. It does this by discarding all pages that cannot be repaired. When this is done, use the ISInteg tool to verify and fix any links between tables in the repaired database.
  - **/r**   Allows you to replay transaction logs to bring a database up to a specific point of time.
  - **/g**   Allows you to verify database at the page level and ESE level. Does not verify integrity at the application level.

- **ISInteg** This tool allows you to remove errors from mailbox databases at the application level. ISInteg is usually run after ESEUtil. ISInteg is deprecated in Exchange 2010 Service Pack 1 and later in favor of the *New-MailboxRepairRequest* and *New-PublicFolderDatabaseRepairRequest* cmdlets.

- ***New-MailboxRepairRequest*** Allows you to repair logical corruption in a specific mailbox or for an entire database. You can only run one database repair request at a time on a server, although you can run up to 100 active mailbox level requests concurrently on a server.

- ***New-PublicFolderDatabaseRepairRequest*** Allows you to repair logical corruption in a specific public folder database.

MORE INFO **REPAIRING MAILBOX DATABASES**

To learn more about repairing mailbox database, consult the following Exchange team blog post: *http://blogs.technet.com/b/exchange/archive/2010/08/23/3410708.aspx*.

Objective Summary

- DAGs can include up to 16 mailbox servers.

- A mailbox server can only be a member of one DAG.

- The round-trip-latency between DAG members in Exchange 2010 SP1 cannot exceed 500 milliseconds.

- A maximum of 14 days of lag is possible for a mailbox database copy.

- Public folders can be made highly available by replicating them to public folder databases on other mailbox servers. Public folders cannot use Database Availability Groups for replication.

- Activation preference allows you to specify which passive mailbox database will be activated in the event that the active mailbox database fails.

- Datacenter Activation Coordination allows DAG mailbox databases to be mounted when the DAG cannot reach quorum.

Objective Review

Answer the following questions to test your knowledge of the information in this objective. You can find the answers to these questions and explanations of why each answer choice is correct or incorrect in the "Answers" section at the end of this chapter.

1. You are considering the creation of a DAG that spans multiple sites in your organization's Australian division. Connections between sites in the Australian division suffer from high latency. You've done some network measurements and discovered the following:

- The round-trip delay between the Melbourne and Sydney sites is 330 ms.
- The round-trip delay between the Brisbane and Adelaide sites is 340 ms.
- The round-trip delay between the Adelaide and Perth sites is 330 ms.
- The round-trip delay between the Brisbane and Perth sites is 580 ms.
- The round-trip delay between the Melbourne and Adelaide sites is 330 ms.
- The round-trip delay between the Melbourne and Brisbane sites is 400 ms.
- The round-trip delay between the Sydney and Adelaide sites is 410 ms.
- The round-trip delay between the Brisbane and Sydney sites is 310 ms.
- The round-trip delay between the Sydney and Perth sites is 560 ms.
- The round-trip delay between the Melbourne and Perth sites is 310 ms.

Each site has Exchange mailbox servers. Which of the following sites can you include in the DAG if your aim is to create the DAG with the largest possible membership? (Choose all that apply.)

A. Melbourne

B. Brisbane

C. Adelaide

D. Perth

E. Sydney

2. Your organization has five branch offices situated across Australia and New Zealand. Mailbox servers are situated in each branch office site. The mailbox server in the Canberra site hosts three public folders. You want to ensure that these public folders will be available in the event that the mailbox server in the Canberra site fails. You also want users in each branch office site to be able to access public folder content locally. Which of the following steps would you take when configuring public folder replication to accomplish this goal? (Choose two. Each answer forms part of a complete solution.)

A. Add all five branch office servers to a DAG.

B. Ensure that each of the five branch office servers has a public folder database.

C. Configure the three public folders to replicate to each of the five public folder databases.

D. Configure database copies of the Canberra public folder database on the four servers at the other sites.

3. You are planning the deployment of Exchange across several islands in a small South Pacific nation. Because of the latency of the communications between each site, you can't create a DAG as a method of minimizing recovery time in the event of mailbox database failure. One mailbox server is deployed at each location and Windows Server Backup has been configured to back these servers up regularly. The mailbox databases are configured so that the transaction logs and database files are all hosted on separate disks. You are developing a set of procedures to be followed by each location's support staff in the event that the disk hosting the mailbox database fails. You want to ensure that users are still able to send and receive mail during the recovery process. Which of the following strategies should the restore procedure focus upon?

   A. Dial-tone recovery

   B. Database restore

   C. Recovery database

   D. Database portability

4. You are developing a disaster recovery plan for the use of lagged mailbox database copies. Which of the following steps should you take prior to using eseutil.exe to replay transaction logs to bring a lagged mailbox database copy back to a specific point in time? (Choose all that apply.)

   A. Suspend replication for the lagged copy.

   B. Resume replication for the lagged copy.

   C. Delete the lagged copy database's checkpoint file.

   D. Move log files created after the recovery point to an alternate location.

5. Five weeks ago a user in the research department deleted several important email messages. Which of the following methods could you use to recover these messages?

   A. Database portability

   B. Dial-tone recovery

   C. Lagged database copy

   D. Recovery database

> **THOUGHT EXPERIMENT**
> **Database Availability Group Backup and Recovery**
>
> In the following thought experiment, you will apply what you've learned about the objective "Design and deploy high availability and disaster recovery for mailbox server role" to design a DAG deployment, backup, and recovery strategy. You can find answers to these questions in the "Answers" section at the end of this chapter.
>
> You are interested in deploying a lagged mailbox database copy as a part of your organization's DAG deployment.
>
> Answer the following questions:
>
> 1. What is the maximum lag time that you can configure for the lagged mailbox database copy?
> 2. Which product should you use to back up the lagged mailbox database copy?
> 3. What three steps should you take to restore a lagged mailbox database copy from backup?
> 4. Which utility should you use to replay the log files up to a specific point in time?

Objective 4.4: Design and Deploy High Availability and Disaster Recovery for Hub Transport Role

Hub Transport servers have built-in technologies that mean that each time you add a Hub Transport server to a site, the routing topology configures itself automatically so that the new Hub Transport server is load balanced with existing Hub Transport servers in the site. This means that you don't need to worry about using technologies like Network Load Balancing, DNS Round Robin, and Failover Clustering to make the Hub Transport role highly available—you just need to ensure that there is more than one Hub Transport server at the site.

> **This objective covers:**
> - Back up and recover the Hub Transport role.
> - Create resilient receive connectors.
> - Scope send connectors.
> - Deploy redundant Hub Transport Services.

Hub Transport Backup

How you back up your organization's Hub Transport servers depends on your existing backup infrastructure and RTO. Of all of the Exchange 2010 roles, the Hub Transport role is the simplest to back up and restore because almost all of the important configuration data related to the role is stored within Active Directory. This means that if you are making a choice between performing a full server recovery using a full restore from backup, or a fresh install and Exchange recovery, you'll need to assess which method takes longer and costs your organization more. If you already have a product like System Center Data Protection Manager and have spare backup capacity, you may be able to achieve a better RTO by planning regular full server backup and restore. If you aren't using a centralized backup solution, it may be quicker, simpler, and cheaper to plan on recovering Hub Transport servers by performing a fresh installation and then performing Exchange recovery.

How you back up Hub Transport servers depends on factors such as whether message tracking logs are important to your organization. The following items are unique and may require backup:

- Message Tracking logs located in the TransportRoles\Logs directory of the Exchange installation path. Most organizations don't need to store or review message tracking logs and don't bother backing them up.

- Certificates and private keys. In general the certificates used on Hub Transport servers are self-signed and automatically created during the installation process. You only need to back them up if you've provisioned certificates from a different source.

- If your organization uses a custom ESE database configuration. This configuration is stored in the EdgeTransport.exe.config file. This is located in the Bin directory of the Exchange installation.

If none of these factors applies to your organization, it may be simpler to plan on full server recovery using the clean installation and Exchange recovery method.

> **MORE INFO** **CUSTOM ESE DATABASE CONFIGURATION**
>
> To learn more about custom ESE database configuration, consult the following TechNet document: *http://technet.microsoft.com/en-us/library/bb232166.aspx*.

Hub Transport Server Recovery

Almost all Hub Transport server configuration settings are stored within Active Directory. The messages that Hub Transport servers process are protected through the shadow redundancy feature. This means that even in the event of a server failure, messages that are transiting your organization's Hub Transport servers are unlikely to be lost.

The full operating system reinstall and Exchange recovery technique that you use to recover a Hub Transport server is the same general technique covered in earlier chapter objectives. Prior to attempting to recover a Hub Transport server using this technique, you must ensure that the following prerequisites are met:

- The replacement server must be running the same operating system as the failed server.
- You must configure the replacement server with the same name as the failed server.
- The replacement server must have a similar volume configuration to the failed server.
- The replacement server should have similar or better performance characteristics as the failed server.

After you have procured and configured the server that will function as the replacement for the failed Hub Transport server, you need to perform the following steps:

- Within Active Directory, you need to reset the computer account of the server for which you will be performing full server recovery.
- Install the operating system on the replacement server. Configure the server with the same name as the failed server.
- Join the replacement server to the same domain.
- Install the necessary Hub Transport server prerequisite components. If you are recovering a server that will host additional Exchange roles, ensure that you install the appropriate prerequisite components as well.
- Log on to the server using an account that has the right to install Exchange 2010, open a command prompt, navigate to the location that hosts the Exchange Server 2010 SP1 (or later) installation files and issue the following command:

```
Setup /m:RecoverServer
```

When the setup process has completed, you may need to follow these steps before returning the mailbox server to production:

- Restore Message Tracking logs.
- Import certificates and private keys.
- Restore custom ESE database configuration.

Redundant Hub Transport Deployment

You can make Hub Transport servers highly available deploying more than one in an Active Directory site. It isn't necessary to configure technologies such as network load balancing, DNS round robin, or failover clustering. Network Load Balancing technology is partially built into the Hub Transport role and does not have to be supported by deploying an external solution such as Windows Network Load Balancing or a hardware network load balancer. The only time you might use Network Load Balancing with a Hub Transport server is if you want to distribute non-Exchange messages among your Hub Transport servers. You'll learn more about this later in the lesson.

Shadow redundancy is an Exchange Server 2010 feature that provides protection for messages while they are in transit across the organization's Hub Transport servers. Shadow redundancy works by delaying the deletion of messages from the transport database until verification has arrived that the next hop in the message's journey has completed delivery. If any of the next hops fail, the message is resubmitted for the delivery.

Shadow redundancy has the following benefits:

- Transport servers can be removed from production without worrying about waiting for queues to clear. This means that you can apply updates to Hub Transport servers and reboot them without risking the loss of messages as long as there is a redundant message path.

- Minimizes the need for redundant storage hardware on Hub Transport servers.

- Simplifies the process of recovering failed transport servers.

- Ensures that as long as a redundant message path exists in the routing topology, any transport server can fail without an impact on overall message transport.

Shadow redundancy works by extending the SMTP service. It only works on Exchange 2010 Hub Transport and Edge Transport servers. When an Exchange transport server that supports shadow redundancy transmits a message to an SMTP server that doesn't support shadow redundancy, the Exchange server marks the message as successfully delivered and deletes it. Shadow redundancy is enabled by default on Exchange Server 2010 transport servers.

You can configure the following shadow redundancy options using the *Set-TransportConfig* cmdlet:

- Use the *ShadowRedundancyEnabled* parameter to enable or disable shadow redundancy.

- Use the *ShadowHeartbeatTimeoutInterval* and *ShadowHeartbeatRetryCount* parameters to configure shadow redundancy heartbeat. This allows you to modify the amount of time that the shadow redundancy manager waits before the message is re-sent.

- Use the *ShadowMessageAutoDiscardInterval* parameter to configure how long shadow copies for a messages are retained for delayed messages.

MORE INFO **SHADOW REDUNDANCY**

To learn more about shadow redundancy, consult the following TechNet document: *http://technet.microsoft.com/en-us/library/dd351027.aspx*.

Resilient Receive Connectors

Receive connectors at a site level can be made highly available by deploying additional Hub Transport servers at the site. Every time you introduce a new Hub Transport server, the routing topology updates. If a Hub Transport server fails at a site that has an additional Hub Transport server, routing fails over to use the remaining Hub Transport server until the failed server returns to service.

Resilience can be more challenging if you are using an internal third-party messaging system that needs to deliver messages to Exchange through custom Receive connectors. Usually you will configure message transport between an internal third-party messaging system and Exchange by providing the third-party messaging system with the address of a Hub Transport server that will accept messages. This becomes problematic if the Hub Transport server that hosts the Receive connector fails. Depending on the way that the internal third-party messaging system functions, it can often be simpler to recover the Hub Transport server than it is to configure the third-party messaging system to route messages to an alternate location.

In these cases, it is possible to add additional network adapters to Hub Transport servers and configure a network load balancing cluster and associate it with the additional network adapter. You can then configure Receive connectors associated with the additional network adapter for the third-party messaging system. This makes the receive connector for the third-party messaging system highly available without impacting the normal functionality of the Hub Transport server.

> **MORE INFO**   **RECEIVE CONNECTORS AND NETWORK LOAD BALANCING**
>
> To learn more about Receive connectors, consult the following TechNet document: *http://technet.microsoft.com/en-us/library/gg476050.aspx*.

Send Connector Resiliency

Send connectors usually are associated with a single source server. When a message is destined for a recipient in a specific email domain associated with a Send connector, the message is routed to a Hub Transport server that is listed as a source server for that Send connector. When designing Send connectors to be highly resilient, ensure that at least two source servers are associated with the Send connector, as shown in Figure 4-7. This way if one of the source servers is not available, the message can be routed through another Hub Transport server.

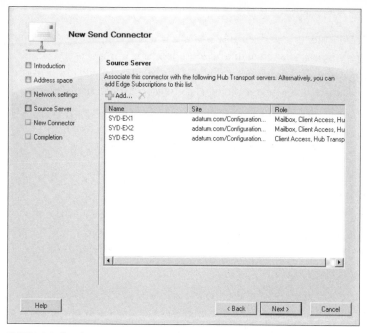

FIGURE 4-7 Send connector source servers

When you configure an Edge Transport subscription, all currently available Hub Transport servers in the site adjacent to the one that hosts the Edge Transport server will be included in the subscription. Each server will be configured with the Send connector that routes mail out to the subscribed Edge Transport server. If you add additional Hub Transport servers at the site adjacent to the perimeter network, you should re-create the Edge subscription to ensure that the Send connector to the Edge Transport server is updated so that the new Hub Transport server is included as a source server.

If you want to limit the Send connector so that it can only be used by Hub Transport servers in a specific site, you select the Scoped send connector option on the Address Space page of the New Send Connector Wizard. You can also accomplish this goal this using the *IsScopedConnector* parameter of the *New-SendConnector* and *Set-SendConnector* cmdlets.

> **MORE INFO SEND CONNECTORS**
>
> To learn more about Send connectors, consult the following TechNet document: *http://technet.microsoft.com/en-us/library/aa998662.aspx*.

 EXAM TIP

Shadow redundancy is used with Hub Transport servers to ensure message delivery when there is a redundant message routing topology. Transport dumpster is used to ensure message delivery to mailbox databases in DAG scenarios.

Objective Summary

- If you use custom certificates or any custom ESE database configuration on your Hub Transport servers, you should back them up and store them.

- You can recover Hub Transport servers using the operating system reinstall and Exchange recovery method.

- You can make Hub Transport servers highly available by deploying more than one in an Active Directory site.

- Scoped Send connectors are only available to other Hub Transport servers in the same site.

- You can make Receive connectors for third-party internal messaging systems resilient using network load balancing.

- Shadow redundancy ensures that messages are retransmitted in the event that another transport server.

Objective Review

Answer the following questions to test your knowledge of the information in this objective. You can find the answers to these questions and explanations of why each answer choice is correct or incorrect in the "Answers" section at the end of this chapter.

1. Your organization has 10 sites, each of which hosts an Exchange 2010 mailbox server. Each mailbox server is a member of a single DAG. You have deployed CAS arrays at three sites. Each CAS array has two members. You want to ensure that message routing is highly available. What is the minimum number of Hub Transport servers that you need to deploy to accomplish this goal?

   A. 2

   B. 10

   C. 15

   D. 20

2. Which of the following technologies provides protection from the loss of messages that are in transit in the event that a Hub Transport server fails?

   A. Database Availability Groups

   B. Transport dumpster

   C. Shadow redundancy

   D. CAS array

3. A Hub Transport server has failed. Which of the following steps should you take before running *Setup /m:RecoverServer*? (Choose all that apply.)

   A. Reset the failed computer's Active Directory account.

   B. Provide the new computer with the same IP address as the failed server.

C. Join the new computer to the same domain as the failed server.

D. Rename the new computer with the failed server's name.

4. You want to configure a Send connector so that it is only available to Hub Transport servers in a specific site. Which of the following should you do to accomplish this goal?

A. Configure a scoped Send connector.

B. Configure the Send connector source servers.

C. Configure the Send connector permissions.

D. Configure Send connector usage type.

5. In which of the following situations should you consider using hardware-based network load balancing with a Hub Transport server?

A. Scoped send connectors

B. Send connectors for internal third-party SMTP messaging systems

C. Receive connectors for internal third-party SMTP messaging systems

D. Edge subscriptions

Objective 4.5: Design and Deploy High Availability and Disaster Recovery for Edge Transport Role

On networks that use them, Edge Transport servers can serve as a single point of failure for messages entering or exiting the Exchange infrastructure. If the Edge Transport server is down, email communication with the outside world may be lost. For this reason if your Exchange 2010 design does include Edge Transport servers, you need to ensure that the solution is highly available so that the loss of one Edge Transport server doesn't block the passages of messages to and from the outside world.

Edge Transport Server Backup and Recovery

The Edge Transport role is installed on standalone servers that are not members of an Active Directory domain. Your data protection strategy for an Edge Transport server should include the following:

- Ensure that all digital certificates are exported and stored in a secure place. This is something that you should do once when you procure the certificate, not something that you need to do on a regular basis.

- Export the Edge Transport server configuration each time you modify the configuration. In many organizations Edge Transport servers have the entirety of their configuration managed through the Edge Subscription process, so this is less important in some cases than in others.

- Some organizations regularly back up message traffic logs. Only do this if it is part of your organization's SLA. There is no need to expend resources backing up logs if the logs themselves are never examined.

You clone an Edge Transport server configuration by exporting it and then importing the configuration. You can import and export Edge Server configuration using the following scripts:

- ExportEdgeConfig.ps1
- ImportEdgeConfig.ps1

To recover an Edge Transport server where you have already performed a configuration export using ExportEdgeConfig.ps1, perform the following general steps:

1. Deploy a replacement server that uses the same name as the failed server.

2. Install the Edge Transport role. There is no need to reset domain accounts as Edge Transport servers are not members of a domain.

3. Run the ImportEdgeConfig.ps1 script to check the previously exported XML configuration file. The script creates an answer file for any problematic settings.

4. Run the ImportEdgeConfig.ps1 script again to import the previously exported XML configuration file, restoring the failed Edge Transport server's configuration.

5. If the original Edge Transport server was synchronized through the EdgeSync subscription process, you'll need to configure a new edge subscription as the cloned configuration restore process will not duplicate the certificates used by the EdgeSync service.

Redundant Edge Transport Server Deployment

You can deploy more than one Edge Transport server on your perimeter network. When you do this, you need to configure the following items to ensure that the redundant configuration works in such a way that message transport continues if one Edge Transport server fails:

- You can use a network load balancing solution to load balance Edge Transport servers on the perimeter network. You can also accomplish equitable distribution of inbound and outbound traffic through external DNS configuration and the use of Edge subscriptions.
- Configure MX records to support the new Edge Transport server configuration. You'll learn more about this later in the objective.
- Ensure that Edge Transport servers have identical configuration. If Edge Transport servers have different configuration, inbound and outbound messages will be processed differently depending on which Edge Transport server they pass across.
- Ensure that each Edge Transport server has its own Edge subscription to the adjacent Active Directory site. Cloning Edge Transport server configuration does not create a new Edge Subscription.

To ensure that Edge Transport servers have the same configuration, you should use the following process to clone the configuration:

1. Run the ExportEdgeConfig.ps1 script to export the original server's configuration. Transfer this file to the new Edge Transport server that will function as the clone.

2. Run the ImportEdgeConfig.ps1 script on the new Edge Transport server to validate the previously exported XML configuration file. The script creates an answer file for any problematic settings.

3. Run the ImportEdgeConfig.ps1 script on the new Edge Transport server again to import the previously exported XML configuration file.

4. If the original Edge Transport server is synchronized through the EdgeSync subscription process, you'll need to configure a new edge subscription for the clone.

You'll also need to configure appropriate SSL certificates for the new server. In most cases, as each Edge Transport server will have a different name—you won't use the same certificate unless you obtained a wildcard certificate.

Configure DNS to Support Redundant Edge Transport

If you aren't using Network Load Balancing to load balance the Edge Transport servers, you need to ensure that the MX records in the external zone that point to the Edge Transport servers on your perimeter network are assigned equal priority. You should avoid DNS round robin, which is not fault tolerant.

MX records with lower priority numbers are preferred over MX records with higher priority numbers. The MX record shown in Figure 4-8 would be preferred over an MX record where the mail server priority is set to a number greater than 10. When you have multiple MX records with the same priority, the DNS server hosting the zone will return those records in a balanced manner. If an Edge Transport server has failed, the SMTP server that is querying the DNS zone for MX record information will use other hosts addresses returned by an MX record query, preferring records with a lower numerical score before moving on to records with a higher numerical score.

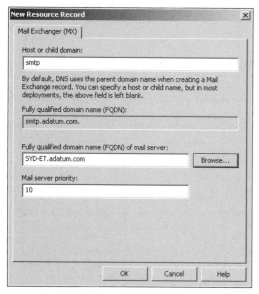

FIGURE 4-8 DNS MX record

You can use the strategy of configuring multiple MX records to split incoming messages across Edge Transport servers in different sites. As long as the internal message infrastructure is working properly, the messages will eventually end up in the correct mailboxes. Spreading message traffic across Edge Transport servers at multiple sites is also a way of ensuring that message delivery during site failure.

EXAM TIP

Remember the process for cloning Edge Transport server configuration.

Objective Summary

- Ensure that Edge Transport server certificates are exported and stored in a safe place.
- Run the ExportEdgeConfig.ps1 to back up the Edge Transport server's configuration. You can also use this script in the Edge Transport server cloned configuration process.
- If an Edge Transport server fails, you can reinstall the operating system, install the Edge Transport role, and then import the exported configuration.
- You have to run the ImportEdgeConfig.ps1 script twice. The first time you need to validate the settings and create an answer file. The second time you are actually importing the configuration.
- You need to create new Edge subscriptions after you recover a server or clone a server's configuration.
- If you have multiple Edge Transport servers, you can either configure DNS load balancing or configure MX records of equal priority.

Objective Review

Answer the following questions to test your knowledge of the information in this objective. You can find the answers to these questions and explanations of why each answer choice is correct or incorrect in the "Answers" section at the end of this chapter.

1. Your organization has a single Edge Transport server that has an EdgeSync subscription to your organization's primary site. An automated task runs the ExportEdgeConfig.ps1 script once a week to a USB stick attached to the server. The server's hard disk drive suffers complete failure, though the contents of the USB stick are unaffected. You replace the hard disk drive, reinstall the operating system, provide the computer with the same name and IP address configuration, and then install the Edge Transport server role. Which of the following steps must you then take to restore the Edge Transport server to full functionality? (Choose three. Each answer forms part of a complete solution.)

   A. Run the ImportEdgeConfig.ps1 script to validate the original server's XML file and generate the answer file.

   B. Run the ExportEdgeConfig.ps1 script to validate the original server's XML file and generate the answer file.

   C. Run the ImportEdgeConfig.ps1 script to import the original server's configuration.

   D. Re-create the Edge Subscription.

2. You are planning to deploy two Edge Transport servers on your organization's perimeter network. Each Edge Transport server is deployed on separate 1U servers hosted in different racks in the datacenter. You want to ensure that in the event that one Edge Transport server fails, incoming message traffic will only be routed to the

Edge Transport server that is still operational. Which of the following high-availability strategies could you pursue to accomplish this goal?

A. DNS round robin

B. Failover clustering

C. Database Availability Groups

D. Network Load Balancing

3. Your organization has two sites, Melbourne and Sydney. Each site is connected to the Internet and has a separate Edge Transport server. Incoming mail comes in through the Edge Transport server on the Melbourne perimeter network. The MX record for the Melbourne Edge Transport server is configured with a priority of 50 in both the internal and external DNS zones Currently the Edge Transport server in the Sydney site is only used to route outbound messages. You want this state of affairs to continue, but also want to ensure that if the Melbourne Edge Transport server suffers an outage, incoming mail will be directed to the Sydney Edge Transport server until the Melbourne server is brought back online. Which of the following steps could you take to accomplish this goal?

A. Add an MX record for the Sydney Edge Transport server to the external DNS zone. Configure this record with a priority of 100.

B. Add an MX record for the Sydney Edge Transport server to the external DNS zone. Configure this record with a priority of 10.

C. Add an MX record for the Sydney Edge Transport server to the internal DNS zone. Configure this record with a priority of 100.

D. Add an MX record for the Sydney Edge Transport server to the internal DNS zone. Configure this record with a priority of 10.

4. Your organization has two Edge Transport servers deployed on its perimeter network. Each Edge Transport server has an identical configuration and is subscribed to the adjacent Active Directory site with an Edge subscription. One of the Edge Transport servers suffers a storage failure. You replace the storage, install an identical operating system, and install the Edge Transport role. Which of the following steps should you take next when attempting to recover the server?

A. Export the configuration of the Edge Transport server that didn't fail using the ExportEdgeConfig.ps1 script.

B. Run the *New-EdgeSubscription* cmdlet on the Edge Transport server that didn't fail.

C. Run the *New-EdgeSubscription* cmdlet on the replacement Edge Transport server.

D. Export the configuration of the replacement Edge Transport server using the ExportEdgeConfig.ps1 script.

THOUGHT EXPERIMENT
Highly Available Edge Transport Design

In the following thought experiment, you will apply what you've learned about the objective "Design and deploy high availability and disaster recovery for Edge Transport role" to design a highly available Edge Transport server solution. You can find answers to these questions in the "Answers" section at the end of this chapter.

Your organization has the following characteristics

There are four main sites that host mailbox servers spread across Europe. These sites are in the cities of Copenhagen, Moscow, Istanbul, and Barcelona.

Each main site has an Internet connection.

Each site connects to the other sites through IPSec tunnels across the Internet.

Your organization has a single Edge Transport server located at the Copenhagen site.

An MX record on the organization's external DNS zone points at the Edge Transport server on the Copenhagen site's perimeter network.

You want to accomplish the following goals:

The Copenhagen site must be able to receive messages from the Internet if an Edge Transport server fails.

The Moscow, Istanbul, and Barcelona sites should be able to receive messages from the Internet if the Copenhagen site fails.

Messages addressed to recipients on the Internet from the Moscow, Istanbul, and Barcelona sites should only route through the Copenhagen site in the event of a local Edge Transport server failure.

With this information in mind, answer the following questions:

1. What is the minimum number of Edge Transport servers that you need to deploy in your organization to meet your goals?

2. What steps should you take to ensure that the objective for inbound communication at the Copenhagen site is accomplished?

3. What steps could you take to ensure that the same rules apply to inbound and outbound communication at the Copenhagen site no matter which Edge Transport server is used to route that communication?

4. What is the minimum number of subscriptions required if all Edge Transport servers are to receive configuration information through EdgeSync?

Chapter Summary

- Active Directory Domain Controllers and Global Catalog servers can be made highly available by deploying more than one in an Active Directory site.

- You can use WSUS and System Center Configuration Manager to deploy updates automatically to Exchange servers.

- You should export and store any certificates used by CAS services.

- The "Operating system reinstall and Exchange recovery" method involves deploying a new server with the same name and operating system as the failed server, resetting the failed server's Active Directory account, joining that server to the same domain, and then running *Setup /m:RecoverServer*.

- You can only have one CAS array per site and CAS arrays cannot span multiple sites.

- DAGs can include up to 16 mailbox servers and a mailbox server can only be a member of one DAG.

- The round-trip latency between DAG members in Exchange 2010 SP1 cannot exceed 500 milliseconds.

- A maximum of 14 days of lag is possible for a mailbox database copy.

- Public folders can be made highly available by replicating them to public folder databases on other mailbox servers.

- You can make Hub Transport servers highly available by deploying more than one in an Active Directory site.

- Shadow redundancy ensures that messages are retransmitted in the event that another transport server fails.

- Run the ExportEdgeConfig.ps1 to back up the Edge Transport server's configuration. You can also use this script in the Edge Transport server cloned configuration process.

- You have to run the ImportEdgeConfig.ps1 script twice. The first time you need to validate the settings and create an answer file. The second time you are actually importing the configuration.

- You need to create new Edge subscriptions after you recover a server or clone a server's configuration.

Answers

This section contains the answers to the Object Reviews and the Thought Experiments.

Objective 4.1: Review

1. **Correct Answer:** D

    A.   Incorrect: You need to deploy a writable domain controller that functions as a Global Catalog server at each site where you deploy Exchange. Even though RODCs can function as Global Catalog servers, this type of Global Catalog server cannot support Exchange Server 2010.

    B.   Incorrect: You need to deploy a writable domain controller that functions as a Global Catalog server at each site where you deploy Exchange. Even though RODCs can function as Global Catalog servers, this type of Global Catalog server cannot support Exchange Server 2010.

    C.   Incorrect: RODCs cannot be used by Exchange Server 2010. Although you need to deploy a writable domain controller that functions as a Global Catalog server at each site where you deploy Exchange, deploying only one writable DC will not provide the redundancy required.

    D.   Correct: RODCs cannot be used by Exchange Server 2010. You need to deploy a writable domain controller that functions as a Global Catalog server at each site where you deploy Exchange. To make this infrastructure redundant, you'll need to deploy at least two writable domain controllers configured as Global Catalog servers at each site.

2. **Correct Answer:** B

    A.   Incorrect: RAID 0 is disk striping. If a disk fails in a RAID 0 set, you will need to replace it and then recover the DC from backup.

    B.   Correct: RAID 1, disk mirroring, provides storage redundancy using a minimum number of disks. A mirroring solution requires a minimum of two disks.

    C.   Incorrect: RAID 5, disk striping with parity, does provide storage redundancy, but requires a minimum of three disks.

    D.   Incorrect: RAID 10, also known as RAID 1+0, is a stripe of mirrored disks. It does provide storage redundancy, but requires a minimum of four disks.

3. **Correct Answers:** A and D

    A.   Correct: You should configure each Domain Controller at the primary site with the DNS role. When configured with Active Directory Integrated Zones, each server hosts a copy of the DNS zone data. This will allow each DNS server to process zone updates with a minimal amount of maintenance.

**B.	Incorrect:** You should not configure three servers as Read Only Domain Controllers (RODCs). When RODCs host Active Directory DNS zones, they are unable to process updates to those zones directly.

**C.	Incorrect:** Stub zones only host the addresses of name servers. You should use an Active Directory Integrated Zone in this case.

**D.	Correct:** Unlike primary zones, Active Directory Integrated Zones can be updated against any server that hosts the zone as long as that server is a writable DC.

4.	**Correct Answers:** C and D

**A.	Incorrect:** Microsoft Baseline Security Analyzer can be used to detect computers that do not have specific software updates installed.

**B.	Incorrect:** System Center Operations Manager 2012 can be used to monitor computers, but cannot be used to deploy software updates to those computers.

**C.	Correct:** You can use System Center Configuration Manager 2012 to automate the deployment of software updates.

**D.	Correct:** You can use Windows Server Update Services to automate the deployment of software updates.

5.	**Correct Answers:** A and C

**A.	Correct:** You use the StargDagServerMaintenance.ps1 cmdlet to put the DAG server into maintenance mode.

**B.	Incorrect:** The CheckDatabaseRedundancy.ps1 script allows you to collect switchover and failover information. You don't need to use this script when applying updates to DAG members.

**C.	Correct:** After you have completed the installation of software updates, you run the StopDagServerMaintenance.ps1 script to return the DAG member from maintenance mode.

**D.	Incorrect:** While Microsoft recommends balancing the active mailbox database copy distribution using RedistributeActiveDatabases.ps1 script, this step is not necessary when manually applying updates to mailbox servers that are members of a DAG.

Objective 4.1: Thought Experiment

1.	You could choose System Center Configuration Manager 2012 or a third-party product that offers similar features. You can't choose Windows Server Update Services because WSUS will not allow you to check what updates have been installed manually or automatically and doesn't allow computer accounts to be members of multiple groups or collections.

2. You use the StartDagServerMaintenance.ps1 script to place a DAG member into maintenance mode.

3. You use the StopDagServerMaintenance.ps1 script to bring a DAG member out of maintenance mode.

4. You can avoid the problem of many servers rebooting at once by configuring staggered maintenance windows in System Center Configuration Manager 2012 and by placing servers in different groups.

Objective 4.2: Review

1. **Correct Answer:** C

   A. **Incorrect:** Microsoft recommends a 5-minute TTL value for DNS records used by Exchange and Exchange clients. A value of 60 minutes will mean that some clients won't receive updated address information in a timely manner during failover events.

   B. **Incorrect:** Microsoft recommends a 5-minute TTL value for DNS records used by Exchange and Exchange clients. A value of 30 minutes will mean that some clients won't receive updated address information in a timely manner during failover events.

   C. **Correct:** You should configure a 5-minute TTL value for DNS records used by Exchange and Exchange clients. This value achieves a balance between the need for quickly updated records during failover events and ensuring that clients do not perform DNS queries to often.

   D. **Incorrect:** Microsoft recommends a 5-minute TTL value for DNS records used by Exchange and Exchange clients. A value of 300 minutes will mean that some clients won't receive updated address information in a timely manner during failover events.

2. **Correct Answer:** C

   A. **Incorrect:** CAS arrays cannot span multiple sites. With 12 sites, the minimum and maximum number of CAS arrays is 12.

   B. **Incorrect:** CAS arrays cannot span multiple sites. With 12 sites, the minimum and maximum number of CAS arrays is 12.

   C. **Correct:** You can have a maximum of one CAS array per site. CAS arrays cannot span multiple sites. With 12 sites, the minimum and maximum number of CAS arrays is 12.

   D. **Incorrect:** You can have a maximum of one CAS array per site. CAS arrays cannot span multiple sites. With 12 sites, the minimum and maximum number of CAS arrays is 12.

3. **Correct Answers:** A, B, and C

   A. **Correct:** A server can be a member of a CAS array if it has other roles installed as long as it is not a member of a DAG.

   B. **Correct:** A server can be a member of a CAS array if it has other roles installed as long as it is not a member of a DAG.

   C. **Correct:** A server can be a member of a CAS array if it has other roles installed as long as it is not a member of a DAG.

   D. **Incorrect:** A server can be a member of a CAS array if it has other roles installed as long as it is not a member of a DAG.

4. **Correct Answer:** C

   A. **Incorrect:** DNS round robin is not used with CAS arrays. You need to configure an NLB cluster prior to running the *New-ClientAccessArray* cmdlet.

   B. **Incorrect:** Database Availability Groups are used to make mailbox servers highly available. You need to configure an NLB cluster prior to running the *New-Client-AccessArray* cmdlet.

   C. **Correct:** You should configure a network load balancing cluster that includes the site's CAS servers before running the *New-ClientAccessArray* cmdlet.

   D. **Incorrect:** Failover clustering is not used by CAS arrays. You need to configure an NLB cluster prior to running the *New-ClientAccessArray* cmdlet.

5. **Correct Answer:** C

   A. **Incorrect:** CAS arrays cannot span multiple sites. To accomplish your goal you need two CAS per site and a total of three CAS arrays.

   B. **Incorrect:** To accomplish your goal you need two CAS per site and a total of three CAS arrays.

   C. **Correct:** To accomplish your goal you need two CAS per site and a total of three CAS arrays. Even when mailbox servers are members of DAGs, they need to be serviced by CAS in the same site.

   D. **Incorrect:** You only need six CAS to accomplish your goal.

Objective 4.2: Thought Experiment

1. You should install Windows Server 2008. The operating system must be the same as that used by the failed server.

2. The new computer should be called ADL-CAS-A.

3. You should reset the computer account of ADL-CAS-A.

4. *Setup /m:RecoverServer.*

Objective 4.3: Review

1. **Correct Answers:** A, B, C, and E

    A. **Correct:** You can include the Melbourne site because it has a round-trip latency of less than 500 ms to all sites in the organization.

    B. **Correct:** You can include the Brisbane site because it has a round-trip latency of less than 500 ms to all sites except Perth. As long as the Perth site is not involved, you can include the Brisbane, Melbourne, Adelaide, and Sydney sites in the DAG.

    C. **Correct:** You can include the Adelaide site because it has a round-trip latency of less than 500 ms to all sites in the organization.

    D. **Incorrect:** You can't add a server to a DAG if the round-trip latency exceeds 500 ms. The Perth site has a round-trip latency that exceeds this figure to both the Brisbane and Sydney sites.

    E. **Correct:** The Sydney site has a round-trip latency of less than 500 ms to all sites except Perth. As long as the Perth site is not involved, you can include the Brisbane, Melbourne, Adelaide, and Sydney sites in the DAG.

2. **Correct Answers:** B and C

    A. **Incorrect:** Public folder replication does not use DAGs.

    B. **Correct:** You need to ensure that each mailbox server that you want to replicate the public folders hosted in Canberra to has a public folder database. You can't replicate public folders to mailbox database.

    C. **Correct:** After you have ensured that each target server has a public folder database, you can configure the existing public folders to replicate to each of these databases.

    D. **Incorrect:** Public folder replication does not use database copies. Database copies are used by DAGs.

3. **Correct Answer:** A

    A. **Correct:** You should include the dial-tone recovery strategy, which will allow people to continue to send and receive messages as the restoration takes place.

    B. **Incorrect:** Although a database restore would allow user mailboxes to eventually be brought back online, it will not allow people to send and receive email during the restore process.

    C. **Incorrect:** Using a recovery database is a good strategy when you want to recover specific items from an Exchange 2010 mailbox database, but is not an appropriate strategy when the disk hosting a mailbox database is lost and the database needs to be restored.

D. Incorrect: Database portability allows you to recover a mailbox database to any mailbox server in the Exchange organization. Because you want to recover locally and you want to ensure that users are still able to send and receive email messages during the recovery process, this strategy is not appropriate.

4. **Correct Answers:** A, C, and D

   A. Correct: You must suspend replication, move unnecessary log files, and then delete the checkpoint file before using eseutil.exe to replay transaction logs to bring a mailbox database copy back to a specific point in time.

   B. Incorrect: You should not resume replication of the lagged copy until the database is in the appropriate state.

   C. Correct: You must suspend replication, move unnecessary log files, and then delete the checkpoint file before using eseutil.exe to replay transaction logs to bring a mailbox database copy back to a specific point in time.

   D. Correct: You must suspend replication, move unnecessary log files, and then delete the checkpoint file before using eseutil.exe to replay transaction logs to bring a mailbox database copy back to a specific point in time.

5. **Correct Answer:** D

   A. Incorrect: You would only recover the entire mailbox database in the event that the database itself was lost. A recovery database or a lagged database copy is an appropriate solution when a small number of messages need to be recovered.

   B. Incorrect: You only use a dial-tone recovery in the event that the entire mailbox database is lost. A recovery database or a lagged database copy is an appropriate solution when a small number of messages need to be recovered.

   C. Incorrect: Lagged database copies can have a maximum lag of 14 days. Transaction logs can be stored for another 14 days. The period specified in the question was 5 weeks or 35 days, which means that you can't recover this data using a lagged database copy.

   D. Correct: In this scenario you would use a recovery database and copy the deleted messages back to the active mailbox database.

Objective 4.3: Thought Experiment

1. The maximum lag time that you can configure for the lagged mailbox database copy is 14 days.

2. You should use System Center Data Protection Manager or a third party Exchange aware VSS-based backup product.

3. You'll need to restore to an alternate location, suspend the passive copy, and then copy the restored database and transaction logs over the current passive copy.

4. You use the Eseutil.exe utility to replay transaction log files against a lagged mailbox database copy up to a specific point in time.

Objective 4.4: Review

1. **Correct Answer:** D

   A. **Incorrect:** You need to deploy 20 Hub Transport servers to accomplish your goal. You need to have a Hub Transport server in every site that has a mailbox server.

   B. **Incorrect:** You need to deploy 20 Hub Transport servers to accomplish your goal.

   C. **Incorrect:** You need to deploy 20 Hub Transport servers to accomplish your goal. 15 Hub Transport servers would allow 5 sites to have redundant message transport, but also leave 5 sites where the failure of a single Hub Transport server would mean message transport to that site would fail.

   D. **Correct:** You must deploy two Hub Transport servers in each site to ensure that message routing is highly available. This means that you need to deploy 20 Hub Transport servers to accomplish your goal.

2. **Correct Answer:** C

   A. **Incorrect:** DAGs protect mailbox databases. They do not provide protection from the loss of messages in transit in the event that a Hub Transport server fails.

   B. **Incorrect:** The transport dumpster is a technology that ensures that DAG member databases remain in a consistent state.

   C. **Correct:** Shadow redundancy is the technology that ensures that messages are only deleted from a transport server when future message hops report that the message has been successfully deleted.

   D. **Incorrect:** CAS arrays make Cient Access Servers highly available.

3. **Correct Answers:** A, C, and D

   A. **Correct:** You need to reset the failed computer's Active Directory account prior to joining the new computer to the domain.

   B. **Incorrect:** The new computer does not have to have the same IP address configuration that the failed computer had.

   C. **Correct:** The new computer must be joined to the same domain as the failed server.

   D. **Correct:** The new computer must be given the same name as the failed server.

4. **Correct Answer:** A

   A. **Correct:** Scoped send connectors can only be used by Hub Transport servers in a specific site.

   B. **Incorrect:** Changing the source servers will not ensure that only Hub Transport servers in a specific site are able to use a specific connector. You need to configure a Send connector to be scoped to accomplish this goal.

   C. **Incorrect:** Send connector permission determine the types of header information that can be sent with an email message. You need to configure a Send connector to be scoped to accomplish this goal.

   D. **Incorrect:** You can configure connector usage types that determine the SIDs that are granted default permission on a connector. This will not allow you to limit the scope of a Send connector to the Hub Transport server in a particular site. You need to configure a Send connector to be scoped to accomplish this goal.

5. **Correct Answer:** C

   A. **Incorrect:** Scoped Send connectors are Send connectors that can only be used by Hub Transport servers in a specific site. You would not consider utilizing NLB in your design to support scoped Send connectors.

   B. **Incorrect:** It isn't necessary to use network load balancing with Send connectors because these will be used equitably when multiple source servers are configured for the Send connector.

   C. **Correct:** Hub Transport servers use elements of network load balancing to evenly distribute internal Exchange traffic. If you want to make a Receive connector for an internal third-party SMTP messaging system resilient, you would include network load balancing in your design.

   D. **Incorrect:** Edge subscriptions already use load balancing to ensure that outbound and inbound messages are distributed across transport servers equitably.

Objective 4.4: Thought Experiment

1. You should back up Hub Transport servers if you need to keep message tracking logs, use a custom ESE database configuration, and are using non-self signed certificates.

2. You can only recover an Exchange server in the domain to which it was originally deployed. In this case you can only recover server ADL-HT1 in the Australia.contoso.com domain.

3. You need to deploy a minimum of 20 Hub Transport servers, 2 in each site, to ensure that message transport is highly available.

4. You should reset the ADL-HT1 computer account in Active Directory.

Objective 4.5: Review

1. **Correct Answers:** A, C, and D

   A. **Correct:** Prior to importing the XML configuration file from the original Edge Transport server deployment you need to validate the file and generate an answer file. This is accomplished using the ImportEdgeConfig.ps1 script.

   B. **Incorrect:** You do not perform validation of the original server's XML file using the ExportEdgeConfig.ps1 script. You perform this validation using the Import-EdgeConfig.ps1 script.

   C. **Correct:** After the XML configuration file has been validated and the answer file generated, you then import the original server's configuration using the ImportEdgeConfig.ps1 script.

   D. **Correct:** After the original server's configuration has been successfully imported, you need to re-create the Edge Subscription.

2. **Correct Answer:** D

   A. **Incorrect:** DNS round robin is not a failure-aware technology. If one of the Edge Transport servers failed, DNS round robin would still direct traffic to the failed server.

   B. **Incorrect:** You can't use failover clustering directly with the Edge Transport role when the role is deployed on separate physical servers.

   C. **Incorrect:** You can't use Database Availability Groups to make Edge Transport servers highly available.

   D. **Correct:** Network Load Balancing is a failure-aware, high-availability solution that is failure aware. The best method of network load balancing Edge Transport servers is to use a hardware-based network load balancing solution.

3. **Correct Answer:** A

   A. **Correct:** MX records with a higher priority number are used only when the servers references by DNS MX records with a lower priority number are unavailable. Placing this record in the external zone will ensure that the Sydney Edge Transport server is used in the event that the Melbourne Edge Transport server is unavailable.

   B. **Incorrect:** MX records with a higher priority number are used only when the servers references by DNS MX records with a lower priority number are unavailable. If you set the value of the MX record to 10, the Sydney Edge Transport server will be prioritized for inbound message traffic over the Melbourne Edge Transport server.

C. **Incorrect:** You should not configure records in the internal DNS zone. The External DNS zone is the one that will be queried during the process of inbound message delivery.

D. **Incorrect:** You should not configure records in the internal DNS zone. The External DNS zone is the one that will be queried during the process of inbound message delivery.

4. **Correct Answer:** A

A. **Correct:** You should export the configuration of the Edge Transport server that didn't fail, so that you can use that configuration as a part of the configuration cloning process.

B. **Incorrect:** You should not run the *New-EdgeSubscription* cmdlet on the Edge Transport server that didn't fail—there will be no need to re-create the existing Edge subscription from that server.

C. **Incorrect:** You will need to resubscribe the replacement Edge Transport server, but you'll need to export the configuration of the Edge Transport server that didn't fail first.

D. **Incorrect:** You should not export the configuration of the replacement Edge Transport server. You'll need to import the configuration of the Edge Transport server that didn't fail, but before you do that, you'll need to export that configuration from that server.

Objective 4.5: Thought Experiment

1. You need to deploy a minimum of five Edge Transport servers to meet your goals. You must deploy two Edge Transport servers at the Copenhagen site and one transport server at each of the Moscow, Istanbul, and Barcelona sites.

2. You need to deploy an additional Edge Transport server at the Copenhagen site.

3. You should use Edge subscriptions as well as exporting and importing the configuration of Edge Transport servers to ensure that the configuration of each server is identical.

4. You will need five Edge subscriptions, one for each Edge Transport server.

Designing and Deploying Messaging Compliance, System Monitoring, and Reporting

In this chapter, you'll learn how Exchange permissions are used by messaging administrators, as well as track messages and prepare for discovery search. You'll learn how to configure mailbox and mailbox database journaling and archive mailboxes. You'll learn how you can include message retention policies so that some old messages are removed and others are archived appropriately. You'll learn how to configure an ethical firewall and message tips as well as learn how to monitor Exchange and evaluate the performance of the servers that host it.

Objectives in this chapter:

- Objective 5.1: Design and deploy auditing and discovery
- Objective 5.2: Design and deploy message archival
- Objective 5.3: Design and deploy transport rules for message compliance
- Objective 5.4: Design and deploy for monitoring and reporting

About 10 years ago I worked at a large company that was being purchased and split by two other companies. This acquisition was unusual in that the companies involved were the three largest of their type in the country. This meant that the Australian Competition and Consumer Commission drew up a substantial set of conditions that my company had to follow as it was split up and shared amongst its two competitors. This involved going as far as to have to use separate file servers and print servers for staff depending on which company they were going to end up working for when the split was completed. Real world ethical firewall situations can seem somewhat ridiculous when you have to live with them. Luckily most of us don't have to live with ethical firewall situations and the closest we come to it is having to know how to implement the process for a certification exam.

Objective 5.1: Design and Deploy Auditing and Discovery

Exchange mailboxes often host an organization's most sensitive data. You can configure Exchange so that access to this data is logged in such a way that you can see who accessed it and when it was accessed. Exchange has a remarkable number of options for recording how it manages information. This objective teaches you about some of the ways you can access this metadata.

This objective covers:

- Administrator audit logging.
- Mailbox audit logging.
- Message tracking.
- Protocol logging.
- Discovery searches.
- IRM logging.

Administrator Audit Logging

You use administrator audit logging when you want to have a record of all of the commands used by messaging administrators within your organization. Administrator audit logging allows you to track the use of Exchange 2010 administrator tools in EMS, EMC and the Exchange Control Panel. Administrator audit logging is enabled by default in new deployments of Exchange Server 2010 with Service Pack 1.

Administrator audit logging tracks the use of specific cmdlets that are on a special list known as the cmdlet auditing list. An event is written to the log if the cmdlet is run from EMS, or indirectly through EMC or Exchange Control Panel. The idea behind audit logging is to have a record of actions taken to modify objects within Exchange rather than when someone views the properties of objects within Exchange. Hence, by default, execution of cmdlets that use the verbs Get, Test, or Search will not be logged in the administrator audit log.

You configure Administrator audit logging using the Set-AdministratorAuditLog cmdlet. You can specify which cmdlets will be audited using the Set-AdminAuditLogConfig cmdlet. Audit logs are stored in a special arbitration mailbox. You can access this mailbox using Exchange Control Panel Auditing Reports, or the Search-AdminAuditLog or New-Admin-AuditLogSearch cmdlet.

The Auditing Reports area of Exchange Control Panel, shown in Figure 5-1, allows you to perform the following tasks:

- **Administrator Role Changes** Allows you to view changes made to management role groups within a specified time frame. The output will list which role groups have been modified, the security principle that modified them, when those changes were made, and the nature of those changes. When you use this report, you can view a maximum of 3000 entries. If you need to view more than 3000 entries, you can export the log or use the Search-AdminAuditLog cmdlet from EMS.

- **Export Configuration Changes** This allows you to export audit log entries to an XML file and then have that file forwarded to a specified mailbox.

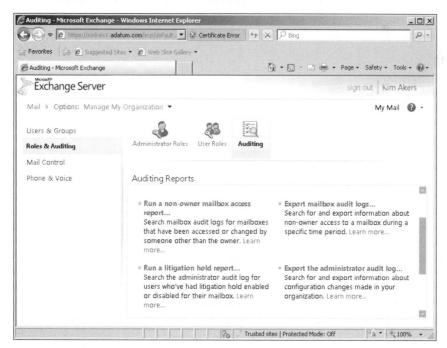

FIGURE 5-1 Audit reports

> **MORE INFO**   ADMINISTRATOR AUDIT LOGGING
>
> To learn more about administrator audit logging, consult the following TechNet document: *http://technet.microsoft.com/en-us/library/dd335144.aspx*.

Mailbox Audit Logging

In many organizations it is necessary to allow multiple people access to certain mailboxes. For example, you may delegate a senior executive's administrative assistant full mailbox access on the senior executive's mailbox. Mailbox audit logging allows you to record access to sensitive mailboxes by mailbox owners, delegates, and administrators. Mailbox audit logging allows you to track the following Administrator access to mailboxes:

- A discovery search is used to access the contents of a mailbox.
- An administrator uses the New-MailboxExportRequest cmdlet is used to export the contents of a mailbox.
- An administrator uses the Microsoft Exchange Server MAPI Editor to access the contents of a mailbox.

You enable Mailbox audit logging on a per-mailbox basis. When you enable mailbox auditing, Exchange creates a special Audits subfolder under the Recoverable Items folder. When you enable this type of auditing, you can specify the types of user actions that you will record for a specific logon type. For example, you could choose to log message deletion for a delegate user or mailbox owner and you could choose to log mailbox access for administrators. The audit log entries will contain data about the client IP address, hostname, and process used to access the mailbox. Mailbox audit logging is enabled through the Set-Mailbox cmdlet.

You can access mailbox audit logs through Exchange Control Panel or by using the Search-MailboxAuditLog cmdlet. You can use the New-MailboxAuditLogSearchCmdlet to search mailbox audit logs for more than one monitored mailbox at a time.

> **MORE INFO**   MAILBOX AUDIT LOGGING
>
> To learn more about mailbox audit logging, consult the following TechNet document: *http://technet.microsoft.com/en-us/library/ff459237.aspx*.

Message Tracking

Message tracking logs contain detailed information about messages transferred to and from Exchange servers running the Hub Transport, Edge Transport, and Mailbox server roles. You use the Set-TransportServer cmdlet to manage all tracking logs on a Hub Transport or Edge

Transport server and the Set-MailboxServer cmdlet to manage tracking logs on a Mailbox server. You can use these cmdlets to configure the following message tracking options:

- Enable or disable message tracking. Message tracking is enabled by default.
- Configure the location of message tracking log files.
- Configure a maximum size for each message tracking log file. The default is 10 MB.
- Configure a maximum size for the message tracking log file directory. The default is 250 MB.
- Configure a maximum age for message tracking log files. The default is 30 days. Message tracking log files older than this setting will be automatically deleted.
- Enable or disable message subject logging. Message subject logging is enabled by default.

You can use several methods to search message tracking logs in Exchange Server 2010:

- You can use the Get-MessageTrackingLog cmdlet.
- You can click on the Message Tracking item in EMC, which will bring up the Mail Control\Delivery Reports item in Exchange Control Panel. This dialog is shown in Figure 5-2. You can use this tool to search the message tracking logs on a Hub Transport server and a Mailbox server. This tool focuses on delivery reports.

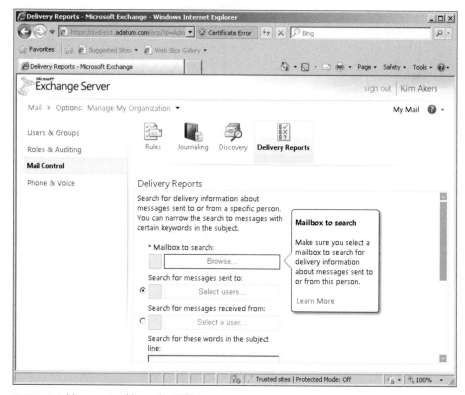

FIGURE 5-2 Message tracking using ECP

- Tracking Log Explorer   This tool is part of the troubleshooting assistant. It allows you to build a command using Get-MessageTrackingLog through a web interface, allowing you to be more precise in your message tracking log queries. You can use this tool on Hub Transport, Edge Transport, and Mailbox servers.

> **MORE INFO**   **MESSAGE TRACKING**
>
> To learn more about message tracking, consult the following TechNet document: *http://technet.microsoft.com/en-us/library/bb124375.aspx.*

Protocol Logging

Protocol Logging records SMTP conversations that occur between SMTP servers during the message delivery process. These conversations occur through Receive connectors and Send Connectors on Exchange 2010 servers that have the Edge Transport or Hub Transport roles installed.

In Exchange 2010, protocol logging is disabled by default on all Send connectors and Receive connectors. You enable protocol logging on a per-connector basis. All Receive connectors on a Hub Transport server or an Edge Transport server use the same protocol log files and options when you enable protocol logging. Send connector protocol log files and options remain separate from Receive connector log files and options.

You can configure the following options for protocol log files:

- Maximum log file size. Default is 10 MB.
- Maximum log file directory size. Default is 250 MB.
- Maximum log file age. Default is 30 days.
- Send connector and Receive connector log file location.

Protocol log files use circular logging by default. When a file exceeds the specified maximum age, it will be deleted automatically. If the log file directory exceeds the maximum size, the oldest log file will be deleted automatically.

You can enable protocol logging on a connector in EMC by editing the properties of that connector and selecting a protocol logging level of either None or Verbose as shown in Figure 5-3. You can use the Set-ReceiveConnector or Set-SendConnector cmdlets with the ProtocolLoggingLevel parameter set to either None or Verbose to configure protocol logging from EMS.

> **MORE INFO**   **PROTOCOL LOGGING**
>
> To learn more about protocol logging, consult the following TechNet document: *http://technet.microsoft.com/en-us/library/aa997624.aspx.*

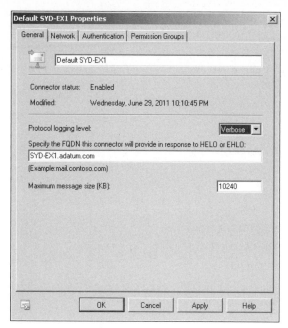

FIGURE 5-3 Enable Protocol Logging

Discovery Searches

Multi-mailbox search allows authorized members of staff to search the contents of all mailboxes in an organization for specific search terms. Reasons for this functionality include the following:

- **Legal discovery** In legal discovery scenarios, it is necessary to perform a multi-mailbox search to comply with an organization's legal obligations during the resolution of a lawsuit.

- **Internal investigations** Multi-mailbox search can assist in responding to requests by management or the organization's legal department as a part of internal investigations.

- **Human Resources surveillance** Depending on the organization, the HR department may carry out routine surveillance on employee communications, or need to perform a specific search as a part of carrying out their duties.

Users must be members of the Discovery Management RBAC role group before they are able to perform discovery searches. This role group is associated with two management roles, Mailbox Search, which allows the user to perform a discovery search, and the Legal Hold role, which allows the role holder to enforce a litigation hold on a mailbox. This RBAC role group has no members by default. You'll learn more about Legal Hold in Objective 5.2, "Design and Deploy Message Archival."

When you perform a discovery search, you need to specify a target mailbox that will host the results of that search as shown in Figure 5-4. When you do this, you select a mailbox configured as a discovery search mailbox.

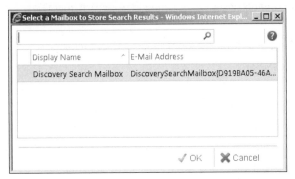

FIGURE 5-4 Choose where to store Discovery Search Results

Discovery mailboxes provide the following functionality:

- **Improved security**   Discovery searches by their nature involve sensitive content. Access to the mailbox is restricted by default to authorized personnel and it is simpler to manage the security and auditing of dedicated discovery mailboxes.

- **Increased mailbox storage quota**   Discovery search mailboxes have a default storage quota of 50 GB.

- **Integrity of data**   Email cannot be sent directly to discovery mailboxes, ensuring the veracity of the results stored in the mailbox.

The default discovery search mailbox is named Discovery Search Mailbox. You can create additional search mailboxes from EMS using the New-Mailbox cmdlet with the Discovery Parameter. For example, to create a new discovery mailbox called AntiTrust, use the following command:

```
New-Mailbox AntiTrust –Discovery –UserPrincipalName AntiTrust@adatum.com
```

Users that have been assigned the Discovery Management role are able to perform searches using Exchange Control Panel. When a search is performed, a search object will be created in Exchange. You can manage this object to start, stop, modify, and delete the search item. You can configure the following discovery search options:

- **Keywords**   The keywords that you are looking for in the search. Logical operators must be capitalized.

- **Senders or recipients**   Allows you to specify who the message was from of who it was addressed to.

- **Date range**   Allows you to limit results to a specific date range.

- **Mailboxes**   Allows you to specify certain mailboxes, rather than all mailboxes in the organization. By default, multi-mailbox search will check all mailboxes in the organization.

- **Personal archive** Included by default in a multi-mailbox search, you can exclude personal archives from the search.

- **Message types** Default searches only check email messages. You can extend searches to look for contacts, documents, instant messaging logs, journal, meetings, and notes.

- **Attachments** Allows the searching of attachment types supported for Exchange search.

- **Unsearchable items** Determines whether unsearchable items will be included in the discovery search.

- **Safe List** File types considered unsearchable.

- **Encrypted items** Allows you to select S/MIME encrypted messages as failed items.

- **IRM-protected items** IRM protected items are returned by multi-mailbox search.

- **Deduplication** Means that search will only return one instance of a unique message.

With Exchange 2010 SP1, discovery managers can annotate messages moved to the discovery mailbox. It is then possible to search the mailbox based on those annotations. This allows them to make comments as a part of the discovery process without compromising the integrity of the discovery evidence.

> *MORE INFO* **DISCOVERY MANAGEMENT**
>
> To learn more about discovery management, consult the following TechNet document: *http://technet.microsoft.com/en-us/library/dd298014.aspx*.

Records Management

Messaging Records Management allows you to accomplish design goals related to legal, business, and regulatory compliance requirements. For example, depending on where your organization is located in the world, there may be complex regulations that govern how long certain types of messages must be stored. Messaging Records Management is a technological solution to this regulatory issue, allowing you to enforce legal policies related to message retention.

There are two basic methods that you can use to ensure that legal requirements related to message retention are observed. These methods are retention policies or managed folders:

- **Retention Policies** Retention policies are new to Exchange Server 2010. These policies allow you to use retention tags to apply retention settings. The Managed Folder Assistant services Mailboxes that have retention policies applied to them. The Managed Folder Assistant runs on a schedule and processes retention tags in mailboxes according to that schedule.

- **Managed Folders** Managed folders were introduced in Exchange Server 2007 and are supported in Exchange Server 2010. The Managed Folder Assistant also processes mailboxes that use managed folders according to its schedule.

For Message Records Management to work effectively, it is necessary for users to participate in the process of appropriately identifying messages based on content and retention value. With Managed Folders users classify messages by moving them into managed folders. By having this process occur manually, you minimize the chance that messages are mishandled by an entirely automatic messaging management solution.

With retention tags, you apply a default retention setting to standard folders such as the Inbox folder and configure a default policy tag (DPT) to the entire mailbox. Any items that a user does not specifically tag will inherit the retention settings configured in the DPT. An advantage of Retention Tags is that they work for users who are organized enough to bother filing email into folders, as retention tags can be applied at the folder or message level. Retention Tags can also be used by users who simply keep everything in their inbox, allowing them to tag each individual message with a specific retention setting.

If a user chooses not to take action, one of the following retention settings will apply:

- **Messages stored in default folders that have a retention tag applied**   If a message is located in a default folder and that folder has a retention policy tag applied, the retention settings specified in the retention policy tag apply.

- **Messages in custom folders that have a personal tag applied**   If a user creates a custom folder and then applies a personal tag, the settings specified in the personal tag apply.

- **Messages in custom or default folders without a retention tag**   If a message does not have a retention tag, the DPT applies.

You'll learn more about retention tags and managed folder in Objective 5.2, "Design and Deploy Message Archival."

> **MORE INFO   RECORDS MANAGEMENT**
>
> To learn more about records management, consult the following TechNet document: *http://technet.microsoft.com/en-us/library/bb123507.aspx*.

Information Rights Management Logging

Information Rights Management (IRM) logging is an Exchange 2010 Service Pack 1 feature that you can leverage to monitor and troubleshoot how IRM operations occur on Mailbox, Hub Transport, Client Access and Unified Messaging servers. IRM logging is enabled by default in Exchange Server 2010 SP1 organizations.

The cmdlet that you use to enable, disable, or configure IRM logging on a particular server depends on the server role. You can configure IRM logging using the following cmdlets:

- *Set-TransportServer*
- *Set-MailboxServer*
- *Set-ClientAccessServer*

A common set of parameters is used with these cmdlets when it comes to configuring IRM logging. These cmdlets are as follows:

- **IrmLogEnabled**   Use this parameter to enable or disable IRM logging on a server.
- **IrmLogMaxAge**   Allows you to specify the maximum age of IRM log files. Files older than this value are automatically deleted from the directory.
- **IrmLogMaxDirectorySize**   Allows you to specify the maximum size of the directory that hosts IRM logs. When the maximum size is reached, the oldest log file is removed. The default size of this directory is 250 MB.
- **IrmLogMaxFileSize**   Specifies how large each IRM log file can grow. The default is 10 MB.
- **IrmLogPath**   Allows you to specify the IRM log directory.

MORE INFO   IRM LOGGING

To learn more about IRM logging, consult the following TechNet document: *http://technet. microsoft.com/en-us/library/ff686962.aspx.*

EXAM TIP

Know which types of logging can be used to diagnose specific types of problems.

Objective Summary

- Administrator audit logging allows you to record all of the commands used by messaging administrators in the performance of their duties.
- Mailbox audit logging allows you to track how authorized users access specific sensitive mailboxes.
- Message tracking logs contain detailed information about messages that transit Hub Transport, Edge Transport, and Mailbox servers.
- Protocol logging allows you to record SMTP conversations between Send connectors and Receive connectors.
- Discovery searches allow authorized people to search the contents of all mailboxes within an organization. A user needs to be a member of the Discovery Management RBAC group to perform a discovery search.
- Message Records Management allows you to ensure that important messages are preserved for an appropriate amount of time and that less important messages are discarded from a mailbox in a way that meets compliance obligations.
- IRM logging allows you to troubleshoot problems that might occur when Active Directory Rights Management Services is used to protect sensitive content.

Objective Review

Answer the following questions to test your knowledge of the information in this objective. You can find the answers to these questions and explanations of why each answer choice is correct or incorrect in the "Answers" section at the end of this chapter.

1. You want to determine if any modifications have been made to role groups and, if so, which user made those changes. Which of the following Messaging Policy and Compliance features of Exchange Server 2010 would you use to accomplish this goal?

   A. Mailbox Audit Logging

   B. Protocol Logging

   C. IRM Logging

   D. Administrator Audit Logging

2. Senior management is concerned that Exchange administrators may be surreptitiously accessing the contents of sensitive mailboxes by using the New-MailboxExportRequest cmdlet to export a sensitive mailbox and then access mailbox contents indirectly. Which of the following Message Policy and Compliance tools could you use to determine if this had occurred? (Choose All That Apply.)

   A. Administrator Audit Logging

   B. Mailbox Audit Logging

   C. IRM Logging

   D. Protocol Logging

3. Which of the following tools can you use to determine why messages to members of the management team, which should automatically be encrypted when sent to members of the management team, are being delivered without the appropriate AD RMS template being applied?

   A. Protocol Logging

   B. Mailbox Audit Logging

   C. Administrator Audit Logging

   D. IRM Logging

4. You want to search the contents of the message tracking log files on your organization's Edge Transport servers. Which of the following tools can you use to accomplish this goal? (Choose All That Apply.)

   A. Exchange Control Panel

   B. Exchange Management Console

   C. Get-MessageTrackingLog EMS cmdlet

   D. Tracking Log Explorer

THOUGHT EXPERIMENT
Design a Messaging Auditing and Discovery Solution

In the following thought experiment, you will apply what you've learned about the design and deploy auditing and discovery objective to design a messaging auditing and discovery solution. You can find answers to these questions in the "Answers" section at the end of this chapter.

You are the messaging administrator at Adatum. You are currently in a committee meeting with several members of senior management. They want to discuss oversight issues with you.

Ken wants to be able to determine which commands administrators are using and how they are being used.

Ian wants to know what steps can be taken to limit the people who are able to perform discovery searches.

Oksana is concerned about tracking the people who have access to the CEO's mailbox

Rooslan wants to know what can be done to diagnose failures in applying rights management templates to messages.

With this information in mind, answer the following questions:

1. What type of logging would you use to address Rooslan's concerns?

2. What type of process would you configure to address Oksana's concerns?

3. Which RBAC role group's membership is Ian concerned about?

4. What steps can you take to provide Ken with the information he is interested in?

Objective 5.2: Design and Deploy Message Archival

Having a message archive and retention strategy is important. Not only does a retention strategy ensure that the size of user mailboxes doesn't keep growing indefinitely, retention policies can allow you to be sure that your organization complies with data retention rules and regulation.

> **This objective covers:**
> - Recoverable Items.
> - Litigation hold.
> - Personal Archives.
> - Messaging Records Management.
> - Retention Tags and Policies.
> - Retention Hold.

Understanding Recoverable Items

In previous versions of Exchange, administrators spent a considerable amount of time restoring items that users had accidentally deleted. The Recoverable Items folder protects messages from accidental or malicious deletion by blocking users from "hard deleting" messages for a specific amount of time. The default is 14 days. The Recoverable Items feature replaces the dumpster feature from Exchange 2007 and is sometimes known as "dumpster 2.0."

The Recoverable Items folder has the following benefits:

- The Recoverable Items folder is attached to the mailbox. If you move the mailbox to another mailbox database, the Recoverable Items folder is also moved.
- The Recoverable Items folder is indexed by Exchange Search. You can discover items in the Recoverable Items folder when performing a Multi-Mailbox Search.
- The Recoverable Items folder has a separate storage quota.
- You can configure Exchange to block the Recoverable Items folder from being purged of content.
- You can configure Exchange to track modifications made to Recoverable Items folder content.

The recoverable items folder hosts the following subfolders:

- **Deletions**   This folder hosts all items that have been deleted from the Deleted Items folder. Users can access this folder through the Recover Deleted Items feature in Outlook and OWA. This feature is accessible when a user right-clicks on the Deleted Items folder and then clicks on Recover Deleted Items.
- **Versions**   Available when litigation hold or single item recovery is enabled. Hosts original and modified copies of deleted items, but is not visible to standard users.
- **Purges**   This folder is only present if litigation hold or single item recovery is enabled. This folder contains all items that have been hard deleted, but is not visible to standard users.
- **Audits**   If you have configured mailbox audit logging, this folder will contain all audit log entries.

When a user deletes an item or empties all items from the Deleted Items folder, those items are moved to the Deletions subfolder in the Recoverable Items folder. Users can then recover items from this location manually without support staff having to restore these deleted items from a backup. Items will remain in this location until the deleted item retention period, by default 14 days, is reached. The deleted items retention period can be configured at either the mailbox database level, as shown in Figure 5-5, or at the individual mailbox level. Once the deleted item retention period expires, the item is shifted to the Purges folder. When the Managed Folder Assistant services the mailboxes, any items in the Purges subfolder will be removed from the mailbox database.

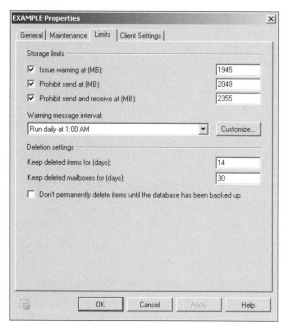

FIGURE 5-5 Deleted Item Retention

MORE INFO   **RECOVERABLE ITEMS**

To learn more about deleted item retention, consult the following TechNet document:
http://technet.microsoft.com/en-us/library/ee364755.aspx.

Single Item Recovery

Users are unable to recover items once they have been removed from the Deletions subfolder. In previous versions of Exchange it was necessary for an administrator to perform a restore from backup operation, which took a substantial amount of effort and time. Single Item Recovery is a new Exchange 2010 feature that allows administrators to recover items without having to perform a restore from backup media.

When the Managed Folder Assistant services the Recoverable Items folder on a mailbox for which you have enabled single item recovery, an item in the Purges subfolder will not be deleted as long as the deleted item retention period for that item has not elapsed. Enabling single item recovery has the additional benefit of placing a copy of an item modified by the user into the Versions subfolder. This process is known as copy-on-write page protection. This allows administrators to recover alternate versions of modified items until the deleted item retention period expires. When Single Item Recovery is enabled, users are unable to purge items from the Recoverable Items folder.

You must use Exchange Management Shell to enable single item recovery for a mailbox. You cannot use EMC to enable single item recovery. Single item recovery is not enabled by default for new mailboxes or mailboxes that have been migrated from previous versions of Exchange. You enable single item recovery using the Set-Mailbox cmdlet with the SingleItem-RecoveryEnabled parameter. For example, to enable single item recovery on a mailbox named Kim_Akers and set the deleted item retention setting for that mailbox to 45 days, use the following command:

```
Set-Mailbox –Identity Kim_Akers –SingleItemRecoveryEnabled $True –RetainDeletedItemsFor 45
```

> **MORE INFO** **SINGLE ITEM RECOVERY**
>
> To learn more about single item recovery, consult the following TechNet document: *http://technet.microsoft.com/en-us/library/ee633460.aspx.*

Litigation Hold

During litigation, courts often require organizations to preserve all communication related to a specific topic or all communication from certain individuals. Depending on what types of electronic discovery practices are in use, you may need to pursue some of the following strategies to preserve e-mail:

- End users may be required to preserve email by not deleting any messages either deliberately or inadvertently.
- Suspend automated deletion mechanisms such as messaging records management.
- Copy or move email to a special archive mailbox to ensure that the messages aren't deleted or modified.

Getting message preservation wrong when an organization is involved in litigation can expose the organization to adverse legal judgments and fines. The litigation hold functionality in Exchange 2010 allows you to minimize the chance that something untoward happens when your organization has to comply with a request related to litigation. Litigation hold allows you to accomplish the following:

- Place a mailbox on hold. This will keep mailbox items in an unaltered state.
- Preserve mailbox items that may have already been deleted or modified by users.

- Ensure that mailbox items that would automatically be deleted by MRM are retained.

- Ensure that litigation hold functions in a way that is transparent to the user.

- Ensure that mailbox items that are placed on hold are discoverable through Exchange's Discovery search functionality.

Users that are members of the Discovery Management RBAC role group are able to place specific mailboxes on legal hold. As of the release of Exchange 2010 SP1, it is possible to use Exchange Management Console (EMC), Exchange Control Panel (ECP) or Exchange Management Shell to place a mailbox on litigation hold. This is done by editing the mailbox properties or using the Set-Mailbox cmdlet with the LitigationHoldEnabled parameter. It can take up to 60 minutes for a litigation hold setting to take effect on a mailbox.

Some organizations have policies in place that make it mandatory to inform a user when their mailbox has been placed on litigation hold. Because litigation hold is transparent to the user, users will not notice that their mailbox has been placed in this state. If your organization does require user notification, you can provide a notification message using the Retention Comment property shown in Figure 5-6.

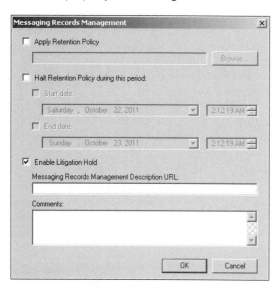

FIGURE 5-6 Litigation hold

Items located in a user's Recoverable Items folder don't count towards their mailbox quota. The Recoverable Items folder has its own separate quota. If you are placing mailboxes on Litigation Hold for an extended period of time, you should monitor this quota as if the quota is exceeded, users will be unable to empty their Deleted Items folder. The default quota setting for the Recoverable Items folder is 30 GB, which in most cases will suffice for all but the most protracted legal battles.

Personal Archives

Personal archives allow you to eliminate the use of Outlook personal store (.pst) files in your organization and to allow users to transfer messages to a special archive mailbox that they can access using Outlook 2010 and OWA. Personal archives can be used with Outlook 2007, Outlook 2010 and OWA, but require that you have Exchange Server 2010 Enterprise Edition Client Access Licenses.

PST files, a traditional way to store messages with Outlook clients, present the following challenges to organizations:

- **Files are unmanaged**   .pst files are often unmanaged in your organization. Users can move messages from their Exchange mailbox to the .pst file, removing them from the mailbox. Systematically backing up client computers is challenging for many organizations and the loss of a volume hosting a .pst file may mean that a large number of important messages become unrecoverable.

- **Discovery problems**   Cataloging data that resides in user .pst files, without 3rd party products, is a costly and manual process. Messages that may be relevant to litigation may remain undiscovered because they are stored in a .pst file rather than stored in a mailbox that is within the scope of a discovery search.

- **Message retention policy problems**   Message retention policies can't be applied to messages in .pst files. If you are unable to do this, your organization is not meeting its compliance obligations.

- **Data security**   Data stored in .pst files may be accessed by unauthorized third parties in the event that the computer or hard disk hosting that data is stolen or lost.

Exchange 2010 RTM required that personal archive mailboxes be stored in the same mailbox database as the user's mailbox. Exchange 2010 SP1 improves archive mailboxes, allowing them to be stored on different mailbox databases that may even be hosted on different mailbox servers. For example, you might store a user's mailbox in an on-premises mailbox database that is configured as part of a DAG and the user's archive mailbox on a mailbox server hosted in the cloud.

Users can move messages manually from their mailbox to their archive mailbox. Users are also able to configure Inbox rules to move or copy messages to their archive mailbox. You can also configure retention policies to automatically move items from the mailbox to the archive mailbox after a certain amount of time has expired. With Exchange 2010 SP1, it is also possible to import messages from a .pst file to a user's primary or archive messages. This functionality greatly simplifies the process of migrating users away from using .pst files.

The default Archive and Retention policy, if applied to a mailbox that is configured with an archive mailbox, will automatically move any message that is more than 2 years of age across to the archive mailbox from the user mailbox. The archive policy also contains personal tags that allow users to specify that messages be moved to the archive mailbox after a year, after five years, or never moved to the archive mailbox. The default Archive and Retention Policy is applied to a mailbox if no other retention policy is applied.

You can enable an archive mailbox during mailbox creation. You can also enable a personal archive for an existing mailbox by right clicking on the Mailbox in EMC and clicking on Enable Archive. This brings up the Enable Archive Mailbox dialog which allows you to specify the location of the archive, which includes being able to select your Microsoft Online Services tenant domain as shown in Figure 5-7.

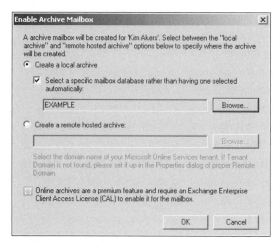

FIGURE 5-7 Enable archive mailbox

> **MORE INFO   PERSONAL ARCHIVES**
>
> To learn more about personal archives, consult the following TechNet document: *http://technet.microsoft.com/en-us/library/dd979795.aspx.*

Managed Folders

Managed Folders are a message records management technology that was introduced in Exchange Server 2007. Managed folders work on the principle that you configure retention settings for folders, and you apply retention settings to messages by placing them in those folders. Although managed folders are supported in Exchange Server 2010, retention policies and tags are now the preferred method of performing message records management as these allow you to apply retention settings on a per-message basis without having to place the message in a specific folder.

You can configure two types of managed folder:

- **Managed default folders**   Managed default folders are folder objects that you use with default folders like Inbox, Deleted Items, and Sent Items. Exchange setup will create a collection of managed default folders, but you can modify this and create different collections for different groups of users.
- **Managed custom folders**   Managed custom folders allow you to create custom folders in user's mailboxes. These folders are created under a top level folder with the name Managed Folders. Managed custom folders can only be used with an Exchange Server 2010 Enterprise CAL.

A managed folder mailbox policy is a collection of managed folders that you can apply to mailboxes. Policies can contain a mix of managed default folders and managed custom folders. You can't add duplicate folders to the same policy. You can add and remove folders from a managed folder mailbox policy as necessary. A mailbox can only have a single managed folder mailbox policy applied to it.

Managed content settings determine the retention and journaling settings for a specific managed folder. You can configure these settings for a specific type of item, such as an email message or calendar item, or you can configure them for all item classes. You can have different types of retention settings for different types of items in the same folder, but all items of the same type in a managed folder must use the same retention settings.

Retention settings involve the type of item, the retention age, and a retention action. The retention age is the length of time that an item will be retained prior to the retention action being performed. You can configure one of the following retention actions:

- **Move to the Deleted Items Folder**   When the retention age expires, the item is moved to the Deleted items folder.
- **Move to a Managed Custom Folder**   When the retention age expires, the item is moved to an existing managed custom folder.
- **Delete and Allow Recovery**   When the retention age expires, the item is moved to the Recoverable Items folder. Items will stay in the Recoverable Items folder until the deleted item retention setting for the mailbox is reached. The deleted item retention setting for the mailbox is different from the managed content retention age.
- **Permanently Delete**   Permanently deletes items so that users are unable to recover them. This does not make the item unrecoverable to an administrator.
- **Mark as Past Retention Limit**   Allow an item to be marked as expired. The item appears in Outlook with strikethrough text.

When configuring retention settings, you can specify whether the retention age is calculated on the basis of its delivery to the mailbox or when it arrives in the current folder. For example, you might have a managed content setting that moves a type of item to one folder after 90 days and then have a managed content setting on that folder that moves that type of item to the archive mailbox when an additional 180 days elapses.

Retention Tags and Policies

As you learned earlier in Objective 5.1, a retention policy is a collection of retention policy tags. A retention policy tag consists of a retention age and a retention action. When the retention age is reached, the retention action is performed. Retention actions include:

- Move to Archive
- Delete and Allow Recovery
- Permanently Delete
- Mark as Past Retention Limit

Only one retention policy can apply to a mailbox at a time. Retention policies allow you to accomplish the following:

- Assign retention policy tags (RPTs) to default folders like the Inbox and Sent Items folders. You can only apply one RPT to a specific folder.
- Configure default policy tags (DPTs) that will automatically manage the retention of any items that aren't tagged.
- Allow users to assign personal tags to individual items or folders that they have created. A policy can contain any number of personal tags.
- Allow the users to file messages in folders according to their own scheme rather than as a way of complying with message records management policy.

To deploy retention tags and policies, perform the following general steps:

1. Create the retention tags that you want to use.
2. Create a retention policy.
3. Link the retention tags that you created to the retention policy.
4. Apply the retention policy to user mailboxes.

Personal tags must be created by an administrator and linked to a retention policy. In Exchange 2010 SP1, users are able to use Exchange Control Panel to select additional personal tags that have been created within the organization but which have not been linked to the retention policy that applies to their mailbox. Users are only able to select additional personal tags if they have the MyRetentionPolicies Role. Personal tags require an Exchange Enterprise CAL.

You can use the Start-RetentionAutoTagLearning cmdlet to configure autotagging. Autotagging works by monitoring how users apply tags and then, when it has enough data, applies tags to new items as they arrive. A user must have manually tagged a minimum of 500 messages before AutoTagging can begin functioning.

You can only apply retention tags and retention policies if the mailbox server that hosts the user's mailbox is running Exchange Server 2010. Clients must access these mailboxes using Outlook 2010 or OWA if they want to view and apply retention tags. It is possible to apply retention policies to mailbox users running earlier versions of Outlook, but the user will be unable to tag specific items.

> **MORE INFO**   **RETENTION TAGS AND POLICIES**
>
> To learn more about retention tags and policies, consult the following TechNet document: *http://technet.microsoft.com/en-us/library/dd297955.aspx.*

Migrate from Managed Folders to Retention Policies

Although Managed Folders are supported for interoperability purposes, it is likely that at some point in the future, retention tags and retention policies will be the only way to perform messaging records management in a future version of Exchange. For this reason, once all of the mailbox servers in your organization have been upgraded to Exchange Server 2010, you should migrate Managed Folders to Retention Policies.

You can migrate a mailbox that has a managed folder mailbox policy so that it uses a retention policy. To do this you must create retention tags that perform the same tasks. You can simplify this process by using Port from Managed Folder To Tag wizard, which you can access from the Actions menu when the Organization Configuration\Mailbox node is selected in EMC. You can also do this by using the New-RetentionPolicyTag cmdlet with the Managed-FolderToUpgrade parameter.

> **MORE INFO**   **MIGRATE FROM MANAGED FOLDERS**
>
> To learn more about migrating from managed folders, consult the following TechNet document: *http://technet.microsoft.com/en-us/library/dd298032.aspx.*

Retention Hold

A retention hold suspends the processing of any retention policy or managed mailbox policy for a mailbox. You usually plan to use retention holds when a user goes on an extended holiday or break from the organization. When a mailbox is placed on retention hold, users are able to log on to their mailbox and change or delete items. Deleted items that have exceeded the deleted item retention period will not be returned in search results.

You can place a mailbox on retention hold by editing the mailbox properties in EMC, selecting the Mailbox Settings tab, selecting Messaging Records Management, clicking Properties and then selecting Halt Retention Policy During This Period and specifying the retention hold duration as shown in Figure 5-8. You can configure a retention hold on a mailbox from EMS using the Set-Mailbox command with the RetentionHoldEnabled parameter.

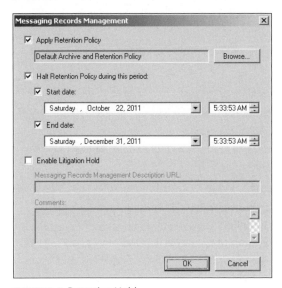

FIGURE 5-8 Retention Hold

MORE INFO RETENTION HOLD

To learn more about retention hold, consult the following TechNet document: *http://tech-net.microsoft.com/en-us/library/dd335168.aspx.*

EXAM TIP

Understand the difference between managed folders and retention policies and tags.

Objective Summary

- Recoverable items allow items that have been removed from the deleted items folder to be recovered without having to restore those items from backup.
- When the deleted item retention period has expired, the item will be removed unless litigation hold or retention hold has been enabled.
- The default deleted item retention period is 14 days.
- Enabling single item recovery will maintain copies of altered items.

- Single item recovery is enabled on a per-mailbox basis.
- Litigation hold preserves mailbox items in an unaltered state and is transparent to the user.
- Users who are members of the Discovery Management RBAC role group are able to place mailboxes on legal hold.
- Items in a user's recoverable items folder don't count towards their mailbox quota.
- The default quota setting for the recoverable items folder is 30 GB.
- Personal archives allow you to eliminate PST files.
- Exchange 2010 SP1 allows archive mailboxes to be stored on different mailbox servers and mailbox databases.
- Managed folders allow you to apply retention settings and actions on a per-folder basis.
- Retention policies and tags allow you to apply retention settings on a per-folder and per-individual message basis.
- Autotagging is a process by which Exchange learns how individuals use personal tags on messages and attempts to automate this process.
- You can migrate from managed folder to retention tags using the Port From Managed Folder To Tag wizard.
- Retention hold allows you to exempt a mailbox from retention policies whilst a user is on vacation or away for an extended period.

Objective Review

Answer the following questions to test your knowledge of the information in this objective. You can find the answers to these questions and explanations of why each answer choice is correct or incorrect in the "Answers" section at the end of this chapter.

1. Your organization's legal team has come up with the following policy regarding the retention of messages:
   - Messages in all user's Inbox folders should be stored for 120 days and then archived
   - Messages in all user's Sent Items folders should be stored for 60 days and then archived
   - Messages in the Deleted Items folder should be stored for 21 days and then permanently deleted

   Which of the following should you use to accomplish this goal with a minimum administrative effort?

   A. A single retention policy and three retention policy tags

   B. Three retention policies and one retention policy tag

   C. A single retention policy and one retention policy tag

   D. Three retention policies and three retention policy tags

2. You are designing a messaging archive strategy for your Exchange 2010 organization. You have the following goals:

   - Users should be able to choose how long a message is kept

   - Messages that have not been classified should be kept for 45 days

   - Users should not have to organize their messages based on retention requirements, but should be able to organize them according to their own filing system

   With these requirements in mind, which of the following elements should you include in your archive strategy? (Choose All That Apply.)

   A. Custom Managed Folders

   B. Personal Tags

   C. Default Policy Tag

   D. Retention Policy

3. You want to ensure that unmodified copies of items are stored in the event that alterations are made to items in a user's mailbox. Which of the following strategies could you use to accomplish this goal?

   A. Configure single item recovery.

   B. Configure a personal archive mailbox.

   C. Configure a managed folder.

   D. Configure a retention policy.

4. One of your design objectives in adopting Exchange Server 2010 is to eliminate the use of .pst files at your organization. Which of the following technologies can you use to accomplish this goal?

   A. Single Item Retention

   B. Litigation Hold

   C. Archive mailboxes

   D. Retention Hold

Objective 5.3: Design and Deploy Transport Rules for Message Compliance

Several compliance technologies are enforced by Hub Transport and Edge Transport servers. These technologies usually involve the transport server examining the contents of the message in transit and taking an appropriate compliance action. Most of the technologies covered in this objective are operationalized through the configuration of transport rules.

Ethical Firewalls

Ethical Walls is a virtual barrier to communication that exists between separate elements of the same Exchange organization. These ethical walls are usually put in place for policy reasons. Ethical firewalls aren't limited to Exchange, but also include telephone, postal mail, and direct fact to fact communication. In some organizations it is necessary to move departments into different locations as a way of ensuring that the ethical firewall remains in effect.

Ethical firewalls can be implemented in Exchange organizations through the use of transport rules. Correctly configured transport rules can block email messages being sent between specific groups within your organization. Ethical firewalls can't block someone creating a private webmail account and using that to contact a person on the other side of the ethical firewall. When you design an ethical firewall for Exchange, you can only take reasonable steps to block communication. It will not be possible to block communication should parties on both sides of the firewall be motivated enough to want to circumvent the measures that you have taken.

When you implement ethical firewalls, it does not matter if both the sender and the recipient's mailboxes reside on the same server, or even within the same mailbox database. All messages that are sent and received within an Exchange Server 2010 organization must pass across a Hub Transport server. This means that transport rules used to block communication between two separate groups will function even if everyone in the organization uses the same mailbox server and mailbox database.

The most straightforward method of enforcing an ethical firewall is to make each affected mailbox a member of one of two distribution groups. You then create a transport rule to reject messages sent between members of these distribution groups. Prior to deploying any transport rules related to ethical firewalls in a production environment, you should test them in a development environment to ensure that they work properly.

> **MORE INFO** **ETHICAL FIREWALLS**
>
> To learn more about ethical firewalls, consult the following TechNet document: *http://technet.microsoft.com/en-us/library/aa996850.aspx.*

Message Journaling

Journaling allows all communications to be recorded. Journaling is primarily used to support a compliance strategy, ensuring that critical communication is recorded in its entirety. Exchange Server 2010 supports the following journaling options:

- **Standard Journaling**   Standard Journaling is configured on a per-mailbox database basis. The journaling agent stores all messages that are sent to and from mailboxes hosted on that database. If you want to journal all messages sent to and from users within your organization, you will need to configure journaling on every mailbox database in your organization. Standard journaling can be used without requiring an Exchange Server 2010 Enterprise CAL

- **Premium Journaling**   Premium journaling requires an Exchange Server 2010 Enterprise CAL. Premium journaling allows you to create more specific journaling rules than recording every message to and from a specific mailbox database. You can use journal rules to store messages sent between specific users or members of distribution groups.

The scope of a Journal Rule determines which messages the journaling agent will forward to the journal mailbox. Journal Rule scope can be configured to the following recipients:

- **Internal**   When this scope is selected, it includes messages sent to recipients and received by senders within the Exchange organization.

- **External**   When this scope is selected, it includes messages sent to recipients and received from senders who are outside the Exchange organization.

- **Global**   The global scope includes all messages, including those that have already been processed by journal rules configured with the Internal or External scope.

When you create a journal rule, you specify recipients on the basis of their SMTP address. A recipient can be an individual mailbox, a distribution group, or a contact. All messages that are sent to or from the recipients that you specify in the journaling rule will be journaled. If you do not specify any recipients, all messages sent do or from recipients that match the journal rule scope will be journaled.

When you create a journal rule, you also specify one or more journaling mailboxes. Journaling mailboxes serve as a repository for journal reports. Depending on your organization's requirements, you may choose to configure one journal mailbox per journal rule, or have a single journal mailbox as the destination for the reports of all journal rules. As journaling mailboxes will contain sensitive information, you need to ensure that they are secure and that access to those mailboxes is audited appropriately.

You use the New-JournalRule EMS cmdlet to configure new journal rules. Journal rules are stored within Active Directory and will replicate to all Hub Transport servers within your Exchange organization.

Alternate Journaling Mailbox

An alternate journaling mailbox is a backup mailbox that is used in the event that the configured journaling mailbox becomes unavailable. You configure an alternate journaling mailbox on an organization wide basis. Journal reports that are rejected by any journaling mailbox within the organization will be redirected to the same alternate journaling mailbox. To configure an alternate journaling mailbox, perform the following general steps:

1. Create a mailbox that will function as the organization's alternate journaling mailbox.

2. Use the Set-TransportConfig cmdlet with the JournalingReportNdrTo parameter to specify the address of the alternate journaling mailbox. For example, to if you created an alternate journaling mailbox with the address alternatejournalbox@contoso.com, issue the following command:

```
Set-TransportConfig -JournalingReportNdrTo alternatejournalbox@contoso.com
```

MailTips

MailTips allow users of Outlook 2010 and OWA to view information about intended message recipients prior to messages being sent. For example, if a recipient has enabled an out-of-office message informing people that they won't be back for two weeks, the sender can be made aware of this prior to actually sending the message. MailTips can also be used to accomplish the following goals:

- Warn users that they are attempting to send a message to a user who doesn't exist, a recipient who is restricted, or a recipient who has exceeded their mailbox quota.

- Warn users they are sending messages to a large number of recipients. By default a MailTip warning will be triggered if the message is targeted to more than 25 users.

- Warn users that they are sending messages to inappropriate distribution groups.

- Warn users that the message they are about to send violates message size restrictions or maximum recipients per message.

- Warn users that a message is addressed to a recipient outside the organization.

You use the Set-OrganizationConfig EMS cmdlet to configure MailTips. For example, to enable MailTips for an organization where MailTips have previously been disabled, use the following cmdlet:

```
Set-OrganizationConfig -MailTipsAllTipsEnabled $true
```

You can configure custom MailTips using the following cmdlets:

- Set-Mailbox
- Set-MailContact
- Set-MailUser
- Set-DistributionGroup
- Set-DynamicDistributionGroup
- Set-MailPublicFolder

For example, you might want to configure a MailTip warning message to be displayed if a user addresses a message to the Executives distribution group. You can do this using the Set-DistributionGroup cmdlet with the MailTip parameter. For example:

```
Set-DistributionGroup -Identity Executives -MailTip "This distribution group is used by
Senior Management. Messages from users not a part of this group will automatically be
rejected"
```

> **MORE INFO** **MAILTIPS**
>
> To learn more about MailTips, consult the following TechNet document: *http://technet. microsoft.com/en-us/library/dd297974.aspx.*

Disclaimers

A disclaimer is a standard statement that is added to inbound or outbound messages. More than one disclaimer can be applied to a single message, though this will only occur if the message matches more than one transport rule in which the disclaimer action is enabled. Disclaimer text is usually designed by an organization's legal team.

You create disclaimers by creating transport rules. You can do this either through EMC or EMS. The key when doing this through EMS is to select the Append Disclaimer Text And Fallback To Action If Unable To Apply option as shown in Figure 5-9. To create a disclaimer using EMS, use the New-TransportRule cmdlet with the ApplyHTMLDisclaimerLocation and ApplyHTMLDisclaimerText, and ApplyHtmlDisclaimerFallBackAction parameters.

> **MORE INFO** **DISCLAIMERS**
>
> To learn more about disclaimers, consult the following TechNet document: *http://technet. microsoft.com/en-us/library/bb124352.aspx.*

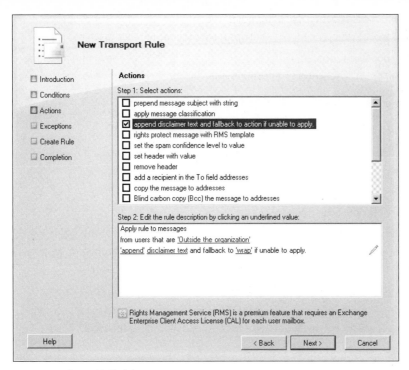

FIGURE 5-9 Append disclaimer

EXAM TIP

Understand the use of transport rules in configuring journaling, ethical firewalls, and disclaimers.

Objective Summary

- Ethical firewalls involve configuring transport rules that block communication between two different groups of people that are members of the same organization.

- The easiest way to create an ethical firewall rule is to create a distribution group for each group of users and configure a transport rule that blocks communication between these two groups.

- You should test transport rules related to ethical firewalls in a development environment before putting them into production to ensure that they function as intended.

- Message journaling involves forwarding a copy of every message sent to or received from a specific mailbox, a collection of mailboxes, or an entire mailbox database to a special journal mailbox.

- You can only perform journaling on a per-mailbox or per –group of mailbox basis if you have an Exchange Enterprise CAL.

- Journal rules can use the Internal, External, or Global scope.

- An alternate journal mailbox is a special mailbox that is used as an alternate in the event that a specified journal mailbox is unavailable. You can only have one alternate journal mailbox in an Exchange organization, but this mailbox can receive Journal reports from any journal rule.

- MailTips are warnings that appear to users of Outlook 2010 or OWA when they are preparing to send messages that meet certain properties.

- Disclaimers are special text that is appended to email messages. They are generally legal in nature.

Objective Review

Answer the following questions to test your knowledge of the information in this objective. You can find the answers to these questions and explanations of why each answer choice is correct or incorrect in the "Answers" section at the end of this chapter.

1. Your organization's legal department has issued a policy that all messages sent by employees to people outside the organization must include standard legal text. Which of the following would you include in your design to accomplish this goal?

   A. Retention Hold

   B. Legal Hold

   C. Disclaimer

   D. Ethical Firewall

2. You need to ensure that users in the Ideas department are unable to send or receive messages from users in the Publicity department. There are currently no distribution groups that represent the membership of these departments. Which of the following steps should you take to accomplish this goal? (Choose 2. Each answer forms part of a complete solution.)

   A. Create two distribution groups

   B. Create a single distribution group

   C. Create a Retention Policy Tag

   D. Create a transport rule

3. You want to ensure that journaling reports are still stored even if the journaling mailbox is not available. Which of the following should you plan to use to accomplish this goal?

   A. Alternate journal mailbox

   B. Personal Archive

   C. Ethical Firewall

   D. MailTips

4. You want to ensure that a MailTip appears if a user addresses an email message to the senior executives distribution group. The membership of this group is static. Which of the following EMS cmdlets would you use to accomplish this goal?

   A. Set-Mailbox

   B. Set-DistributionGroup

   C. Set-DynamicDistributionGroup

   D. Set-MailUser

THOUGHT EXPERIMENT
Design Transport Rules for Message Compliance

In the following thought experiment, you will apply what you've learned about the design and deploy transport rules for message compliance objective to design a transport rules scheme to enforce message compliance. You can find answers to these questions in the "Answers" section at the end of this chapter.

You are the messaging administrator at a large financial company. You need to ensure that all messages sent by senior executives are journaled for compliance purposes. It is also necessary to restrict communication between users in the Auditing department and users in the Finance department to minimize conflicts of interest. Finally after several damaging leaks, management has asked you to find some way of reminding users that they should be careful when sending messages to recipients outside the organization.

With this information in mind, answer the following questions:

1. What type of CAL is required if you want to configure a journal rule for a specific distribution group?

2. How will you ensure that users in the Auditing department are unable to communicate with users in the Finance department?

3. How can you ensure that users are warned in the event that they appear to be sending an email message to a recipient who is outside the organization?

4. What client software must users be using to receive these warnings?

Objective 5.4: Design and Deploy for Monitoring and Reporting

Monitoring an Exchange organization falls into two general categories: availability and performance. Availability monitoring is when you configure an infrastructure to alert you in the event that some aspect of your Exchange infrastructure, from a critical service on a CAS to an entire mailbox server, fails. Performance monitoring involves being able to accurately measure how well aspects of your Exchange infrastructure are performing, from ensuring that the hard disks that host mailbox databases are not overwhelmed with input/output operations, to ensuring that critical message queues are not flooded with excess traffic.

> **This objective covers:**
> - Monitoring Exchange.
> - Exchange 2010 Performance Monitoring.
> - Connectivity Logging.
> - ActiveSync Reporting.

Monitoring Exchange

By planning a comprehensive Exchange 2010 monitoring strategy, you can ensure that your organization's Exchange infrastructure functions reliably and efficiently. There are several different methods that you can use to monitor an Exchange server infrastructure:

- **Windows Server 2008 Event Viewer**   This tool collects data related to server events. Generally you only use this tool against a particular Exchange server. You can run it locally or connect to the event log remotely. While you can configure event log forwarding to centralize event log data, it is often difficult to monitor events in real time using this tool. Event Viewer is helpful in performing historical analysis, for example, if you are trying to determine what factors may have led to the occurrence of a specific failure.

- **Windows System Resource Manager**   This tool doesn't function as a performance monitor tool, but does allow you to configure how system resources, such as CPU, are allocated to applications, services, and processes. You can use Windows System Resource Manager to ensure that no single process monopolizes Exchange resources.

- **Network Monitor**   Network Monitor allows you to view, capture, and analyze network data. Generally used as a real time analysis tool to determine precisely what traffic is crossing the network to the Exchange server.

- **Exchange Server 2010 Management Pack for System Center Operations Manager**   The Exchange Server 2010 management pack for System Center Operations Manager 2007 and 2012 is the most comprehensive monitoring solution available for Exchange. Operations Manager is Microsoft's operations monitoring and management platform. The Exchange Server 2010 specific management pack is designed to alert administrators to all important Exchange-related events.

While the Exchange Server 2010 management pack for Operations Manager will provide you with the most comprehensive picture of the state of your Exchange Organization, it also requires that you purchase both Systems Center Operations Manager 2007 or 2012 and SQL Server 2008 or SQL Server 2008 R2 to host the Operations Manager database. While this type of monitoring can be invaluable for large organizations, it may not be necessary for smaller organizations.

> **MORE INFO**
>
> To learn more about the Exchange 2010 Management Pack for Operations Manager 2007 and 2012, consult the following link on Microsoft's website: *http://www.microsoft.com/download/en/details.aspx?id=692*.

Connectivity Logging

You can use connectivity logging to record connection activity for outbound message delivery queues on Hub Transport and Edge Transport servers. The connectivity log records connection activity from the sending queue to the target Mailbox server, smart host, or domain. The connectivity log records the following information:

- **Source Queue**   This can be the remote delivery queue or the mailbox delivery queue.
- **Destination Mailbox server**   When the message is going to be delivered to a mailbox server within the local site.
- **Destination Smart Host**   When the delivery is to a smart host that will forward outbound traffic to the appropriate destination.
- **Destination Domain**   When the delivery is to a remote SMTP server.
- **Connection Failures**   Connection errors that have occurred during transmission.
- **Number of Messages and bytes transmitted**   The total number of messages and bytes transmitted to the destination.

Connectivity log configuration is performed using the Set-Transport server cmdlet in EMS. You can configure the following connectivity log options using this cmdlet:

- Enable or disable connectivity logging. Connectivity logging is disabled by default.
- Specify connectivity log file location.
- Specify maximum log file size. The default is 10 MB.
- Specify maximum size for connectivity log file directory. Default maximum is 250 MB.
- Specify maximum age for connectivity log files. Default is 30 days.

As is the case with other transport log files, connectivity logging uses circular logging. This means that if the maximum size of the log file directory is exceeded, the oldest log file will be deleted as a way of ensuring that the limit is observed. Similarly when a log file reaches the maximum age, it will be deleted.

> **MORE INFO** **CONNECTIVITY LOGGING**
>
> To learn more about connectivity logging, consult the following TechNet document: *http://technet.microsoft.com/en-us/library/bb124500.aspx.*

Exchange 2010 Performance Monitoring

Exchange server performance monitoring involves taking measurements using performance monitor over time to determine which, if any, hardware resources are constraining Exchange performance. Generally you can improve performance by determining which component has the poorest performance and then remediating that performance. If performance is still not acceptable after you have remediated that component, you perform the process again to determine the next component with poor performance. You then remediate that component.

You perform this process iteratively until you reach a stage where the performance of your organization's Exchange infrastructure is acceptable to all stakeholders. You generally use Performance Monitor to monitor Exchange in real-time, or to record Exchange performance at certain peak usage times as a way of determining which components constitute performance bottlenecks.

> **MORE INFO** **EXCHANGE PERFORMANCE**
>
> To learn more about Exchange performance monitoring, consult the following TechNet document: *http://technet.microsoft.com/en-us/library/dd351192.aspx.*

Monitoring Mailbox Servers

Your primary concern when monitoring the performance of mailbox servers will be to make assessments around disk response time. Microsoft recommends that you aim to have an average response time for data read operations of under 20 milliseconds (ms) and that the average data write response time should not exceed 100 ms. You should also monitor disk queue length to ensure that disk queue lengths do not grow.

Mailbox server-related counters that you should monitor include:

- **Logical Disk\Avg. Disk sec/Read**   Below 20 ms
- **Logical Disk\Avg. Disk sec/Write**   Below 100 ms
- **Logical Disk\Avg. Disk sec/Transfer**   Below 20 ms on average; spikes below 50 ms
- **MSExchangeIS Mailbox\Messages Queued For Submission**   Below 50

- **MSExchangeIS\RPC Requests**   Below 70
- **MSExchangeIS\RPC Averaged Latency**   Less than 25 ms on average
- **MSExchangeIS\RPC Num Slow Packets**   Less than 3

MORE INFO   **MAILBOX SERVERS**

To learn more about the performance counters that are relevant to the Mailbox role, consult the following TechNet document: *http://technet.microsoft.com/en-us/library/ff367871. aspx.*

Monitoring CAS

When monitoring CAS, you should keep an eye on disk queue lengths, especially when the CAS is collocated with the Hub Transport and Mailbox Server roles. You should also keep an eye on ASP.NET services and applications response time. Specific CAS related performance counters that you should keep an eye on include:

- **Logical Disk\Avg. Disk sec/Read**   Below 20 ms
- **Logical Disk\Avg. Disk sec/Write**   Below 20 ms
- **ASP.NET\Application Restarts**   Below 10
- **ASP.NET\Worker Process Restarts**   Below 10
- **ASP.NET\Requests Current**   Less than 5000
- **ASP.NET\Requests Wait Time**   Less than 1000 ms
- **ASP.NET Applications\Requests in Application Queue**   Less than 5000
- **MSExchange OWA\Average Response Time**   Less than 100 ms
- **MSExchange OWA\Average Search Time**   Less than 100 ms
- **RPC/HTTP Proxy\Number of failed backend connection attempts per sec**   0 at all times
- **MSExchangeFS:OAB\Download Task Queued**   0 at all times

MORE INFO   **CLIENT ACCESS SERVERS**

To learn more about the counters that are relevant to the CAS role, consult the following TechNet document: *http://technet.microsoft.com/en-us/library/ff367877.aspx.*

Monitoring Transport Servers

Your two primary concerns when monitoring transport servers are disk and network performance. In most cases, the bottleneck with a transport server will be its disk performance and this is only exacerbated if you co-locate the transport server role with the

CAS and Mailbox server roles. The Transport server related counters that you should keep an eye on include:

- **Logical Disk\Avg. Disk sec/Read**   Below 20 ms
- **Logical Disk\Avg. Disk sec/Write**   Below 100 ms
- **Logical Disk\Avg. Disk Queue Length**   Should be 0 at all times
- **MSExchange Database\Log Generation Checkpoint Depth**   Below 1000
- **MSExchange Database\Version buckets allocated**   Below 200
- **MSExchange Database\Log Record Stalls/sec**   Less than 10 per sec on average with spikes no greater than 100 per sec
- **MSExchangeTransportQueues\Aggregate Delivery Queue Length (All Queues)**   Less than 5000
- **MSExchangeTransportQueues\Active Remote Delivery Queue Length**   Less than 250
- **MSExchangeTransportQueues\Active Mailbox Delivery Queue Length**   Less than 250
- **MSExchangeTransportQueues\Retry Mailbox Delivery Queue Length**   Less than 100
- **MSExchangeTransportQueues\Unreachable Queue Length**   Less than 100
- **MSExchangeTransportQueues\Largest Delivery Queue**   Less than 200
- **MSExchangeTransportQueues\Poison Queue Length**   0 at all times

---

MORE INFO   **TRANSPORT SERVERS**

To learn more about the performance counters that are relevant to the Hub Transport and Edge Transport server roles, consult the following TechNet document: *http://technet.micro-soft.com/en-us/library/ff367923.aspx.*

ActiveSync Reporting

Exchange ActiveSync reporting uses Windows PowerShell to analyze IIS logs and processes to create a series of reports related to your organization's ActiveSync deployment. You can use the Export-ActiveSyncLog cmdlet to generate the following reports.

- **Exchange ActiveSync Usage Reports**   Provides information about the total amount of data that was sent and received in bytes. Also provides a count of each type of item, such as mail messages, calendar items, contact items, and task items, sent and received.
- **Hits Report**   This report allows you to view the total number of synchronization requests that are processed every hour. This report also allows you to view the total number of unique devices that are initiating synchronization requests.

- **HTTP Status Report** This report provides general overview information on CAS performance. The report also provides information on error code responses and how often the errors related to the codes occur.

- **Policy Compliance Report** Provides information on the number of fully compliant, partially compliant, and noncompliant mobile devices that utilize ActivSync to connect to Exchange. Fully compliant devices are those that accept the Exchange ActiveSync policy and are able to implement all aspects of the policy. These devices are likely to run the Windows Mobile 6.5 operating system as the Windows Phone 7 operating system does not support all ActiveSync policy options.

- **User Agent List** Provides you with information about the total number of unique ActiveSync users, organized by mobile phone operating system.

MORE INFO **ACTIVESYNC REPORTING SERVICES**

To learn more about ActiveSync reporting services, consult the following TechNet document: *http://technet.microsoft.com/en-us/library/bb201675.aspx.*

Objective Summary

- Event viewer allows you to see past events, but is not a good tool for real-time monitoring of Exchange.

- Windows System Resource Manager allows you to allocate quotas to system resources such as CPU.

- Network monitor allows you to capture, view, and analyze network traffic.

- The Exchange Server 2010 Management Pack for System Center Operations Manager is the most comprehensive solution provided by Microsoft for monitoring Exchange Server 2010.

- Connectivity Logging allows you to record connection activity from the sending queue to a target Mailbox server, smart host, or domain.

- You can use performance monitor to determine which components are causing performance bottlenecks.

- You can use the Export-ActiveSyncLog cmdlet to generate ActiveSync reports.

Objective Review

Answer the following questions to test your knowledge of the information in this objective. You can find the answers to these questions and explanations of why each answer choice is correct or incorrect in the "Answers" section at the end of this chapter.

1. You want to track the number of messages sent from the Hub Transport servers in your organization's Melbourne site to the Edge Transport servers on the Melbourne site's perimeter network. Which of the following tools should you use to accomplish this goal?

   A. Message tracking

   B. Connectivity logging

   C. Protocol logging

   D. Agent logging

2. Which Exchange ActiveSync report should you use to determine the number of mail messages and calendar items sent and received through ActiveSync?

   A. Exchange ActiveSync Usage Reports

   B. Hits Reports

   C. User Agent List

   D. Policy Compliance Reports

3. You want to generate a report for management that will show the total number of unique ActiveSync users organized by mobile phone operating system. Which of the following reports would you use to accomplish this goal?

   A. Exchange ActiveSync Usage Reports

   B. Hits Reports

   C. User Agent List

   D. Policy Compliance Reports

4. Management is concerned that a large number of mobile devices that are used to sync mailbox data do not support all of the security features required to ensure that organizational data does not fall into the hands of unauthorized third parties in the event that the mobile device is lost. Which of the following ActiveSync reports can you use to determine how many devices are partially compliant and non-compliant with current Exchange ActiveSync mailbox policies?

   A. User Agent List

   B. Policy Compliance Reports

   C. Exchange ActiveSync Usage Reports

   D. Hits Reports

THOUGHT EXPERIMENT
Design a Monitoring and Reporting Solution

In the following thought experiment, you will apply what you've learned about the Design and deploy for monitoring and reporting objective to assess the performance of particular Exchange servers. You can find answers to these questions in the "Answers" section at the end of this chapter.

You are in the process of analyzing a performance report on three computers that have Exchange roles installed. These computers are located at the Traralgon, Warragul, and Yarragon branch offices of your organization. You have been provided with the following information.

Mailbox Server Traralgon Alpha:

      Logical Disk\Avg. Disk sec/Read   15 ms

      Logical Disk\Avg. Disk sec/Write   200 ms

      Logical Disk\Avg. Disk sec/Transfer   12 ms

      MSExchangeIS\RPC Requests   40 ms

Client Access Server Warragul Beta:

      ASP.NET\Requests Current   2000

      ASP.NET\Requests Wait Time   800 ms

      ASP.NET Applications\Requests in Application Queue   4000

      MSExchange OWA\Average Response Time   250 ms

Hub Transport server Yarragon Delta:

      MSExchangeTransportQueues\Active Remote Delivery Queue Length   150

      MSExchangeTransportQueues\Active Mailbox Delivery Queue Length   500

      MSExchangeTransportQueues\Retry Mailbox Delivery Queue Length   70

With this performance information in mind, answer the following questions:

1. Which performance counter is cause for concern on Traralgon Alpha?
2. Which performance counter is cause for concern on Warragul Beta?
3. Which performance counter is cause for concern on Yarragon Delta?

Chapter Summary

- Administrator audit logging allows you to record all of the commands used by messaging administrators in the performance of their duties.

- Mailbox audit logging allows you to track how different authorized people access specific sensitive mailboxes.

- Message tracking logs contain detailed information about messages that transit Hub Transport, Edge Transport and Mailbox servers.

- Protocol logging allows you to record SMTP conversations between Send connectors and Receive connectors.

- Discovery searches allow authorized people to search the contents of all mailboxes within an organization.

- Recoverable items allow items that have been removed from the deleted items folder to be recovered without having to restore those items from backup.

- Litigation hold preserves mailbox items in an unaltered state and is transparent to the user.

- Users who are members of the Discovery Management RBAC role group are able to place mailboxes on legal hold.

- Managed folders allow you to apply retention settings and actions on a per-folder basis.

- Retention policies and tags allow you to apply retention settings on a per-folder and per-individual message basis.

- Retention Hold suspends the processing of retention policies or managed mailbox policies. Retention hold is usually activated when a user goes on holiday.

- Ethical firewalls block communication between two different groups of people that are members of the same organization.

- Message journaling involves forwarding a copy of every message sent to or received from a specific mailbox, a collection of mailboxes, or an entire mailbox database to a special journal mailbox.

- An alternate journal mailbox is a special mailbox that is used as an alternate in the event that a specified journal mailbox is unavailable.

- Disclaimers are special text that are appended to email messages.

- Connectivity Logging records connection activity from the sending queue to a target Mailbox server, smart host, or domain.

- Use performance monitor to determine which components are causing performance bottlenecks.

Answers

This section contains the answers to the Object Reviews and the Thought Experiments.

Objective 5.1: Review

1. **Correct Answer:** D

   A. Incorrect: Mailbox Audit Logging allows you to track access to sensitive mailboxes. You can't use this type of logging to track modifications made to role groups.

   B. Incorrect: Protocol logging allows you to track SMTP conversations that occur between messaging servers during the message delivery process. You can't use this type of logging to track modifications made to role groups.

   C. Incorrect: IRM Logging allows you to monitor and troubleshoot IRM related operations on Mailbox, Hub Transport, and Client Access Servers. You can't use this type of logging to track modifications made to role groups.

   D. Correct: Administrator Audit Logging allows you to track how administrators use cmdlets when managing an Exchange Server 2010 environment. This includes tracking modifications made to role groups.

2. **Correct Answers:** A and B

   A. Correct: Administrator Audit Logging will audit use of the New-Mailbox-ExportRequest cmdlet by default, though in most cases you would use Mailbox Audit Logging for this specific task.

   B. Correct: Mailbox Audit Logging allows you to track who uses a particular mailbox and what actions that person takes. This includes access through Discovery search, mailbox export, or the Exchange Server MAPI editor.

   C. Incorrect: IRM Logging allows you to monitor and troubleshoot IRM related operations on Mailbox, Hub Transport, and Client Access Servers. You can't use this type of logging to track whether a sensitive mailbox has been exported.

   D. Incorrect: Protocol logging allows you to track SMTP conversations that occur between messaging servers during the message delivery process. You can't use this type of logging to track whether a sensitive mailbox has been exported.

3. **Correct Answer:** D

   A. Incorrect: Protocol logging allows you to track SMTP conversations that occur between messaging servers during the message delivery process. You can't use this type of logging to diagnose IRM issues.

   B. Incorrect: Mailbox Audit Logging allows you to track who uses a particular mailbox and what actions that person takes. You can't use this type of logging to diagnose IRM issues.

C. **Incorrect:** Administrator Audit Logging allows you to track the use of cmdlets, either directly through EMS or indirectly through EMC or the Exchange web console, by administrators. You can't use this type of logging to diagnose IRM issues.

D. **Correct:** IRM Logging allows you to diagnose Information Rights Management issues on Client Access, Hub Transport, and Mailbox servers.

4. **Correct Answers:** C and D

A. **Incorrect:** You can't use Exchange Control Panel to access message tracking logs on an Edge Transport server. You can only use this method on Hub Transport and Mailbox servers.

B. **Incorrect:** You can't use Exchange Management Console to access message tracking logs.

C. **Correct:** You can use the Get-MessageTrackingLog EMS cmdlet on an Edge Transport server to access the message tracking logs.

D. **Correct:** You can use the Tracking Log Explorer, which functions as a web-front-end to the Get-MessageTrackingLog EMS cmdlet to access Edge Transport Server message tracking logs.

Objective 5.1: Thought Experiment

1. You can use IRM logging to assist in diagnosing failures in applying rights management templates to messages.

2. You can configure mailbox audit logging on the CEO's mailbox to address Oksana's concerns about tracking access to that mailbox.

3. Ian is concerned about the membership of the Discovery Management group.

4. You can use the Administrator Audit Logs to allow Ken to determine which commands are being used and how they are being used.

Objective 5.2: Review

1. **Correct Answer:** A

A. **Correct:** A retention policy tag allows you to specify the retention period and what action will be taken. A retention policy can hold more than one retention policy tag.

B. **Incorrect:** Only one retention policy can apply to a mailbox at a time.

C. **Incorrect:** You need three retention policy tags to accomplish the goal of having three separate actions related to how long messages are stored and how they are dealt with after the retention period expires.

D. **Incorrect:** Only one retention policy can apply to a mailbox at a time.

2. **Correct Answers:** B, C, and D

   A. **Incorrect:** Custom Managed Folders would require users to organize their messages based on retention requirements, rather than letting them use their own filing system.

   B. **Correct:** Personal tags allow users to specify how long a message is retained.

   C. **Correct:** A default policy tag allows you to configure retention settings for unclassified messages.

   D. **Correct:** A retention policy allows users to control the retention of their messages without having to move those messages to specific folders.

3. **Correct Answer:** A

   A. **Correct:** When single item recovery is enabled, original mailbox items are stored as well as any modifications made to those items.

   B. **Incorrect:** Personal archive mailboxes allow users to store items in a separate mailbox for archiving purposes. You can't use personal archive mailboxes to ensure that original mailbox items are stored as well as any modifications made to those items.

   C. **Incorrect:** Managed folders allow you to manage what actions are taken to items after a certain amount of time has expired. You can't use personal archive mailboxes to ensure that original mailbox items are stored as well as any modifications made to those items.

   D. **Incorrect:** Retention policies allow you to manage what actions are taken to items after a certain amount of time has expired. You can't use personal archive mailboxes to ensure that original mailbox items are stored as well as any modifications made to those items.

4. **Correct Answer:** C

   A. **Incorrect:** Single item retention allows you to retain deleted items. You can't use single item retention as a substitute for .pst files.

   B. **Incorrect:** Litigation hold is used to stop items being permanently deleted from a user mailbox. You can't use Litigation hold as a substitute for . pst files.

   C. **Correct:** Archive mailboxes can be used as a replacement for .pst files. You can import . pst files and store the imported contents in archive mailboxes.

   D. **Incorrect:** Retention hold is used to suspend message records management processes on a mailbox, usually when a person is on extended vacation. You can't use Retention Hold as a substitute for .pst files.

Objective 5.2: Thought Experiment

1. You can implement retention hold to ensure that items are not removed from user mailboxes by existing message records management processes while those users are on sabbatical.

2. You can place the mailboxes of the employees who may be involved in the lawsuit on litigation hold. This will ensure that their mailboxes will not be modified in such a way that may cause problems if the issue goes to trial at a later date.

3. You can use the Port From Managed Folder To Tag wizard to migrate existing managed folders to retention tags.

4. By enabling autotagging, users' tagging choices will be monitored. Once Exchange has enough data, it will attempt to replicate users' tagging strategies by automatically applying personal tags.

Objective 5.3: Review

1. **Correct Answer:** C

   A. **Incorrect:** Retention Hold allows you to block messaging records management processes on the mailbox of a user for a certain period of time. You can't use retention hold to ensure that legal text is appended to messages sent from internal users to external recipients.

   B. **Incorrect:** Legal Hold ensures that modifications cannot be made to the contents of mailboxes. You can't use legal hold to ensure that legal text is appended to messages sent from internal users to external recipients.

   C. **Correct:** A disclaimer is text that is appended to a message by a transport rule. This text is usually of a legal nature.

   D. **Incorrect:** An ethical firewall blocks communication between groups in the same organization. Although it is implemented through a transport rule as disclaimers are, you do not use ethical firewalls to append disclaimer text to messages.

2. **Correct Answers:** A and D

   A. **Correct:** To create an ethical firewall, you should create a distribution group for both the Publicity and the Ideas departments. You should then use these distribution groups with a transport rule that blocks communication between these groups.

   B. **Incorrect:** You need to have two distribution groups, one for each department to create an ethical firewall.

   C. **Incorrect:** Retention Policy tags allow you to manage how long messages are stored and what action to take when the retention period expires. You can't use retention policy tags when building an Ethical Firewall.

D. **Correct:** Once you have distribution groups that represent the membership of each department, you can create a transport rule that block communications between these departments.

3. **Correct Answer:** A

A. **Correct:** Alternate journal mailboxes can be used to ensure that journal reports are still stored in the event that the specified journal mailbox is not available.

B. **Incorrect:** Personal Archives are additional mailboxes. You can't use personal archives as a method of ensuring that journal reports are still stored in the event that the specified journal mailbox is not available.

C. **Incorrect:** Ethical firewalls allow you to block communication between two different groups of users. You can't use ethical firewalls as a method of ensuring that journal reports are still stored in the event that the specified journal mailbox is not available.

D. **Incorrect:** MailTips allow messages to be displayed to users prior to them sending a message. You can't use MailTips as a method of ensuring that journal reports are still stored in the event that the specified journal mailbox is not available.

4. **Correct Answer:** B

A. **Incorrect:** You would not use the Set-Mailbox cmdlet to configure a MailTip. You only use Set-Mailbox if you want to configure a MailTip related to a specific mailbox.

B. **Correct:** You use the Set-DistributionGroup cmdlet to configure a MailTip for users that address messages to the distribution group.

C. **Incorrect:** You would not use the Set-DynamicDistributionGroup to configure this MailTip as the target group was described as static.

D. **Incorrect:** You would not use the Set-MailUser cmdlet to configure a MailTip. You only use Set-MailUser if you want to configure a MailTip related to a specific mail user.

Objective 5.3: Thought Experiment

1. You need an Exchange Enterprise CAL if you want to configure a journal rule for a specific distribution group.

2. You can configure an Ethical Firewall to block communication between users in the Auditing department and users in the Finance department.

3. You can configure a MailTip to warn users in the event that they appear to be sending an email message to a recipient outside the organization.

4. Users need to be running Outlook 2010 or later, or OWA on Exchange 2010 to be able to view MailTips.

Objective 5.4: Review

1. **Correct Answer:** B

   A. **Incorrect:** Message tracking records information about the routing and delivery of email messages. You should use connectivity logging to determine the number of messages sent from Hub Transport servers.

   B. **Correct:** Connectivity logging allows you to record connection activity of outbound message delivery queues on Hub Transport and Edge Transport servers. This includes recording the number of messages and bytes transmitted.

   C. **Incorrect:** Protocol logging allows you to view the SMTP interaction that occurs between Send and Receive connectors. You should use connectivity logging to determine the number of messages sent from Hub Transport servers.

   D. **Incorrect:** You use Agent logging to track the functionality of the anti-spam agent. You should use connectivity logging to determine the number of messages sent from Hub Transport servers.

2. **Correct Answer:** A

   A. **Correct:** The Exchange ActiveSync Usage Reports provide information about the total amount of data sent and received. These reports also provide count information of each type of item send and received.

   B. **Incorrect:** Hits Report provides you with the total number of synchronization requests processed every hour. You can't use this report type to determine the number of mail messages and calendar items sent and received through ActiveSync.

   C. **Incorrect:** The User Agent List report provides information on the total number of unique ActiveSync users, organized by mobile phone operating system. You can't use this report type to determine the number of mail messages and calendar items sent and received through ActiveSync.

   D. **Incorrect:** The Policy Compliance report provides information on the number of fully compliant, partially compliant, and noncompliant mobile devices that use ActiveSync. You can't use this report type to determine the number of mail messages and calendar items sent and received through ActiveSync.

3. **Correct Answer:** C

   A. **Incorrect:** The Exchange ActiveSync Usage Reports provide information about the total amount of data sent and received. These reports also provide count information of each type of item send and received. You can't use this report to provide information on the total number of unique ActiveSync users, organized by mobile phone operating system.

B.   **Incorrect:** Hits Report provides you with the total number of synchronization requests processed every hour. You can't use this report to provide information on the total number of unique ActiveSync users, organized by mobile phone operating system.

C.   **Correct:** The User Agent List report provides information on the total number of unique ActiveSync users, organized by mobile phone operating system.

D.   **Incorrect:** The Policy Compliance report provides information on the number of fully compliant, partially compliant, and noncompliant mobile devices that use ActiveSync. You can't use this report to provide information on the total number of unique ActiveSync users, organized by mobile phone operating system.

4.   **Correct Answer:** B

A.   **Incorrect:** The User Agent List report provides information on the total number of unique ActiveSync users, organized by mobile phone operating system. You can't use this report to learn how many devices are partially compliant, and noncompliant with Exchange ActiveSync mailbox policies.

B.   **Correct:** The Policy Compliance report provides information on the number of fully compliant, partially compliant, and noncompliant mobile devices that use ActiveSync.

C.   **Incorrect:** The Exchange ActiveSync Usage Reports provide information about the total amount of data sent and received. You can't use this report to learn how many devices are partially compliant and noncompliant with Exchange ActiveSync mailbox policies.

D.   **Incorrect:** Hits Report provides you with the total number of synchronization requests processed every hour. You can't use this report to learn how many devices are partially compliant and noncompliant with Exchange ActiveSync mailbox policies.

Objective 5.4: Thought Experiment

1.   Logical Disk\Avg. Disk sec/Write should be below 100 ms on a server that hosts the Mailbox role.

2.   MSExchange OWA\Average Response Time should be less than 100 ms on a server that hosts the CAS role.

3.   MSExchangeTransportQueues\Active Mailbox Delivery Queue Length should be less than 250 on a server that hosts the Hub Transport role.

Index

A

accepted domains
  configuring, 144–145
    as internal relay domain, 31
  and email addresses, 46
  planning, 28–38
Actions, in transport rules, 146
activation preference number, of mailbox database copy, 315
Active Directory
  administrators, 239
  functional level requirements, 97–98
  Hub Transport server for each site, 20
  infrastructure
    and cloud-based deployments, 4
    requirements, 99
  integrated DNS zones, 5
  network topology and, 10
  preparing for Exchange 2010, 96, 101–102
  redundancy and recovery, 288–290
  schema preparation, 100–101
  split permissions, 239
  synchronization, 106
    with cloud, 12–35
Active Directory domain, Mailbox server role and, 161–213
Active Directory Federation Services (AD FS)
  for single sign-on to cloud service providers, 13
Active Directory Integrated Zone, 290
Active Directory Lightweight Directory Service (AD LDS), 112
  deletion of replicated data in, 114
Active Directory objects, restoring deleted, 289
Active Directory Recycle Bin feature, 289
Active Directory Replication Monitor (replmon.exe), 101

Active Directory Rights Management Services (AD RMS), 223
  applying templates based on message properties, 226
Active Directory sites, Hub Transport server in, 143
Active Manager, 314–316
ActiveSync, 61, 134
  Autodiscover and, 135
  with Information Rights Management, 224–225
  policies, 257–260
  reporting, 388–389
Add-ADPermission cmdlet, 136, 220, 270
Add-AttachmentFilterEntry cmdlet, 252
Add-AvailabilityAddressSpace cmdlet, 136
Add-DatabaseAvailabilityGroupsServer cmdlet, 312
Add-IPAllowListEntry cmdlet, 247
Add-IPBlockListEntry cmdlet, 246
Add-MailboxDatabaseCopy cmdlet, 312, 317
Add-PublicFolderAdministrativePermission cmdlet, 177
Add-PublicFolderClientPermission cmdlet, 177, 269
Address Book Service, 61
address lists
  deployment, 167–170
  in Outlook Web App, 132
address rewriting, configuring, 120–213
Address Rewriting Inbound agent, 118
Address Rewriting Outbound agent, 118
Add-RoleGroupMember cmdlet, 177, 269
Administration tools, multiphase upgrade and user access to, 71
administrative privileges, assignment of, 232
administrator audit logging, 352–354
administrators, 176
  Exchange vs. Active Directory, 239
  granting rights to manage public folders, 177
ADSI Edit, 132

Agent logs, disk space requirements, 26
Allow lists, 247
alteration, protecting message from, 217
anonymous relay, 119, 218
    configuring, 155–156
anonymous SMTP connections, Receive connector to accept, 30
anti-malware software, 243–244
anti-spam features of Exchange 2010, 244–254
AntiTrust discovery mailbox, 358
antivirus scanners, 226
Application identifier (AppID), 14
approval process for updates, 293
Approved Application List, ActiveSync policies and, 259
arbitration mailbox, 353
Archive and Retention policy, default, 369
archive mailbox, enabling, 369
archives. *See* message archives
arrays, Client Access, deployment, 301–302
Attachment Filtering agent, 118
attachments
    discovery search of, 359
    filtering, 252–253
    maximum size, 154
auditing and discovery, 352–363
    administrator audit logging, 352–354
    discovery searches, 357–359
    Information Rights Management (IRM) logs, 360–361
    mailbox audit logging, 354
    message tracking logs, 354–356
    protocol logging, 356–357
    PST files and, 368
    records management, 359–360
Audits folder, 364
authentication
    for ActiveSync, 134
    between Hub Transport server and third-party email gateway, 119
    Outlook Web App (OWA), 260–262
authoritative domains, 28, 144
Author role, 176, 269
Autodiscover service, 61
    planning, 64–65
autotagging, 372
availability, 61
    CAS and, 136
    Service Level Agreement and, 8

B

back pressure, 25
backup
    for alternate journaling mailbox, 379
    of CAS, 299
    Database Availability Groups and, 306, 318
    Hub Transport servers, 325
backup and recovery objectives, 295
bandwidth, Exchange server placement and, 3
Basic authentication, 119
    for OWA, 260
benchmarking, performing for I/O, 70
bidirectional mail flow, routing group connectors for, 193
Blocked Senders Lists, 244
block lists, 246–248
block mode, continuous replication, 313
Bluetooth, ActiveSync policies and, 257
bridgehead server, 194
browser, ActiveSync policies and, 257

C

Cached Exchange Mode, 170
calendars
    Availability service and, 136
    Federation to share with third parties, 103
    multiphase upgrade and user access to information, 71
camera, ActiveSync policies and, 257
capacity analysis, for hardware, 70
CDOEX (CDO for Exchange 2000 Server), 75
certificate authority (CA), 66
    trusted third-party, 218
certificates, 217–218
    backup, 299
    for Client Access Servers, 66–67, 126–128
    for Edge Transport servers, 115, 333
    for Hub Transport servers, 115
        backup, 325
    for Microsoft Federation gateway, 14
    recovery, 216
change management, 295
Character Settings, in Outlook Web App, 132

checklists
    for deploying Exchange 2010 in Exchange 2003 environment, 183–184
    generating, 76
circular logging, 42, 165
    connectivity logging and, 386
    for protocol log files, 356
Client Access arrays, deployment, 301–302
client access roles, 176
Client Access security, 257–267
    ActiveSync policies, 257–260
    Outlook Web App
        authentication, 260–262
        segmentation settings, 262–264
Client Access Servers (CAS), 59–69
    Autodiscover service, 64–65, 134–136
    Availability service, 136
    certificates, 66–67
    deployment, 125–142, 185
        ActiveSync, 134
        certificate request, 126–128
        Outlook Web App (OWA), 128–132
        POP3 and IMAP4 access, 137
        prerequisites, 125
        verifying functionality, 137–140
    Exchange Control Panel (ECP), 61–63
    hardware requirements, 64
    high availability and disaster recovery, 298–305
        backup, 299
        multi-site deployment, 302
        recovery, 300–301
        site failover, 302
    location planning, 59–60
    monitoring, 387
    Offline Address Book distribution, 170
    Outlook Anywhere, 133–134
    planning services, 60–61
    proxying and remote access, 60
    testing performance, 63–64
Client usage type, for Receive connector, 151
cloning Edge Transport server configuration, 116–117, 333, 334
Closed group membership, 271
cloud
    directory synchronization with, 12–14
    placing mailboxes in, 54
cloud-only deployments, 4
cloud service providers, AD FS for single sign-on to, 13

Cluster Continuous Replication, 75
cmdlets, tracking use of, 353
coexistence
    deployments, 4–5
    with Exchange 2003, 182–184
    vs. Exchange 2003 upgrade, 72–74
    with Exchange 2007, 184–186
    Exchange 2007 transport rules functionality, 191–192
    vs. Exchange 2007 upgrade, 74–75
    multiphase upgrade with, 71
    routing group connector configuration, 193–194
    with SMTP-based messaging systems, 77
    with third-party email systems, 188–191
    transport rules and, 191–192
common shared namespace, DNS support planning for, 6
computers, standalone for Edge Transport role, 111
concurrent mailbox deliveries, configuring maximum, for message throttling, 23
concurrent mailbox submissions, configuring maximum, for message throttling, 23
Conditions, in transport rules, 146
confidential information, filtering from email, 145
Configuration read scope, 236
Configuration scope, 237
Configuration write scope, 236
Connection filtering agent, 117
ConnectionInactivityTimeOut parameter, of Set-TransportServer cmdlet, 24
connection rate per minute, configuring maximum, for message throttling, 23
ConnectionTimeOut parameter, of Set-TransportServer cmdlet, 24
connectivity logs, 385–386
    disk space requirements, 26
Connect-MsolService cmdlet, 13
constraints, for existing infrastructure, 2
consumer mail, ActiveSync policies and, 257
contacts
    Federation to share information with third parties, 103
    mail forest, 46
content filter, 251–252
    agent, 118, 250
    safelist aggregation and, 244
Content Filtering Properties dialog box, 250, 251
content index, and mailbox database storage requirements, 41

content replica, 174, 319

continuous replication, 75, 313

Contributor role, 176, 269

Convert-MsolDomainToFederated cmdlet, 13

copy-on-write page protection, 366

corrupt mailbox databases, repairing, 320–321

cost of spam, 243

counters

    CAS-related, 387

    mailbox server-related, 386

CreateItems right, 176, 268

CreateSubfolders right, 176, 268

cross-forest topologies, 11

    Autodiscover and, 65

    IRM in, 225

    mailboxes in, 44

Custom connector type, 149

custom folders, managed, 370

custom management role groups, 235

custom management role scopes, 237

Custom usage type, for Receive connectors, 152

D

Database Availability Groups (DAGs), 41, 43, 161, 309–318

    and backup, 306, 318

    creating, 311

    deploying updates to members, 294–295

    deployment across multiple locations, 318

    and disk space requirements, 27

databases. *See also* mailbox databases

    default public folder, 165

    portability, 309

Datacenter Activation Coordination (DAC) mode, 316

decryption, transport protection rules and, 226–227

default Archive and Retention policy, 369

default folders, managed, 370

default manager, of distribution group, 50

default policy tag (DPT), 360

default public folder database, 165

default reply-to address, configuring, 48

default settings, for message size limits, 153

Delegated Setup role group, 234

delegation tokens, Security Assertion Markup Language (SAML), 14

DeleteAllItems right, 176, 268

deleted Active Directory objects, restoring, 289

deleted item retention window, disk space for, 41

deleted mailboxes, in mailbox database, 307

DeleteOwnedItems right, 176, 268

Deletions folder, 364

delivery agents, 77, 191

Desktop Sync, ActiveSync policies and, 258

dial-tone recovery, 309

Digest Authentication, for OWA, 261

digital signature, for message, 220

Direct File Access, 130–131

direct Internet mail flow, 156–157

Directory Services Restore Mode (DSRM), 289

directory synchronization server, 4

Directory Synchronization tool, 106

DirectPush, 63

Disable-TransportAgent cmdlet, 118

Disable-TransportRule cmdlet, 147

disaster recovery, 288–298

    Active Directory, redundancy and recovery, 288–290

    backup and recovery objectives, 295

    for CAS role, 298–305

disclaimers, 226, 380–381

discovery. *See* auditing and discovery

Discovery Management role, 358

    ECP use and, 61

Discovery Management role group, 234, 357, 367

discovery searches, 354, 357–359

Discovery Search Mailbox, 358

disjointed namespaces, 6–8

disk space requirements

    Mailbox server performance and, 42–44

    for transport server, 26–27

disk-write caching, 44

Dismount-Database cmdlet, 164

distribution groups

    blocking creation of, 273

    configuring users ability to join, 51

    default manager, 50

    expansion servers for, 22

    policies, 49–53

    security, 270–273

distribution of out-of-office messages, 148

DNS

    configuration for SMTP, 107–108

    planning, 5–8, 32–34

    redundancy and recovery, 290–292

    split namespace, 5

to support redundant Edge Transport, 335
text (TXT) records for federation, 105–106
DNS Manager console, 33
DNS Suffix Search List group policy item, 7
document archives, mailboxes as informal, 39
documents, WebReady document viewing, 130–131
domain controllers
  for Exchange, 290
    requirements, 288
  NetBIOS name of, 6
  operating systems, and domain functional level, 97
domain functional level, 97
  viewing and managing settings, 98
domain object container, msDS-AllowedDNSSuffixes
Active Directory attribute, 7
domains
  configuring remote, 148–149
  multiple, in single forest, 11
  preparing for Exchange 2010, 102
Domain Security, 221–222
Do Not Forward template, 223
dumpster feature, 364
dynamic distribution groups, 49

E

Edge Rule agent, 118
edge subscriptions, 112–115
  cmdlets to manage, 113
  creating, 113
  limitations, 112
  removing, 114
  and Send connector, 149
EdgeSync process, replication, 112
EdgeTransport.exe.config file, 325
Edge Transport servers, 20, 30
  anti-malware software, 243–244
  compliance technologies enforced by, 376–383
  configuring accepted domains for, 144
  creating Receive connector on, 151
  deployment, 111–124
    cloning configuration, 116–117
    configuring address rewriting, 120–121
    configuring transport agents, 117–118
    direct configuration, 115–116
    Edge subscriptions, 112–115
    third-party email gateways, 118–120

direct communication with Hub Transport
servers, 115–116
DNS resolution, 32–34
DNS to support redundant, 335
firewalls between Hub Transport servers and, 34
high availability and disaster recovery, 332–338
  backup and recovery, 333–334
  redundant deployment, 334
limiting number of messages accepted, 23–24
role, 111
tracking logs, 354
Edge Transport subscription, 329
and connectors creation, 29
EditAllItems right, 176, 268
Editor role, 176, 269
EditOwnedItems right, 176, 268
email
  direct Internet flow, 156–157
  message flow, multiphase upgrade and user access
  to, 71
  message size restrictions, 153–154
  personal, ActiveSync policies and, 257
  third-party gateways, 118–120
email address policies, 46. *See also* recipient policies
email relay, deploying, 155–156
EMC. *See* Exchange Management Console (EMC)
EMS. *See* Exchange Management Shell (EMS)
Enable-OutlookAnywhere cmdlet, 134, 136
Enable Outlook Anywhere Wizard page, 133
Enable-TransportAgent cmdlet, 118
Enable-TransportRule cmdlet, 147
encrypted items, discovery search and, 359
encryption of messages, public key access for, 221
end users. *See* users
Enterprise Admins group, 101
ESEUtil command-line tool, 320
ethical firewalls, 377
Event Viewer, 384
exam questions, 2
Exceptions, in transport rules, 146
Exchange, explaining capabilities to non-technical
users, 96
Exchange 2000, 99
Exchange 2003
  coexistence with, 182–184
  planning transition from. *See* transition planning
  removal recommendations, 73
  upgrade or coexistence, 72–74

Exchange 2003/2007, installing Exchange 2010 in mixed environment, 186–187

Exchange 2007
   basic steps for upgrading to Exchange 2010, 74
   coexistence with, 184–186
   features not supported in Exchange 2010, 74–75
   order for removing, 75
   upgrade or coexistence, 74–75

Exchange 2010
   Exchange 2003 features not supported, 73
   full server recovery process, 300
   planning transition. *See* transition planning

Exchange 2010 Hub server, limiting number of messages accepted, 23–24

Exchange 2010 Mailbox Server Role Requirements Calculator, 43

Exchange ActiveSync Usage Reports, 388

Exchange administrators, vs. Active Directory, 239

Exchange Control Panel (ECP), 61–63, 238
   Auditing Reports, 353

Exchange Deployment Assistant, 15–17

Exchange federation
   installation design and, 14–15
   preparing, 103–106
   text (TXT) records in DNS, 105–106

Exchange Hosted Services, Internet mail flow through, 155

Exchange Management Console (EMC)
   configuring accepted domain, 144
   to create address list, 168–169
   to create distribution group, 50
   to create dynamic distribution group, 52
   to create email address policy, 47
   to create linked mailbox, 44–45
   to create OAB, 170–171
   to create public folder, 172–173
   to create public folder database, 172
   to create Receive connector, 152, 189
   to create Send connector, 150–151, 188
   to create static distribution group, 49–50
   to create transport rules, 146–147
   to enable Outlook Anywhere, 133
   Operation Configuration Mode, 103

Exchange Management Shell (EMS). *See also* specific cmdlet names
   cmdlets for verifying CAS functionality, 139–140
   and single item recovery, 366
   to create federation trust, 104

Exchange Object permissions, 268–275
   distribution group security, 270–273
   mailbox permissions, 270
   public folder security, 268–269

Exchange Online, 54

Exchange permissions model, 231–242
   Role-based access control (RBAC), 232–237
   split permissions model, 239–240

Exchange Pre-Deployment Analyzer, 15

Exchange remote procedure call (RPC), 20

Exchange Server 2010
   built-in management roles, 233
   infrastructure preparation, 96–97
      Active Directory functional requirements, 97–98
      Active Directory preparation, 101–102
      Active Directory preparation with existing Exchange deployment, 99–100
      Active Directory schema preparation, 100–101
      Active Directory synchronization, 106
      DNS configuration for SMTP, 107–108
      domain controller role requirements, 98–99
      domain preparation, 102
      Exchange Federation preparation, 103–106
   validating deployment, 187
   vs. Exchange Server 2010 SP1, 99

Exchange Server 2010 installation wizard, background operation, 2

Exchange Server 2010 Management Pack for System Center Operations Manager, 384

Exchange Server 2010 Service Pack 1 setup wizard, 239

Exchange Server Deployment Assistant (ExDeploy), 76–77

Exchange Server Jetstress 2010, 70

Exchange Server Load Generator 2010, 70

Exchange Server Remote Connectivity Analyzer, 138

Exchange servers, consolidatiing, 70–71

Exchange Server User Monitor (ExMon), 139

Exchange-specific routing costs, and default routing topology change, 21–22

Exchange Trusted Subsystem universal security group, 314

Exchange Web Services, 61
   Outlook Protection rules and, 227

exclusive scope, for management roles, 235

ExDeploy (Exchange Server Deployment Assistant), 15, 76–77

ExOLEDB, 75

expansion servers, for distribution groups, 22

expletives, restricting email containing, 145
Export-ActiveSyncLog cmdlet, 388
ExportEdgeConfig.ps1 script, 117, 333, 334
Export-TransportRuleCollection cmdlet, 146
Extensible Storage Engine format, 39
external DNZ zone, MX records for, 107
Externally secured connection, 119
External Message Routing, 20
external relay domains, 28, 144
external SLAs, 9

mailboxes in multiple-forest topologies, 44–46
multiple, 11–12
multiple domains in single, 11
formats, for email addresses, 46
Forms-Based Authentication, for OWA, 260
Full Access to user mailbox, 270
full operating system reinstall and Exchange recovery
technique, 308
fully qualified domain names, translating IP
addresses to, 33

F

Fail status value, for sender ID, 245
fax gateways, third-party, 191
Federated Delivery mailbox account, 225
federated organization identifier (OrgID), 15, 105
Federation. *See* Exchange federation
federation trust, creating, 103–104
file mode, continuous replication, 313
filtering
    attachments, 252–253
    content, 251–252
    recipients, 253–254
firewalls
    between Edge Transport servers and Hub Transport
    servers, 34
    ethical, 377
    perimeter network between, 111
Flexible Single Master Operations (FSMO) roles, domain
controllers hosting, 98
FolderContact right, 177, 269
FolderOwner right, 177, 268
folders
    for mailbox databases, 39
    managed, 369–371
    Recoverable Items, 364
FolderVisible right, 177, 269
Forefront Identity Lifecycle Manager (ILM) 2010, 12
Forefront Identity Manager (FIM), 54, 78
Forefront Protection 2010 for Exchange server, 243
foreign connectors, 77, 191
forest functional level, 97
    viewing and managing settings, 98
forests
    Autodiscover service in, 65–66, 135
    IRM in multiple forest environments, 225–226

G

Get-AcceptedDomain cmdlet, 144
Get-AddressRewriteEntry cmdlet, 121
Get-ADForest cmdlet, 98
Get-ADForest | FT SchemaMaster command, 100
Get-AttachmentFilterEntry command, 253
Get-EdgeSubscription cmdlet, 113
Get-EdgeSyncServiceConfig cmdlet, 113
Get-EmailAddressPolicy cmdlet, 48, 192
Get-ExchangeServer cmdlet, 187
Get-FederatedDomainProof cmdlet, 105
Get-Mailbox command, 307
Get-MessageTrackingLog cmdlet, 355
Get-OwaVirtualDirectory cmdlet, 129
Get-PublicFolderAdministrativePermission cmdlet, 178
Get-PublicFolderClientPermission cmdlet, 178
Get-ReceiveConnector cmdlet, 220
Get-TransportAgent cmdlet, 118
Get-TransportConfig cmdlet, 222
Get-TransportPipeline cmdlet, 118
Get-TransportRule cmdlet, 147
Global Address List (GAL), 5
    multiphase upgrade and user access to, 71
    segmentation, 11
    synchronization, 78
Global Catalog servers, 288
    domain controllers as, 98
Gzip Compression Settings, in Outlook Web App, 132

H

hardware requirements, for Client Access Servers, 64
header, maximum size through Receive connector, 154
HELO/EHLO analysis, Sender Reputation Level and, 248

Help Desk role group, 234
high availability and disaster recovery, 288–298
   Active Directory redundancy and recovery, 288–290
   backup and recovery objectives, 295
   for CAS, 298–305
      backup, 299
   for Edge Transport servers, 332–338
      backup and recovery, 333–334
   for Hub Transport servers, 324
      backup, 325
   for mailbox server role, 306–324
   vs. scalability, 22
   sites, 292
   storage, 292
   updates, 293–295
Hits Report, 388
Hosted Archive service, in Exchange Hosted Services, 155
Hosted Continuity service, in Exchange Hosted Services, 155
Hosted Encryption service, in Exchange Hosted Services, 155
Hosted Exchange 2010, coexistence supported by, 5
Hosted Filtering service, in Exchange Hosted Services, 155
HTML E-mail, ActiveSync policies and, 258
HTTP Status Report, 389
hub sites, configuring, 21
Hub Transport servers
   accepted domains configuration, 144–145
   for Active Directory site, 20
   adding additional, 22
   anti-malware software, 243–244
   compliance technologies enforced by, 376–383
   configuring to accept email directly, 156–157
   default routing topology and, 21
   deployment, 143–160
      direct Internet mail flow, 156–157
      message size restrictions, 153–154
      in multi-site and multi-forest environment, 143
      Receive connectors, 151–152
      remote domain configuration, 148–149
      Send connector management, 149–151
      special case scenarios, 155–157
      transport rules configuration, 145–148
   direct communication with Edge Transport servers, 115–116
   and distribution group expansion, 22

firewalls between Edge Transport servers and, 34
high availability and disaster recovery, 324
   backup, 325
inclusion in Edge Transport subscription, 329
recovery, 325–326
redundant deployment, 326–327
tracking logs, 354
and witness servers, 313
Human Resources surveillance, discovery searches and, 357
Hygiene Management role group, 234

I

IMAP4, 61, 137
implicit scopes, 236
ImportEdgeConfig.ps1 script, 117, 333, 334
Import-TransportRuleCollection cmdlet, 146
inbound domain security, 222
information leakage, protection from, 217
Information Rights Management (IRM), 223–225
   ActiveSync policies and, 258
   ActiveSync with, 224–225
   in multiple forest environments, 225–226
   logging, 360–361
infrastructure, constraints for existing, 2
installation design of Exchange Server 2010, 2–19
   Active Directory and network topology, 10
   directory synchronization with cloud, 12–14
   DNS support planning, 5–8
   Exchange Deployment Assistant, 15–17
   Exchange federation, 14–15
   Exchange Pre-Deployment Analyzer, 15
   location choices, 3–5
      cloud-only deployments, 4
      coexistence deployments, 4–5
      on-premises demployments, 3
   in mixed Exchange 2003/2007 environment, 186–187
   multiple domains in single forest, 11
   Service Level Agreement (SLA), 8–10
installation packages, unsigned, ActiveSync policies and, 258
Integrated Windows Authentication, for OWA, 261
Integrated Zone, Active Directory, 290
interception, protecting message from, 217
internal certificate authority, 218

Internal connector type, 149
internal investigations, discovery searches and, 357
Internal Message routing, 20
internal network, perimeter network and, 111
internal relay domains, 28, 144
    Send connectors for, 150
internal service level agreements, 9
internal SMTP relay, 31
Internal usage type, for Receive connector, 151
Internet
    Autodiscover for clients, 65
    direct mail flow, 156–157
Internet connector type, 149
Internet firewall, perimeter network and, 111
Internet Information Server (IIS), backup of configuration, 299
Internet Information Services (IIS) console, 129
Internet Sharing, ActiveSync policies and, 258
Internet usage type, for Receive connector, 151
Inter-Organization Replication Tool, 73
IP addresses
    bindings, 137
    translating to fully qualified domain names, 33
IP Block List Properties dialog box, 246
IP Block List Providers Properties dialog box, 247
IP block lists, 246–248
IPsec connection, for externally secured Receive connectors, 219
IPv4 reverse lookup zone, 33
IPv6
    and DAG network, 310
    reverse lookup zone, 33
IrDA, ActiveSync policies and, 258
IRM-protected items, discovery search and, 359
ISInteg tool, 321

J

journaling
    managed folder settings, 370
    message, 378–379
journal recipient, for mailbox database, 165
journal reports, redirecting to alternate journaling mailbox, 379
"Just a Bunch of Disks" (JBOD), 43

K

keywords, for discovery search, 358

L

lagged mailbox database copy, 316–317
Language Settings, in Outlook Web App, 132
legacy Exchange permissions, 99
legacy host name, configuring, 184
legal discovery, 357
licenses, for virtualized instances, 289
Lightweight Directory Access Protocol (LDAP)
    converting to OPATH filters, 192–193
    replication scripts, 78
linked mailboxes, 44
linked role groups, 235
Link State Updates, disabling, 194
litigation hold, for message archive, 366–368
load balancing
    and CAS arrays, 301
    Edge Transport servers, 334
    Hub Transport servers and, 324
    mailbox assignment to database and, 54, 167
Load Generator (LoadGen) tool, 63, 70
Local Continuous Replication, 75
local deployments, as exam focus, 3
logon method, for POP3 and IMAP4, 137
logs. *See also* transaction logs
    administrator audit, 352–354
    connectivity, 385–386
    Information Rights Management (IRM), 360–361
    mailbox audit, 354
    message tracking, 354–356
        disk space requirements, 26
    protocol, 356–357
    replaying for recovery, 317
lookup zones, reverse, 33–34
Lotus Domino, Microsoft Transport Suite for, 75
Lotus Notes, 77

M

mailbox database copy
  activation preference number, 315
  back up volumes hosting, 318
  creating, 312
  criteria for, 312
  lagged, 316–317
mailbox databases
  configuration and quota policies, 165–166
  deployment, 162–165
  moving, 164
  provisioning policies, 166
  recovery, 308–309
  removing, 164
  repairing, 320–321
  sizing, 39–42
mailboxes
  arbitration, 353
  audit logging, 354
  deprovisioning policy, 55
  Exchange server placement and, 3
  Journaling, 378
  location for, 54
  permissions, 270
  provisioning policies, 54–55
  quarantine, 250
  retention, 307
  retention policy for, 371
  services to access, 60
  synching mobile devices with, 63
  user access to, 128
mailbox policy, managed folder, 370
Mailbox Resources Management Agent, 166, 167
Mailbox server role design, 39–58
  database sizing, 39–42
  distribution group policies, 49–53
  Mailbox provisioning policies, 54–55
  multiple-forest topologies and, 44–46
  public folders, 53
  recipient policies, 46–48
  storage performance requirements, 42–44
  transaction logs sizing, 42
mailbox servers
  Active Directory domain and, 161–162
  anti-malware software, 243–244
  backup, 306–307
  CAS for site hosting, 125
  database configuration and quota policies, 165–166
  deployment, 161–181
    address lists, 167–170
    mailbox database, 162–165
    Offline Address Book (OAB), 170–171
    public folder database, 172–178
    validating access, 178
  designing role, 39
  high availability and disaster recovery, 306–324
  monitoring, 386–387
  recovery, 307–308
  tracking logs on, 355
mail-enabled security groups, 49
Mail Exchange (MX) records, 30, 107
  and Edge Transport server, 334
  priority numbers of, 335
mail flow
  bidirectional, routing group connectors for, 193
  distribution group settings, 272–273
  through Exchange Hosted Services, 155
mail forest contact, 46
mailing lists. *See* distribution groups
mail server priority number, 108
MailTips, 61, 379–380
maintenance mode, 294
Manage Database Availability Group Membership
dialog box, 312
Managed Folder Assistant, 359, 366
managed folders, 369–371
  migrating to retention policies, 372
management role entries, 233
management role groups, custom, 235
management roles, 233
  assignments, 237
  scopes, 235–237
manager of distribution groups, default, 50
MAPI networks, DAGs and, 310
MaxDumpsterSizePerDatabase parameter, of Set-
TransportConfig cmdlet, 27
MaxInboundConnection parameter, of Set-
ReceiveConnector cmdlet, 24
MaxInboundConnectionPErcentagePerSource
parameter, of Set-ReceiveConnector cmdlet, 24
MaxInboundConnectionPerSource parameter, for Set-
ReceiveConnector cmdlet, 24
MaxOutboundConnections parameter, of Set-
TransportServer cmdlet, 23

MaxPerDomainOutboundConnections parameter, of Set-TransportServer cmdlet, 23
MaxProtocolErrors parameter, of Set-ReceiveConnector cmdlet, 24
meeting schedules, Availability service and, 136
MemberDepartRestriction cmdlet, 272
MemberJoinRestriction cmdlet, 272
membership, approval for distribution group, 271–272
message archives, 363–376
    litigation hold, 366–368
    managed folders, 369–371
    personal, 368–369
    recoverable items, 364–365
    retention hold, 372–373
    retention tags and policies, 371–372
    single item recovery, 365–366
message compliance
    disclaimers, 380–381
    ethical firewalls, 377
    journaling, 378–379
    MailTips, 379–380
    transport rules for, 376–383
Message Delivery Restrictions, for distribution group, 272
message hygiene, 243–256
    anti-spam features, 244–254
    antivirus features, 243–244
message journaling, 378–379
message retention policies, 368
message routing infrastructure design, 20–38
    accepted domains planning, 28
    default topology modification, 21–22
    DNS planning, 32–34
    message transport design, 20–21
    Send and Receive connectors planning, 29–31
    shadow redundancy, 25–26
    transport server ports planning, 34–35
    transport server scalability, 22–25
    transport storage requirements, 26–27
messages
    maximum size, 154
    planning outbound flow, 30
    sanitation, 111
Message Size Restriction, for distribution group, 272
message throttling, 23–24
message tracking logs, 354–356
    disk space requirements, 26
    and Hub Transport server backup, 325

message traffic logs
    backup, 333
message transport design, 20–21
messaging policies, applying to email, 145
Messaging Records Management, 359, 373
messaging security, 216–231
    certificates, 217–218
    Domain Security, 221–222
    Information Rights Management (IRM), 223–225
    IRM in multiple forest environments, 225–226
    Outlook protection rules, 227–228
    requirements, 217
    secure relaying, 218–220
    S/MIME (Secure/Multipurpose Internet Mail Extensions), 220–221
    transport protection and decryption, 226–227
messaging system, mailboxes on third-party, 31
Microsoft Exchange Replication service, 318
Microsoft Exchange Server MAPI Editor, to access mailbox, 354
Microsoft Federation Gateway, 14, 73, 103
Microsoft Identity Integration Server (MIIS) synchronization, 46
Microsoft Online Services Directory Synchronization Configuration Wizard, 106
Microsoft Online Services Module for Windows PowerShell for Single Sign On, 13
Microsoft Outlook client
    Availability service and, 136
    testing connectivity, 178
Microsoft SmartScreen, 250
Microsoft Transport Suite for Lotus Domino, 75
migration, 70
    converting LDAP to OPATH filters, 192–193
    third-party email system to Exchange, 190
MIME encryption algorithm, ActiveSync policies and, 258
mobile devices
    ActiveSync policies and, 257–260
    synching mailbox information with, 63
    user access to mailboxes with, 128, 134
Mobile OTA Updates, ActiveSync policies and, 258
monitoring Exchange organization, 384–391
    ActiveSync reporting, 388–389
    connectivity logging, 385–386
    monitoring CAS, 387
    performance monitoring, 386–388
    transport servers, 387–388

Moore's Law, 39

Mount-Database cmdlet, 163

Move-DatabasePath cmdlet, 165

moving mailbox database, 164

msDS-AllowedDNSSuffixes Active Directory attribute
on domain object container, 7

MSOL_AD_SYNC account, 106

MTLS (Mutual Transport Layer Security), 221

multi-mailbox search, 357

multiphase upgrade with coexistence, 71

MX (Mail Exchange) records, 30, 107
and Edge Transport server, 334
priority numbers of, 335

MyDistributionGroups implicit scope, 236

MyGAL implicit scope, 236

N

names
for DAG, 310
organization changes, address rewriting for, 120

namespaces
common shared, 6
disjointed, 6–8

native mode, and Exchange 2003 upgrade, 182

NetBIOS name of domain controllers, 6

Network Monitor, 384

Network News Transfer Protocol (NNTP), 73

network topology, Active Directory and, 10

Neutral status value, for sender ID, 245

New-AcceptedDomain cmdlet, 144

New-AddressList cmdlet, 169

New-AddressRewriteEntry cmdlet, 120

New-AdminAuditLogSearch cmdlet, 353

New-ClientAccessArray cmdlet, 302

New-DatabaseAvailabilityGroup cmdlet, 311

New-DeliveryAgentConnector cmdlet, 154

New-DistributionGroup cmdlet, 50

New-DynamicDistributionGroup cmdlet, 52

New-EdgeSubscription cmdlet, 113

New Edge Subscription Wizard, 113

New-EdgeSyncServiceConfig cmdlet, 113

New-EmailAddressPolicy cmdlet, 48

New E-mail Address Policy Wizard, 47

New-ExchangeCertificate cmdlet, 104

New Exchange Certificate Wizard, 126

New-FederationTrust cmdlet, 104

New Federation Trust Wizard, 14, 103

New-ForeignConnector Exchange Management Shell
cmdlet, 191

New-JournalRule cmdlet, 378

New-Mailbox AntiTrust command, 358

New-MailboxAuditLogSearch cmdlet, 354

New-Mailbox cmdlet, 45

New-Mailbox database cmdlet, 163

New-MailboxExportRequest cmdlet, 354

New-MailboxRepairRequest cmdlet, 321

New-ManagementRoleAssignment cmdlet, 237

New-ManagementRole cmdlet, 233

New-ManagementScope cmdlet, 237

New-OABVirtualDirectory cmdlet, 170

New-OfflineAddressBook cmdlet, 171

New-OutlookProtectionRule cmdlet, 228

New-OwaVirtualDirectory cmdlet, 129

New-PublicFolder cmdlet, 173

New-PublicFolderDatabase cmdlet, 172

New-PublicFolderDatabaseRepairRequest cmdlet, 321

New-ReceiveConnector cmdlet, 152, 189

New Receive Connector Wizard, 189

New Resource Record dialog box, 105, 107

New-RetentionPolicyTag cmdlet, 372

New-RoleGroup cmdlet, 235

New-RoutingGroupConnector cmdlet, 194

New-SendConnector cmdlet, 149, 188, 329

New-SendConnector EMS cmdlet, 151

New Send Connector Wizard, 149, 150, 188, 329

New-TestCasConnectivityUser.ps1 script, 178

New-TransportRule cmdlet, 147, 154, 380

next hop delivery failure, 25

NNTP (Network News Transfer Protocol), 73

Non-EditingAuthor role, 176, 269

None status value, for sender ID, 245

Novell GroupWise, 77

Novell GroupWise connector, 73

nslookup command-line utility, 33

O

Office Outlook Mobile Access, 73

Offline Address Book (OAB), 167
deployment, 170–171

on-premises deployments, 3

OPATH filters, converting LDAP to, 192–193

Open group membership, 271

open relay, 218
Operating system reinstall and Exchange recovery, 300
OrganizationConfig implicit scope, 236
organization identifier (OrgID), federated, 15, 105
Organization implicit scope, 236
Organization Management role, 162
Organization Management role group, 233, 235
organization name changes, address rewriting for, 120
OU scope, 237
outbound connections, configuring maximum, for message throttling, 23
outbound domain security, 222
outbound message flow, 30
Outlook
    Address Book, 168
    Autodiscover for configuring, 64
Outlook Anywhere, 61, 133–134
Outlook clients
    Availability service and, 136
    testing connectivity, 178
Outlook protection rules, 227–228
Outlook Web App (OWA), 60, 128–132
    advanced features, 131–137
    authentication, 260–262
    Availability service and, 136
    segmentation settings, 262–264
    virtual directories for, 129–130
    WebReady document viewing, 130–131
out-of-office messages, controlling external distribution, 148
Owner Approval of group membership, 271
Owner role, 176, 269
ownership of distribution group, 271

P

parent management role, 233
Partner connector type, 149
Partner usage type, for Receive connectors, 152
passive mailbox database copies, backup, 318
Pass status value, for sender ID, 245
passwords
    ActiveSync policies and, 258, 259
    for private or public keys, 216
    synchronization, 106

performance
    monitoring, 386–388
    Service Level Agreement and, 8
perimeter network
    Edge Transport servers on, 111
    multiple Edge Transport servers on, 334
PermError status value, for sender ID, 245
permissions. *See also* Exchange permissions model
    Exchange Object, 268–275
    for public folders, 176–178
personal archives, 368–369
    discovery search of, 359
personal email, ActiveSync policies and, 257
Phishing Confidence Level (PCL), 250
PickupDirectoryMaxMessagesPerMinute parameter of Set-TransportServer cmdlet, 23
policies
    ActiveSync, 257–260
    Archive and Retention, 369
    for distribution groups, 49–53
    mailbox deprovisioning, 55
    mailbox provisioning, 54–55
    managed folder mailbox, 370
    retention, 359, 363, 371
Policy Compliance Report, 389
POP3 access, 137
POP3/IMAP4 service, 61
POPIMAPEmail, ActiveSync policies and, 258
portability of database, 309
Port from Managed Folder To Tag wizard, 372
ports
    for IMAP4 and POP3, 137
    planning for transport servers, 34–35
Premium Journaling, 378
primary DNS suffix, 6
Primary zones, 290
private keys
    Hub Transport server backup, 325
    password for, 216
privilege structure, 231
project-based distribution groups, 49
Protocol Analysis agent, 118
protocol logging, 356–357
    disk space requirements, 26
proxying, CAS and, 60
.pst (Outlook personal store) files, 368
public certificate, access for message encryption, 221

public folder databases, 40
    default, 165
    deployment, 172–178
    replication, 319–320
Public Folder Management Console, 176, 319
Public Folder Management role group, 234
public folder replicates, synchronization, 319
public folders
    creating, 172–173
    for mailbox servers, 53
    multiphase upgrade and user access to, 71
    for Offline Address Book distribution, 170
    permissions, 176–178
    replication
        configuring, 173–176
        and high availability, 306
    security, 268–269
Public Key Infrastructure (PKI), 221
public keys
    of message recipient, 221
    password for, 216
PublishingAuthor role, 176, 269
PublishingEditor role, 176, 269
Purges folder, 364

Q

quarantine mailbox, 250
queued messages, number of Hub Transport servers for, 22
quota limits on per mailbox-database basis, 165
quota policies, mailbox database configuration and, 165–166

R

RAID, 44
    striping, 39
RBAC (role-based access control), 231, 232–237
    split permissions, 240
ReadItems right, 176, 268
Read Only Domain Controllers (RODCs), 289, 290
Receive As permission, 270
Receive connectors, 151–152
    for anonymous SMTP connections, 30
    coexistence and, 188
    on Edge Transport server, 116
    externally secured, 219
    for email from third-party system, 189
    planning, 29–31
    relay permissions to anonymous connections, 220
    resilience, 328
    SMTP conversation through, 356
received messages, maximum size for, 153
Recipient Filter agent, 118
recipient filtering, 253–254
Recipient filter scope, 237
Recipient Management role, 233
recipient policies for mailboxes, 46–48
Recipient read scope, 236
recipients per message, maximum number of, 153
Recipient write scope, 236
records management, 359–360
Records Management role group, 234
Recoverable Items folder, 364–365
    and user quota, 367
recovery
    of CAS, 300–301
    Hub Transport servers, 325–326
    mailbox databases, 308–309
    mailbox servers, 307–308
    Service Level Agreement and, 8
Recovery Point Objective (RPO), 295
Recovery Time Objective (RTO), 295
Recycle Bin, for Active Directory, 289
redundancy, 43
Regular scope, for management roles, 236
relay domains, 28
remote access, CAS and, 60
Remote Desktop, ActiveSync policies and, 258
remote domains, 28
    configuring, 148–149
Remote-EdgeSubscription cmdlet, 114
Remove-AcceptedDomain cmdlet, 144
Remove-AddressRewriteEntry cmdlet, 121
Remove-DatabaseAvailabilityGroupServer cmdlet, 312
Remove-EdgeSubscription cmdlet, 113
Remove-EmailAddressPolicy cmdlet, 48
Remove-MailboxDatabase cmdlet, 164
RemoveMailboxDatabaseCopy cmdlet, 312
Remove-OwaVirtualDirectory cmdlet, 129
Remove-TransportRule cmdlet, 147
repadmin.exe tool, 101
Replay Lag Time setting, 317

replication
  Active Directory Integrated Zone for, 290
  of Active Directory schema changes, 101
  continuous, 313
  DNS zone data, 290
  EdgeSync, 112
  public folder databases, 319–320
  of public folders
    configuring, 173–176
    and high availability, 306
  of transport rules, 146
replmon.exe (Active Directory Replication Monitor), 101
reply-to address, configuring default, 48
resilience
  of Receive connectors, 328
  of Send connectors, 328–329
  of witness servers, 313–314
resource-forest topology, 12
  linked role groups in, 235
  mailboxes in, 44
Resource Manager, 384
Resume-PublicFolderReplication cmdlet, 176
retention, managed folder settings, 370
retention hold, 372–373
retention policies, 359, 363
  migrating managed folders to, 372
retention policy, 371
retention policy tag, 371
retention tags, 360
Reverse DNS lookup
  Sender Reputation Level and, 248
reverse lookup zones, 33–34
Reviewer role, 176, 269
rich coexistence, 5
RODCs (Read Only Domain Controllers), 289, 290
role-based access control (RBAC), 231, 232–237
  split permissions, 240
role groups
  built-in, 233–235
  modifying membership, 235
roles, adding users to, 176
routing group connector
  coexistence and, 193–194
routing loop, 150
routing topologies, 10
RPC Client Access, 60

S

Safelist aggregation, 244–245
Safe List, discovery search and, 359
Safe Recipients Lists, 244
Safe Senders Lists, 244
sanitation of messages, 111
scalability of transport server, 22–25
schema for Active Directory, 100–101
Schema Master role, domain controller hosting, 98
scope
  of management roles, 235–237
  of Journal Rule, 378
Search-AdminAuditLog cmdlet, 353
searches, discovery, 357–359
Search-MailboxAuditLog cmdlet, 354
Secondary zones, 290
secure relaying, 218–220
Secure Sockets Layer certificates. *See* certificates
security, 215. *See also* Client Access security; messaging security
Security Assertion Markup Language (SAML) delegation tokens, 14
segmentation, for Outlook Web App, 131
Self implicit scope, 236
self-signed certificates, 217
  for Exchange, 66
  for federated trust, 103
  for Microsoft Federation gateway, 14
Send As permission, 270
Send connector
  on Edge Transport server, 116
  for Hub Transport servers, 116
  maximum message size through, 154
Send connectors, 21
  coexistence and, 188
  edge subscription and, 112
  managing, 149–151
  planning, 29–31
  resilience, 328–329
  SMTP conversation through, 356
Sender Filter agent, 118
Sender ID, 245–246
Sender ID agent, 118
sender of message, verifying identification, 217
Sender open proxy test, 249
Sender Policy Framework (SPF) records, 245
Sender Reputation Level (SRL), 248–249

Sender Reputation Properties dialog box, 249

sensitive information, 352

    controlling flow, 223

sent messages, maximum size for, 153

Server Management role group, 234

servers

    capacity, Exchange server placement and, 3

    checking previous configuration, 288

    determining capacity of new, 70

service catalog, maintenance, 9

Service Level Agreement (SLA), 8–10

    review, 9

service level monitoring, 9

service level reporting, 9

Set-AcceptedDomain cmdlet, 144

Set-ActiveSyncVirtualDirectory cmdlet, 134, 135

Set-AddressList command, 193

Set-AddressRewriteEntry cmdlet, 121

Set-AdminAuditLogConfig cmdlet, 353

Set-AdministratorAuditLog cmdlet, 353

Set-ADSiteLink cmdlet, 22, 154

Set-AttachmentFilterListConfig cmdlet, 252

Set-ClientAccessServer cmdlet, 135

    and IRM logging, 360

Set-DatabaseAvailabiltyGroup cmdlet, 316

Set-DeliveryAgentConnector cmdlet, 154

Set-DistributionGroup cmdlet, 50, 51, 271, 272, 380

Set-EdgeSyncServiceConfig cmdlet, 113

Set-EmailAddressPolicy cmdlet, 48, 193

Set-FederatedOrganizationIdentifier command, 105

Set-ForeignConnector cmdlet, 154

Set-IMAPSettings cmdlet, 137

Set-IRMConfiguration cmdlet, 223, 227, 233

Set-Mailbox cmdlet, 354, 366, 367, 373

Set-MailboxDatabase cmdlet, 166, 167

Set-MailboxDatabaseCopy cmdlet, 315, 317

Set-MailboxServer cmdlet, 315, 355

    and IRM logging, 360

Set-MsolAdfscontext cmdlet, 13

Set-OABVirtualDirectory cmdlet, 136

Set-OrganizationConfig cmdlet, 380

Set-OutlookAnywhere cmdlet, 134

Set-OwaMailboxPolicy cmdlet, 264

Set-OwaVirtualDirectory cmdlet, 128, 129, 131, 132, 264

Set-POPSettings cmdlet, 137

Set-PublicFolder cmdlet, 175, 319

Set-PublicFolderDatabase cmdlet, 175, 320

Set-ReceiveConnector cmdlet, 219, 222, 356

Set-RecipientFilterConfig cmdlet, 253

Set-RoleGroup cmdlet, 235

Set-RoutingGroupConnector cmdlet, 154, 194

Set-SendConnector cmdlet, 222, 329, 356

Set-SenderIDConfig cmdlet, 246

Set-SenderReputationConfig cmdlet, 249

Set-TransportConfig cmdlet, 26, 27, 153, 222, 327, 379

Set-TransportRule cmdlet, 147, 154

Set-TransportServer cmdlet, 23, 154, 354, 385

    and IRM logging, 360

Setup /PrepareAD command, 101, 183, 185

Setup /PrepareAllDomains command, 102, 183, 185

Setup /PrepareLegacyExchangePermissions command, 99, 183, 185

Setup /PrepareSchema command, 100, 183, 185

shadow redundancy, 327, 329

    message queues and, 25–26

ShadowRedundancyEnabled parameter, of Set-TransportConfig cmdlet, 26

Shadow Redundancy Manager, 25

SharePoint, vs. public folders, 53

Sign-In and Sign-Out Pages, customizing in Outlook Web App, 132

simple coexistence, 5

Single Copy Cluster, 74

Single Item Recovery, 306

    from archive, 365–366

single-phase upgrades, 71

single sign-on

    and Active Directory synchronization, 106

    configuring, 12

site affinity, Autodiscover and, 65, 135

sites, high availability, 292

sizing

    mailbox databases, 39–42

    transaction logs, 42

smart cards, OWA configuration to require for authentication, 261

smart host, 29

smartphone operating system, accessing Exchange 2010 mailboxes, 134

S/MIME (Secure/Multipurpose Internet Mail Extensions), 220–221

SMTP service, 31, 188

    DNS configuration for, 107–108

    internal relay, 31

    messaging system based on, coexistence with, 77

Receive connector and, 29
recording conversations, 356
Send connector and, 29
and shadow redundancy, 25
Soft fail status value, for sender ID, 245
spam, 111
anonymous relay and, 218
cost of, 243
source of, 247
Spam Confidence Level (SCL), 245, 250–251
split DNS namespace, 5
split permissions model, 239–240
spoofing, combatting, 245
SSL settings, for OWA virtual directory, 129
standalone computers, for Edge Transport role, 111
standard certificates, 218
Standard Journaling, 378
Standard zones, 290
Standby Continuous Replication, 75
StartDagServerMaintenance.ps1 script, 294
Start-EdgeSynchronization cmdlet, 113
Start-OnlineCoexistenceSync cmdlet, 106
Start-RetentionAutoTagLearning cmdlet, 372
static distribution groups, 49
StopDagServerMaintenance.ps1 script, 294
storage
high availability, 292
storage card, ActiveSync policies and, 258
Subject Alternative Names, 218
Suspend-MailboxDatabaseCopy cmdlet, 315, 317
Suspend-PublicFolderReplication cmdlet, 176, 319
synchronization
of Active Directory, 106
of Global Address List (GAL), 78
of passwords, 106
of public folder replicates, 319
System Center Configuration Manager 2012, 294–295
System Center Data Protection Manager (DPM), 42, 299, 318
System Center Operations Manager, Exchange Server 2010 Management Pack for, 384
System Center Orchestrator, 294
System Center Service Manager, 10
System Properties dialog box, 7

T

tablet operating systems, user access to mailboxes with, 128, 134
TarpitInterval parameter, of Set-ReceiveConnector cmdlet, 24
TempError status value, for sender ID, 245
Test-ActiveSyncConnectivity cmdlet, 139
Test-EcpConnectivity cmdlet, 139
Test-EdgeSynchronization cmdlet, 113
Test-ImapConnectivity cmdlet, 139
testing Microsoft Outlook client connectivity, 178
Test-Mailflow cmdlet, 178
Test-OutlookConnectivity cmdlet, 139, 178
Test-OutlookWebServices cmdlet, 140
Test-OwaConnectivity cmdlet, 139
Test-PopConnectivity cmdlet, 139
Test-SmtpConnectivity cmdlet, 139
Test-WebServicesConnectivity cmdlet, 140
text messaging, ActiveSync policies and, 258
Text Messaging Delivery Agent connector, 191
text (TXT) records, in DNS for federation, 105–106
themes, in Outlook Web App, 132
third-party CA certificates, 66
third-party email gateways, 118–120
third-party email systems
coexistence with, 188–191
mailboxes on, 31
migrating to Exchange, 190
Time To Live (TTL) records, 291
TLS, 31, 115
SMTP and, 31
tokens
Security Assertion Markup Language (SAML) delegation, 14
Tracking Log Explorer tool, 356
transaction logs
for mailbox databases, 39, 162
and replication, 313
sizing, 42
transition planning, 70–81
coexistence with SMTP-based messaging systems, 77
Exchange 2003 upgrade or coexistence, 72–74
Exchange 2007 upgrade or coexistence, 74–75
Exchange consolidation, 70–71
Exchange Server Deployment Assistant (ExDeploy), 76–77

transition planning *(continued)*
   Global Address List synchronization, 78
   mixed Exchange 2003 and 2007 environments, 75–76
   for multiple sites, 72
   upgrade approaches, 71
transport agents, configuring, 117–118
transport dumpster, 27, 329
transport protection rules, and decryption, 226–227
transport rules
   components, 146
   configuring, 145–148
transport servers, 20
   disk space requirements, 26–27
   monitoring, 387–388
   ports planning, 34–35
   scalability, 22–25
Transport Settings Properties dialog box, 153
   General tab, 27
Truncation Lag Time setting, 317
trust broker, 14
Trusted Third-Party Certificate Authority (CA), 218
trust relationships, between forests, 11

U

UM Management role group, 234
unsigned applications, ActiveSync policies and, 258
Update-AddressList cmdlet, 169
Update-EmailAddressPolicy cmdlet, 48
Update-PublicFolder cmdlet, 319
Update-PublicFolderHierarchy cmdlet, 176
updates
   deploying DAG members, 294–295
   high availability, 293–295
upgrade, 70. *See also* transition planning
usage type for connectors, 149
User Agent List, 389
User Principle Names (UPNs), 13
user profile configuration settings
   Autodiscover and, 134
users
   access to Exchange objects, 268
   adding to roles, 176
   configuring ability to join distribution groups, 51
   and litigation hold, 367
   security requirements enforcement, 217

V

validating Mailbox server access, 178
Versions folder, 364
View-Only Organization Management role group, 233
virtual directories for Outlook Web App, 129–130
virtualized instances, licenses to run, 289

W

Web-based distribution, 170
Web Beacon and HTML Form Filtering, in Outlook Web App, 132
WebDAV, 75
WebReady document viewing, 130–131
Wi-Fi, ActiveSync policies and, 258
wildcard certificates, 67, 218
Windows Failover Clustering, for DAGs, 309
Windows Mobile 6.5, ActiveSync policy and, 257
Windows Phone 7, ActiveSync policy and, 257
Windows PowerShell, 388
   Microsoft Online Services Module for, 13
Windows Server 2008
   Event Viewer, 384
   licenses to run virtualized instances, 289
Windows Server Backup, 318
Windows Server Update Services (WSUS), 293–295
   vs. System Center Configuration Manager, 294
Windows System Resource Manager, 384
witness servers, resilience, 313–314

X

X.509 certificate, for Microsoft Federation Gateway, 14

About the Author

ORIN THOMAS holds multiple MCITP certifications, including the Enterprise Messaging Administrator 2010 credential. His first job managing a production Exchange deployment was running Exchange 5.5 at one of Australia's biggest manufacturing companies more than a decade ago. He is an MCT, a Microsoft MVP, and is a contributing editor at *Windows IT Pro* magazine. He regularly speaks at events in Australia and around the world, including TechED and Microsoft Management Summit. Orin founded and runs the Melbourne System Center Users Group, and has authored more than 20 books for Microsoft Press, including books on Exchange 2003, Exchange 2007, and Exchange 2010. You can follow him on Twitter at *http://twitter.com/orinthomas*.

What do you think of this book?

We want to hear from you!

To participate in a brief online survey, please visit:

microsoft.com/learning/booksurvey

Tell us how well this book meets your needs—what works effectively, and what we can do better. Your feedback will help us continually improve our books and learning resources for you.

Thank you in advance for your input!